Doing Climate Justice

Religion and Transformation in Contemporary European Society

Edited by

Kurt Appel,
Christian Danz,
Jakob Helmut Deibl,
Rüdiger Lohlker,
Richard Potz,
Sieglinde Rosenberger

VOLUME 21

Jan Niklas Collet, Judith Gruber,
Wietske de Jong-Kumru, Christian Kern, Sebastian Pittl,
Stefan Silber, Christian Tauchner (Eds.)

Doing Climate Justice

Theological Explorations

BRILL
SCHÖNINGH

RaT
Religion and Transformation
in Contemporary Society

Cover illustration: Global Warming, 2017 © Pete Linforth / Pixabay

Bibliographic information published by the Deutsche Nationalbibliothek.

The Deutsche Nationalbibliothek lists this publication in the Deutsche Nationalbibliografie; detailed bibliographic data available online: http://dnb.d-nb.de

www.schoeningh.de

Cover design: Evelyn Ziegler, Munich
Production: Brill Deutschland GmbH, Paderborn

ISSN 2198-5235
ISBN 978-3-506-79531-1 (hardback)
ISBN 978-3-657-79531-4 (e-book)

Table of Contents

Introduction: Doing Climate Justice

Jan Niklas Collet / Judith Gruber / Wietske de Jong-Kumru / Christian Kern / Sebastian Pittl / Stefan Silber / Christian Tauchner

The online workshop "Doing Climate Justice—Theological Contributions Between Concernment and Resistance" took place on October 24–25, 2020. More than 60 scholars and practitioners from different fields, including theology, philosophy, religious studies, and education, met online to discuss the workshop's central question: How can climate justice be realized in contemporary societies, and what could be the particular contribution of theology—especially liberation theology—for this task? The workshop was organized by the Centre for Liberation Theologies (KU Leuven), in collaboration with members of the University of Tübingen, TU Dortmund, the Steyler Missionswissenschaftliches Institut at Sankt Augustin, and Plattform Theologie der Befreiung. It continued a biannual series of workshops that address social, and political challenges from the perspectives of critical contextual theologies and liberation theologies.

The workshop *Doing climate justice* took a threefold approach: The workshop operated, first, with a praxeological perspective. Our point of departure was the concrete situations of people who are affected by and concerned with climate change in particular ways. Organizers and participants drew attention to people who live under precarious conditions with increased vulnerability to climate change, and who have limited or no visibility in political, economic and ecological systems of decision making. Starting from these contexts, the workshop highlighted concrete practices of resistance through which people oppose the excessive exploitation of natural resources and the emission of climate-damaging gasses. We looked for possible theological qualities in these critical tactics.

Second, the workshop followed an analytic perspective: by taking concrete practices of resistance as its point of departure, we tried to explicate the deeper economic and structural causes of environmental exploitation and the logic of economic growth that fosters climate change. With an explicitly theological perspective, the workshop shed light on theological motives in the respective contexts: Which theological arguments, frameworks, and images contribute(d) to the legitimization of the exploitation of the Earth's resources, and to climate pollution—in the past and in the present? Which alternative frameworks and imaginaries do Christian theology and belief offer, which can help us to critically open up and possibly overcome climate-damaging practices and the logics of exploitation that they are based on?

By doing so, the workshop unfolded, third, a constructive dimension: together, the organizers and the participants opened a space for exchange on climate actions and theories, for the re-consideration of forms of resistance and for the creative imagination of innovative, alternative ways of climate protection and sustainable futures—while drawing from biblical, spiritual, and theological heritage.

This volume presents the contributions of the workshop in revised and expanded versions. In its structure, this publication mirrors the threefold approach of the workshop itself: with concrete practices as the starting point, followed by the analysis of frameworks and their theological components underpinning climate-damaging structures and behavior, and the imagination of different ways of shaping human and non-human relations in the search for more sustainable, ecologically and economically just lifestyles.

The opening part of this volume starts with two concrete situations in which people are confronted with the power of excavation industries, and massive exploitation of natural resources: the coal-mining area in North Rhine-Westphalia, Germany ("Braunkohlerevier NRW"), and the hard coal mining area in La Guajira, Colombia. After a brief outline of the concept "climate justice" in a praxeological perspective (Christian Kern), two introductory texts describe concrete practices of resistance by climate activists in the respective contexts—and reflect on them from the perspective of theological ethics (Benedikt Kern and María Fernanda Herrera Palomo).

Part I then initiates an investigation of different frameworks and epistemologies that mark current discourses on climate change: i.e. eco-fascism and its influence on the social climate in today's societies (Elizabeth Pyne); the critical and constructive impulses of eco-feminism (Irmgard Klein); and possibilities of overcoming anthropocentrism in social structures and theological discourse (Sybille Trawöger, Dan Horan, and Michael Nausner). Each of these contributions develops a critical theological perspective that shows how theology can either contribute to an objectification of nature or to an alternative, more open, less dominant and non-instrumental relation between human and non-human beings, and their environment.

Part II deepens the praxeological aspects and moves into concrete practical fields: i.e. eco-activism (Sebastian Salaske-Lentern); school education and pedagogy (Claudia Gärtner); and poetry of young people (Petr Jandejsek). The contributions explicate both the challenges and the conflicts that mark the respective fields. They discuss forms of theology and spirituality that are able to contribute to the development of more sustainable and economically critical lifestyles.

Finally, Part III presents reflections for the imagination of alternative futures, with the horizon of biblical eschatological hope (Susana Vilas Boas), and apocalyptic thinking (Gregor Taxacher). A collaborative article then develops a critical reflection on modern state territoriality and presents impulses to overcome the correlated logic of exploitation on the basis of a biblical understanding of land stewardship.

The volume closes with a final chapter by the editors that brings together, in a heterogeneous collage, important remarks, open questions and criticism that came up before, during, and after the workshop—and which require further consideration.

Doing climate justice does not simply imply constructing a framework in which costs and benefits of climate justice are calculated in adequate ways and where the respective capacities of the agents involved and the people affected by climate change are taken into account. As the introductory remarks indicate, "doing climate justice" means opening up a space of negotiation where the "common concern of humankind"—the fight against the climate crisis—is connected to concrete, particular contexts and situations. From there, the measures and means of climate action are re-considered so that the experiences and conditions of the respective places become visible and start to play a decisive role in the design of climate action and the initiation of structural change on political, social and economic levels.

Theology—especially with its long and strong tradition of liberation theologies—can contribute to "doing climate justice." It is part of its practice to cultivate a particular sensitivity for human and non-human lives in precarious situations. Its discourse offers a place for the articulation of the "other", for the excluded, marginalized or weakened experiences and realities. In these particular situations, it searches for structural causes of injustice and precariousness and brings them to light in critical analyses. At the same time, theology raises awareness of the creativity and potentiality of practices, beliefs, lifestyles and knowledges of cultures that were invisible, inaudible before. Theological discourse opens up a space for the discovery of transformed social structures that move beyond the destructive mechanisms of exclusion and exploitation, be it of human beings, animals or environment as a whole. This, finally, modifies and enlarges the meaning and practice of "climate justice". In the framework of the UNFCCC [United Nations Framework Convention on Climate Change] as well as in the Paris Agreement, there is a widespread understanding of justice as *distributive* justice. Costs and benefits of climate action are calculated and distributed with regard to the responsibilities and the capacities of agents involved, especially from the perspective of the CBDR-RC-principle

[Common but Differentiated Responsibilities and Respective Capabilities]. Climate action becomes fairer when it pays attention to the different circumstances, historical contributions and the current capacities of diverse agents. "Doing climate justice" in this regard means to calculate and organize climate action in a way that meets the requirements, capacities, needs and the potential of the agents involved. In this sense, justice is an endeavor of human intelligence, calculation and planning—a human product. The meaning of justice emerges within a framework of productivity and manufacturing, prolonging an instrumental way of reasoning.

Theology broadens this view on justice critically, by referring to a kind of justice that is not simply a product of human intelligence and creativity alone. Instead, theology deals with a meaning of justice that integrates, crucially, a moment of unavailability, indeterminability, and non-instrumental openness. Justice, theologically speaking, comes as a divine gift, without the possibility of being anticipated and/or calculated. Rather than a clear and distinct calculation and distribution, it has the character of a visitation or a haunting. Doing justice theologically, then, implies taking the risk to move beyond a framework or attitude of calculation, planning and—thus—domination. Instead, the risk is to enter a space of vulnerable openness. However, wouldn't this risky movement allow us, on a very fundamental level, to cultivate relationships towards other human and non-human lives, relationships that pay attention to the dignity and worth of all beings? Such an attitude helps us to resist the temptation to subjugate the "other" to a regime of successful calculation in means-ends frameworks. Such an attitude can be seen as a critical resistance to logics of exploitation which stand at the basis of the climate crisis.

The articles collected in this volume invite readers to trace the theological dimension of climate justice in multiple ways. The texts open up a space of negotiation in which different realities of life under the conditions of the current climate crisis are made visible and discussed critically. This kaleidoscope of perspectives invites readers to discover theological reflections and impulses on how to do climate justice and take responsibility in the face of the climate crisis.

OPENING

In Practice: Points of Disrupture

Doing Climate Justice: Spaces of Negotiation

A Conceptual Outline

Christian Kern

Abstract

This article traces the changing, multifaceted use of the term climate justice on the basis of documents from international relations. It elaborates that climate justice is conceptually and practically characterized by a double tension: particularity and universality as well as stabilization and contestation. With these characteristics, climate justice represents a normative principle, a binding agent of climate policy, as well as a tool for its critique. It opens spaces of negotiation not only for efficient but also for just climate protection measures.

Keywords

Paris agreement; justice; critique; conceptual polarity; space; negotiation

1 Paradise lost?

The "Weserbergland" is a low mountain range in the middle of Germany, somewhere between Hannover and Göttingen. It is a region with large woods, rivers, only a few tourists at any season, and many possibilities for walking, hiking, relaxing, and closeness to nature. A small valley is located in the middle of the Weserbergland, called "Silberbachtal"—"Silver Creek Valley"—which is one of the best known areas for hiking in the region: deep forests, a very divers fauna, foxes under the roots of the trees, winds in the willows, and clear water in small brooks inhabited by fishes like trouts or perches.

A view years ago, the Silberbachtal was still a shimmering, colorful, beautiful and paradisiacal area, but during the last four years, from 2016 on, the situation has changed dramatically.[1] After two very dry summers with high temperatures far above average, with only little rain and many dusty days, the valley has changed intensively. The trees—especially the pines—couldn't deal with the

1 Möller, *Der Trend.*

 | DOI:10.30965/9783657795314_002

dry local climate anymore and quietly began to wither. The Silver Creek lost about 75% of its average water level, became slow and musty. Simultaneously, a well-known parasite—the bark beetle—took its opportunity and spread over a large area. After three years, the pine forest couldn't bear the burden anymore and died little by little. After the fir trees lost their needles, the foresters decided to cut them down, 70% of the former tree population. What remained on the now emerging open areas was a moonscape, a dry area peppered with tree stumps.—The Silver Creek Valley, a lost paradise?

There is much evidence and proof of the reality of climate change in our living environments worldwide. Science tells us about it, and so does as well our own everyday experience. De-forestation like described in the Silberbachtal is only one of many symptom of the reality of climate change: sea level rise, ice mass loss in the alps and at the poles, loss of land and the decline of biodiversity. With the growing amount of evidence of human-induced the number of coordinated actions to react on climate change has grown as well. Countermeasures were taken in many different forms, on local, national and global level that involve diverse agents, associations, community institutions from all societal realms: street movements, activities of civil disobedience, institutional cooperation on the international level, global governance activities. "Climate action" is a name for a large range of activities, including actions to analyze and assess the impact of climate change, actions to reveal historical and structural causes and to oppose to the deeper factors of climate exploitation, actions to mitigate the effects of changed climate and weather conditions, actions to adapt to changed conditions of live in order to prevent future climate harm, actions to protest against economic structures and logics of exploitation, actions to take responsibility and to respond to the challenge of changing live conditions on earth.

To take responsibility—the questions and challenges raised by climate change transcend a purely pragmatic dimension. They do not simply affect and challenge people all over the world and ask for action, they are marked by deep ethical questions: questions of justice.

Because: Who has to take responsibility?—in which form and in regard to which concrete problem? Are there different degrees to which people bear responsibility on and in climate change? What should and must be done and by whom? Where to set priorities? And how is it possible to design a fair way of addressing the climate crisis? Questions like these point to differences in regard to causes, responsibilities and capacities connected with climate change. It is true that climate change threatens, challenges and changes the whole planet and is therefore a challenge for all human and non-human agents. However, there are differences to be respected and be paid attention to. People in different parts of the world have played different roles in climate pollution and have contributed in different degrees to climate change. Some individuals, groups, nations are more capable to react on climate change more effectively—due to divergent economic, topographical, financial infrastructural reasons. The vulnerability to climate change is distributed in different ways: people at coasts on small islands are more affected and threatened by rising sea levels than people living in rural areas or secure urban centers.[2] Last but not least there are temporal questions to be addressed: former generations have profited by environmental pollution. Which responsibility do they take in regard to young people today and in regard to children not yet born—a question of intergenerational justice.

In the midst of climate action, the question arises of climate justice: How is it possible to deal with the realities of climate change in a just manner which takes the different responsibilities, capacities into account, as well as the different grades of climate vulnerability?

2 Climate Justice in International Politics

Climate justice is a normative principle and a critical tool in the discourse on climate change and the design of climate action. Like a golden thread, it runs through the negotiations on climate policies on the level of national and especially international politics.

The *United Nations Framework Convention on Climate Change* (UNFCCC)[3] from 1992 does not make explicit use of the term itself, however, it formulates several guiding principles for the coordination of international climate action that can count as indirect articulation of climate justice.[4] The principles are formulated to foster fair and effective actions against the climate crisis and to guarantee that the main objective of the convention is reached: the "stabilization of greenhouse gas concentration in the atmosphere at a level that would prevent dangerous anthropogenic interference with the climate system" (Art. 2).

One of the guiding ideas which the convention formulates is the "principle of common but differentiated responsibilities and capacities" (CBDR-RC-principle). The parties of the convention are seen as individual agents with different histories in regard to climate pollution, and with different capacities to react on climate change. To different degrees, nations have contributed to

2 Füssel, *Vulnerability*.

3 United Nations, *United Nations Framework*.

4 Lienkamp, *Klimagerechtigkeit*, esp. pp. 171–173.

the emission of greenhouse gases, and to different degrees are they capable to answer its effects. The contributions in the past and the capacities to react in the present vary from each situation and the respective people involved. The CBDR-RC-principle takes these differences into account and prepares the ground for a differentiated design of international cooperation/action, building on a detailed knowledge about economic, political, social capacities of compensation, adaption, mitigation, and adequate distribution of costs and resources.

The UNFCCC connects the CBDR-RC-principle with another regulative idea: the right to sustainable development. By this, climate measures are embedded in a larger context and goal: International climate policies have to be organized in such a way that they foster the sustainable development of the parties involved, especially of so called "less developed" countries. In the framework of the convention, sustainable development is understood primarily as economic growth on the basis of the possibility to participate in a "supportive and open international market system" (UNFCCC, Art. 3, Nr. 5).

The Paris Agreement from 2015[5] builds on the UNFCCCC and develops the main contents and principles of the latter further. It specifies the main objective of the international climate cooperation on the level of the UN and reformulates the decisive guiding principles of climate action. The Preamble states accordingly:

> *The Parties to this Agreement,* [...]
>
> [i]*n pursuit* of the objective of the convention, and being guided by its principles, including the **principle of equity** and **common but differentiated responsibilities and respective capabilities**, in the light of different national circumstances, [...]
>
> [e]*mphasizing* the intrinsic relationship that climate change actions, responses and impacts have with **equitable access to sustainable development and eradication of poverty** [...],
>
> [a]*cknowledging* that climate change is a common concern of humankind, Parties should, when taking action to address climate change, respect, promote and consider their respective obligations on **human rights**, the right to health, the rights of indigenous peoples, local communities, migrants, children, persons with disabilities and people in vulnerable situations and the right to development, as well as gender equality, empowerment of women and intergenerational equity,

5 United Nations, *Paris Agreement.*

> [n]*oting* the importance of ensuring the integrity of all ecosystems, including oceans, and the protection of biodiversity, recognized by some cultures as Mother Earth, and noting the **importance for some of the concept of "climate justice"**, when taking action to address climate change, [...] Have agreed as follows [...].

What follows is a more detailed definition of the general objective of the convention and the planned climate measures based on it. While the UNFCCC of 1992 has spoken only in a generalizing way of the aim to stabilize the concentration of greenhouse gas in the atmosphere, the Paris Agreement now specifies the target idea: The main objective of the Agreement is to strengthen the global response to climate change in order to hold the global average temperature rise below 2°C, better below 1.5°C.

In order to reach this goal, the Agreement does not only formulate a bundle of concrete measures to be undertaken by the subscribing Parties, but it reformulates and enhances the guiding principles already presented in the UNFCCC: It makes explicit use of the term "climate justice" and connects it with the "principle of equity" (Paris Agreement, Preamble). It quotes again the CBDR-RC-principle and underlines the importance of circumstances, conditions, and contexts of people affected by climate change, and the different degrees of climate vulnerability which have to be taken into account in the organization, financing and calculation of climate measures. At the same time, it picks up the sustainable development rule, enlarging it with the main goal of "eradication of poverty" and the realization and protection of human rights.

3 A Complex Set of Norms, a Space of Negotiation

As this very brief look into the major documents of climate policies on the international level shows, there is not one single definition or interpretation of "climate justice". Climate justice is a name for a set of perspectives, norms and regulative principles that are applied and accentuated by agents of climate protection in different, nuanced ways. The UNFCCC and the Paris Agreement intertwine, under the title of "climate justice", the analysis of historical contributions to climate protection with the present capacities to react on climate change effects and with the different degrees of vulnerability to climate change effects. The meaning of "climate justice" shifts further when we take a look on other agents of climate protection, such as scientific institutions or climate activists. Some of the latter connect climate justice to questions of social justice and plead for a profound system change: the overcoming of liberal market-based economies with their belief in the self-regulation of economic processes and the establishment of fair structures of trade and exchange.[6] With a modified perspective on international relations and global governance, scholars plead for strengthening international cooperation structures in order to make climate change measures more effective and to expand the participate possibilities of the people, especially those who are affected by climate change more directly, in processes of decision making.[7]

The fact that the different principles that are brought together under the title "climate justice" are controversial themselves increases the complexity again. This concerns, for instance, the so-called polluter-pays-principle. At a first glance, it seems to be evident that those agents/nations that have contributed more to climate pollution (and benefitted more form it) in the last 150 years, should also pay more for climate mitigation, adaption, and compensation today. However, it remains difficult to deduct directly an obligation to pay or, more generally speaking, an ethical responsibility from the historical facts when we take into account that people, at least until the 1950s, did not and/or could not know have a clear knowledge and consciousness of the long-term effects of their energy production, gas emissions or consumption habits.[8]

Despite this complexity of "climate justice", one can identify certain components that appear regularly and on different levels in the discourse about just climate measures and policies. These components represent crucial aspects and nodes of meanings of climate justice. Mutually intertwined and correlated, they form a normative network and outline of what we can understand by climate justice: responsibility, capacity, vulnerability, visibility, human rights, livability. The mentioned documents address all parties as *equal partners* in the common endeavor of climate protection and the commitment to the development of more sustainable cultures of life on earth. At the same time, the agents involved in climate protection measures are to be perceived in their respective social, economic, cultural, political *situations*, with different *capacities* to react on climate change effects. The different degrees of *vulnerability* to climate change are connected with different degrees of *visibility*: Often, those who are more directly affected by climate change effects, with lower capacities to compensate their impact, are less visible in the dominant discourses and less represented in the systems of decision-making than others. This observation implies different forms of *responsibility* in regard to climate change and climate action: All are equally responsible for the protection of the

6 System Change not Climate Change.

7 Skillington, *Climate Justice*.

8 Moellendorf, *Climate Change Justice*.

earth's ecosystem and the global climate, as the latter forms the basis of human and non-human lives. However, the ways and forms of climate change action has to be decoded and designed in the light of different social, economic, political contexts in the past and in the present.

Climate justice implies a *mutual awareness of differences* and a respectful perception of the other, a sensitivity and view for the particular circumstances, needs, and limits that mark one's situation. The most general component of climate justice in the horizon of the documents and discourses mentioned above are human rights. Climate action has to be done in a way that it helps to realize and protect sustainably *human rights* and for the "eradication of poverty" on the basis of structural changes in economic, political and societal regards.

Climate justice, as such a set of norms and principles guiding climate action, is characterized by two internal tensions which are constitutive of it and give it a critical and creative dynamic. The first is the polarity between universality and particularity. On the one hand, climate change challenges all people on earth equally insofar everyone is part of the global system of live whose interconnectedness is becoming more and more visible in the last years. The global climate is seen more and more as a common good which is there for all, and, thus, all should engage in its protection in order to enable livable live on earth for present and future generations, including those not yet born. Climate protection takes place in this universal horizon and only seems to be successfully possible if all people support it, with equal rights and a fundamentally equal responsibility.

On the other hand, there are specific and particular situations that require priority and special attention because the impact of climate change is stronger there and makes urgent reactions necessary. The vulnerability to climate change effects is distributed in different ways, depending on infrastructural, political, topographical, cultural contexts and conditions. Vice versa, the potential to react to climate change effects varies as well from agent to agent, community to community, nation to nation producing different degrees to which people are able to take responsibility and react efficiently on the climate crisis. Climate action becomes (more) fair when it addresses climate change as a common concern of all human beings as bearers of equal rights, and, at the same time when it addresses and involves them differently, in correlation to respective situation, contexts, conditions, and capacities.

A second crucial tension in climate justice as a set of norms and guiding principles is the difference between stabilization and contestation. It is directly connected to the polarity of universality and particularity. Climate justice, understood as a principle that takes account of the contexts of climate change impact and the variant distribution of capacities to react on it, contributes to the integrative character of climate action. Individuals, groups, communities, nation states will only take part in climate action and submit themselves to climate policies if the latter do not exceed the capacities of the respective agents and if they are perceived as fair in regard to other agents involved. To the extent that an international climate regime or agreement is sensitive to specific situations and takes into account the different capacities of the actors involved, the likelihood that the agreement will be upheld and applied effectively increases. In short, climate justice strengthens the binding power of conventions on climate change and stabilizes the normativity of a climate regime.

At the same time, climate justice as a bundle of normative principles marked by the tension between universal claims and particular situations and needs has a critical function. As shown above, it draws the attention again and again to concrete contexts where people experience the impact of climate change and bring up the question how and on the basis of what cooperation or support, reaction to climate change effects are possible. Climate justice serves, then, as a critical lens for a permanent reviewing of agreements, rules and measures of climate actions, the distribution of costs and resources, starting from concrete situations and respective conditions of life.

In this sense, "climate justice" has a paradoxical nature: By paying particular attention to specific circumstances, conditions, and capacities in regard to climate action, it strengthens the universal binding force of international cooperation, agreement or regimes, yet, at the same time, by doing so, it reproduces permanently a critical re-consideration that questions the status quo. Climate justice oscillates between universality and particularity, stabilization and contestation. As a bundle of normative principles, it does not establish a homogeneous set of rules able to regulate or orient climate action once and for all, but opens a permanent critical space of negotiation in which climate action can be forged, applied, criticized and re-considered anew.

If we understand climate justice not simply as a stable set of rules, but as a dynamic principle that oscillates between universalizing integration and stabilization on the one hand, and contextualization and contestation on the other hand, it becomes finally possible to outline a particular understanding of "doing climate justice". Climate justice is not simply done where people draw utopian images of peaceful worlds where human and non-human beings live together in harmony in a peaceful, harmonic environment. Climate justice is not simply done when/where people come up with well calculated masterplans on how costs of climate change mitigation, adaption or compensation should be distributed in a fair manner that pays attention to circumstances and capacities in the past and the present. Climate justice is not done where an international a carbon market is established based on the belief in an efficient self-regulation of the system itself. Instead, against the background of the previous considerations, climate justice is done in and by opening a space of negotiation where existing frameworks, distribution mechanisms, economic rules, regimes of visibility are transformed on a way that human and non-human experience can start to play an active and efficient role in the discourse on and the design of climate action and the imagination of a post-climate-crisis-world.

References

Füssel, Hans-Martin, "Vulnerability to Climate Change and Poverty," in: Ottmar Edenhofer et al. (eds.), *Climate Change, Justice and Sustainability*, Dordrecht: Springer Netherlands, 2012, 9–17.

Lienkamp, Andreas, "Klimagerechtigkeit: Fairness in Zeiten globaler Erwärmung," in: Markus Vogt/Peter Schallenberg, *Soziale Ungleichheiten: Von Der empirischen Analyse zur gerechtigkeitsethischen Reflexion*, Paderborn: Ferdinand Schöningh, 2017, 167–192.

Moellendorf, Darrel, "Climate Change Justice," in: *Philosophy Compass* 10, no. 3 (2015), 173–186; https://doi.org/10.1111/phc3.12201 [accessed 20.05.2021].

Möller, Sonja, "Der Trend ist sehr besorgniserregend", https://www.westfalen-blatt.de/OWL/Kreis-Paderborn/Altenbeken/4318500-Waldzustandsbericht-2020-zeigt-gravierende-Schaeden-im-Wald-auf-Hochstift-Paderborn-stark-vom-Borkenkaefer-betroffen-Der-Trend-ist-sehr-besorgniserregend [accessed 20.05.2021].

Skillington, Tracey, *Climate Justice and Human Rights*, New York: Palgrave Macmillan, 2017.

System Change not Climate Change, "Unser Selbstverständnis," https://systemchange-not-climatechange.at/de/unser-selbstverstaendnis/ [accessed 20.05.2021].

United Nations, "Paris Agreement," https://unfccc.int/sites/default/files/english_paris_agreement.pdf [accessed 20.05.2021].

United Nations, "United Nations Framework Convention on Climate Change," https://unfccc.int/resource/docs/convkp/conveng.pdf [accessed 20.01.2021].

Spirituality at the Abyss

The Coal-Mining Area in Rhineland, Germany as a Liberation-Theological Field of Intervention

Benedikt Kern

Abstract

This article deals with the practice of the ecumenical initiative "Die Kirche(n) im Dorf lassen" ("Leaving the churches in the village") in the Rhenish coal mining area in Western Germany for the preservation of creation and in resistance against the local and global capitalist destruction of villages and forests. To what extent do Christians see themselves challenged as part of the global climate justice movement to take a stand against this destruction through coal mining, which produces the global catastrophic consequences of climate change? What are Christian forms of action such as worship in this and how do politicization processes come about through a "spirituality of conflictivity"?

Keywords

Climate justice; theology and social movements; ecology; liturgy; spirituality and liberation theology

Introduction

The coal-mining area in Rhineland/Germany is the largest lignite deposit in Europe and the coal-fired power generation in the region is one of the largest sources of carbon dioxide in Europe. It is now clear that without an immediate coal phase-out, the Paris climate goals will not be achieved. However, lignite mining is to continue until 2038 and the approved destruction of five more villages, the contamination and lowering of groundwater reservoirs and the further loss of valuable soils is continuing, with serious, irreversible consequences for global warming and the living space of the affected local people, 1,500 of whom are still to be forcibly resettled. There have been protests against the energy company RWE for years, which culminated in the Hambach Forest in 2018 and attracted international attention. In the meantime, the initiative

 | DOI:10.30965/9783657795314_003

"Alle Dörfer bleiben" [*all villages must remain*] and activists who have settled in the villages are fighting to preserve the threatened villages. The climate crisis, produced by capitalist economy, is thus essentially contested in the Rhenish coal mining area as well. This is why the conflicts in the region are relevant for a liberation-theological practice and reflection concerning climate justice.

In 2019, the *Institut für Theologie und Politik* (*Institute for Theology and Politics, ITP*) in Münster, Germany organized a Climate Synod,[1] taking place parallelly to the Roman Amazon Synod, in order to contextualize the ecological and social question in relation to the Rhenish coalfield. Since then, our institute has been actively involved in the initiative "Die Kirche(n) im Dorf lassen" [*Keep the church(es) in the village*].[2]

This Christian initiative, along with other actors, fights for global climate justice, an immediate coal phase-out and, in particular, for the preservation of the threatened churches in the Rhenish lignite mining area. The aim of the initiative is to take action with regard to the churches as buildings, as institutions and as communities. People are involved for a variety of reasons: they want to preserve the churches as cultural assets, but they also want to stand up for the integrity of creation and for global climate justice, i.e., the living conditions of future generations and of people living in different parts of the world. "Die Kirche(n) im Dorf lassen" expands the resistance and practice of the climate justice movement in the Rhenish coal mining area to include a perspective of organized Christians. A Christian perspective within the climate justice movement is not as self-evident today as it used to be in the peace movement or the anti-nuclear movement, in which decidedly Christian actors have always played a role. At the same time, Christians do participate in the climate justice movement, even if they are not necessarily visible as such in it.

The initiative "Die Kirche(n) im Dorf lassen" exists since the demolition of the so-called "Cathedral of Immerath" in 2018 (i.e. the church of one of the villages next to the coal-mining pit) and has been active particularly since the beginning of 2020. Its activities are also about looking for forms to oppose the madness of climate destruction in the Rhenish coal mining area. The experiences in 2020, which were marked by the Corona crisis, have shown that despite all external difficulties, the group has been able to continue to build up and stabilize itself in order to make the protest more permanent.

---

1 Https://www.itpol.de/klimasynode-im-rheinischen-braunkohlerevier/ [last accessed 24.04.2021].

2 Https://www.kirchen-im-dorf-lassen.de/ [last accessed 24.04.2021]. "Keeping the church(es) in the village" is a common expression in German and means sticking to the facts or refusing to be unobjective.

1 Services at the Edge: Protest and Celebration of Hope

An important form of creating visible places of gathering in public were open-air services in the threatened villages at the edge of the open-cast mine, which are in line with the tradition of the "political night prayers" of the circle of activists around protestant theologian Dorothee Sölle in post-war Germany. For many people, these services offer the opportunity to make a public statement and to be visible with their own attitude of opposition to the existing situation, as well as to draw strength, to be sure of their own perspective and to deepen the motivation for the common confrontations. The "Services on the Edge" of the Garzweiler open-cast mine, for instance, are an attempt to open up a space to give the conflicts and disputes a place, to reflect on them, to endure them together and to draw strength for moving forward. Liturgy in public space is something completely new for many people. At the same time, it ties in with well-known and often little-present traditions, which are, even in secular context, often still known especially by older people. Perhaps this marks what is special about "Die Kirche(n) im Dorf lassen": that the two dimensions of protest on the one hand and that of the expression of one's own faith in the ritualized form of liturgy on the other hand, are brought together. In the liturgical celebration, affirmation and disappointment, doubts and certainties, powerlessness in the face of overwhelming, destructive violence and hope for the Kingdom of God are given their place. Thus, on the one hand, these liturgies are characterized by a traditional ecclesial character, i.e. they include biblical scripture readings, sermons, prayers, blessing rites, songs, times of silence, mutual exchange, processions, erection of a cross, commemoration of the dead, liturgical vigils, carol singing blessing of houses threatened with demolition, etc. Traditional Catholic Eucharistic celebrations also belong to these forms. On the other hand, these services take place without ministers, but they are carried out by the self-confident understanding of the celebrants and participants and as collectively as possible. Those participating are invited to contribute with their own words, comments and experiences. It is an ongoing challenge to encourage those who are not trained in theology to prepare and preside over services themselves.

In addition to traditional liturgical elements, the services also integrate aspects that are rather unusual for a church liturgy: On the one hand, this is the choice of place and time for the service, such as in close proximity to the demolition excavators at work in the village of Lützerath,[3] in front of trees

3 Https://www.kirchen-im-dorf-lassen.de/beitr%C3%A4ge/pressemitteilung-polizei-st%C3%BCrmt-in-gottesdienst/ [last accessed 24.04.2021].

threatened by immediate clearing,[4] on a road connecting the villages that was to be demolished,[5] in memory of the destroyed Immerather Cathedral at its original location[6] or in front of the church door on the occasion of the announced de-consecration of the church of Keyenberg.[7]

2 Liturgy and Civil Disobedience

In any case, church service as an executed transgression of rules may seem extraordinary. For example, church services took place with the direct presence of police task forces and also with violent attacks on their part, on the company grounds of *RWE Power*[8] symbolically re-appropriated by the celebration, at the edge of the open-cast mine,[9] at symbolic locations in the villages during ongoing demolition work or in front of a village pub in Keyenberg[10] occupied and "reopened" by activists, surrounded by police forces. Disobedient actions like keeping the Keyenberg St. Cross Church open in 2020 by singing for hours on the "Day of the Open Monument", when the church was supposed to be closed to the public, are encouraging examples of self-determined action.

These celebrations took place directly at the sites of destruction, even when it was not allowed, and so the content of the liturgy and the local and temporal context were closely related. Due to the direct proximity to activities of groups of the climate justice movement, such as during the *Ende Gelände*[11]action days in September 2020 or on the occasion of the actions of civil disobedience to prevent the demolition works, there was not only a verbal solidarity with all

4 Https://www.kirchen-im-dorf-lassen.de/beitr%C3%A4ge/offener-brief-l%C3%BCtzerath/ [last accessed 24.04.2021].

5 Https://www.youtube.com/watch?v=omAIsSeXxwo&feature=youtu.be und https://www.kirchen-im-dorf-lassen.de/beitr%C3%A4ge/liturgische-nachtwache/ [last accessed 24.04.2021].

6 Https://www.youtube.com/watch?v=oD8OBD3Lt4I&feature=youtu.be [last accessed 24.04.2021].

7 Https://www.youtube.com/watch?v=oD8OBD3Lt4I&feature=youtu.be [last accessed 24.04.2021].

8 Https://www.youtube.com/watch?v=LhBJwgz6Awc&feature=youtu.be and https://www.kirchen-im-dorf-lassen.de/beitr%C3%A4ge/gottesdienst-sie-hatten-alles-gemeinsam/ [last accessed 24.04.2021].

9 Https://www.youtube.com/watch?v=F1AzuNH1Vbo&feature=youtu.be [last accessed 24.04.2021].

10 Https://www.youtube.com/watch?v=fzh1nZ7mnGE&feature=youtu.be [last accessed 24.04.2021].

11 For further information about "Ende Gelände" see https://www.ende-gelaende.org/en/ [last accessed 24.04.2021].

those activists who committed civil disobedience, but the services themselves partly became part of the action. Thus, in addition to the symbolic character, the liturgical celebrations and processions also have a character of direct intervention, which on the one hand refers directly to forms of protest in solidarity and on the other hand has a real impact on what is happening on the ground. It is precisely here that questions arise about the intrinsic value of a political church service for activist action.

For "Die Kirche(n) im Dorf lassen" it is important that liturgy is not simply a trick of activists to get attention for themselves and their concerns. For example, accusations were made by the police to the media that these services are held solely to camouflage political gatherings, or to avoid falling under the law on assembly, or to make police repression more difficult. Likewise, the accusation was repeatedly spread on social media that the form of these liturgical celebrations of "Die Kirche(n) im Dorf lassen" was being instrumentalized for political purposes. Such accusations are untenable in view of the motivation of those participating as well as in view of the content of the service. At the same time, it remains important to address them. For those involved in "Die Kirche(n) im Dorf lassen", it is important to emphasize that these services are not simply creative and religiously packaged forms of protest, but that they always have an intrinsic value as services, not only because of their traditional liturgical elements. It is absolutely a theological and not a legal question whether a public gathering is a worship service: The intrinsic value of these services is precisely to give a resistant Christian perspective a form of expression that fits it, which existentially concerns actions and thinking of Christians and which involves a common perspective in light of the "Kingdom of God". In any case, an assessment of the legitimacy and authenticity of a service by a police force is impossible and definitely not compatible with the freedom of religious practice.

3 And the Constituted Church?

The activities of "Die Kirche(n) im Dorf lassen" and especially the church services have often been taken up by the media. This causes resistance among those who do not subscribe to corresponding political options. Contact with local ecclesial communities is very difficult to arrange, especially with the local Catholic community, which is essentially in charge of handling the resettlement. The local parish priest and church council have been very strongly involved in the processes by RWE in recent years, so that the three remaining churches were already sold to RWE Power at the beginning of 2020. Especially

Christians in the threatened villages feel abandoned by the Catholic Church because they feel that clear political signals on the part of the church would have been possible and in order (such as the option of a mining expropriation process of the church buildings, instead of a sale). Thus, there was a great wave of protest when in January 2021 the unofficially ongoing preparations of the parish to desecrate the church of Keyenberg were already announced for March 2021, rather than for the end of the year 2021. An accelerated desecration was finally stopped by the diocese of Aachen with reference to the still pending guiding decision of the NRW state government on how to proceed with the Garzweiler II open-cast mine and the future of the villages which depended on it.[12]

There was only little solidarity with the protests of "Die Kirche(n) im Dorf lassen" on the part of representatives of the churches. At the end of 2020, however, several Protestant superintendents and the Diocesan Council in the diocese of Aachen took a clear stand in favor of the preservation of the villages and an accelerated coal phase-out.[13]

4 Congregational Education in the Face of Destruction

Experimenting with forms of political liturgy in 2020, in the midst of the Corona pandemic, was one of the most important fields of experience for "Die Kirche(n) im Dorf lassen". Increasing one's own capacity to act, coping with experiences of powerlessness and developing awareness of collective forms of action are important elements of this practice. In the process, possibilities as well as limitations were redefined. In the face of chainsaws and demolition excavators, it is not easy to stop the destruction, and yet it is right and important to be present on the ground and to oppose it, for both public perception and for the activists themselves. It makes a difference whether protest and mutually experienced solidarity take place or not, even if the desired effect is not achieved immediately.

In addition to the actions of other actors such as "Alle Dörfer bleiben" or the "Mahnwache Lützerath" ["Picket of Lützerath"], the liturgical forms developed above were able to bring together people from the villages threatened with demolition, committed people involved in the climate justice movement,

12 Https://www.bistum-aachen.de/aktuell/nachrichten/nachricht/Entscheidung-zur-Entwidmung-der-Keyenberger-Kirche-vertagt/ [last accessed 24.04.2021].

13 Https://dioezesanrat-aachen.de/a-media/Forderung-fuer-den-Erhalt-der-bedrohten-Doerfer-im-Rheinischen-Revier/ [last accessed 24.04.2021].

activists who have settled locally in the permanent picket or the forest occupation as well as the many people who repeatedly come from far away to these places to participate in demonstrations, events and church services. In addition to committed Christians who are more or less active in church contexts, numerous people without any affiliation to the churches have also been able to connect to this liturgical form of resistance. Thus, very different people with a more or rather less pronounced connection to Christian tradition meet in the services and events. They are united by common goals of climate justice and the protection of villages. Especially among anarchist-influenced, often very young activists, awakening understanding for explicitly Christian forms of expression of resistance and protest is a fruitful challenge due to mutual fears of contact, which can contribute to a closer cooperation.

Some of those who regularly participate in services of "Die Kirche(n) im Dorf lassen" have repeatedly expressed that it is precisely through this form of service in these respective places that they have found a completely new approach to liturgy or that they were able to find an expression of their faith through it in the first place. In this respect, it is also an interesting field from a pastoral-theological perspective that people articulate their faith here who could not otherwise find a place for it, at least not a collective one.

5 A Spirituality of Conflictivity

Spirituality necessarily plays a role in the reflection on the practice of "Die Kirche(n) im Dorf lassen". But how can spirituality be grasped and meaningfully applied to the experiences of people in the climate hotspot in the Rhineland? According to the Brazilian liberation theologian Alberto da Silva Moreira, spirituality is a physical, existential, at the same time spiritual, deeply human basic experience; it is the persistent breathing of the spirit "which longs for authenticity of existence through all situations in life."[14] For da Silva Moreira, the struggle for the survival of people and nature has a direct spiritual density, since it fundamentally affects the existence of human beings, and as such must be taken seriously: If and when Christians and all those with whom they struggle live in the "here and now" of history with all its hopes and illusions, advances and setbacks, expectations and disappointments, and therein choose to be partisan.[15] Spirituality understood in this way (Moreira calls it the spirituality of conflictivity) also has room for anger about structural, violent

14 Da Silva Moreira, *Spiritualität in der Konfliktivität*, p. 62.
15 Da Silva Moreira, *Spiritualität in der Konfliktivität*, p. 70.

injustice and does not let up in confronting this injustice, not allowing itself to be demobilized by setbacks and holding on to the possibility of overcoming conditions.[16] Moreira emphasizes that a spirituality in conflict also counteracts solo effort and isolation when a community of strugglers emerges "that is always fed by faith and includes in faith many other strugglers of whom one knows without ever knowing them."[17]

Through the experiences of solidarity and common worship practice in "Die Kirche(n) im Dorf lassen", spirituality becomes visible for many as an assurance of one's own thinking, as a source, long breath and grounding of one's own actions in this conflict-ridden field of the Rhenish mining area. A spirituality of conflictivity anchored in this way is not at all any form of escapism, but is closely connected with or even the starting point of a partisan confrontation with the violent and destructive conditions that are particularly visible at the edge of the open-cast mine. Becoming aware of the liberation experience of biblical Israel and the Jesus movement at the abyss of the coal mine and the demolished villages is an incentive to no longer accept the idea that conditions are unchangeable or even natural, but to collectively hold on to the possibility of a good life for all in a world worth living in.

References

Alberto da Silva Moreira, Alberto, Spiritualität in der Konfliktivität. Eine Sicht aus der Befreiungstheologie, in: Giancarlo Collet/Dorothea Sattler (eds.), *In Konflikten leben. Mit Zorn und Zärtlichkeit an der Seite der Armen*, Berlin: Lit 2012, 57–82.

16 Da Silva Moreira, *Spiritualität in der Konfliktivität*, p. 73.
17 Da Silva Moreira, *Spiritualität in der Konfliktivität*, p. 76.

The West Colonizes on a Daily Basis

The El Cerrejón Open-Pit Mine in La Guajira/Colombia and the Coloniality of the World Energy System

María Fernanda Herrera Palomo

Abstract

Our cultural way of thinking and beliefs affect not only our daily life but also our way of how we treat our neighbor and our whole environment. The coal mine problematic in La Guajira (Colombia) between the Wayuú people and Western energy companies is a good example. It shows how the way of Western beliefs allows the exploitation of people, nature and landscapes with long-term consequences for all humankind since the beginning of colonial times.

Keywords

Indigenous peoples; Wayúu; Emberá, development; La Guajira; coal; contamination; water

1 How Our Way of Thinking Influences the Planet[1]

The millenary sociopolitics of multiple peoples who have resisted the colonial and postcolonial system to this day—such as the Awa, Lakota, Wayúu, Maya, Emberá and Navajo, to name a few[2]—is based on their knowledge of the Earth as Mother, as a living being, as the whole each of us is part of, and as the source of life. That precludes seeing it as an object of sale. The sense of community is of maximum cultural importance. On the contrary, the sociopolitics of Western culture continues to be based on the idea that the Earth is a mere resource at the service of man for the "development" of each individual, culture

1 This article is based on a text published in German; Herrera Palomo: *Und täglich kolonisiert.*

2 I have known the worldview of these peoples through my direct contact with the Emberá in 2009, the Lakota of North America through various historical documents such as "God is Red" or "The World we used to live in" by the Lakota Author Vine de Loria; the Wayuú through direct contact in 2009 and 2017, the Awa through accounts of their struggle in Catatumbo in 2017, the Maya through various historical documents, the Navajo through indirect contact.

 | DOI:10.30965/9783657795314_004

or country according to its capacities. With the colonial system, the concepts of civilization, wealth and poverty were introduced with great violence on all continents. These concepts gave rise to racist and classist structures that today are the basis for the exploitation of the Earth and its inhabitants and create policies that continue to devastate numerous peoples and their territories in the name of industrial and economic "development". This idea of the Earth as a mere resource not only prevents harmonious coexistence with the environment, its inhabitants and other cultures, but also encourages the displacement and mass murder not only of entire communities on all continents, but also of millions of beings and forms of life and those who wish to protect them, as demonstrated by the case of La Guajira in Colombia.[3]

2 The Resistance of the Wayúu People and the Mestizo and Afro-Descendant Peasant Communities of La Guajira

The arrival of the Spanish to the continent they called America meant the death and dispossession of millions of its native inhabitants. One of those peoples that managed to survive to this day is the Wayúu people, located in the north of Colombia, in the Guajira region.

Due to the lack of manpower after the genocide carried out by the Spanish against the native peoples, whom they described as inferior and from whom they stole their lands, men and women were brought from the African continent, kidnapped and forced to work as slaves. Thus, the exploitation of humans and of the usurped territories could continue. Some of these men and women escaped and hid in the Guajira territory and formed several free communities. These men and women, together with the Wayúu and mestizo peasants (descendants of whites and indigenous people) resisted for more than 400 years, first to the slave armies, then to the white landowners, and now, in the 20th and 21st century, to the Colombian state and the multinationals that have dispossessed them to make way for one of the largest open-pit coal mines in the world. The mine supplies above all the energy needs and follies of countries such as Germany, Netherlands, Italy, Turkey, and England, among others.[4]

---

3 Colombia's history has left a great legacy of violent deaths of human rights defenders and environmentalists throughout the country. In 2017, Colombia suffered about 186 murders of activists, 44 of which were indigenous. See https://www.elcolombiano.com/colombia/paz-y-derechos-humanos/homicidios-de-indigenas-en-colombia-FM7842135 [accessed 24.05.2021]. Not only Colombia suffers from this phenomenon, the fight against defenders of life is worldwide.

4 See https://www.bing.com/videos/search?q=asi+desterro+la+mina+de+carbon+a+los+negros+de+la+Guajira&view=detail&mid=A94631608C13032F54F3A94631608C13032F54F3&FORM=VIRE Asi desterró la mina de carbón a los negros de la Guajira [accessed 24.05.2021].

3 Arrival of the Energy Companies and "Development"

In 1976, the Colombian government granted a concession for coal exploitation in Guajira. This exploitation began in 1984 under the leadership of the U.S. oil giant Exxon. Until the late 1990s, Colombia owned 50% of the mine; since 2000, the mine has been fully owned by three multinationals: Glencore, BHP Billington and Anglo American. In 2008, the mine extracted 31.1 million tons of coal. Between 1990 and 2010, the mine earned US$ 44,527,379,000.[5] In 2013, it achieved a turnover of US$ 2.3 billion.[6] La Guajira is, despite of this contribution of wealth, the second poorest department in Colombia and the multinationals continue to argue that its expansion is decisive for the progress of La Guajira.

Since its inception, the mine has displaced 35 communities, of which only five have been resettled. The Colombian State extended land titles to some of the native communities of the Guajira and thus suggested them to sell their properties to the company at very low prices under the pretext of making them part of the "development" through new housing, new types of work, health and education. On the other hand, the Wayúu were assigned reservations and part of their territory was declared as wasteland. This is how the government prepared the ground to give it to the multinationals.[7] Those who did not want to sell were forcibly displaced, as Rogelio Ustate, a displaced person from the Afro-descendant community of Tabaco on August 9, 2001, recounts:

> "I remember that it was 10:30 a.m. when arbitrarily, Judge Marta Peñaloza and Intercor[8] officials ordered, pregnant with happiness, to demolish the houses, without any contemplation. That fateful day left only sadness when the bulldozers rammed against the humble houses, thus ending the repeated dreams of a community". He continues: "In a few minutes those machines […] put an end to that site of sacred sentiment and to the peace of the good spirits that never thought they would be touched by the criminal hands of the multinationals from which hangs a bloody greed that has left dire consequences in the territory of Guajira."[9]

The dire consequences of the companies actions were the contamination of the main river of the Guajira, the Ranchería River, the disappearance of

5 http://extractivismoencolombia.org/el-cerrejon-carbon-para-las-potencias-y-miseria-y-pobreza-para-colombia-y-la-guajira/, 8 [accessed 24.05.2021].
6 http://www.labuenavida-pelicula.com/mina-el-cerrejon/: Transfondo [accessed 24.05.2021].
7 Cf. note 4: Así desterró la mina carbón a los negros de la Guajira.
8 Intercor: International Colombia Resources Corporation.
9 Centro Nacional de Memoria Histórica: *Del ñame espino*, p. 67.

17 streams, the diversion of two[10], as well as the destruction of several aquifers (groundwater). Thus, numerous natural wells on which the Wayúu population have depended for hundreds of years, dried up and increased droughts in a territory that is only suitable for artisanal agricultural work.[11] In 2015, the company used approximately 35 million liters of water per day, while families in the region have to meet their basic needs with only seven liters per day.[12]

With the water problem and the worsening climatic conditions, corn, bean, cassava and sorghum crops have started to disappear, as well as agricultural and livestock activities and, finally, handicraft activities such as textile manufacturing. Lack of water and air pollution have brought hunger, real poverty and serious health problems. The company has produced high-risk jobs and many of its workers suffer, as well as a large part of the population, from serious respiratory problems, especially the children. Territorial destruction has endangered the culture and community life of all its inhabitants.[13] As Rogelio Ustate describes in his Chronicle:

> Today we cannot work because we have no land to do so. For such an obvious reason, today we are consumers and not producers, we carry in our souls an infinite pain and many illnesses due to the contamination that the Cerrejón multinational is leaving in the Guajira territory.[14]

4 Resistance Today

From the moment of displacement, the communities have been fighting for the defense of human rights and territory and have been supported by NGOs such as CINEP and human rights lawyers, among others, with a large number of legal actions. As an example, in 2002, they achieved a ruling in favor of the

10 Las huellas que dejó el Cerrejon—Documental explotación de carbón mina El Cerrejón—La Guajira Colombia, in: https://www.youtube.com/watch?v=ryssy7pJhJI, posted 10.07.2017, Minute 20:04.

11 Las huellas del Cerrejón—Documental explotación de carbón mina El Cerrejón—La Guajira, Colombia, in: https://www.youtube.com/watch?v=ryssy7pJhJI, posted 10.07.2017. See also: Colombia: Guajira entre la riqueza y el olvido, at: https://www.youtube.com/watch?v=BlYU6-2qafE, accessed 24.09.2016.

12 Colombia: Guajira entre la riqueza y el olvido: https://www.youtube.com/watch?v=BlYU6-2qafE [the link doesn't exist anymore], accessed 24.09.2016. Minute 16:16 to 17:04.

13 Las huellas del Cerrejón—Documental explotación de carbón mina El Cerrejón—La Guajira, Colombia, posted 10.07.2017, también: Centro Nacional de Memoria Histórica: *Del ñame espino al calabazo: Objetos que despiertan memoria*. Also: Guajira, entre pobreza y olvido, in: https://www.youtube.com/watch?v=BlYU6-2qafE 4/9/2016.

14 Centro Nacional de Memoria Histórica: *Del ñame espino*, p. 68.

community of Tabaco, which demanded that the mayor of Hatonueva rebuild the community of Tabaco within 48 hours, a reconstruction that until now has not been fulfilled.[15]

The defense for life led not only to unite the strength of the Wayúu women, the Wayúu and the peasant communities, but has also earned the solidarity of international movements and organizations such as Kolko e.V.[16], Ende Gelände, and Misereor, among others, to defend the life and territory, and to prevent the company from continuing to expand and divert more rivers and streams as is currently the urgent case of the Bruno stream, so that the company can extract an additional 40 million tons of coal. The detour of the stream was initiated without prior consultation with the affected communities and towns.[17]

Coal mining means for the communities, as Jackelyn Romero, a Wayúu leader, expressed in an interview, "taking from the Earth what is in its belly."[18]

It is for this reason that land and life defenders like Jackelyn Romero and Samuel Arregoces (who, like many other human rights and land defenders, live under constant threat by illegal armed actors and by the State) have come to Europe in the company of Catalina Caro Galves, of the CENSAT Agua Viva Organization, in the summer of 2017, to inform and make coal-consuming peoples understand the situation they and the territories where they live are facing. They have also shown solidarity with the German movement in defense of the Hambach Forest and warn us in general of the threat that we all will have to face because of the economic system that turns us into mere consumers and continues to exhaust ever faster the last sources of life and ancestral communities of the planet and thus ourselves.

Today more than ever we need to strengthen alliances and above all change our way of thinking in order to change our values, policies and economies for values, policies and economies that protect life, the Earth, the people and especially those who are least accountable for the destruction of the planet on which we all depend and for which we are all responsible.[19] As far as the case of La Guajira and continued colonization on a global level is concerned, taking

15 Ibid.

16 Kolko: Menschenrechte für Kolumbien e.V: www.kolko.net.

17 El caso del Arroyo Bruno https://www.elespectador.com/tags/arroyo-bruno/. Also: Las Huellas del Cerrejón—Documental explotación de carbón mina El Cerrejón—La Guajira, Colombia, at: https://www.youtube.com/watch?v=ryssy7pJhJI. Posted 10.07.2017.

18 *La defensora del agua.*

19 In 2017 I had the possibility to accompany Jackelyn Romero Epiayú, Samuel Arregoces, and Catalina Caro Galves, I went with them to Hambacher Forst and this article was inspired by their visit to Cologne.

responsibility implies putting an imminent end to the era of coal and the idea of "development" on a purely industrial and economic level.

Translated from Spanish: Stefan Silber

References

Centro Nacional de Memoria Histórica: *Del ñame espino al calabazo, objetos que despiertan memoria.* Bogotá: CNMH, 2015.

Herrera Palomo, Maria Fernanda: *Und täglich kolonisiert der Westen. Der Steinkohleabbau in Kolumbien und seine Folgen für Menschen und Umwelt,* in: ila 413 (2018), 4–5.

Kolko: Menschenrechte für Kolumbien e.V: www.kolko.net [accessed 24.05.2021].

La defensora del agua en medio de la sed de La Guajira, in: https://www.radionacional.co/especiales-paz/jakeline-romero-epiayu-una-voz-medio-de-la-sed-de-la-guajira [accessed 24.05.2021].

PART I

Frameworks and Epistemologies

Dangerous Forecasts for a Climate of Justice: Far-Right Environmentalisms and a Planet on Fire

Elizabeth Pyne

Abstract

The urgency of the climate crisis is becoming increasingly visible in far-right politics in the United States and Europe, as ecological themes are rearticulated through nationalist visions of ethnic and racial identity and connected to issues like global migration. While these shifts connect to a well-established history of right-wing ecological discourse, including ecofascism, the outsized influence of climate change denialism on the right and the common association of environmentalism with progressive aims have tended to obscure these worrying trends. This contribution to theological cultivation of climate justice is primarily diagnostic—an account of fast-moving political developments that merit attention from theologians who are committed to struggles against racism, xenophobia, and Christian supremacy in efforts toward planetary transformation.

Keywords

Climate change denial; ecofascism; Naomi Klein; political ecology; populism; white nationalism

1 Change Is in the Air?

Liberative theologies seeking just responses to the climate catastrophe face challenges both numerous and substantial, many of which are well known to the environmental movement writ large. Among these challenges are: the gap between knowledge and action; the inertia of consumerism, whether comfortable or conflicted; bureaucratic idling and insufficient political leadership; deep-rooted structural inequalities; and tangled webs of cause and effect. Then there is the entrenched resistance of financiers and the fossil-fuel industry. This last is tied to an ideological position that contests not only more strenuous calls for eco-social transformation or particular policy responses but the very claim that there is a problem to begin with. Buoyed by a vocal handful of

 | DOI:10.30965/9783657795314_005

high-level scientists, a well-funded and politically-connected "climate change counter-movement" has sought to cast doubt on the overwhelming scientific consensus that climate change constitutes a serious threat to vast swathes of plant, animal, and human life and thus on the need to make any real changes to existing political and economic systems—let alone the need to rethink nearly everything about them. Climate change denial has not, in fact, materialized spontaneously from the ground up, but has been consciously manufactured and disseminated.[1] For the past decade or so, such denialism has exerted an outsized influence on the cultural and political landscape in the United States and has made significant inroads elsewhere, including Brazil, Australia, the United Kingdom, and parts of Europe.

My interest in this chapter lies in pursuing the distinction between climate action and climate justice at a moment when it seems that the tide is finally shifting and outright denialism is increasingly embattled. I am motivated by the concern that "taking climate change seriously"—among the powers that be, among those who did not before—creates a profoundly ambivalent situation rather than a necessarily hopeful one.[2] As Naomi Klein maintains, convincing people that there is a crisis does not indicate how they will be inclined to act; experience shows that the naming of an emergency can lead to opportunistic abuses and the retrenchment of powerful interests rather than their dislodging.[3] So, while there is no doubt that the refusal to give credence to climate change contributes to an array of socio-ecological harms, a move toward climate action is not tantamount to climate justice. Indeed, some ways of conceiving and reacting to the climate crisis are profoundly at odds with any just vision of environmental transformation.[4]

In what follows I examine aspects of the "lethal dialogue" that Klein contends is underway between two "planetary and political trends" characteristic of the past decade: on the one hand, the intensification of climate-driven pressures

1 See Klein, *This Changes Everything*, especially Ch. 1, "The Right is Right"; the quoted phrase is sociologist Robert Bulle's (44). See also Oreskes/Conway, *Merchants of Doubt*.

2 In case it has not been clear enough, I want to emphasize that this recognition is differential. The ability to come to awareness in one's own time is itself deeply unequal: residents of some island nations and coastal communities, and many others in the Global South, know that the crisis is long since arrived.

3 Klein, *On Fire*, p. 21; Stephenson, *Against Climate Barbarism*.

4 I use "climate justice" as something of a placeholder throughout this piece, acknowledging the sweep of debate about what specific socio-ecological conditions are sought under this rubric. It should be clear in what follows that the kinds of racism, religious intolerance, and global brutality in the ideologies I describe are inconsistent with even a minimal standard of justice. I also note that my focus is on its human dimensions, though not to the exclusion of more-than-human facets addressed in more sustained ways elsewhere in this volume.

across the globe and, on the other, the rise in visibility and political impact of "an increasingly violent hard right."[5] To be sure, this political sector remains responsible for a great deal of indifference and often hostility to environmental regulation generally and climate measures specifically. The already dramatic contrast between ignorance and evidence suggests that sustained denial will persist in some quarters with astonishing tenacity; it is not clear that a situation, however dire, can force the hand of those who have thus far resisted. (And one must mention, again, the damage already done and ongoing.) Yet, the picture is changing. If it is premature to count denialism out entirely, there is also something true in the oft-heard claim that the consequences of climate change are growing more difficult to disregard. As people across more varied demographics come to recognize the presence of a "real" problem, it is increasingly the case that strands of ecological discourse are emerging amidst nationalist, populist, and authoritarian right-wing politics, sometimes with explicit reference to the need to address climate change. What results is cause for concern: new justifications for defensive and exclusionary ethnocentric policies; new tangles of crude biologism with racist beliefs; an atmosphere of exigency seized upon by strongmen and fanatics to stoke resentment and murderous rage. A recent headline puts the projection bluntly: "Far-right climate denial is scary. Far right climate acceptance might be scarier."[6]

That article, which discusses the resurgence of ecofascism, is part of a wave of journalistic interest in the volatile territory Klein identifies, a territory that also exposes the shortcomings of a common reflex to assume that recognition of the gravity of the climate crisis goes hand in glove with progressive intentions. Such an assumption is, at least in part, structural. For many climate advocates, the overwhelming burden of having to persuade the (supposedly) unbelieving and the unwilling *that* there is a problem has made the dangers of ecofascism and associated discourses—as modes of climate action, however insidious—comparatively more difficult to see or, where visible, more remote than they actually are. The pressures of this positioning are especially acute in contexts where confrontation with climate change denialism has loomed large. In the US, for one, the recent presidential transition is emblematic of a framing that locates climate justice on one side of a chasm: acceptance and action versus denial. Indeed, after a Trump presidency characterized from start to finish by a devastating anti-environmental agenda emboldened by denialist claims, the environmental priorities of Biden's administration mark a

5 Klein, *On Fire*, p. 13.
6 Levitz, *Far-Right Climate Denial*.

momentous shift.[7] There are key reversals of some of his predecessor's moves, including a renewed commitment to climate goals agreed at Paris; the White House as host to an Earth Day 2021 summit for world leaders; and plans for renewable energy and reduced emissions put front and center in a two trillion dollar infrastructure plan. The question is not whether but how best to respond to a situation whose gravity is now acknowledged. This new ethos, paired with shifts in public opinion concerning the need to take action on climate issues, leads some to think that "[t]he Trump years may well have been the death rattle of influential denialism."[8] Biden's political identification in a two-party system and, more pointedly, his embrace of language around environmental justice compounds the sense that where denial gives way, where people wake up and take action, progressive leadership on climate action results. I have suggested, however, that while any prospective decline of denialism must be counted a positive development, this is a moment of planetary transitions that, in the US and elsewhere, requires careful scrutiny.

This chapter focuses on the dangers posed by the growth of right-wing environmentalism, especially as an area that is often occluded by the framing—illustrated in the Trump-Biden contrast—of a linear passage toward socially transformative climate remediation. In drawing theological attention to these dangers, I build on the work of theorists and activists (within and beyond theological circles) who have already shown that while the prospects for climate justice may be improving, they are, as ever, tenuous and uneven. As has been noted with respect to promising considerations of equity and fairness in Biden's program, for instance, these gains are a result of struggle and targeted advocacy—not an inevitability.[9] Their presence, and the extent to which similar concerns have entered the mainstream environmental movement's discussion of urgent climate action, depends on the work of those who have long had to insist that an ecological consciousness is not automatically attuned to the wellbeing of minoritarian and marginalized populations. Even as these thinkers name the cost of climate change denialism, they bring perspicacious analysis to the gaps, failures, and hypocrisies of liberal discourse about a secure future for all people and the planet. Such groups already navigate the

7 This overall characterization of Trump's environmental record holds despite his occasional protestations that he is a "great environmentalist" and a few policy decisions—presented in deeply nationalist rhetoric—with salutary implications for local ecology. See, e.g., Landler/Plumer/Qiu, *Trump*.

8 Milman, *Dizzying Pace of Biden's Climate Action*. Should this assessment prove to be correct, a steady stream of dissenters in Congress still intent on challenging the premise of anthropogenic climate change will appear ever more the exception that proves the rule.

9 Kurtzleben, *Ocasio-Cortez Sees Green New Deal.*

pitfalls within a rhetoric of urgency and crisis, knowing that the push to convince people to *do something* is, on its own, insufficient to the demands of fairness and that capitalism's capacity for "greenwashing" is immense. Insofar as they expose the difference between climate action and climate justice, their leadership continues to be essential in confronting what else comes after denialism. There is now increasing need for proponents of climate justice to contest responses to climate change that contain little to no pretense of equality, oppose the principle that benefits and harms should be distributed as fairly as possible, and indirectly or directly align themselves with reactionary currents of the extreme right.

In a volume that explores the relationship of Gospel-inspired justice and the lives we seek to make possible on a warming and ever more unpredictable planet, the aim of this chapter is largely limited to a critical diagnosis. Theologians working in liberationist, decolonial, and political traditions have increasingly engaged political ecology as a useful apparatus for understanding and intervening in a host of inseparable dynamics—between nature and society; politico-economic and environmental systems; material and discursive factors—that function to the detriment of human beings and habitats along lines of race, gender, class, and citizenship.[10] I contend that the confluence of far-right politics with elements of ecological thought and climate-driven pressures represents a crucial and complementary sphere for developing this analysis.

2 A "Lethal Dialogue": Ecofascism, Far-Right Environmentalism, and Climate Barbarism

Thus far I have argued that the prevalent association of environmental concern with left-leaning objectives in many contemporary contexts—compounded by scenes like the denialist drama in the US and Brazil—can obscure the way nature protection has functioned in tandem with right-wing aims and, at times, far-right politics. But various "green" initiatives have often been the territory of aristocrats intent on preserving both flora and fauna and a social order shaped by conservative ideals.[11] In an American context, those who seek to show that "conservation is conservative" have plied a language of self-sufficiency that draws on the mythos of "rugged individualism" in the country's foundational wilderness narrative as support for what they see as a superior form of

10 See, e.g., Castillo, *An Ecological Theology of Liberation*, and Lloyd, *Environmental Justice*.

11 Coates, *Nature*, pp. 162–65. Coates focuses on British conservation history.

stewardship.[12] Where environmentally friendly policy is often tarred as the bureaucratic cudgel of centralized government, these efforts carve out a model of environmental consciousness that champions "individual liberty, limited government, and free markets."[13] Such selective recounting, combined with hyperbolic barbs from other self-identified conservatives regarding the threat of the contemporary environmental movement as a socialist-cum-ecofascist assault on American freedom,[14] diverts attention away from an important history that environmentalists of all stripes—including progressives—must consider: namely, an overtly racist, nationalist, and/or totalitarian tenor that pervades formative sources of ecological thought and environmental politics.[15] Especially to the extent that elements of this kind of thinking have not been thoroughly exposed and expunged from subsequent developments, those arguing for the imperative to redress the eco-social devastation wrought by climate heating are bound to consider the "specter of ecofascism" in more than hypothetical fashion.[16]

There is troubling historical precedent for the convergence of "ecologism" with authoritarian violence. Nazi devotion to "blood and soil" exemplified a vicious fusion of nationalist ethnocentrism, fantasies of racial purity, and a quasi-mystical connection to the German homeland, all under the aegis of a conception of Nature as a law-governed organism. Practices like tree planting and organic farming, and the recommendation of vigorous hiking, fed on popular aspects of romantic irrationalism and antimodernism while bolstering a contrast with Jews who were propagandized as urban, materialistic, and rootless.[17] The precise ways in which the exterminationist program of

12 See Bliese, *Traditionalist Conservatism*. William Cronon, among others, calls attention to the elitism, masculinism, and Indigenous erasure bound up with this ethos: *The Trouble with Wilderness*, pp. 13–16. See also Taylor, *The Rise*.

13 Gordon, *Individuals*.

14 On this charge against greens, see, e.g., Klein's introduction to *On Fire*, and Zimmerman, *The Threat of Ecofascism*.

15 For example, Ernst Haeckel, credited with founding "ecology" as a discipline, was a known eugenicist; see Weikart, *The Role of Darwinism*. John Muir, hero of the American conservation movement, maligned Black and Indigenous people; see Melley, *Sierra Club Apologizes*. Appropriate nuance about differences between correlation and causation does not obviate the seriousness of such connections.

16 Klein, *On Fire*, p. 22. While here I share Klein's focus on right-wing threats, I also want to keep in view the degree to which this history burdens the mainstream environmental movement, as well as radical perspectives where the traditional designators of "left" and "right" begin to break down. Scholarly assessment of deep ecology has been one such area; see, e.g., Ferry, *The New Ecological Order*.

17 See Coates, *Nature*, pp. 165–72, for an overview. One classic study is Staudenmaier/ Biehl, *Ecofascism*.

staving off foreign intrusion and acquiring *Lebensraum* was fueled by an "ecological panic" (entailing Malthusian notions of resource scarcity and pseudo-Darwinian notions of competition)[18] and likewise the degree to which concern for non-human nature and ecological sustainability was an essential element in German National Socialism (rather than a fringe position of select advisers or a convenient window-dressing for Hitler's industrial and imperial expansionism) are debated points. Nonetheless, it is crucial today to recognize the destructive and alluring power of "a connection between healthy races and healthy land."[19]

Although these ideas took shape well before climate change emerged as a global issue, they are being mobilized in the present. As Jason Wilson wrote in *The Guardian* in 2019, "eco-fascism is a longstanding political ideology that is currently undergoing a revival in the fetid culture of the contemporary extremist right."[20] His piece appeared in March on the heels of the massacre of over fifty people at two mosques in Christchurch, New Zealand by a white supremacist who, in a manifesto posted online before the attack, self-identified as an "eco-fascist." In August of the same year, an individual who expressed similar positions regarding the supposedly interconnected ills of immigration ("Hispanic invasion"), overpopulation, and environmental despoliation killed twenty-three people at a Walmart in El Paso, Texas, which was targeted because of the preponderance of Mexican shoppers.[21] An uptick in far-right online forums in which such ideas appear includes various configurations of hateful screeds ranging across issues of pollution, urbanization, industrialization, technology, consumer culture, animal rights, eugenics, white supremacy, neo-Nazism, racial purity, border control, birth rates, resource scarcity, masculinity, nature spirituality, and terrorism.[22] Albeit loosely organized and to some degree internally diverse, this internet subculture shows how prior eco-fascist conceptions of eco-social threats and what are perceived as necessary responses to them are being amplified by the stakes of a climate crisis often described in apocalyptic terms.

The "ecologically justified neo-fascism" that Nils Gilman calls "Avocado Politics" ("green on the outside but brown(shirt) at the core") is not limited to chat boards and terrorist manifestos but may also be discerned among intellectuals, political commentators, and those who occupy, or would wish to,

18 Snyder, *Black Earth*.
19 Zimmerman, *Ecofascism: An Enduring Temptation*, p. 398.
20 Wilson, *Eco-fascism*.
21 Achenbach, *Two Mass Murders*.
22 See Lawrence, *The Regrowth of Eco-Fascism*.

halls of government.[23] Indeed, a figure such as the American white supremacist Richard Spencer is a lesson against making too sharp or too secure a distinction between the margins and the mainstream. While Spencer's one-time political ambitions appear to have stagnated, the violence of his platform and its consequences remain potent.[24] Within a cocktail of specious claims about race and world history, overt anti-Semitism and sexism, and vague fearmongering, Spencer's statement on the meaning of being alt-right touches on the value of wilderness, wildlife, and sustainable agriculture—a vital natural heritage to complement an ethnic and cultural heritage—all of which is predicated on understanding "the natural world—and our experience of it—[as] an end in itself."[25] Though he prefaces his comments by "putting aside contentious matters like global warming and resource depletion," his rhetoric is nevertheless instructive for tracking how an ecofascist rendering of nature protection is being rearticulated in an era of climate anxiety.[26] While remarks elsewhere demonstrate that Spencer "believes" in climate change, he navigates a US far-right milieu wherein, for the time being, ecofascists mix with climate denialists.[27] However, as and when current pillars of right-wing politics—that is, denial of anthropogenic climate change plus dedication to unrelenting extractivism—begin to erode, Spencer's old-new vision of a "natural" White ethno-state provides a ready formula for hard-righters so inclined to take on board ecological goals.[28]

In Europe, where outright climate denialism has had less traction and right-wing populism is notably on the rise, there are further indicators of the contours of a far-right environmentalism. A study of right-wing populist parties in

---

23 Gilman, *The Coming Avocado Politics*.

24 Lee, *White Nationalist Richard Spencer*. Spencer gained national notoriety as a proponent of the "alt-right" and a vocal supporter of Donald Trump in the 2016 presidential election. He helped to organize the "Unite the Right" rally in Charlottesville, Virginia in August 2017, which resulted in the death of a counter-protestor.

25 Spencer, *What It Means*. This document was published in conjunction with the Charlottesville rally, an event at which some of the torch-bearing marchers chanted "Blood and Soil."

26 See Rueda, *Neoecofascism*. Rueda quotes the relevant passage from Spencer as an epigraph for his article, but curiously omits the clause in which Spencer distances climate concerns; cf. Gilman, *The Coming Avocado Politics*.

27 Knights, *The Climate Movement*.

28 Phelan, *The Menace of Eco-Fascism*; he writes, "In that disturbing and carefully calibrated statement, Spencer clearly hoped to bridge the divide between those on the far right who believe that climate change is a hoax ... and those who actually find the science undergirding environmental causes persuasive ... Spencer's goal here is to build a consensus on preserving the natural environment—for the privileged ownership, use, and pleasure of Western ethno-states."

the European parliament from 2009–2018—who held about fifteen percent of seats during this time—revealed a range of positions on climate science. Some form of climate skepticism or inconsistent messaging was most common, with clear denial of anthropogenic climate change a significant minority stance and clear affirmation of it a smaller one.[29] These MEPs showed little appetite for the multilateral cooperation associated with climate mitigation/adaptation and sustainable energy policy. Such resistance to EU-led and international efforts also cut across voting patterns on other environmental issues; proposals that were perceived to disentangle environmental conservation, clean air, and renewable energy from "threats" to national sovereignty tended to garner considerable support among right-wing parties.[30] Taking a broad view, the study's authors rightly worried about poor prospects for effective climate policy due to the likelihood of an increased presence of right-wing populist parties (an accurate prediction: as of the 2019 elections, they hold nearly a quarter of seats) and the influence of their cool to lukewarm climate stances on centrist and progressive governments.[31]

At the same time, some of the nuances and exceptions the study notes, and contradictory dynamics it is less able to capture, appear especially salient in light of more recent developments. For instance, Hungary's Fidesz party is highlighted as one of the small minority that affirms the scientific consensus on climate change and regularly votes in favor of EU policies to curb its effects.[32] However, commentary on this topic from Prime Minister Viktor Orbán and his inner circle has interspersed suspicion about the reality at hand, and in June 2019 Hungary voted against a major EU plan to reach net zero carbon levels by 2050; critics allege a cynical political calculus, largely oriented around obtaining European climate funding.[33] Moreover, when the authors observe that "[m]ost of the 'anti-migration' parties do not draw links between global environmental change, climate change and the wellbeing of other countries, and forced migration," Hungary is not mentioned as a counter-example.[34] Yet precisely these links are now being adduced; they are

29 Schaller/Carius, *Convenient Truths*, pp. 9–12.

30 Schaller/Carius, *Convenient Truths*, pp. 31–32. A further factor is the way in which "environmental" arguments can be made against certain climate policy proposals—negative impacts of wind turbines on animals and habitats is a common example; see Schaller/Carius, *Convenient Truths*, p. 37.

31 Schaller/Carius, *Convenient Truths*, Abstract, p. 38.

32 E.g., Schaller/Carius, *Convenient Truths*, p. 87. They note that domestic environmental policy has fared poorly.

33 See, e.g., Walker, *Migration v Climate*.

34 Schaller/Carius, *Convenient Truths*, p. 24.

associations that, taken alongside border walls and screeds against "Muslim invaders," can only reproduce and energize the anti-migrant nativism Fidesz has long cultivated.[35] These complications suggest that while it may remain politically expedient for far-right parties to pit concerns about migration and climate against one another it is also timely to examine those places where these issues are connected, with the expectation that more will emerge.[36] Where climate an increasingly important issue for voters, especially younger ones, the wager for these far-right parties is that they cannot afford to remain indifferent or hostile to the topic. Green parties across Europe also fared well in the 2019 contest. Following one such strong performance in Germany, the leadership of the far-right Alternative for Germany was rebuked for its climate denialism by the party's Berlin-based youth wing.[37] From the perspective of climate justice and this chapter's interest in ecofascist trends, the xenophobic manner in which authoritarian and right-wing populist politicians are interpreting the mandate to take action on climate change is a troubling if wholly unsurprising development.

France's National Rally (formerly the National Front) merits consideration in this respect. The merging of "green patriotism" with anti-migrant ideology by Marine Le Pen marks a departure from her father's dismissive attitude toward ecological concerns during his tenure as party leader.[38] Lately, Marine Le Pen is increasingly frank in addressing the role of climate-related pressures. A spokesperson expressed the key connection in the party's 2019 European platform: "Borders are the environment's greatest ally; it is through them that we will save the planet."[39] So too will this implicit "we" save France and its culture for the properly French. If the National Rally has adopted an ecological "localism" to back conservation programs, restricted imports, and domestic energy independence, the sentiment applies equally to ethnocentric/racist demographic politics: hardening borders and strengthening the national homeland. Or, in any case, a "Europe of nations," as Le Pen and like-minded party members describe their vision for a European "ecological civilization"

35 Eldarov, *Hungarian President*. The quoted phrase reflects language Orbán has used on multiple occasions.

36 Another recent shift appears in the UK, where the Brexit Party's 2019 campaign included modest signals of environmental consciousness—a departure from its leaders' years of ignoring or flatly denying any problem. However, as David Lawrence observes, ecological threats are demarcated from anthropogenic climate change per se because, crucially, "[t]his denial of climate change allows for the denial of responsibility, which is instead placed on immigrants and progressive politicians": *From Climate Denial*.

37 Aronoff, *The European Far-Right*.

38 Legrand, *Le Rassemblement National*.

39 Mazoue, *France's National Rally*.

in opposition to "nomadic" people whose transience inhibits proper respect and care for a given territory and its traditions.[40] The nationalist bent of the National Rally's ecological proposals leads to obvious limitations in their effectiveness: neither can air pollution in northern France be addressed absent cooperation with neighboring Germany nor decarbonization of the global economy be sufficiently accomplished by trade protectionism.[41] Rightly, therefore, some will not be persuaded that this kind of program qualifies as *real* climate action, but, for others, showing how certain ecological elements complement and even enhance the party's core principles (strengthening national identity and curbing immigration) has an appeal, particularly when this connection is made manifest and meaningful in institutions and conditions that affect daily life.[42]

It is easy to critique the adoption of an environmental agenda by online extremists as well as far-right parties as opportunistic—an exploitation of selective aspects of ecological concern that weaponizes them against already identified opponents. If, conversely, the ideas that coalesce are taken to be sincere, then intellectually and ethically they are low-hanging fruit for condemnation. Somewhere in the middle, we can say that disingenuous political and economic calculations bleed into deeply held convictions about people and nature, and vice versa. None of these observations make the phenomena in question less dangerous. The situation I have sketched points, fundamentally, to unprecedented planetary pressures that demand a response. The crucial questions have to do with how to adapt, and what is increasingly clear is that the hard right is invested in providing an answer. As the consequences of climate catastrophe continue to stress existing systems, explicitly racist and xenophobic environmental messaging as well as somewhat tempered revisions—from dog-whistles in right-wing media outlets to putatively more reputable forms with ties to the academy and recognized social institutions—will all get more of a hearing.[43] Like the non-linear patterns of climatic

40 Aronoff, *The European Far-Right*. The way this language echoes some of the antisemitic tropes discussed above is far from incidental, though in the present French context it is particularly laden with Islamophobia.

41 Onishi, *France's Far Right*.

42 Onishi highlights local National Rally initiatives such as LED lights on neighborhood streets (*France's Far Right*) and Daniel Trilling notes how its associated movement, "Le Collectif Nouvelle Écologie," organizes social infrastructure (*Flag, Faith and Fear*).

43 To note just a few of many precedents, Pentti Linkola and Renaud Camus, both of whom "specifically justify their virulent anti-immigrant politics in terms of the need to protect the natural ecology of their respective countries [i.e. Finland and France]," have had prominent platforms (Gilman, *The Coming Avocado Politics*). In a chapter that details right-wing environmentalism's "significant overlap with organized white supremacy in

alteration that scientists have identified, it seems plausible that correlatively abrupt and cascading ideological shifts will feature in the coming decades. In these fast-moving and diverse conditions, no single model obtains, but there are significant blueprints in place, all differently disquieting. The practices of ideological repurposing and construction visible today—of which the examples I have treated are only a sample—suggest that ecofascism is resonant among pernicious associations of environmental responsibility with frequently racialized and ethnically discriminatory notions of belonging, nature, and nation.

The ease and imprecision with which accusations of "ecofascism" have been launched and its headline-grabbing potential should give us pause.[44] As is true of "fascism" generally, this charged term is prone to "semantic inflation," so it is analytically important to be clear that ecofascism is neither coterminous with every version of right-wing environmentalism and eco-nationalism nor applicable to every conceivable instance of draconian environmental policy or environmental racism.[45] Yet, the term is in view right now for a reason (recall that the Christchurch killer self-identified as an "ethno-nationalist eco-fascist") and certain forms of discourse in circulation no doubt match the criteria. Moreover, even if "ecofascist" is raised as a possible descriptor only to be subsequently found wanting, its presence can help to clarify dynamics at work in other systems of thought and practice. Qualifying a given position as being adjacent to or resonant of ecofascism, or as sharing some but not all of its tendencies, might usefully indicate both its present violence and its potential for a very problematic direction of travel.

I would argue that a similar insight lies behind Naomi Klein's discussion of "climate barbarism," which calls attention to the cruelty—indelibly inflected by racism and xenophobia—of a band of current responses to climate-related

the United States," Rajani Bhatia shows that core ideas of this "anti-immigrant" "population environmentalism" have gained a degree of academic legitimacy and impacted moderate environmental organizations: *Green or Brown?*

44 I referred above to the use of this tactic by conservative critics keen to shut down any push for environmental responsibility. Writing in the left-wing *Jacobin*, Sam Knights also observes a parallel one among some of his compatriots: "There is … an unhelpful tendency on the Left to categorize any right-wing response to the climate crisis as a direct product of 'eco-fascism.' Often, what they are actually referring to is a natural product of capitalism. Environmental racism is, after all, not the preserve of fascists" (Knights, *The Climate Movement*).

45 Rueda, *Neoecofascism*, p. 97. See also Lubarda, *Beyond Ecofascism?* In his carefully argued piece, Lubarda contends that "contemporary far-right ecological values are too complex and elusive to be reduced to (neo)fascism" (p. 716).

pressures, especially as they bear on migration.[46] She uses this term to describe those border-fortifying, death-dealing policies enacted by climate denialists like Trump, Italy's Matteo Salvini, and Australia's Scott Morrison, who are *already* adapting to a planetary crisis, even if they won't name it as such. Yet at times the term functions as an umbrella category that also describes those measures advocated in extremist manifestos. The movement around Klein's use of these two terms, ecofascism and climate barbarism, reflects (accurately, I think) her recognition of the porosity between the phenomena they name. For despite the still consequential gap between denial and acceptance of climate catastrophe, in some respects it is bridged by a commitment to supremacist ideas of nation, race, and religion; on immigration, at least, the politics that flow from this commitment look strikingly similar, whether environmental themes are voiced or not. From this vantage, a move by one-time climate change deniers to position themselves as climate defenders is only a partial reversal of ideology, one that very much facilitates a continuation of practice.

By this route we reach the terrifying prospect broached earlier in the chapter: that the adoption of some kind of ecological sensibility or avowed climate concern by those who have refused it tooth and nail—far from dampening antipathy to international frameworks, collective responsibility, and just cooperation—stands to add fuel to an already dangerous fire. Per Klein: "The climate science will no longer be denied; what *will* be denied is the idea that the nations that are the largest historical emitters of carbon owe anything to the black and brown people impacted by that pollution. This will be denied based on the only rationale possible: that those non-white and non-Christian people are lesser than, are the other, are dangerous invaders."[47] She is not alone in seeing overlap between the "sinister worldview" of a mass killer and vilifications of migrants and minorities that are more widespread in conservative rhetoric.[48] It takes no great leap to see how alarmism around the climate crisis can be fitted in to this vicious nexus of normalization and radicalization. For white nationalists on the extreme right who seek to amp up Trumpian racism,

46 Klein clarifies that climate change can be both a direct and indirect driver of migration, one that intensifies complex dynamics around "war, gang violence, sexual violence, [and] deepening poverty" (*On Fire*, p. 25).

47 Klein, *On Fire*, p. 24, her emphasis. Of course, she is clear that the "rationale" of this white power eco-fascism is really "a ferocious rationalization for refusing to live up to our collective climate responsibilities" (p. 23).

48 Klein refers to the work of Murtada Hussain, who argues that the Christchurch shooter's manifesto demonstrates the possibility of radicalization in plain sight (*On Fire*, p. 25), while Jeet Heer writes that "the striking thing about the [El Paso shooter's] manifesto … is how banal most of it is, echoing many of the nativist passions of mainstream Trumpism" (*After the El Paso Massacre*).

"The very real dangers of climate change provide race war fantasists the dystopian background they need to give urgency to their violent agenda."[49] Even where the ecological philosophy is relatively more fleshed out and the overt violence muted, it is worth emphasizing again that the varieties of "climate action" proposed by ecofascists and right-wing populists are far from commensurate with the kinds of transformation necessary to address planetary warming (though that empirical failure is simultaneously rendered moot by their ethical bankruptcy). Still, the warning persists: these factions have a stake in trying to redefine what it means to take climate change seriously.

3 Theological Directions

That ecofascism and climate barbarism are inimical to the work of climate justice is clear enough. Yet there is a real risk, as I suggested in the first section, of overlooking these dangerous forecasts in so far as a binary framing shaped by climate denialism obtains. Indeed, a need to interrogate the pervasiveness of this denial among certain Christian constituencies, notably white evangelicals, may heighten this risk in theological analyses (which is not to contest the necessity of such interrogation).[50] If Klein and others are right about shifting configurations forged by right-wing politics and climate-driven pressures, then it is equally time to prepare for what emerges where denialism gives way. Cruelty repackaged under the aegis of climate action is on the rise; it poses different questions and thus merits more scrutiny than it has received to date in Anglophone theology. My claim is that theologians pursuing the narrow way of liberation and climate justice, including those who already probe the co-implication of climate denial with white ethno-nationalism and settler colonialism, while also naming the "corrupting" contexts that mar many climate responses, will find complementary lines of inquiry in far-right environmentalisms.[51] This chapter is an initial step toward familiarity with that terrain.

Beyond outlining key features that warrant attention, an extended theological critique would entail recognizing where certain theological language and arguments, which aim to convey the gravity of climate change and the perils of denying it, may inadvertently lend credence to problematic aspects of the alternative discourses in question. For instance, ecotheologians have often emphasized the reality of a divinely created order to underscore nature's limits

---

49 Heer, *After the El Paso Massacre.*

50 See, e.g., Paul Tyson's recent study, which features Australia, *Theology and Climate Change.*

51 See, e.g., Jenkins, *Working With Politics.*

on economic growth and the care that must be taken with finite resources. They join other environmental theorists in contrasting respect for nature's interconnected integrity to an individualistic and instrumental approach to the world. Questions of anthropology, morality, and social life cannot be divorced, many contend, from their organic connections to ecosystemic health; thus these thinkers contest the subordination of family, community, and obligations of care rooted in regional belonging to the dictates of an impersonal, value-less market. Such critiques are often apposite, but the fact that these themes circulate in ecofascist territory should raise a red flag. However impossible to avoid any possibility of co-optation, taking responsibility remains essential.

Negotiations of responsibility are inevitably difficult and contextually specific. Nonetheless, some overarching questions may be limned. Following on the themes just mentioned, I would highlight the central yet ambivalent position of modernity critique for theologies that hope to foster a climate of justice. It has become almost a truism in diagnoses of the ecological and climate crises that paradigmatically modern attitudes and industrial systems are to blame. But, as we have seen, it is also the case that in criticizing these destructive deficits the environmental movement can display a "romantic-reactionary tendency," one that the language of apocalyptic crisis can ratchet up in ways amenable to ecofascists and their ilk.[52] One alternative is posed by "ecomodernism," the self-styled corrective to mainstream environmentalism that lauds the marriage of liberal politics and market-led economic growth as the best repudiation of climate alarmism and its potential for abuse. Per ecomodernists, the common diagnosis gets it backwards: current circumstances demand more modernization, not less.[53] However, as a number of critics have argued, ecomodernism fails to accurately reckon the inextricable link between capitalist modernity's productivity, on the one hand, and its appropriative and exploitative dynamics, on the other—that is to say, with real questions of history and power.[54] Contra ecomodernism, a theology of climate justice must pursue more modernity critique, not less, and in a way that locates the pull of far-right environmentalisms within the globally defining set of eco-social relations structured by capitalism in its various instantiations over the past five centuries. For this, the integration of political ecologies with perspectives from decolonial studies and critical race theory is essential.

Given this chapter's focus on the far right, it is important to stress the extent to which the climate cruelty to which I refer is enacted within a

52 Phelan, *The Menace of Eco-Fascism*.
53 Asafu-Adjaye et al., *An Ecomodernist Manifesto*.
54 Examples of these critiques and others may be found in Crist/ Van Dooren, *Replies*.

neoliberal framework—even as the nationalism on display here accents certain tensions—and is in many ways consistent with liberal capitalism's record of environmental and cultural destruction—the latter's rhetoric about progress, freedom, fairness, and global inclusivity notwithstanding.[55] Whether the agendas that stand to materialize on the radical right would represent a definitive move away from the neoliberal order or instead demonstrate yet another rapacious adaptation of modern capitalism would require further examination. For one, it is difficult to generalize regarding the status and depth of anti-modern and anti-capitalist critiques leveraged in some versions of far-right thought, including ecofascism. At least on an aesthetic level, there are certainly differences between, for example, the communal agrarian ideal extolled by Marine Le Pen and the plug for solar energy by Debbie Dooley, a self-identified "free market conservative" who sounds certain recognizable notes in her appeals to Americans: individual empowerment, small government, and consumer choice. The convergence around anti-immigrant policies in their respective "Europe for Europeans" and "America first" platforms is both a further counterpoint to the assumption that ecological awareness has an ennobling effect and a caution against being too eager to see environmental causes as apolitical.[56] Wariness regarding slippage *and* existing overlap between far-right positions and climate responses more amenable to the liberal-conservative consensus must come into focus for liberative theologies as experiences of climate-related precarity touch more and more people who have thought themselves immune.[57] Not all onetime climate deniers will become ecofascists, and race-war fantasists' impact on the political landscape may be limited to the episodic and the extreme, but violence already spirals in the mundane and coming decades stand to cut new grooves of immiseration. Klein flags how climate measures enacted under neoliberal austerity regimes have led to resistance by already put-upon people, whose resentment far-right populists have in some cases successfully tapped and channeled.[58] One salient

55 For an impassioned argument that the "genocidal white nationalism" currently attributed to ecofascism in fact falls squarely within the bounds of economic liberalism, see McDonald, *It's Not 'Ecofascism'*.

56 Phelan makes similar points with reference to Dooley's collaboration with liberal environmental groups in the US who are eager to work with a Republican bucking the party's denialist stance (*The Menace of Eco-Fascism*).

57 For one discussion, see Lustgarten, *How Climate Migration*. Lustgarten, a scholar of environmental migration, reflects on the ongoing burden of climate change on poor communities and its likelihood to expand economic insecurity and resource competition across the country.

58 A signature example (see Stephenson, *Against Climate Barbarism*): in 2018, Emmanuel Macron's imposed a fuel tax that put a disproportionate share of the country's

lesson is, as ever, the error of trying to trace ideological investments apart from material conditions; another is the need to understand the intertwining of planetary changes with economic, political, and cultural factors—without flattening differences among them.

This chapter's effort to bring far-right environmentalisms into view thus redoubles the importance of distinguishing transformative climate justice from climate action; sheds light on the blurred edges between climate denialism and reactive/reactionary climate adaptation; and insists on a critique of ecofascism and associated ideologies that carefully tracks their parasitic embeddedness in capitalism's fundamentally unjust social relations. These are, I maintain, key issues for scholars and communities who have found in Christian faith and praxis radical potential for reshaping the political ecology of God's beloved creation. At the same time, the conscription of Christianity into the far right's exclusionary discourses of cultural, racial, and national identity remains an obvious spur for critical self-reflection. The way in which contemporary manifestations of this historical pattern intersect with environmental rhetoric presents a crucial area for further research—one where existing interventions into forms of racial, ethnic, and religious supremacism take on new significance for theologies of climate justice.

References

Achenbach, Joel: "Two Mass Murders a World Apart Share a Common Theme: 'Ecofascism,'" in: *Washington Post*, August 18, 2019, https://www.washingtonpost.com/science/two-mass-murders-a-world-apart-share-a-common-theme-ecofascism/2019/08/18/0079a676-bec4-11e9-b873-63ace636af08_story.html [25.05.2021].

Aronoff, Kate: "The European Far-Right's Environmental Turn," in: *Dissent*, May 31, 2019, https://www.dissentmagazine.org/online_articles/the-european-far-rights-environmental-turn [25.05.2021].

Asafu-Adjaye, John, et al., "An Ecomodernist Manifesto," April 2015, http://www.ecomodernism.org/manifesto-english [25.05.2021].

carbon-cutting burden on the shoulders of working-class people, who kicked back in the *gilets jaunes* movement, which in turn has been sought as an ally by leaders like Le Pen. Her party's environmental alternative, as I have indicated, is itself insufficient and deeply flawed.

Bhatia, Rajani: "Green or Brown? White Nativist Environmental Movements," in *Home-Grown Hate: Gender and Organized Racism*, ed. Abby L. Ferber. New York: Routledge 2004, pp. 194–214.

Bliese, John R. E.: "Traditionalist Conservatism and Environmental Ethics," in: *Environmental Philosophy: From Animal Rights to Radical Ecology*, ed. Michael Zimmerman et al., 3rd edition. Hoboken: Prentice Hall 2001.

Castillo, Daniel P.: *An Ecological Theology of Liberation: Salvation and Political Ecology*. Maryknoll, NY: Orbis 2019.

Coates, Peter: *Nature: Western Attitudes Since Ancient Times*. Cambridge: Polity 1998.

Crist, Eileen/Thom Van Dooren, eds., "Replies to an Ecomodernist Manifesto," in: *Environmental Humanities* (7, no. 1, May 2016).

Cronon, William: "The Trouble with Wilderness: Or, Getting Back to the Wrong Nature," in: *Environmental History* 1, no. 1 (January 1998): 13–16.

Eldarov, Nijat: "Hungarian President Calls for Fight Against Climate Change to Reduce Migratory Pressures," in: *Emerging Europe*, October 5, 2018, https://emerging-europe.com/news/hungarian-president-calls-for-fight-against-climate-change-to-reduce-migratory-pressures/ [25.05.2021].

Ferry, Luc: *The New Ecological Order*, trans. Carol Volk. Chicago: University of Chicago Press 1995.

Gilman, Nils: "The Coming Avocado Politics: What Happens When the Ethno-Nationalist Right Gets Serious about the Climate Emergency," in: *Breakthrough Journal* no. 12 (Winter 2020), https://thebreakthrough.org/journal/no-12-winter-2020/avocado-politics [25.05.2021].

Gordon, Robert: "Individuals, Liberty, and the Environment: Challenging the Foundations of the Green Establishment," report for *The Heritage Foundation*, October 10, 2012, https://www.heritage.org/environment/report/individuals-liberty-and-the-environment-challenging-the-foundations-the-green [25.05.2021].

Heer, Jeet: "After the El Paso Massacre, the Choice is Green Socialism or Eco-Fascism," in: *The Nation*, August 6, 2019, https://www.thenation.com/article/archive/el-paso-mass-shooting-fascism/) [25.05.2021].

Jenkins, Willis: "Working With Politics," in *The T & T Clark Handbook of Christian Theology and Climate Change*, ed. Ernst M. Conradie and Hilda P. Koster. London: T & T Clark 2019.

Klein, Naomi: *On Fire: The (Burning) Case for a Green New Deal*. New York: Simon & Schuster 2019.

Klein, Naomi: *This Changes Everything: Capitalism vs. the Climate*. New York: Simon & Schuster 2014.

Knights, Sam: "The Climate Movement Must Be Ready To Challenge Rising Right-Wing Environmentalism," in: *Jacobin*, November 16, 2020, https://www.jacobinmag.com/2020/11/climate-change-right-wing-environmentalism-alt-right-eco-fascism [25.05.2021].

Kurtzleben, Danielle: "Ocasio-Cortez Sees Green New Deal Progress in Biden Plan, But 'It's Not Enough,'" in: *NPR*, April 2, 2021, https://www.npr.org/2021/04/02/983398361/green-new-deal-leaders-see-biden-climate-plans-as-a-victory-kind-of [25.05.2021].

Landler, Mark/Brad Plumer/Linda Qiu: "Trump, Prioritizing Economy Over Climate, Cites Disputed Premises," in: *New York Times*, June 1, 2017, https://www.nytimes.com/2017/06/01/us/politics/fact-check-climate-change-trump.html [25.05.2021].

Lawrence, David: "From Climate Denial to Blood and Soil," in: *Hope not Hate*, March 21, 2021, https://www.hopenothate.org.uk/from-climate-denial-to-blood-and-soil/ [25.05.2021].

Lawrence, David: "The Regrowth of Eco-Fascism," in: *Hope not Hate*, February 10, 2019, https://www.hopenothate.org.uk/magazine/climate-change-far-right/the-regrowth-of-eco-fascism/ [25.05.2021].

Lee, Kurtis: "White Nationalist Richard Spencer Considers a Run for Montana Congressional Seat," *Los Angeles Times*, December 20, 2016, https://www.latimes.com/nation/la-na-pol-richard-spencer-congress-20161220-story.html [25.05.2021].

Legrand, Thomas: "Le Rassemblement National et L' Écologie," in: *FranceInter*, September 11, 2019, https://www.franceinter.fr/emissions/l-edito-politique/l-edito-politique-11-septembre-2019 [25.05.2021].

Levitz, Eric: "Far-Right Climate Denial Is Scary. Far-Right Climate Acceptance Might Be Scarier," in: *New York Magazine*, March 6, 2019, https://nymag.com/intelligencer/2019/03/climate-science-invites-liberal-solutions-or-fascist-ones.html [25.05.2021].

Lloyd, Dana, ed., "Environmental Justice and Settler Colonialism: A Political Theology of Climate Change," in *Political Theology Network* symposium, May 25, 2020, https://politicaltheology.com/symposium/environmental-justice-and-settler-colonialism-a-political-theology-of-climate-change/ [25.05.2021].

Lubarda, Bal a: "Beyond Ecofascism? Far-Right Ecologism (FRE) as a Framework for Future Inquiries." in: *Environmental Values* (29, no. 6, December 2020), pp. 713–32.

Lustgarten, Abrahm: "How Climate Migration Will Reshape America," in: *The New York Times*, September 15, 2020, https://www.nytimes.com/interactive/2020/09/15/magazine/climate-crisis-migration-america.html [25.05.2021].

Mazoue, Aude: "France's National Rally Goes Green in Bid for European Election Votes," in: *France24*, April 20, 2019, https://www.france24.com/en/20190420-le-pen-national-rally-front-environment-european-elections-france [25.05.2021].

McDonald, Samuel Miller: "It's Not 'Ecofascism'—It's Liberalism," in: *Current Affairs*, March 19, 2020, https://www.currentaffairs.org/2020/03/its-not-ecofascism-its-liberalism [25.05.2021].

Melley, Brian: "Sierra Club Apologizes for Founder's Racist Views," in: *Associated Press*, July 23, 2020, https://apnews.com/article/c52ccd3ac1c127289cf5b1a5c0dc070d [25.05.2021].

Milman, Oliver: "Dizzying Pace of Biden's Climate Action Sounds Death Knell for Era of Denialism," in: *Guardian*, January 30, 2021, https://www.theguardian.com/environment/2021/jan/30/joe-biden-climate-change-action [25.05.2021].

Onishi, Norimitsu: "France's Far Right Wants to Be an Environmental Party, Too," in: *New York Times*, October 17, 2019 (updated March 13, 2021), https://www.nytimes.com/2019/10/17/world/europe/france-far-right-environment.html [25.05.2021].

Oreskes, Naomi/Erik M. Conway: *Merchants of Doubt: How a Handful of Scientists Obscured the Truth on Issues from Tobacco Smoke to Climate Change.* New York: Bloomsbury 2010.

Phelan, Matthew: "The Menace of Eco-Fascism," in: *New York Review of Books*, October 22, 2018, https://www.nybooks.com/daily/2018/10/22/the-menace-of-eco-fascism/?lp_txn_id=1234438 [25.05.2021].

Rueda, Daniel: "Neoecofascism: The Example of the United States," in: *Journal for the Study of Radicalism* (14 no. 2, Fall 2020), pp. 95–125.

Schaller, Stella/Alexander Carius: *Convenient Truths: Mapping Climate Agendas of Right-Wing Populist Parties in Europe.* Berlin: adelphi 2019.

Snyder, Timothy: *Black Earth: The Holocaust as History and Warning.* New York: Tim Duggan Books 2015.

Spencer, Richard B.: "What It Means to Be Alt-Right. A Meta-Political Manifesto for the Alt-Right Movement," in: *AltRight*, 11 August 2017, http://archive.fo/vuZGm [25.05.2021].

Staudenmaier, Peter/Janet Biehl, eds.: *Ecofascism: Lessons From the German Experience. San Francisco and Edinburgh: AK Press 1995.*

Stephenson, Wen: "Against Climate Barbarism: A Conversation with Naomi Klein," in: *Los Angeles Review of Books*, September 30, 2019, https://lareviewofbooks.org/article/against-climate-barbarism-a-conversation-with-naomi-klein/ [25.05.2021].

Taylor, Dorceta E.: *The Rise of the American Conservation Movement: Power, Privilege, and Environmental Protection.* Durham: Duke University Press 2016.

Trilling, Daniel: "Flag, Faith and Fear for the Planet: How the Far Right Is Exploiting Climate Change for Its Own Ends," in: *Prospect*, August 28, 2020, https://www.prospectmagazine.co.uk/magazine/far-right-climate-change-orban-wilders-salvini-eco-fascism) [25.05.2021].

Tyson, Paul: *Theology and Climate Change.* Abingdon/New York: Routledge 2021.

Walker, Shaun: "Migration v Climate: Europe's New Political Divide," in: *Guardian*, December 2, 2019, https://www.theguardian.com/environment/2019/dec/02/migration-v-climate-europes-new-political-divide [25.05.2021].

Weikart, Richard: "The Role of Darwinism in Nazi Racial Thought," in: *German Studies Review* (36, no. 3, 2013), pp. 537–56.

Wilson, Jason: "Eco-fascism Is Undergoing a Revival in the Fetid Culture of the Extreme Right," in: *Guardian*, March 19, 2019, https://www.theguardian.com/world/commentisfree/2019/mar/20/eco-fascism-is-undergoing-a-revival-in-the-fetid-culture-of-the-extreme-right [25.05.2021].

Zimmerman, Michael E.: "The Threat of Ecofascism," in: *Social Theory and Practice* (21, no. 2, 1995), pp. 207–38.

Zimmerman, Michael E.: "Ecofascism: An Enduring Temptation," in *Environmental Philosophy*, From Animal Rights to Radical Ecology, fourth edition, ed. Michael E. Zimmerman, et al. (Upper Saddle River: Prentice Hall, 2004).

Fully-lived Theologies of Creation from the "Grandmothers' University": A Communicative-Theological Approach

Irmgard Christine Klein

Abstract

In Western canonical Christian theology rationalist, abstract perspectives are prevailing. An alternative approach to Climate Justice in order to nourish practically informed ecotheology allows appreciating narrative structures in concrete experiences. Through biographical conversations with elderly Bolivian farm-wives their sets of values have been analyzed. The rich data material offers insights on: relationship and experience of nature, nature as a source of life and a commodity, natural spirituality, cyclic or teleological experience of nature. Finally, there is an outline and discussion of ecofeminist strands with the conflictive findings in the fully lived theologies of Grandmothers' University.

Keywords

Women; Chiquitano; ancestor wisdom; experience; eco-theology; communicative theology; campesinas; natural space; eco-feminism

1 Introduction

In ancient Greek the term αφ' εστίας means "starting from the fireplace, the goddess Hestias altar, the center of the house" in order to say "starting something—an inquiry—from the ground, from the core point, from the root". The following practical theological investigation about a feminist reformulation of nature and creation as a theological issue took the fireplace as a starting point. For their theological treatment, questions of climate justice are often located within social ethics or within the theology and spirituality of creation. By collecting and interpreting life stories of Bolivian *campesinas*, their lived "theologies of creation", I locate my study in the latter section. The urgency of dealing with women's experiences still seems to be indicated because throughout history (rich, white, male) men's experience and thinking

 | DOI:10.30965/9783657795314_006

has set the usual frame for Western canonical Christian theology. Thus, Kutzer with reference to Gebara emphatically demands "an evaluation of the concrete experiences of people, particularly of women, as knowledge about the world and its ecological connections."[1] The approach of the "grounded", "lived theologies of creation", rooted in a qualitative-empirical procedure, contributes to drawing attention to "blind spots" in the existing sketches of a theology of creation and to promoting women by talking to the wisdom of Bolivian peasant women.[2] The ecofeminist thinker Vandana Shiva answered the difficult question of "what to do" in the face of the climate crisis and found the following answer:

> One way to resist is to build an alternative: [... Elderly women] are the resources, where the teachings for the younger generation will come from. We call this the "grandmothers' university".[3]

Since technicist, rationalist concepts and behavior have led to abusive exploitation of nature the inquiry opens up to "fully lived" wisdom, supposing this is a different kind of thinking about creation. As a result, this type of thinking will nourish practically informed ecotheology and provide new paths of behavior. Therefore, I have collected biographical conversations (following the Rosenthal-paradigm[4]) with "grandmothers" about their life and work in and with nature in the Bolivian lowlands. The following short presentation of a larger work[5] focuses on four major points of interest. First, I shall briefly sketch methodological remarks on the concept of "fully lived theologies" in order to reconstruct the philosophical and theological standpoints behind it. In part two I will discuss the data collection and analysis of my empirical investigation. Third I shall offer selected perspectives and results out of the rich data material mainly on the social, economic, spiritual implications of nature that contrast some ecofeminist perceptions. A fourth section shall finally outline and discuss ecofeminist strands by contrasting them with the conflictive findings in the fully lived theologies of Grandmothers' University.

---

1 Kutzer, *Befreiung der Schöpfung?*, p. 106.

2 Cf. Pemsel-Maier, *Von der Geburt bis zum Tod*, p. 59.

3 Shiva, *Monocultures of Minds*, p. 37.

4 Rosenthal, *Interpretative Sozialforschung*.

5 Klein, *Ganz Welt*.

2 Methodological Remarks on the Concept of "Fully Lived Theologies"

The research design applied in this paper is committed to the communicative-theological working method.[6] This means that the study evolves in a dialogical process between several loci theologici. One of them: biographical conversations with campesinas in the third age. Whereas canonical Western Christian theology focuses more on abstract terms and concepts and less on narrative dimensions in order to solve problems, the fundamental theological and philosophical intuition at the "Grandmothers' University" is based on narrators that have struggled all their lifetime to survive. They have tried to come to terms with their specific households, husbands, children, parents, animals, plantations embedded in nature, creating and re-creating life day after day. The study was conducted in Spanish during four stays in Chiquitania (Province Velasco/Bolivia) in 2009, 2010, and 2012. A total of 23 conversations with 16 female interlocutors were recorded in over 14 hours of audio and partly video material.

What are the theoretical premises to use these rural biographies to gain touching points to nature, worldviews, and stories of creation—more familiar with the conception of *creatio continua?* The proposed kind of fully lived theologies is based on three main assumptions. (a) Daily life phenomena are theory-laden—a phenomenological view (Gräb, Failing, Heimbrock); (b) there is practical philosophy/theology in all actions—Lived Worldview (Rahner, Muck); (c) promises and concepts of theology should be brought back into history—"historizar" (Ellacuría). All three of them address conceptual frameworks that nourish oppressive devaluation-mechanisms rooted in dichotomies: nature-culture, practical-theoretical, historical-universal.

(a) Phenomenology[7] focuses on "Lebenswelt"[8]. Note that it is possible in a phenomenological perspective to place the term "lived theology" in the area of encounter between systematic and practical theology. A plurality of life-world processes, thus also religious processes, can be situated in the Lebenswelt without preliminary dichotomous selection. As a consequence, "fully lived theology" is proposed as a search term that may—or must—remain theoretically and methodologically open or else it is impossible to keep the plurality of content. Aesthetic expressions of human societies and groups—for example

6 Forschungskreis Kommunikative Theologie/Communicative Theology Research Group, Kommunikative Theologie.

7 See Gräb, *Wahrnehmen und Deuten;* Failing/Heimbrock, *Praktische Theologie;* Heimbrock, *Wahrnehmung.*

8 Cf. Korsch, *Leben.*

the recorded rural biographies—promise to provide information about "fully lived theology because the "Lebenswelt" can be considered as a space and time for concrete as well as abstract aspects. Everyday life and lifeworld are therefore places of "fully lived theology". One of my basic assumptions: Everyday life is theory-laden.[9]

(b) At the core of all human asking, talking, acting lies a very personal constructed world-view, integrating practical and theoretical aspects. For the present study, following the positions of Otto Muck[10] and Karl Rahner[11], I consider it justified to understand the life stories as an expression of a lived worldview. It is to be assumed that there is an original unity of action and reflection. In this model, the confrontation with the mystery of life, which is given to every human being, is understood as theology. Life-bearing convictions unfold in a confused way. They are woven into each unique life as silent speech of the whole in the fragmentary, as a speech of God in the very human.[12] The interlocutors in the study are restricted to human subjectivity and the study remains within a humanistic point of view. This does not exclude different subjectivities (the Earth, nature as a whole, divine entities, nonhuman animals ...).

(c) Ellacuría's thinking on "universalidad historizada" [historicized universality][13] contextualizes rigid theological concepts in dynamic history. From such a perspective the questions are less concerned with the inherited theoretical edifices of tradition, in our present case theology of creation as taught in dogmatics, but more with the search for actualization of the events represented in these traditional edifices in specific historical processes. Salvation history happens according to theologies of liberation in down-to-earth, actual history. The interviewees in my investigation about "fully lived theologies" actualize and historize Godtalk about beginning the "life/world", maintaining beings in life/world—it is a form of "historizar"[14].

Some epistemological and ontological dualisms became obstructive in Western canonical theology of creation throughout time. For the "fully lived theologies" it is central to address them in a balanced, intertwined model.

---

9 See Klein, *Ganz Welt*, pp. 65–78.

10 Muck, *Rationale Strukturen;* Muck, *Der Beitrag.*

11 Rahner, *Hörer des Wortes*, pp. 45–46.

12 See Klein, *Ganz Welt*, pp. 79–89.

13 Ellacuría, *Geschichtlichkeit des christlichen Heils*, p. 313.

14 See Klein, *Ganz Welt*, pp. 89–106.

3 Data Collection and Analysis

One strand in the paradigm of interpretive social research (Rosenthal) assumes that if the research topic is placed in the overall scope of the interlocutor's biographical narration everyday relevance systems, i.e. the talking partner's own set of relevancies, become apparent. The initial question I used as a narrative stimulus to elaborate a biographical narration (a) and place the research interest (b) in the specific interview situation was: (*a*) *I collect biographies of* campesinas. *I am interested in the life of women farmers and what they mainly do and I would like you to tell me about it.* (*b*) *Especially your work with nature and what you think about the nature that surrounds you. Please tell me about your life and about your work*. This was to be followed by the self-representation of the interviewees in a free impromptu narrative. In the free narrations so-called constraints of story-telling (Schütze)—"constraint to close the form (Gestalt)"[15], "constraint to go into details"[16], "constraint to condense"[17]—take place.

> If the interviewees can be motivated to produce narrations, then they are bound by the so-called 'constraints of storytelling'. This may lead to the interviewees telling more than they perhaps first intended, because they remember more and more details as the story proceeds. On the other hand, it obliges them to set limits to their narrations in order to avoid losing themselves in too many details.[18]

How can the hidden structure be brought to the surface from life narratives, episodes, dreams, stories, arguments, the multifaceted data material that the interviewees have spoken on tape, which provides information about the interviewees' talk and practice of God *as, in, with* and *about* creation? Together with other theologians working in communicative theology[19] I have analyzed the conversations with the documentary method.[20] A basic distinction in analysis with the documentary method is between immanent meaning and documentary meaning.[21] The first level of meaning is thematically known by

15 Rosenthal, *Interpretive Social Research*, p. 137.
16 Rosenthal, *Interpretive Social Research*, p. 137.
17 Rosenthal, *Interpretive Social Research*, p. 138.
18 Rosenthal, *Interpretive Social Research*, p. 137.
19 See Volume 5 and 15 of *Kommunikative Theologie—interdisziplinär:* Langhammer, *"Ist Gott drin?!"*; Peter, *Von der Angst zu gehen.*
20 Nohl, *Interview.*
21 Nohl, *Interview*, p. 8.

the speaker and the text; the latter is implicitly underlying the speaker's manufacturing process and the manufacturing process of the text. The documentary method opens up these habitual actions and atheoretical knowledges in which experience-structuring orientations are anchored.

Because the documentary method depicts texts to have "a public or social meaning on the one hand and a non-public or milieu-specific meaning on the other hand,"[22] a discussion, an interview or a text always have a share in the collective memory, in the conjunctive space of experience of the text producers. The documentary method directs its efforts towards gaining an insight into this condensed, atheoretical space of action. The "fully lived theologies" rely on common and shared experiences and actions, common to the interlocutors' biographies.

The core of the documentary method according to Bohnsack is the consistent "comparative sequence analysis"[23] used from the very beginning, which can bring to light the orientation framework that is not reflexively accessible to the interviewees, i.e. the implicit, atheoretical knowledge. Comparison takes place at all levels of interpretation.

Nohl's tabular summary[24] is suitable for illustrating the analytical steps applied in the material:

Table 7.1

Stages	**Intermediate stages**
Formulating Interpretation	Topical structures and selection of segments for transcription
	Detailed formulating interpretation of a segment
Reflecting Interpretation	Formal interpretation and differentiation of text genres
	Semantic interpretation and comparative sequential analysis
Type Formation	Sensegenetic Type Formation
	Sociogenetic Type Formation

22 Bohnsack, *Dokumentarische Methode*, p. 561.
23 Nohl, *Interview*, pp. 50–56.
24 Nohl, *Interview*, p. 45.

I elaborated selected case structures in detail.[25] During the arrangement, selection, and interpretation of the biographical experiences pieces of the lived theologies of creation were (re)constructed along the following aspects:

1) about their individually narrated relationship to themselves as "worldliness"/"to be nature," "to be creation;"[26]
2) regarding their relationship to "living, working with/in world/nature/creation;"
3) concerning the speech of the divine, of other realities "in/above the world/nature/creation".

These aspects provide insights into the subjunctive experience of the interlocutors. This is the "space of implicit, atheoretical knowledge, based on a similar practice and experience"[27], which connects people who share certain experiences—in this case, experiences of nature. The comparative analysis condenses orientations or frames that summarize habitual actions into statements about the subjunctive (communicative) space of experience.[28] These reconstructed frames of orientation are understood in the present study as "fully lived God-talk" because they document or articulate the shared practical-theoretical horizon of the interlocutors.

4 Detailed Perspectives and Results

How do the texts of the interlocutors document the tacit knowledge of nature experiences in specific? It is beyond the scope of this presentation to consider the large systems of relevance at work throughout the data. But I am going to present four detailed perspectives as outcome of the comparative analysis concerning nature. First, nature experiences are connected with relationships. Second, nature appears in economic terms as a commodity but also in the concept of a deeper source of life. Third, spirituality connected with nature experience can be found as well as a non-animistic view. Fourth, concerning the models or visions of nature, a cyclic view is predominant.

25 See Klein, *Ganz Welt*, pp. 183–252.

26 Through biological, hormonal cyclic events, through birth-giving women's bodies get remembered of being "a natural thing" frequently. This aspect offers all narrative reasoning about being this "part of creation/nature" and depending on that "nature", the body is.

27 Nohl, *Interview*, p. 11.

28 Cf. Nohl, *Interview*, pp. 10–11.

4.1 *Relations between Social Space and Natural Space*[29]

First of all, the interlocutors did not explicitly address nature to the extent and clarity I had hoped for. Much more important for them are interpersonal relationships—i.e. the I-We relation dominates and is superimposed on the natural phenomena in the texts. The "lived theologies of creation" document a very strong connection between the human-social and natural experience. Most of the time descriptions of nature are very intensively intertwined with the I-We, i.e. the relationship foil.

In most cases the relationship foil—the narrated I, the narrated We—is intensively interwoven with the natural conditions (clearing, garden, water, forest). In a few cases, a distance between natural space and the relationship events becomes apparent; then the field and the bed, the watering-place, and the forest are less explicitly connected with the persons involved in the life story.

Community and relationships are the basic outline of the orientation framework. Thus, the agricultural fieldwork is usually told about family ties. The natural living environment is a place of relationships. Veiled experiences of violence[30] in the life stories also document the destructiveness of the relationality.

A close interweaving of social space and natural space is strongly documented in the "lived theologies of creation" of the Chiquitano women. There is no "nature per se" in the system of relevance of the interlocutors. Social relationships are far more important. Adding the overall large absence of descriptions of nature this first result leads to a strong emphasis on the significance of socio-historical mediation. Nature opens up and is mediated through social relationships. Creation is tied back to the community.

---

29 See Klein, *Ganz Welt*, pp. 259–263.

30 Veiled experiences of violence in the life stories also document the destructiveness of relationality. Systems of dependence include for example landlord—indigenous people, husband—woman, father—daughter, nature—farm wives and families. "Not like in the past, there was slavery, because my mother still saw/experienced that, they were whipped if they drank until the morning hours, scuffled, they were whipped at the highest cacique [indigenous authority], I still saw that, that my grandfather whipped the other people, because there was nothing where you could go to complain, not like nowadays, there are the police, where you can go and complain and before there was nothing, there was only with the chief cacique, whipping, that happened in the past, yes. If my husband beat me beyond measure, I went to the chief cacique so that they punished him, and if he didn't give anything, went on to the next booze-up, came back and did the same thing and where should one have gone to complain, it was there, but fortunately, no nothing, not even my husband did that to me, he's only good." Doña Tomichá Posiabó (Z. 219–228)—See Klein, *Ganz Welt*, p. 208.

4.2 *Relations between Economy and Natural Space*[31]

Does the "lived theology of creation" of the interlocutors show the—in the initial expectation hoped for—money-free, forest-related way of life, which represents nature as a source, as a giver of abundance? Or does a market-economic view prevail, dealing with nature as a commodity?

The texts document the perspective that "working with nature frees us from buying." The nature-loving way of life is independent of the money economy. The longing backward and the knowledge about that intensive connection with e.g. forest, water, garden, clearing is stored in some parts of the subjunctive experience space of the interlocutors. This view is found for example in the retrospective, which praises the forest as a source of life, as well as in the pride that addresses the harvest stocks that are still available. Also, the documents of community work, the traditional giving in mutuality called *minga* is visible in several places, for example documented in the mastery of agriculture, house building (from natural materials), gardening based on mutual relations and obligations, and not on means of payment. However, the model of a money-free, forest-based way of life is not presented exclusively positively, and certainly not uncritically. This type of nature-bound lifestyle is also obstructive. All of the interviewees regret the fact that they have received no or only inadequate school education. The reasons for this are, among other things, the constant work in the field, the great dependence on the yield of agricultural production. Dependence on nature prevents the interlocutors' liberative aspirations in this respect. Constant, hard work keeps the first-person-narrators away from schooling. Moreover, patriarchal family structure ads to this forest-bound experience of nature. It is another element that usually interrupts the educational path of the interlocutors too early. Most fathers are depicted as violent and denying their daughters wish for education. Although the figure of the patriarchal father is also portrayed as enabling school education and seeking ways to educate their daughters.

Nature appears as the economic basis for the children's education. The lack of education, experienced as a deficit in one's own life, is followed by another element of the orientation framework: the wish and the active implementation of this wish, to provide a material basis for the education of one's children, especially daughters. Natural resources are paid in exchange for the improvement of children's lives.

In this view of nature, economization is already inscribed. Nature as a commodity as orientation frame especially occurs in the texts close to the living space of the city. It is connected with leaving the village, going away, bringing

31 See Klein, *Ganz Welt*, pp. 263–266.

the harvest to the city. Nature becomes a commodity when it enters the urban economic concepts. Documents for this are, for example, the work processes at the rubber plantation, the "preservation" of the flexible peasant "capital" (harvesting, supplying, slaughtering, processing) for the life in the city, the selling of bananas against her husbands' will in the capital. With the sold goods from the field and garden, the livelihood of the family and especially children can be achieved.

The closeness to nature that has been detached from the money economy in addition to the economization and capitalization of natural phenomena lie in the subjunctive, experiential knowledge of the farmwives. Both poles are handled relatively unrivalled side by side in the life stories. Positive and negative aspects can be seen in both perspectives. The memories may be evaluated in one respect, namely the extent to which freedom or dependence is increased. Freedom can be associated with market economy entrepreneurship or with detachment from the money economy and thus with a way of life that is closely linked to the forest.

4.3 *Relations between Cosmovision and Natural Space*[32]

At first glance, the initial expectation that biographical conversations shall show an intensive treatment of the Chiquitano's world view, was disappointed. In particular I had hoped for narrations about those natural-spiritual elements that show the intensive interweaving of the Chiquitano communities with their living environment. The ambivalent spirits of nature, called "jichis", who according to the worldview of the Chiquitano protect and possess streams and water holes, hills, forests, grasslands, and also every species of animal, have not been addressed in the life testimonies and stories recorded during the study.

Only at a second glance could the indigenous cosmovision embedded in the depth structure of various text passages be discerned. Where emotionality is in its full range, where the conditions and qualities of life are intimately connected with natural scenes, the other world view shines through.

If, for example, the opening passage of a life story deals intensively with the problems of the sinking waterhole, the illegal use of water to wash motorcycles and cars, and the lack of spiritual respect for water, it sets in at the neuralgic point of the natural-religious cosmic map. Here the essential importance of the element of water for the physical and cultural integrity of the narrative community from which this ego text comes and to which the first-person narrator belongs is emphasized. If the touching, heart-opening scene with tears and an intimate mother-son conversation takes place where the landscape

---

32 See Klein, *Ganz Welt*, pp. 266–270.

is vast, then in the inner scenery of the text at least the natural presence of the open pampas landscape is a trigger for the free flow of emotions. If "puro del monte/pure from the forest" is longed for as the source of the good life, this indicates the supply connection to the protective and nourishing lifeline of the forest through hunting, imagined in retrospect as "intact". When the "chaco", the plantation, holds "everything" ready for the childlike narrated ego and the corresponding we of the mother with her group of children, then a transcendent quality of the giving dimension of the tilled soil is revealed. In these exemplary passages, we can see the "jichis" that are never expressed in the texts explicitly but work indirectly. There is a fluid boundary between the people acting in the narratives and the respective spiritual presence of nature.

At times the interlocutors narrate their life stories with sober realism and Christian-Catholic piety. Thus, for example, the blessing of the newly occupied house with holy water all around, both inside and outside, reflect the holiness in a Christian style. The Christian socialization is particularly intense in the narrators' subjunctive space of experience when consecrated life as a religious sister is longed for as a paradisiacal state, when rest is found in the house of prayer and Bible reading, with the catechists and in participation in their work.

My initial expectation of finding an obvious indigenous transformation of the natural experiences present in life stories was disappointed. I could not find the holiness of nature as depicted by some concepts of the Gaia-hypothesis or ecofeminist-thinking.[33] Elements of the traditional cosmovision do appear in the frames of orientation studied. However, in the subjunctive experiential space of the Chiquitano peasant women, in those insights which the collected and evaluated conversations provide, the traditional world view is mute.

4.4 *Relations between Cyclical and Teleological Models of Nature*[34]

Does a rhythmic, cyclical experience of nature prevail or is nature represented in a purposeful teleology in the "lived theologies of creation"?

The ego texts testify to cyclical frames. They also indicate the larger dimension, i.e. the integration of different rhythms into the rhythm of coming and going of life as a whole. The experiences of nature consider the disturbed, fragile, and changing rhythms in the natural matrix and thus also in the effects on the lives of the interviewees. The "lived theologies of creation" of the Chiquitano women also know about the vulnerable bodies woven into the changeable, natural up and down.

---

33 Western ecological movements with spiritual dimensions sometimes base their believes in a large, all-embracing organism they consider as holy.

34 See Klein, *Ganz Welt*, pp. 271–274.

The rhythm of cultivation, which structures years, memories, and also life, and which includes a time of preparation, a time of planting and sowing, a time of weeding, a time of harvesting, a time to consume and sell, a time of fallow land and a time to burn down the *chaco* again, is not extensively described in the life-memories. The cycle occurs, for example, in "calendar function" on the rubber plantation. The perspective of agriculture as a kind of "game of chance" is documented. It is not clear from the outset what will prosper and what will spoil. This mirrors the experience of the great dependence of rural life on uninfluenceable natural factors.

On the one hand, in the "lived theologies of creation" of the interlocutors it becomes clear that the cycles are predetermined. On the other hand, they are extremely fragile and change or can easily get out of balance. Some of the documented perceptions of nature discuss shifting sowing times. These times are no longer reliable as before due to the absence or abundance of rain. The interlocutors sense a change in the climate of their region compared to the past. This change is also a symbol of the changeable nature of life as a whole.

Natural things in people are also subject to a cycle, an up-and-down movement. The "fully lived theologies of creation" of the Chiquitano women do not only see the natural matrix surrounding them as cyclical but also the human beings inherent in them are by their nature taken back and forth and up and down. Health and illness are a fluctuating state. The physical, mental, and spiritual state of health is always in a precarious situation throughout the narrations.

The findings show that nature is primarily experienced as a circular, recurring fabric of life. The integration into cosmic, larger dimensions, and their tides also becomes visible. The agricultural cycles of cultivation are not detailed, but rather, in their often concise and condensed presentation, point to the eternal recurrence of these processes. The climatic changes and disturbances in the rhythms are documented in the recorded life histories. As a predominant orientation frame nature is anchored in the narrators' subjunctive richness of experience as a complex system of cycles rather than a purposeful process.

5 Ecofeminist Spiritualities Thinking Strands

The ecofeminist core argument in theology points out that women such as nature have been understood as material for exploitation. Hence woman-nature connections have to be reformulated on a variety of levels. I agree with the ecofeminist critique that is trying to break with dualistic and negative correlations of women and nature, but after listening to the lectures at

Grandmothers' University we should underline the orientation frames developed from the legitimate aspirations for liberation and longings for a sound life for all.

According to Susan Roll, eco-feminism can be seen as a distinctive branch of discourse in feminist theology:

> Ecofeminism as a distinctive discourse within feminist theology grapples explicitly with the nature/culture dualism in which women are arbitrarily identified with nature, because under patriarchy both women and nature are identified as the Other, the Object upon which the Subject acts, to be brought under control, dominated, tamed, and made to serve useful purposes.[35]

According to Roll, the main point of critique is that the subject-object division of Western philosophy is combined with the dominium terrae and patriarchal women's oppression and both are mutually reinforcing each other.

Historically ecofeminist thinkers such as Susan Griffin[36], Rosemary Radford Ruether or Sallie McFague introduced the topic into European theological debates. Triggered by the controversy in the USA, theologians like Halkes, Moltmann-Wendel and Sölle dealt with eco-feminist ideas in Europe.[37] From the 1980s onwards, the emancipating non-Western eco-feminist theologies developed separate scenes and discourses.[38]

The term eco-feminism was coined in the 1970s for the alliance between feminist and ecological political movements, but is now used as a "collective term […] for theoretical concepts that […] investigate the connections between nature and women […]."[39] In addition to more theoretical and scientific debates, it also includes a "socio-political grassroots movement"[40] which wants to achieve a fairer, non-dominant relationship to nature and between the sexes, as well as a "spirituality […] which places the holiness of all life at

35 Roll, *Time and the Cosmic Rhythms*, p. 111.

36 Griffin, *Frau und Natur.* "Susan Griffin traces the dualisms between soul-flesh, mind-feelings and culture-nature as the outcome of men being confronted with the terror of mortality. Instead of facing such mortality, she suggests that men oppress women and nature. Hence, for her, the solution is to identify with the earth in its mortality. The voice of nature that is joined with those of women becomes embodied and impassioned." Deane-Drummond, "Eco-feminist theology," p. 147. Deane-Drummond elaborates on the various directions of ecofeminist spirituality, especially in the Anglo-Saxon world, from their beginnings—Griffin, Christ, Radford Ruether, and Grey.

37 For basic bibliography cf. Hartlieb, *Ökofeminismus.*

38 Kutzer, *Befreiung der Schopfung*, p. 92 (footnote 5); p. 106.

39 Hartlieb, *Ökofeminismus*, pp. 249–250.

40 Hartlieb, *Ökofeminismus*, p. 250.

the center."[41] The central element of the ecofeminist tendencies in spirituality, which are quite different in content—historically past as well as currently growing—, is the equation woman=nature. The feminist critique of the patriarchal understanding of creation, which places the (male) human being at the center and declares him to be the crown, unites all those designs that practice a sense of connectedness and focus on a mostly female-conceived large organism—often called Gaia. Mies/Shiva argue, among other things, for a different, helpful imagining of the divine of nature in the form of the Gaia hypothesis[42] which imagines nature as an interrelational large organism, sacred and integrating everything.

Gudmarsdottir[43] sharpens the essential characteristics of the ecological and eco-feminist movement to parallel the connection between sexist-sexual violence against women and the human-exploitative rape of Mother Earth.

> When the earth is declared a body, violated by human consumption and greed, powerful transformations of language take place. On the one hand symbolic connections between nature and women are affirmed; on the other the experience of sexual violence that women especially suffer are addressed and intensified to a cosmic scale. For many ecothinkers, the body of the earth came to be seen as a sacred body, identified with a motherly or a goddess deity. Consequently, if

---

41 Hartlieb, *Ökofeminismus*, p. 250.

42 Cf. Mies/Shiva, *Ökofeminismus*. p. 357. Compare also the familiar baptizing as "Mother Earth": Mies/Shiva, *Ökofeminismus*, pp. 22, 29, 31, 142, 172, 328. Also Radford Ruether, *Gaia & Gott*, pp.14–15. The earth mother Gaia emphasizes "the powerful and creative aspects in the understanding of nature as well as of femininity," argues Hartlieb, *Ökofeminismus*, p. 252. Kutzer points out that the "Gaia hypothesis" plays an important role in the elaboration of "new cosmologies" and was originally imported from discussions in the natural sciences: "The name of the Greek earth goddess was used in the mid-1960s by the microbiologist Lynn Margulis and the biophysicist James Lovelock to designate the hypothesis that the earth, together with its biosphere, forms a dynamic system that enables the organization of complex organisms by means of the capacity of autopoiesis, and in this sense can be regarded as a living being as a whole": Kutzer, *Befreiung der Schöpfung*, p. 90. Not only ecofeminist thinkers rely on the "Gaia hypothesis". See also Latour, *Kampf um Gaia*.

43 Gudmarsdottir, *Rapes of Earth*, p. 207. Gudmarsdottir is very skeptical concerning the parallelization of languages. "Important as it [the metaphor of earth rapes, I.K.] was for early ecofeminisms, does the image of rape serve for contemporary ecofeminist purposes as helpful metaphors for the environmental crisis? The question automatically spawns new questions of language and images, such as: Should we describe the earth as having a body? And if such metaphoric body language is deemed helpful for contemporary feminist enquiry, how is that body gendered? Do rape metaphors adequately express the condition of women and nature, or does it cast female bodies and the cosmos into a role that is too passive, too victimized, too hopeless for the tastes of third wave feminists? If women struggle for subjectivity, dignity and power, in language, how helpful is it to land once more on the 'wrong' side of the nature/culture scale?"

> nature was identified as a female body; the ecological crisis which the contemporary world faces was depicted as the abuse, rape or slaughter of the sacred mother. If thinking about the earth as a body is common in diverse ecotheological circles, the main contribution of ecofeminists to this kind of thinking was to apply feminist analyses of patriarchal oppression and ravishment of female bodies to the environmental debate.[44]

The diversity of ecofeminist attitudes and practices is illustrated by Bauhardt's distinction between three major currents of ecofeminism,[45] which, starting from a similar fundamental analysis of social natural conditions using the gender perspective, each concentrate on different drafts for action. Bauhardt distinguishes (1) cultural and social ecofeminism,[46] (2) queer ecology,[47] and (3) ecofeminist political economy.[48]

Towards some ecofeminist spiritualities which operate with the Gaia-hypothesis, a large, sacred, female being, the orientation frames concerning nature documented in the rural biographies in the present study stand in critical objection.[49]

(a) Cultural ecofeminism tends to spiritualize, idealize and dismiss real women's needs: The Gaia-hypothesis especially in neopagan or Wicca goddess spirituality[50] is sometimes very spiritual, very idealizing or romanticizing and hyper-feminine. Therefore, there is no overcoming the dualistic scheme and cultural or symbolic eco-feminist theories then miss real women's experiences and needs.

(b) Language of corporeality has disadvantages: Ecofeminist spirituality and theology sometimes addresses nature and earth in terms that are derived from the thematic field of the body. This metaphor can lead to a reductionist and materialist impression that would reinforce a rigid image of women and establish an exclusive naturalness in them. To talk to third aged *campesinas* somehow fell into the troubling area of patriarchal mindsets of a supposed greater closeness of women that have given birth and have already seen their grandchildren alive.

44 Gudmarsdottir, *Rapes of Earth*, pp. 206–207.
45 Bauhardt, *Gesellschaftliche Naturverhältnisse*.
46 Cf. Bauhardt, *Gesellschaftliche Naturverhältnisse*, pp. 49–50.
47 Cf. Bauhardt, *Gesellschaftliche Naturverhältnisse*, pp. 50–51.
48 Cf. Bauhardt, *Gesellschaftliche Naturverhältnisse*, pp. 51–52.
49 See for a deeper discussion Klein, *Ganz Welt*, pp. 288–301.
50 Some parts of ecofeminist movements worship "Mother Earth" as a long-forgotten Goddess of former matriarchal times. On 22 of April for example, the UN day for Mother Earth, rituals to harmonize and walk in peace with Mother Earth are held.

(c) One-dimensional perspective and a simplified woman=nature equation vs. multidimensional reality: Ecofeminist spirituality can be tempted to be blind to socio-economic differences between women, to power and dominance gaps.

(d) Woman=Nature as a theoretical-mental-spiritual problem vs. Woman= Nature as a complex relationship in the economy: Ecofeminism spirituality sometimes tends to neglect the concrete economic connections and entanglements in which women find themselves with nature. The orientation frames documented a longing for independence from nature through using nature as commodity.

(e) Unclear, universalizing use of the terms "woman" and "nature" vs. differentiation and clarification: Ecofeminist spirituality should bear in mind that the disadvantageous equation woman=nature has not been represented in this way everywhere and pay attention to sharpness in the use of the different understandings of nature.

6 Summary and Consequences

What could climate justice mean in the light of Grandmothers' University "life lectures"? Will these "fully lived theologies" contribute some important focuses to climate protection debates? Of course, the talking about "Mother Earth" or "Gaia" is helpful to accelerate human actions towards a less harmful using of natural resources. It is useful to shape environmental and natural systems like a large, motherly organism in order to become aware of humans' strong relation as earth-bound creatures. But some pictures are contradictory to the fully lived perceptions to be found in the subjunctive experience at Grandmothers' University.

At the "fireplace, the center" of the "fully lived God-talk" lies a strong emphasis on relationality. The recorded texts remind us of the importance of social-closeness in connection with the natural space and foreground how intensely the community is interwoven and relationships are a first level to deal with. Relationality in the life stories has also a destructive side. Debates on climate justice that will not take action towards gender justice and social justice miss key issues.

The orientation frames testified in the "fully lived theologies" also remind us of women's legitimate longings for freedom and autonomy. And they recall that processes of autonomy are conquered by using nature as a commodity. This empirical approach is an attempt to make voices heard, that are not placed in the center of discourses for a new praxis towards Climate Justice. For

Western Christian theology the "fully lived God-talk" encourages to listen to the subjunctive and collective experiences of real people.

References

Bauhardt, Christine: "Gesellschaftliche Naturverhältnisse und globale Umweltpolitik—Ökofeminismus, Queer Ecologies, (Re)Produktivität und das Konzept 'Ressourcenpolitik'," in: Barbara Rendtorff/Claudia Mahs/Verena Wecker (eds.): *Geschlechterforschung. Theorien, Thesen, Themen zur Einführung*. Stuttgart, 2011, pp. 44–58.

Bohnsack, Ralf: "Dokumentarische Methode und sozialwissenschaftliche Hermeneutik," in: *Zeitschrift für Erziehungswissenschaft 6*, no. 4 (2003), pp. 550–570.

Deane-Drummond, Celia: "Eco-feminist theology," in: Celia Deane-Drummond (ed.): *Eco-theology*. London, 2008, pp. 146–163.

Ellacuría, Ignacio: "Geschichtlichkeit des christlichen Heils," in: Jon Sobrino/Ignacio Ellacuría (eds.): *Mysterium liberationis I*. Luzern, 1995, pp. 313–360.

Failing, Wolf-Eckart/Hans-Günter Heimbrock: "Praktische Theologie als Theorie Gelebter Religion," in: Wolf-Eckart Failing/Hans-Günter Heimbrock/Thomas A. Lotz (eds.): *Religion als Phänomen. Sozialwissenschaftliche, theologische und philosophische Erkundungen in der Lebenswelt*. Berlin/New York, 2001, pp. 15–45.

Forschungskreis Kommunikative Theologie/Communicative Theology Research Group, *Kommunikative Theologie. Selbstvergewisserung unserer Kultur des Theologietreibens*. Münster, 2006.

Gräb, Wilhelm: "Wahrnehmen und Deuten", in: Albrecht Grözinger/Georg Pfleiderer (eds.), *"Gelebte Religion" als Programmbegriff Systematischer und Praktischer Theologie*, Zürich, 2002, pp. 43–65.

Griffin, Susan: *Frau und Natur. Das Brüllen in ihr*. Frankfurt a. M., 1987.

Gudmarsdottir, Sigridur: "Rapes of Earth and Grapes of Wrath. Steinbeck, Ecofeminism and the Metaphor of Rape," in: *Feminist Theology 18*, no. 2 (01/2010): pp. 206–222.

Hartlieb, Elisabeth: "Ökofeminismus," in: Irene Leicht/Claudia Rakel/Stefanie Rieger-Goertz (eds.): *Arbeitsbuch Feministische Theologie. Inhalte, Methoden und Materialien für Hochschule, Erwachsenenbildung und Gemeinde*. Gütersloh, 2003, pp. 255–256.

Heimbrock, Hans-Günter: "Wahrnehmung als Element der Wahr-Nehmung," in: Albrecht Grözinger/Georg Pfleiderer (eds.), *"Gelebte Religion" als Programmbegriff Systematischer und Praktischer Theologie*, Zürich, 2002, pp. 65–90.

Klein, Irmgard: *Ganz Welt. Gelebte Schöpfungstheologien—eine frauenspezifische Studie anhand bäuerlicher Lebensgeschichten im Tiefland Boliviens*. Dissertation. Innsbruck, 2013.

Korsch, Dietrich: "'Leben' als Thema gelebter Religion," in: Albrecht Grözinger/Georg Pfleiderer (eds.), *"Gelebte Religion" als Programmbegriff Systematischer und Praktischer Theologie*, Zürich, 2002, pp. 191–207.

Kutzer, Mirja: "Befreiung der Schöpfung? Die Suche nach einer 'neuen Kosmologie' als Antwort auf die ökologische Krise," in: Gunter Prüller-Jagenteufel/Hans Schelkshorn/Franz Helm (eds.): *Götzendämmerung? Die Zivilisationskrise und ihre Opfer*. Aachen 2013, pp. 90–106.

Langhammer, Elke: *"Ist Gott drin?!" Erfahrungen der Gottespräsenz im pastoralen Alltag von Gemeindeseelsorgerinnen*. Kommunikative Theologie—interdisziplinär 15. Wien/Berlin, 2011.

Latour, Bruno: *Kampf um Gaia. Acht Vorträge über das neue Klimaregime*. Berlin, 2017.

Mies, Maria/Vandana Shiva: *Ökofeminismus. Beiträge zur Praxis und Theorie*. Zürich, 1995.

Muck, Otto: "Der Beitrag der Wissenschaftstheorie zur Klärung der Rationalität von Glaube als lebenstragender Überzeugung," in: Otto Muck/Winfried Löffler (eds): *Rationalität und Weltanschauung, Philosophische Untersuchungen*. Innsbruck/Wien, 1999, pp. 100–105.

Muck, Otto: "Rationale Strukturen des Dialogs über Glaubensfragen," in: Otto Muck/Winfried Löffler (eds): *Rationalität und Weltanschauung, Philosophische Untersuchungen*. Innsbruck/Wien, 1999, pp. 106–151.

Nohl, Arnd-Michael: *Interview und dokumentarische Methode. Anleitungen für die Forschungspraxis*. Wiesbaden, 2006.

Pemsel-Maier, Sabine: "Von der Geburt bis zum Tod. Geerdete Schöpfungstheologie aus Frauenperspektive," in: Margit Eckholt/Sabine Pemsel-Maier (eds.): *Unterwegs nach Eden. Zugänge zur Schöpfungsspiritualität*. Ostfildern 2009, pp. 58–75.

Peter, Teresa: *Von der Angst zu gehen und vom Gehen in der Angst. Angsterfahrungen als Herausforderung an theologisches Denken, Reden und Handeln*, Kommunikative Theologie—interdisziplinär 5. Münster, 2006.

Radford Ruether, Rosemary: *Gaia & Gott. Eine ökofeministische Theologie der Heilung der Erde*. Luzern, 1994.

Rahner, Karl: *Hörer des Wortes. Zur Grundlegung einer Religionsphilosophie*, neu bearbeitet von Johann Baptist Metz. Freiburg, 1971, pp. 45–46.

Roll, Susan K.: "Time and the Cosmic Rhythms in Transition. A perspective from feminist creation theology," in: Brigitte Enzner-Probst/Elisabeth Moltmann-Wendel (eds.): *Im Einklang mit dem Kosmos. Schöpfungsspiritualität lehren, lernen und leben. Theologische Aspekte—Praktische Impulse*. Ostfildern, 2013, pp. 100–116.

Rosenthal, Gabriele: *Interpretative Sozialforschung. Eine Einführung*. Weinheim, ²2008.

Rosenthal, Gabriele: *Interpretive Social Research—An Introduction*. Göttingen, 2018.

Shiva, Vandana: "Monocultures of Minds create Monocultures on the Field. The inevitable shift or why organic farming is the answer," in: Petra Gruber (ed.): *Die Zukunft der Landwirtschaft ist biologisch! Welthunger, Agrarpolitik und Menschenrechte*. Opladen, 2009, pp. 37–56.

Scientific Findings on Microbiome and on Microplastic—Stimulations for Theology of Creation

Sibylle Trawöger

Abstract

It is important to incorporate current scientific findings into creation theology. Findings on microbiome and microplastics call for an update of classical theologies of creation both on a material level and on a basic theoretical level. On the material level, there is a relativization of anthropocentrism, without degrading human beings. On the level of basic theory, the question of relational ontologies in contrast to substance ontologies is raised. These updates place the issue of sustainability at the center of theology of creation.

Keywords

Natural science; theology of creation; microbiom; microplastic; evolution theory; intraaction; performativity

Theology of creation is based on scientific-theoretical considerations of "possible connections between natural science and theology",[1] to which, for example, Ian Barbour has assigned four models.[2] Models linking science and theology are popular right now. The *dialogue* model and the *integration* model are two examples of modelling that do not allow for a theology of creation to be addressed, independent of scientific findings.[3] That said, it is extremely rare when a theology of creation includes individual scientific findings. Instead, several individual scientific findings are usually gathered up and then systematized and structured, according to a certain overarching vision, before being included in a theology of creation. Philosopher Reinhold Esterbauer employs the distinction between "area- and universal-ontology" ("Bereichs- und

1 Barbour, *Wissenschaft und Glaube*, p. 113 (translated by S. T.).—I am grateful to Carlton Chase for his helpful comments on the text.

2 Barbour, *Wissenschaft und Glaube*, p. 113ff.

3 Compare in more detail: Trawöger, *Zum Zusammenspiel von Glauben und Wissen.*

 | DOI:10.30965/9783657795314_007

Universal-Ontologie") to help clarify this.[4] "Area ontologies" are methodologically regulated and are constructed from the findings of scientific research. "Universal ontologies" claim instead to offer an understanding of reality in its entirety. (Creation) theology, for example, is a "universal ontology," according to such classifications. Esterbauer stresses the importance of these classifications of area- and universal ontology, in the hope that any engagement between natural science and theology respects equally the specific contents, methods and the scientific-theoretical foundations of the respective disciplines.

It is important to pay attention to the fact with which area ontology a universal ontology such as creation theology operates! For each concrete area ontology already gives a basic orientation to an implicit theology of creation. This can be seen better in the following illustration, using Darwin. It is conspicuous that (German-speaking) theologies of creation use Darwinian theory in a way that highlights his "survival of the fittest" thesis, and rarely do such theologies of creation employ an alternative evolution theory, such as the one evinced by biologist Lynn Margulis. Margulis endorses and publishes on endosymbiont theory. The mitochondria in eukaryotes offer us an entry into endosymbiont theory. Mitochondria, the so-called power plants of animal and human cells, were originally independent cells before becoming incorporated into eukaryotic cells, through symbiogenesis. Lynn Margulis' area ontology emphasizes that all living beings have evolved with the help of microorganisms through a process of symbiosis, according to an understanding of evolution known as symbiogenesis.[5] "We are symbionts on a symbiotic planet, and if we care to, we can find symbiosis everywhere. Physical contact is a non-negotiable requisite for many differing kinds of life".[6] Together with the natural scientist James Lovelock, Margulis developed the Gaia hypothesis, featured in her monograph *Symbiotic Planet*, which connects evolution with symbiosis, otherwise known as symbiogenesis. The Gaia hypothesis underlines vividly the mutual relatedness of living beings among each other and to the vitality of earth.

It matters greatly, for example, whether a universal ontology interacts with area ontologies that summarize scientific findings on evolution, under the Darwinian paradigm "survival of the fittest" or whether such interactions occur under a symbiogenetic paradigm. Under the latter, a shift of emphasis can take place that calls for a relativization of anthropocentrism, without degrading human being.

---

4 Esterbauer, *Methodenbewusstsein*, p. 35.

5 See, for example: "My claim is that, like all other apes, humans are not the work of God but thousands of millions of years of interaction among highly responsive microbes": Margulis, *Symbiotic Planet*, p. 4.

6 Margulis, *Symbiotic Planet*, p. 5.

At this point, I would like to note the work of Sarah Coakley and Martin A. Nowak. In *Evolution, Games, and God*, Coakley and Nowak argue that, with respect to Darwin's theory of evolution, the notion of the 'survival of the fittest' does not do adequate justice to Darwin's theses.[7] From an interdisciplinary perspective, their anthology attempts to identify interfaces between the talk of evolution and the talk of God, by means of the concept of cooperation:

> The aim of the book is to assess the place and significance of cooperation within the dynamics of evolution, and to do so in a radically interdisciplinary way, bringing to bear not only the insights of evolutionary biology (both mathematical and empirical), but also of the social sciences, philosophy, and theology.[8]

Cooperation is distinguished from altruism by all authors of the anthology:

> From the Introduction on, the various authors agree (by and large) that cooperation is a "form of working together in which one individual pays a cost (in terms of fitness, whether genetic or cultural) and another gains a benefit". Altruism is a logical subset of cooperation, defined as "a form of (costly) cooperation in which an individual is motivated by goodwill or love for another".[9]

The term cooperation avoids the moral charge of interconnectedness and it implicitly suggests that Darwin's theory points to more than individualism and competitivism. Coakley and Nowak point out, that in the theological and religious environment, Darwin's theory was often inadequately shaped, by an overreliance on these key points:

> The genius of Charles Darwin was to disclose and clarify the crucial role of "mutation" and "selection" in the constraining of evolutionary processes. But Darwin himself, especially in his later work, was well aware that there was something else going on in evolution that could not be accounted for solely in terms of these two fundamental principles.[10]

7 Nowak/Coakley, *Evolution, Games, and God*.—Only one of the twenty-one articles also mentions Lynn Margulis' theory, that of biologist Jeffery P. Schloss: Schloss, *Unpredicted Outcomes*. The anthology aims to: "Humans who more accurately understand how cooperation works, both biologically and culturally (qua 'altruism'), can potentially extend the range of its efficacy" (Schloss, *Introduction*, p. 26).

8 Nowak/Coakley, *Evolution, Games, and God*, p. 1.

9 Clayton, *Evolution, Altruism, and God*, p. 344. See also, there is "the crucial distinction between a form of 'cooperation' which just happens, and 'altruism' proper, which is motivated by specific goals or affective commitments" (Nowak/Coakley, *Evolution, Games, and God*, p. 4).

10 Nowak/Coakley, *Evolution, Games, and God*, pp. 5–6.

They also criticize the charging of the term cooperation with valence:

> Certainly it is naïve and misleading to assume that "cooperation," in *se*, is a good, while its opposite, "defection," is somehow morally culpable. But we shall nevertheless need to return to this issue of whether a natural evolutionary phenomenon like "cooperation" could, according to any particular "metaethic," be seen as intrinsically value laden.[11]

What is evident in Lynn Margulis' theory can also be found in Darwin's theory. Interconnectedness and cooperation are essential moments of our human existence. I would like to build upon this and the above-mentioned "relativization of anthropocentrism without degrading human being", with some considerations on the *microbiome*. The so-called microbiome, which consists of a multitude of microorganisms such as bacteria, yeasts or even viruses, covers all surfaces and, thus, also the "outer" and "inner surfaces" of the human body in a characteristic composition. Artist Sonja Bäumel works with the microbiome in a way that reveals microorganisms as actors directly connected to the human body. Since 2012, she has been working on the series *Expanded Self*[12] and *Expanded Self II*,[13] in cooperation with natural scientists Erich Schopf and Manuel Selg. The invisible microbiome, or the invisible "material" on her body, is made visible by means of appropriating a laboratory procedure. In the laboratory, microorganisms are cultivated on nutrient-containing agar, in small round petri dishes. This is done to make these organisms visibly detectable after suitable incubation periods. Following this principle, Bäumel places her naked body on an oversized agar plate and pulls the trigger, whereupon at least some of the microorganisms that are settled on her body surface continue to grow on the agar and form recognizable colonies. A microbiological imprint of the artist's body is thus made visible and exhibited. Bäumel shows that the surfaces of the body are littered with microorganisms, and makes clear, right from the start, that the human body is not viable without microorganisms. "She creates images of her body that can be understood as a living biotope, a hybrid, and a symbiotic ecosystem".[14] Lynn Margulis' area ontology reveals an aspect of the microbiome that I will examine in more detail below: the fact that the subject status of humans is deeply connected to microorganisms, which are usually assigned to the object status. Scientific insight apparently puts to the test,

11 Nowak/Coakley, *Evolution, Games, and God*, p. 7.

12 See: http://www.sonjabaeumel.at/work/bacteria/expanded-self [last modified April 10, 2021].

13 See: http://www.sonjabaeumel.at/work/bacteria/expanded-self-2 [last modified April 10, 2021].

14 Various, *Trees of Life*, p. 35.

here, the subject-object-separation to which many approaches in the history of philosophy but also in theological anthropology refer.

The concept of microperformativity, as illustrated by Jens Hauser, helps to draw attention to the agency of the microbiome, which is normally called object.[15] Hauser is concerned with research topics that are located at the interface of art and science, in particular technology; he is interested in bio-art. With the term microperformativity, the agentive/active moment of microorganisms also moves into the field of vision, whereby, for example, the "staging modalities of corporeality" shift:

> In both the visual and the performing arts, "body" can consequently no longer simply be understood as the mesoscopic human body as the central instance. In an art of transforming biological systems in vivo and in vitro, the focus shifts, on the one hand, to the microscopic minute level of molecules, cells, enzymes, etc., and, on the other hand, this opens up perspectives of staging a continuum of life that expands the spectrum of human actions to include the action potentials of the animal and the vegetable and relates it to these epistemologically and ontologically.[16]

Bruno Latour uses the term *performativity*, as well, to highlight the agency of a wide variety of actors, and thus also of microorganisms. Writes Latour, "It is no longer only humans who transport information through transformations, but nonhuman beings do likewise when they transform themselves underhand from barely existing attributes into fully valid substance".[17] It comes to light that microorganisms are independent actors, which, in turn, act upon the actor "human" or, on a macro level, upon the actor "society".

The findings on the microbiome, Bäumel's artistic work with the microbiome, and Margulis' area ontology make it clear: *life takes place in relationships*.[18]

15 Hauser, *Molekulartheater*.

16 Hauser, *Molekulartheater*, p. 173. (The German quote is: "Sowohl in den bildenden als auch in den darstellenden Künsten kann demzufolge als 'Körper' nicht einfach mehr nur der mesoskopisch-menschliche Körper als zentrale Instanz verstanden werden. In einer Kunst der Transformation biologischer Systeme in vivo und in vitro verlagert sich der Fokus einerseits auf die mikroskopische Kleinstebene von Molekülen, Zellen, Enzymen etc., andererseits eröffnen sich dadurch Perspektiven der Inszenierung eines Lebenskontinuums, welches das Spektrum menschlicher Handlungen um die Aktionspotentiale des Tierischen und des Pflanzlichen erweitert und es zu diesen epistemologisch und ontologisch in Beziehung setzt.")

17 Latour, *Die Hoffnung der Pandora*, p. 147. (The original quote is: "Es ist nicht länger nur der Mensch, der Information durch Transformationen transportiert, sondern nichtmenschliche Wesen tun dies ebenfalls, wenn sie sich unterderhand aus kaum existierenden Attributen in eine vollgültige Substanz verwandeln.")

18 See Trawöger, *Impulse*.

However, as already mentioned in the work of Coakley and Nowak, relationship and interconnectedness are not necessarily good in and of themselves. Challenging moments of relationship and interconnectedness become clear when we look at disease-causing microorganisms or at the invasive presence of microplastics. I would like to take a closer look at this phenomenon of microplastics.

Scientific findings on microplastics also illustrate the interconnectedness of the human with environment. The term *microplastic* was coined by Thompson et al. in 2004. Thompson, in concert with others, observed that "microscopic plastic fragments and fibres are [...] widespread in the oceans".[19] Currently, in natural science research, plastic particle sizes are differentiated again into microplastics and nanoplastics. Microplastics range, in size, from 0.1 to 5 μm, and nanoplastics range from 0.001 to 0.1 μm.[20] The size of the particles can result in different interactions with nature and humans. The so-called secondary microplastics are formed in the decay process of plastic products.

> Plastics are synthetic or semisynthetic organic materials with high molecular weight, molecular chains mainly consist of carbon, hydrogen, oxygen, chlorine and silicon atoms. Plastics are easy to mould into complex shapes and forms, extremely durable, lightweight, corrosion resistant, thermally and electrically insulating and offer a wide mechanical and even multifunctional performance range.[21]

Due to plastic's versatility and cost-efficiency, the annual global plastic production reached 368 million tons in 2019.[22] Because the material does not degrade under natural circumstances, post-consumer recycling process is important. In many countries, the recycling return is very low; plastic is burned or, in the worst case, released directly into nature. There, plastic waste decomposes into smaller parts, creating microplastics and nanoplastics. Scientific research on microplastics in the environment, especially in oceans, is ongoing.[23] How microplastics and nanoplastics interact with the human organism and which diseases can be caused or accelerated by it, still needs to be researched in detail. There are indications that nanoplastics, in particular, interact with the

19 Thompson et al., *Lost at Sea*, p. 838.

20 See for example the European Food Safety Agency (EFSA). They distinguished between these two main groups of plastic particles by size that contaminate the food chain. Cf. EFSA Panel on Contaminants in the Food Chain [last modified April 30, 2021].

21 Gruber et al., *To Waste or not to Waste*.

22 PlasticsEurope 2020, *Plastics*, p. 16.

23 For a cultural perspective on microplastics, see: Bergman, *Schleimige Assoziationen im Meer*.

human organism on the cellular and protein level, which can have harmful consequences for whole generations, in the long run.

Analyses investigating the effects of microplastics and nanoplastics on environment, non-humans, and humans, are particularly important in this era of Anthropocene. In 2000, Paul J. Crutzen, Nobel laureate in chemistry in 1995 for his work on the destruction of stratospheric ozone, proposed a new geological age, the Anthropocene. He pointed out, that humans are the most important factor influencing biological and geological processes on Earth. Science theorist Donna Haraway coined the term *Chthulucene* instead, to illustrate that humans are not masters of their activities. Thus, Chthulucene clarifies that humans are deeply interconnected with other living beings and the environment.[24] Between these two characterizations of our present age, it is important to map out this problem of microplastics and nanoplastics. On the one hand, humans continue to produce plastic, despite knowing the problems of microplastics and nanoplastics. On the other hand, microplastics and nanoplastics already act as "agents;"[25] they already affect our environment and health in ways that we do not (yet) fully understand and, consequently, cannot begin to control. Moreover, the possible catastrophic consequences of microplastics and nanoplastics pollution show that we need to have a different approach toward plastics and, by extension, toward the practice of a different lifestyle. For example, as Sallie McFague exhorts, we have to leave the "culture of consumerism".[26]

The interconnectedness between microplastics, especially nanoplastics, and human body bears a health risk that may be irreversible: the more plastic is produced, the more the next generation will be affected by effects, which are

24 Haraway, *Unruhig bleiben*. Chthulucene is a neologism. Starting from the name of a small creature, the spider "Pimoa cthulhu", which belongs, so to speak, to the chthonic creatures, Haraway makes a change to "chthulu". Thus, she designs "a name for an elsewhere, for another time, that was, still is and could be: the Chthulucene" (Haraway, *Unruhig bleiben*, 49; translation S. T.).

25 For non-humans as agents compare more precisely: Latour, *Die Hoffnung der Pandora*.

26 McFague, *Blessed are the Consumers*, p. X. Sally McFague's *Kenotic Theology* includes the findings of Nowak and is also based on interconnectedness and relation: "It all works by symbiosis—living off one another. Nothing in an old-growth forest can go it alone; nothing could survive by itself; everything in the forest is interrelated and interdependent […]" (McFague, *Blessed are the Consumers*, p. 21). "Like the plants and animals in an old-growth forest, we are interrelated and interdependent" (McFague, *Blessed are the Consumers*, p. 22). She pleads for new approaches: "What I have been trying to do with these thought and feeling experiments is to loosen the hold of the predominant model of subject/object, human/nature, and to entertain the possibility that a different model—one in which all have a voice and the goal is sustainable well-being—might guide our actions" (McFague, *Blessed are the Consumers*, p. 27).

not yet fully understood. Plastic, in its ability to interact with other substances and materials, challenges the plasticity of the human body. Philosopher Catherine Malabou differentiates "creative plasticity" from "pathological plasticity". Her work is primarily based on a phenomenological analysis of the human brain, but her differentiation could be addressed to the whole human body.[27] Creative plasticity affects all life and takes place in a balance of destruction and construction. Pathological plasticity underscores the reality that this balance cannot be kept; it changes the human being in a primarily destructive way. In relation to plastics, especially to microplastics and nanoplastics, it remains to ask how we can avoid this state of "pathological plasticity" on a physical level. To what extent does global plastic production introduce microplastics and nanoplastics into the world? To what extent is this done in a manner that changes the human, on a biological level, in such a way that we are confronted with diseases that we do not know, or are left reckoning with new accelerations of known diseases? Because the human body does not consist entirely of elastic material and cannot be completely freed from the microplastic and nanoplastic particles once they have "stepped in", it is necessary to reduce plastic consumption. The transhumanistic potential of these small particles must not be underestimated.[28] Humans have produced new agents that are now impacting humans, in new ways. Every human ingests an average of 5g of plastic per week. How will this change the human body, how will it then change the gut microbiome? Will microplastics and nanoplastics affect the fertility of humans? How do nanoplastics affect organs, do they promote cancer? Will nanoplastics, which are currently difficult to detect in vivo, affect protein folding in our brains, in a way that, for example, accelerates the progression of dementia? These are open questions that also need to be framed within both debates of posthumanism and transhumanism, as well as within debates about sustainability. If we now move further into a creation theology with a relational focus, I want to stress that sustainability issues are not some incidental strands of thought but are woven into the very fabric of concern.

Starting points such as Margulis' area ontology, a reading of Darwin's theory of evolution as suggested by Coakley and Nowak, scientific findings on the microbiome, and scientific findings on microplastics, all could support creation theologies based less on a "substance ontology" but on a "relational ontology". Several decades ago, Jürgen Moltmann presented an "ecological theology of creation", which considered the relational moment and thus

27 Malabou, *Ontologie*.

28 For a more in-depth look at the subject area, cf. also: Loh, *Trans- und Posthumanismus*.

the integration of human beings in creation to be central.[29] The religious educationist Katrin Bederna makes the following observation, regarding Moltmann's approach: "Important first-generation ecotheologies such as Jürgen Moltmann's or Rosemary Radford Ruethers' want [...] to surround nature again with an aura of the sacred. Yet they remain appellatively and philosophically underexposed".[30] A philosophical deepening of relation can be found in other theological approaches, such as those of Catherine Keller[31] or Peter Knauer.[32] Keller's approach has a process-theological basic tenor; Knauer tries to keep the nature grace difference high. Though different in their respective points of departure, Keller's and Knauer's theologies both place emphasis on the relational moment.

I would like to deepen this relational moment by looking at a recent concept of physicist and philosopher Karen Barad. On the basis of "agential realism," she has coined the term "intra-action".[33]

> The notion of intra-action is a key element of my agential realist framework. The neologism "intra-action" signifies the mutual constitution of entangled agencies. That is, in contrast to the usual "interaction", which assumes that there are separate individual agencies that precede their interaction, the notion of intra-action recognises that distinct agencies do not precede, but rather emerge through, their intra-action. It is important to note that the "distinct" agencies are only distinct in a relational, not an absolute, sense, that is, agencies are only distinct in relation to their mutual entanglement; they do not exist as individual elements.[34]

An essential accompaniment to this notion of intra-action is the question of the subject-object-division that has been handed down in the history of philosophy. If the starting point of consideration is not the subject or the object, but the (eventful) relation, and if, in turn, this intra-action is also attributed to

29 Moltmann, *Gott in der Schöpfung*.

30 Bederna, *Every Day for Future*, pp. 160–161 (translated by S. T.).

31 Keller, *Über das Geheimnis*; Keller, *Face of the Deep*.

32 Knauer, *Der Glaube kommt vom Hören*.

33 "Importantly, agential realism rejects the notion of a correspondence relation between words and things and offers in its stead a causal explanation of how discursive practices are related to material phenomena. It does so by shifting the focus from the nature of representations (scientific and other) to the nature of discursive practices (including technoscientific ones), leaving in its wake the entire irrelevant debate between traditional forms of realism and social constructivism. Crucial to this theoretical framework is a strong commitment to accounting for the material nature of practices and how they come to matter" (Barad, *Meeting the Universe Halfway*, pp. 44 45).

34 Barad, *Meeting the Universe Halfway*, p. 33.

the capacity of apparently "objective matter" to act, then the self-evident separation of subject and object is fundamentally put into question.

Two points of note:

1. The concept of intra-action can lead creation theologies to a deeper reflection about relation. Existing "relational ontologies" could be examined to see whether static subjects or objects are not again placed before the relation. Focusing on relation also allows its diversity to emerge and can concretize the theological talk of relation (between human and God).

2. Ascribing to "objective" matter the capacity to act probably represents a challenge for a contemporary theology of creation. Often the environment is called the "house" in which we live.[35] This static metaphor can obscure the capacity of matter to act and the intra-action of humans with it. Of course, if microorganisms and microplastics are regarded as agents or actors, the question remains to be asked, whether the subjectivity and freedom of human is thereby too strongly restricted? Freedom must in any case be (re)thought through. Further-more, intra-action must not be idealized. Intra-action with different people and diverse "matter" can also be a challenge, as I have shown about the debate on microplastics and nanoplastics. It also becomes clear, for example, when Keller speaks of the "stickiness"[36] of relationships and Margulis' area ontology highlights the moment of "becoming engulfed".

On a formal level, I would like to state that one will never (be allowed to) abolish substance-ontological thinking, but relational ontology must be emphasized even more strongly in view of the complexity of our time, in which the interwovenness of everything becomes apparent! Relational ontology highlights the focus on the process. As Catherine Keller emphasizes, because we are relational beings, we are also always in the process of becoming.[37] The view of the changeable and processual in (human) being, also highlights Catherine Malabou in her *Accidental Ontology*. It is a not completely controllable process, since many actors are involved in it, also smallest living beings and particles from our garbage. This is what the talk of microperformativity makes us aware of. With this knowledge, we have to be sensitive especially where we would overlook the small actors.

The reflections starting from the microbiome also made clear how closely especially theological anthropology, epistemology and theology of creation are interwoven. It is important to keep this in mind when taking first steps

35 See, for example: Gruber, *Im Haus des Lebens*.

36 See, for example: Keller, *Über das Geheimnis*, p. 194.

37 Keller, *Über das Geheimnis*, p. 34.

into ethics.[38] The relational integration of all life requires a very careful handling of all visible and invisible relationships respectively intra-actions. The view that the active human being protects the passive "house" of the environment should be replaced with another image of the human: a human being who openly engages in intra-actions with life and therefore acts ethically. This human being could be aware of how strongly he or she is involved in the most diverse intra-actions and not always only attributing the active moment in his or her actions to him-/herself (even if he/she unfortunately has the ability to destroy all relationships with other people and with the environment, as shown by climate change).

References

Barad, Karen: *Meeting the Universe Halfway. Quantum Physics and the Entanglement of Matter and Meaning*. Durham, London: Duke University Press 2007.

Barbour, Ian G.: *Wissenschaft und Glaube: Historische und zeitgenössische Aspekte*. Göttingen: Vandenhoeck&Ruprecht 2003.

Bederna, Katrin: *Every Day for Future: Theologie und religiöse Bildung für nachhaltige Entwicklung*. Ostfildern: Grünewald 2019.

Bergman, Sven: "Schleimige Assoziationen im Meer—die Plastisphäre", in: Friederike Gesing/Michi Knecht/Michael Flitner/Karin Amelang: *NaturenKulturen: Denkräume und Werkzeuge für neue politische Ökologien*. Bielefeld: transcript 2019, pp. 353–384.

Clayton, Philip: "Evolution, Altruism, and God: Why the Levels of Emergent Complexity Matter," in: Nowak/Coakley, *Evolution, Games, and God*, pp. 343–361.

EFSA Panel on Contaminants in the Food Chain: Presence of microplastics and nanoplastics in food, with particular focus on seafood, Statement, 2016, https://efsa.onlinelibrary.wiley.com/doi/full/10.2903/j.efsa.2016.4501, [last modified April 30, 2021].

Esterbauer, Reinhard: "Methodenbewusstsein: Zu einer wichtigen Voraussetzung für den Dialog zwischen Theologie und Naturwissenschaften," in: Christian Tapp/Christoph Breitsameter (EDS.): *Theologie und Naturwissenschaften*. Berlin/Boston: De Gruyter 2014, pp. 21–37.

Gruber, Elisabeth et al.: To Waste or Not to Waste: Questioning Potential Health Risks of Micro- and Nanoplastics with a Focus on Their Ingestion and Potential

38 See, for example. "Objectivity is simultaneously an epistemological, ontological and axiological issue, and questions of responsibility and accountability lie at the core of scientific practice" (Barad, *Meeting the Universe Halfway*, p. 37; cf. also pp. 353–396).

Carcinogenicity, in: Expo Health (2022). https://doi.org/10.1007/s12403-022-00470-8 [last modified April 16, 2022].

Gruber, Franz: *Im Haus des Lebens. Eine Theologie der Schöpfung*. Regensburg: Pustet 2001.

Haraway, Donna J.: *Unruhig bleiben. Die Verwandtschaft der Arten im Chthuluzän*. Frankfurt am Main: Campus 2018.

Hauser, Jens: "Molekulartheater, Mikroperformativität und Plantamorphisierungen," in: Susanne Stemmler (ed.): *Wahrnehmung, Erfahrung, Experiment, Wissen: Objektivität und Subjektivität in den Künsten und den Wissenschaften*. Zürich/Berlin: Diaphanes 2014, pp. 173–189.

Keller, Catherine: *Face of the Deep. A Theology of Becoming*. New York: Routledge 2003.

Keller, Catherine: *Über das Geheimnis: Gott erkennen im Werden der Welt: Eine Prozesstheologie*. Mit einem Geleitwort von Jürgen Moltmann. Freiburg im Breisgau: Herder 2013).

Knauer, Peter: *Der Glaube kommt vom Hören: Ökumenische Fundamentaltheologie*. Norderstedt: Books on demand 2015.

Latour, Bruno: *Die Hoffnung der Pandora*. Frankfurt am Main: Suhrkamp 2002.

Loh, Janina: *Trans- und Posthumanismus zur Einführung*. Hamburg: Junius 2020.

Malabou, Catherine: *Ontologie des Akzidentiellen*. Berlin: Merve 2011.

Margulis, Lynn: *Symbiotic Planet: A New Look at Evolution*. Amherst: Basic Books 1998.

McFague, Sally: *Blessed are the Consumers: Climate Change and the Practice of Restraint*. Minneapolis: Fortress Press 2013.

Moltmann, Jürgen: *Gott in der Schöpfung: Ökologische Schöpfungslehre*. Gütersloh: Chr. Kaiser/Gütersloher Verlagshaus 1993.

Nowak, Martin A./Sarah Coakley (eds.): *Evolution, Games, and God: The Principle of Cooperation*. Cambridge/London: Harvard University Press 2013.

PlasticsEurope 2020, Plastics—the Facts 2020. An analysis of European plastics production, demand and waste data (Brussels: PlasticsEurope 2020), https://www.plasticseurope.org/en/resources/publications/4312-plastics-facts-2020, [last modified April 30, 2021].

Schloss, Jeffrey P.: "Introduction: Why Cooperation Makes a Difference," in: Nowak/Coakley, *Evolution, Games, and God*, pp. 1–34.

Schloss, Jeffrey P.: "Unpredicted Outcomes in the Games of Life," in: Nowak/Coakley, *Evolution, Games, and God*, pp. 201–219.

Thompson, Richard C./Ylva Olsen/Richard P. Mitchell/Anthony Davis/Steven J. Rowland/Anthony W. G. John/Daniel McGonigle/Andrea E. Russell, "Lost at Sea: Where is all the Plastic?" in: *Science* 304 (May 2004).

Trawöger, Sibylle: "Impulse aus Bruno Latours Wissenschaftsforschung für den Dialog zwischen Naturwissenschaft und Theologie," in: Daniel Bogner/Michael Schüßler/

Christian Bauer (eds.): *Gott, Gaia und eine neue Gesellschaft? Theologie anders denken mit Bruno Latour*. Bielefeld: Transcript 2021, pp. 195–218.

Trawöger, Sibylle: "Zum Zusammenspiel von Glauben und Wissen im Spannungsfeld zwischen Naturwissenschaft und Theologie," in: Franz Gmainer-Pranzl (ed.): *"... mit Klugheit und Liebe" (Nostra aetate 2): Dokumentation der Tagungen zur Förderung des interreligiösen Dialogs 2019–2021*. Salzburg (forthcoming).

various: *Trees of Life. Stories for a Damaged Planet. Ausstellungskatalog Frankfurter Kunstverein meets Senckenberg Naturmuseum*, Frankfurt am Main, 10.10.19–19.01.20. Frankfurt am Main 2019.

The Recognition of Nonhuman Animal Agency as a Form of Decolonial Resistance

Daniel P. Horan

Abstract

This article offers both a critical and constructive contribution in response to the need for climate justice. Critically, it interrogates classic epistemological structures of exclusive human agency, particularly present in theological projects touched by Western intellectual and cultural hegemony. What is called for is a decolonial option that de-centers the human person and anthropocentric forms of knowledge production. Constructively, this reflection invites to engage in an imaginative exercise to consider the possible Umwelten (environments, worlds, etc.) of nonhuman creatures as a form of resistance to anthropocentric and colonial epistemological frameworks that reproduce forms of ecological injustice and erase the experiences, worldviews, and bodies of subjugated populations—human and nonhuman alike.

Keywords

Decolonial; ecology; ecospirituality; Umwelten; integral ecology; nonhuman animal agency; Pope Francis; Leonardo Boff

In light of the global climate catastrophe we currently face, I believe that recognition of nonhuman creaturely agency is needed and the epistemological shifts necessary to achieve that recognition amounts to a kind of decolonial resistance. My theological wager is centered on the conviction that doing climate justice first requires paradigmatic shifts along hermeneutical lines. Recognizing the intrinsic fallacies of anthropocentrism is a first step toward the necessary praxis of climate justice, and the implications that arise from such preliminarily theoretical reflections can inform the way we engage with and deploy practical strategies.

As decolonial theorist Arturo Escobar keenly observes in his survey of ecological anthropologies and indigenous wisdoms about the world, there is a primordial story that Christian theologians generally call "creation," which has been obfuscated by an anthropocentric emphasis on the constructed category of "nature" as something exterior to humanity. Escobar writes:

 | DOI:10.30965/9783657795314_008

> The story suggests that there is a deep interconnection between levels or domains of the real—biophysical, human, and supernatural. It also makes clear the imbrication of nature with our knowledge and significations of it. We moderns tend to overlook this fact—nature is one thing, external to us, and our knowledge of it, especially our scientific knowledge, is another thing altogether. This is why one of the most sustained questions moderns have asked is, 'What is nature?,' and we have done so without much trepidation, expecting to arrive at an unequivocal answer.[1]

The questioning of "nature" in this modality has been a preoccupation of post-Western Enlightenment philosophical and theological inquiry for centuries, reifying the modern presumption of "human separatism" apart from the rest of creation (what is thereby categorized as "nature").[2] Nature is understood in this context of alterity as something that we humans can analyze or study as an object without self-implication. But, as I have argued elsewhere, we are creation too and therefore equally part of what is commonly described as "nature."[3] Recognition of this scientific, philosophical, and theological fact ought to shift our attention not only away from the false paradigm of species exceptionalism but also toward greater recognition of nonhuman creaturely agency, which has been occluded by our anthropocentrism and commitment to human separatism.

This brings us to some theoretical dynamics that underlay the problematics of global climate change, rampant species extinction, and environmental degradation. I believe that we can conceptualize these anthropocentric and solipsistic tendencies according to a colonial framework. Like the way fellow human beings have deployed strategies of power and control against other humans *ad intra*, so too the human species writ large has similarly deployed essentializing logics against nonhuman creation *ad extra*. Just as the historical experience of colonization reduces or seeks to erase human agency among the colonized, our anthropocentric framework for thinking about and acting toward nonhuman creation has likewise sought to eliminate the possibility of nonhuman creaturely agency, which has contributed to the justification of the destructive paradigms and practices during the anthropocene. As José Martínez describes it, "an essentialized notion of nature as wilderness that is outside of the human domain becomes subject to a new kind of domination."[4] While the consequences of human-exacerbated global climate change have rendered this "new

1 Escobar, *Territories of Difference*, p. 112.
2 I borrow the phrase "human separatism" from Clough, *On Animals*.
3 See Horan, *Catholicity and Emerging Personhood*, pp. 23–52.
4 Martínez, *Critical Anthropo-Geographies*, p. 74.

kind of domination" more broadly apparent, few theologians have embraced a colonial framework to describe this enduring phenomenon.

Escobar offers us a short summation of the coloniality of nature and the intersectional consequences of this sort of worldview:

> Very schematically, the main features of the coloniality of nature, as established by myriad discourses and practices in post-Renaissance Europe and beyond, include classification into hierarchies ("ethnological reason"), with nonmoderns, primitives, and nature at the bottom of the scale; essentialized views of nature as being outside the human domain; the subordination of the body and nature to the mind (Judeo-Christian traditions; mechanistic science; modern phallogocentrism); seeing the products of the earth as the products of labor only, hence subordinating nature to human-driven markets; locating certain natures (colonial and third world natures, women's bodies, dark bodies) outside the totality of the male Eurocentric world; the subalternization of all other articulations of biology and history to modern regimes, particularly those that enact a continuity between the natural, human, and supernatural worlds—or between being, knowing, and doing.[5]

With this colonial framework in mind, we can approach the pressing climate catastrophes of our time and begin to reconceive our relationship to nonhuman creation and the ways in which our deployment of colonizing power strategies has contributed to creational injustice or what Pope Francis has referred to as "sins against creation."[6]

In this short chapter I intend to accomplish three things: First, I offer a critique of classic epistemological structures of exclusive human agency, particularly as it is found in theological projects touched by Western intellectual and cultural hegemony. I argue that what is needed today is what theorists call a "decolonial option" that, in this applied context, de-centers the human person and anthropocentric forms of knowledge production within the broader community of creation in order to create a space for considering the ways in which nonhuman creatures are also real loci of experience, moral agency, intelligence, and meaning-making. Second, I want to invite readers to engage in an imaginative exercise to consider the possible *Umwelten* ("environments" or "worlds," etc.) of nonhuman creatures as a form of resistance to anthropocentric and colonial epistemological frameworks that reproduce forms of ecological injustice and erase the experiences, worldviews, and bodies of subjugated populations—the human and nonhuman alike, or what Leonardo Boff and

5 Escobar, *Territories of Difference*, p. 121.

6 Pope Francis, *Laudato Si'*, no. 8. Here Pope Francis also references a similar theme developed in the thought and writings of Ecumenical Patriarch Bartholomew. See Chryssavgis, ed., *On Earth as in Heaven*.

Pope Francis have both called attending to "the cry of the earth and the cry of the poor."[7] And, finally, I present three areas in which our critical analysis of epistemological presumptions might inspire constructive practices that are informed by our reflection on nonhuman creaturely agency. My hope is that this chapter might serve as a springboard for robust reflection, rich discussion, and renewed praxis.

1 We Do Not Know What We Do Not Know

The renowned primatologist Frans De Waal cleverly titled his 2016 book about the breadth and depth of nonhuman animal cognition, *Are We Smart Enough to Know How Smart Animals Are?*[8] It's an instructive question, the honest answer to which can only be "no." If we take the premise of the question as our starting point, it reflects back to us an anthropocentric presumption about knowledge and meaning making that rests on the Western Enlightenment epistemological foundation of Cartesian rationality. Accordingly, only human beings have the capacity to know, to emote, to discern, and to act rationally. One widespread and commonly held assumption of the Western intellectual enterprise is that subjectivity is limited to human beings, and history reflects that only certain categories of *homo sapiens* have been considered to be fully human (more specifically, white, straight, cisgender, male human beings of European descent). Descartes infamously contributed at the outset to what would become the growing Enlightenment divide between the human and nonhuman world. What he distinguished in terms of *res cogitans* and merely *res extensa*, was later appropriated by several lines of philosophical and theological reasoning and taken to its logical and, ultimately, destructively anthropocentric ends.[9] Emblematic of this manner of thinking, Descartes rejected outright that nonhuman animals were capable of reason, language, or moral discernment, writing in his 1637 treatise *Discourse on Method*, that nonhuman animals "have no intelligence at all, and that it is nature that acts in them, according to the disposition of their organs—just as we see that a clock composed exclusively of wheels and springs can count the hours and measure time more accurately than we can with all our carefulness."[10] This notion of

7 Boff, *Cry of the Earth*; and Pope Francis, *Laudato Sí'*, nos. 49 and 107.

8 De Waal, *Are We Smart Enough*.

9 A full analysis exceeds the scope of this chapter, but for more on the historical development of this phenomenon from the medieval and renaissance eras through the industrial revolution, see Horan, *All God's Creatures*, pp. 3–21.

10 Descartes, *Discourse on Method*, p. 73.

nonhuman animality as akin to "fleshy machines" has persisted throughout subsequent centuries and has negatively influenced theological attempts to account for the totality of creation and humanity's distinctive place as one creature among others within it.

Returning to De Waal's keen titular question, and my decisive answer in the negative, what I mean to say is that our philosophical and theological anthropocentrism—especially as it pertains to discerning varieties of knowledge—has prevented us from recognizing the possibility of nonhuman animal agency. Elsewhere, I have described this phenomenon as "anthropocentric privilege," a form of advantage accrued to humans as the other side of environmental injustice.[11] This way of thinking about human exceptionalism has cast an occluding shadow over the ability of humans to recognize the proximity—biologically and theologically—that we share to the rest of creation. As a result, ecological devastation, rampant pollution, and species endangerment and extinction have risen. The standard by which all nonhuman creation has been measured is according to anthropocentric models. The late environmental philosopher Val Plumwood saw in this exclusive epistemological tendency an iteration of a "colonizing conceptual structure." She noted that we have long been aware of the hierarchical and epistemological presuppositions that shape the logic of colonization among different peoples, part of which included the plundering and damaging of the land on which the colonized had lived. Yet, she claims:

> What we are less accustomed to acknowledging is the idea that the concept of colonization can be applied directly to non-human nature itself, and that the relationship between humans, or certain groups of them, and the more-than-human world might be aptly characterized as one of colonization.[12]

With this in mind, I believe that what is needed is a methodological and hermeneutical turn that is characterized as "the decolonial option."

There is not enough space here to do justice to the richness and development of decoloniality having risen to greater prominence as a deliberate hermeneutical approach in recent years.[13] In brief, as theorists Catherine Walsh and Walter Mignolo explain, decoloniality "is not a new paradigm or mode of critical thought. It is a way, option, standpoint, analytic, project, practice,

---

11 See Horan, *Deconstructing Anthropocentric Privilege*.

12 Plumwood, *Decolonizing Relationships with Nature*, p. 52.

13 For more on this, see Mignolo, *The Darker Side*; and Quijano, *Coloniality of Power*, pp. 181–224; among others.

and praxis."[14] One of the key dimensions of a hermeneutic of decoloniality is the critical interpretation of standards of knowing and experiencing, which have been conscripted by singular forces that align with the expansion of the Western European colonial enterprise. To get at this reality, we might ask: what constitutes *real* or *legitimate* knowledge, science, or scholarship? Put in a broad ecological context, we might ask: what constitutes *real* or *legitimate* knowledge, intelligence, language, emotional capacity, or moral agency? Oftentimes, the gatekeepers to what is considered *real* or *legitimate* are the same in both cases: that is, those who maintain and deploy this colonial power, in broader society, in the church, and in the creaturely community writ large. Generally speaking, such centers of power tend to be maintained and protected by small populations of select human beings.

Those who pursue a decolonial turn or embrace a decolonial option seek "conceptual instruments, other ways of theorizing, and other genealogies" in an effort to broaden what has typically been limited in terms of the "real" or "legitimate."[15] Such a shift in prioritization of knowing and interpretation moves from the centers of power to the colonial peripheries. Within human discursive contexts, such a shift might include the prioritization of historically marginalized or subjugated sources and voices. Among decolonial (and, earlier, postcolonial) theorists, this has generally taken the form of attention to the subaltern and non-Eurocentric archives of knowledge. For our purposes, I want to suggest that our de-centering of the human species in the broader planetary and cosmic community in order to better recognize nonhuman animal agency is an analogous form of decolonial resistance at the species level in the age of climate catastrophe.

This is where my constructive invitation begins to emerge. I believe that embracing a decolonial option in forming our theologies of creation and ecological ethics opens up the possibility for at least two things: First, a more expansive exercise of human knowing, which is to say that we broaden our own epistemological and analytical horizons; and Second, recognition of the diverse array of genuine knowing and being of nonhuman creatures reflective of their actual, if underappreciated, agential capacities.

---

14 Walsh/Mignolo, *On Decoloniality*, p. 5.

15 Walsh/Mignolo, *On Decoloniality*, p. 7.

2 Considering Nonhuman Animal Agency as a Form of Decolonial Resistance

So much of our way of viewing the world around us is shaped by a kind of anthropological hubris grounded in a sense of human separatism presupposed in the classical modern approaches to theology. More recently, various scholars have been considering the ways that creaturely distinctiveness need not be demarcated only along the lines of human and nonhuman, but might be broader and more relative. The work of Jakob von Uexküll (d. 1944), the founder of so-called "semiotic biology," comes to mind as a useful analog in thinking about creaturely agency in its myriad manifestations.[16] Uexküll has gained some renewed attention in recent years, especially for his research into the social and physical *Umwelten* (roughly translated "environments" or "worldviews") of various species and inquiry into the unity of nature.[17] During his graduate studies, he was strongly influenced by two biological schools of thought that represented two poles on the spectrum of the then-contemporary biological frontier: First, the relatively new theories of Charles Darwin (1809–1882) and, second, the contemporaneous thought of Karl Ernst von Baer (1792–1876).[18] Uexküll sought to develop something of a middle ground between Darwin's emphasis on the somewhat random natural selection and Baer's strict teleological approach,

16 Most of his work remains untranslated, but in recent years several key texts have been translated into English, including his *A Foray into the World*.

17 It is also worth noting that the influence, reception, and personal legacy of Uexküll is somewhat controversial. Most notably, the German philosopher Martin Heidegger, who was affiliated with the Nazi Party, appropriated some of Uexküll's work. Still others within the Nazi scientific community engaged his work more explicitly. Questions about Uexküll's own personal political and ideological commitments continue to surface and have been described by scholars as "contradictory." However, it is generally agreed upon that he never joined the Nazi Party, even as his own personal views on National Socialism remain the subject of scholarly and historical debate. Despite the deplorable usage of his thought by some affiliated with the Nazis (as well as others affiliated with forms of Marxism), and the ongoing lack of clarity about his own personal political thought, his work in the areas of theory and semiotic biology offer instructive resources for breaking out of the hubris of anthropocentric epistemologies. In this way, this chapter aims at reading and applying Uexküll's scholarship in a liberative modality.
For more on the state of the question regarding Uexküll's political thought and scholarly reception, see Michelini/Köchy, eds., *Jakob von Uexküll and Philosophy*, esp. pp. 5–8 and 17–35; and Brentari, *Jakob von Uexküll*, esp. pp. 21–46; and Mazzeo, *Il biologo degli ambienti*, pp. 7–33.

18 See Buchanan, *Onto-Ethologies*, p. 9.

articulating what he called the "conformity with a plan" (or *Planmäßigkeit* in German) approach to biology.

In addition to his formation in the biological sciences, Uexküll's outlook was deeply shaped by the philosophy of Immanuel Kant (1724–1804). In fact, Uexküll opens his 1926 masterwork *Theoretical Biology* with neither Baer nor Darwin, but with Kant. He writes that the task of biology consists in expanding the results of Kant's investigations, which he summarizes succinctly stating that: "all reality is subjective appearance."[19] Uexküll's interpretation of Kant's philosophy serves as the foundation for his guiding thesis: "that the reality we know and experience is ultimately what we subjectively perceive in the world. There is no objective reality in the form of objects, things, or the world; there is nothing outside of the individually subjective experiences that create a world as meaningful." In other words, "Reality is created through the experiences of each and every subject, and this, as we shall see, holds for all animals just as much as it does for humans."[20] Because we have for so long constructed a worldview in which human beings are the only subjects, we have neglected to consider that all creatures—human and nonhuman—do not perceive the world in the same way. Just because we do not perceive the world as other animals do and, conversely, they do not perceive the world as we do does not mean that nonhuman animals do not have subjective experiences of the world and, we might add theologically, of the Creator.

Uexküll boldly and insightfully argued that *all* creatures are meaning-makers, but we are blinded by a pervasive anthropocentrism, which prohibits us from recognizing the nuanced and variably complex ways nonhuman creatures experience the world through active, dynamic, and constructive engagement as subjects. Uexküll writes in his 1934 book, *A Foray Into the Worlds of Animals and Humans*, that:

> We comfort ourselves all too easily with the illusion that the relations of another kind of subject to the things of its environment play out in the same space and time as the relations that link us to the things of our human environment. This illusion is fed by the belief in the existence of one and only one world, in which all living beings are encased. From this arises the widely held conviction that there must be one and only one space and time for all living beings. Only recently [*this was written in the 1930s*] have physicists raised doubts as to the existence of one universe with one space valid for all beings.[21]

In terms of the contention of many philosophers and theologians that nonhuman animals do not have access to "world," Uexküll would concur insofar

19 Jakob von Uexküll, *Theoretical Biology*, p. xv.

20 Buchanan, *Onto-Ethologies*, p. 13.

21 Uexküll, *A Foray into the Worlds*, p. 54.

as what was meant by "world" was *this particular human person's* "world" or *Umwelt*. However, Uexküll strongly argues against the hegemony of human experience as determinative or absolute for all creation. Instead, Uexküll reacts to the then (and even now) pervasive physiological presupposition that denies any kind of subjectivity to nonhuman animals. This inherited way of thinking, so prominently displayed in the work of the influential twentieth-century philosopher Martin Heidegger and in the uncritically accepted foundations of many theologians and ethicists today, posits "one objective environment for all life forms and, subsequently, proceeds to analyze animals from the outside in."[22]

This way of viewing the world around us, of making judgments about nonhuman aspects of creation from our vantage point alone, reflects a fundamental anthropological hubris. In his 1940 text, *A Theory of Meaning*, Uexküll likens this present analysis of nonhuman creation to studying a house. He writes:

> If we compare an animal's body with a house, then the anatomists have studied closely the way it is built and the physiologists have studied closely the mechanical appliances located in the house. Ecologists, too, have demarcated and investigated the garden in which the house is located. But the garden has always been depicted as it offers itself to our human eye, and it has therefore been neglected to take into account how the garden changes when looked at by the subject who lives in the house.[23]

We cannot be content to presume that because a squirrel is not a human it therefore does not experience meaning or even the world-building that Heidegger and others withhold for humans alone. Nonhuman creatures are just as much subjects as human creatures are, and they also have worlds of their own, integrated and complex worlds in which meaning is made and in which they themselves are constructed just as we are in our own world.

Using human language and experience, Uexküll judges what we might call the "relative complexity" of each creature's world. "All animal subjects," he writes, "from the simplest to the most complex, are inserted into their environments to the same degree of perfection. The simple animal has a simple environment; the multiform animal has an environment just as richly articulated as it is."[24] What we know for certain (more or less) is the experience of our *human world*, our *Umwelt*. What Uexküll likewise affirms is that all creatures similarly have their own *world*, their *Umwelt*. We cannot know apodictically what that world of another creature is like, for it is ultimately a view

22 Winthrop-Young, *Afterword*, p. 231.

23 Uexküll, *A Theory of Meaning*, p. 200.

24 Uexküll, *A Foray into the Worlds*, p. 50.

reserved for the resident of the "house" Uexküll described earlier. However, we can, through our observation and imagination, consider what the experience of the other might be like. At the very least, we can gain an appreciation for the fact that other creatures indeed *have* a subjective experience of meaning making. "Organisms, according to Uexküll, actively interpret their surroundings as replete with meaningful signs. They are not merely passive instruments or message bearers, but actively engaged in the creation of a significant environment."[25]

Creatures, human and nonhuman alike, have *a priori* perceptive capacities for objects within our respective *Umwelten*. There are things that human beings perceive and interpret that have, as it were, no meaning for a squirrel. The converse is also true. Some of Uexküll's most famous theoretical contributions center on intellectual case studies involving different types of creatures and extrapolating their possible *Umwelten* based on observation and biological study. Some of the classic examples include amoebas, sea urchins, fish, dogs, snails, birds, spiders, flies, bears, ants and, famously, the tick.[26] The phenomenon of meaning making, of exercising creaturely agency, varies in form according to the respective capacities of the creature. But it is not simply a matter of what this or that creature, human or otherwise, can "sense" with the sensory receptors with which each species is endowed. Rather, it is a matter of *how* those things that are perceived in the "world" are networked together to constitute "objects of experience"."[27]

Perhaps Uexküll's greatest gift to theologians is the articulation that all creatures experience a world and make meaning according to their respective *Umwelt*. Nonhuman creatures are not simply "objects" or biological "machines," as traditional anthropocentric theologies have contended. Rather, all creatures are makers of meaning within their environments—as limited or capacious as each is (and how to judge that should not be limited to the human person via human experience alone). This understanding of nonhuman creaturely agency in manifold forms challenges longstanding Western Christian epistemological presumptions and invites renewed consideration of humanity's place within God's vast and diverse community of creation. It does not diminish the inherent dignity and value of human creatures, but instead broadens our conceptualization of what constitutes legitimate creaturely agency and therefore calls us to reorder not only our theoretical consideration of creation

---

25 Buchanan, *Onto-Ethologies*, p. 32.

26 The example of the tick as described by Uexküll fascinated, among others, the Italian philosopher Giorgio Agamben. See his *The Open*, esp. pp. 45–47.

27 Deely, *Umwelt*, p. 127.

but also to adjust our practices and strategies to better reflect the embodied contributions to doing climate justice.

3 From "Thinking" to "Doing" Climate Justice

In the face of the global climate catastrophe that threatens the existence of all life on this planet, it is not merely enough to rethink our insufficient epistemological frameworks or preconceived notions of agency and human exceptionalism. We need reflective action, a *decolonial praxis* that finds its grounding in renewed frameworks and paradigm shifts. What I mean by praxis here follows the description of Paulo Freire, who describes it as "an act of knowing that involves a dialogical movement that goes from action to reflection and from reflection upon action to a new action."[28] This dynamic process of theory and reflection informing and subsequently being informed by action is what is required for genuine climate justice. Decolonial theorists are keen to remind us that such a hermeneutical option is never devoid of or in opposition to praxis but, as Walsh and Mignolo attest, "theory is doing and doing is thinking."[29]

This final section of the chapter is dedicated to closing the theory-praxis circle by suggesting several trajectories for reflective action shaped by a commitment to decolonial readings of creation that restores nonhuman animal agency as a form of resistance. Given the limitations of space, I am proposing three general areas in which this recognition of nonhuman animal agency is a form of decolonial resistance in action. These include: discursive practices, social practices, and ecclesial practices.

First, how we think ought to inform how we speak and communicate. Because words matter and language functions, we must be attentive to our discursive practices. What we say arises from how we view the world while also informing it, which can be for either good or ill. Given all that is archived and presented in this volume, we do not need to dwell again here on the myriad ways anthropocentric views of creation have negatively impacted human and nonhuman creatures alike. Presumptions of human separatism and the inert and non-agential status of nonhuman creation expressed in both scholarly discourse and colloquial discussion have contributed to a false sense of human sovereignty, which has led to increasingly dire outcomes for the planet and all its inhabitants.

28 Freire, *The Politics of Education*, p. 50.
29 Walsh/Mignolo, *On Decoloniality*, p. 7.

But what if we thought and spoke in a different way? Imagine, for example, the potential impact of rejecting overly determined boundaries between human and nonhuman creatures in our everyday discourse. What if instead of speaking about "nature" or "the environment" as objects outside of human existence and therefore subject to our objectification and utilization, we were to recognize our inherent interconnectedness and interdependence? Every time we elect to use language that presumes strict human exceptionalism, we reinscribe false notions of sovereignty and species superiority that can be used to justify ecologically destructive behaviors and policies. While some people may view such an admonition to be insufficient or inconsequential, I would argue that nothing is more significant in effectuating concrete change. We regularly see the ways in which shifts in discursive practices can raise awareness of systemic injustices in our human communities such as in the case racism or misogyny or clericalism. How we imagine our role and that of other creatures in the community, and then articulate such conceptions, inevitably informs worldviews, modes of discernment, and decisions leading to actions.

Broadly speaking, decolonial praxis is a mode of being-in-the-world that reflects dynamic commitment and ongoing reflection about the intersections among thinking, speaking, and doing. Walsh and Mignolo remind us that,

> decoloniality seeks to make visible, open up, and advance radically distinct perspectives and positionalities that displace Western rationality as the only framework and possibility of existence, analysis, and thought. Such perspectives and positionalities evoke and convoke what [Nelson] Maldonado-Torres refers to as a *decolonial attitude.*[30]

De-centering the Western Christian hegemonic legacy of anthropocentrism and prioritizing other ways of thinking about the rest of creation, especially nonhuman animals and their agential capacities, reflects precisely this "decolonial attitude." When we consciously engage in discursive practices that emphasize nonhuman creaturely agency we deploy a kind of decolonial resistance that is a concrete form of working toward climate justice.

The second form of decolonial praxis I wish to highlight is what we might call social practices. Admittedly, that which may fall under this conceptual aegis is nearly infinite, for what I mean by "social practices" are all those systems, structures, and institutions that arise from and reinstate what Mignolo calls the "colonial matrix of power" (CMP).[31] Framed within the context of cli-

30 Walsh/Mignolo, *On Decoloniality*, p. 17.

31 See Walsh/Mignolo, *On Decoloniality*, pp. 111–116.

mate justice, I am thinking about the various ways the "coloniality of nature," as Escobar described it, informs our social interactions from the elevation of human comfort and institutional economic growth over the necessity of grappling with our inherent creatureliness, corporeality, and interdependence (both within and beyond the human species). To highlight several examples where anthropocentrism and the denial of nonhuman animal agency has resulted in devastating ecological consequences, one only has to think about the rise in so-called "factory farming," rampant mineral and fossil-fuel extraction, deforestation, and the ever-expanding efforts of human communities to "civilize" nonhuman animal habitats with little or no regard for these other creatures. In each case, individual wealth or the rise of nation-state power supersedes the concerns, safety, and longevity of the collective community of creation.

Social practices reflecting decolonial attitudes can take several forms in the work of climate justice. Legislatively, one thinks of the move in several countries in recent years to grant nonhuman creation—both the planet earth in general and several spaces and tributaries in particular—juridical rights and legal status recognized in courts of law.[32] Politically, one might think of some British and European efforts to promote "Green Deal" policies or what in the United States has been called the "Green New Deal."[33] But for all the large, structural efforts at reform, there is a need to rethink and then act in accordance with the decolonial option at the personal and local levels too. I am not proposing an absolute refusal to harm any creature, which from a Christian ethical perspective introduces a problematic flattening of creation in terms of ethical discernment and subject valuation. Rather, a Christian decolonial attitude in this context seeks to dislodge the trenchant presupposition of anthropocentrism that reduces nonhuman animals and other creatures to a mere utility or "natural resource" for human persons to use at will.[34] What is needed instead is a reconfiguration of our juridical, political, and ethical outlooks to be shaped as much by the recognition of the inherent dignity and value of all creatures independent of our desire for their utility and the inevitable necessity we

32 Some examples include Ecuador in 2008; Bolivia in 2010; New Zealand in 2014; and Colombia in 2016.

33 For example, see the United Kingdom "Green Deal" policies, available online: https://www.gov.uk/green-deal-energy-saving-measures; and, for the United States, see Friedman, *What is the Green New Deal*.

34 For more, see Meyer, *Inner Animalities*.

face in instrumentalizing some nonhuman creatures for our survival.[35] Beyond applying such evaluative decolonial frameworks to those creatures we humans "use" for food, shelter, and so on, we can also expand this outlook to the whole of the community of creation of which we are also a part.

Finally, recognizing nonhuman animal agency as a form of decolonial resistance can help shape our ecclesial practices. As the now-classic 1968 essay by historian Lynn White, Jr. boldly asserted, Western religions in general and Christianity in particular are ineluctably responsible for bolstering a distorted (and we might add, colonial) anthropocentrism, which has been used to justify the most egregious forms of environmental degradation before, during, and since the industrial revolution.[36] The persistent erasure of nonhuman animal agency is one factor among many that coalesce to form this problematic colonial view of the world, and within the Christian tradition this has been supported by willfully ignorant approaches to the natural sciences, myopic and eisegetical readings of sacred scripture, anthropocentric theological ethics and doctrinal formulation, naïve or irresponsible liturgical preaching, and a restrictive interpretation of *Imago Dei*.[37]

Indeed, there have been improvements within certain ecclesial circles and Christian ecumenical contexts, but the vast majority of contemporary Christians continue to assume a limited anthropocentric view of the world. One way to enact climate justice within an ecclesial context is to bring this decolonial attitude into the sanctuary, incorporate it into the liturgical life of the community, and engage pastoral ministry and religious education through an inclusive lens that recognizes the diversity of creaturely agency and dignity within the family of creation. There are numerous passages from the Hebrew Bible and the Christian New Testament that affirm this paradigmatic outlook. However, the failure of many ministers and theologians to engage with this normative source for theology in a decolonial frame has resulted in the reinscription of problematic and destructive social imaginaries and practical actions.[38] One step in the direction of climate justice is to bring this hermeneutic of decoloniality into ecclesial contexts, challenging the deep-seated assumptions

35 To this end, I have elsewhere proposed critically re-appropriating the medieval framework of "*usus pauper*" by the Franciscan theologian John of Peter Olivi (d. 1298) for negotiating the tension between the inherent dignity and value of all creatures with necessary instrumentalizing of some of them, some of the time. See Horan, *All God's Creatures*, pp. 161–166.

36 See White, *The Historical Roots*; and White, *Continuing the Conversation*, pp. 55–64.

37 On this last point, see Horan, *Catholicity and Emerging Personhood*, pp. 87–119.

38 Some recent exceptions to this include Edwards, *Ecology at the Heart of Faith*; Johnson, *Ask the Beasts*; and Horan, *All God's Creatures*; among others.

of human separatism held by many Christians. And this can take a variety of forms, requiring creativity in both theological and pastoral contexts.

4 Conclusion

This chapter opened with a challenge to epistemological humility. For centuries, Christians have deployed strategies of colonial logic to subjugate not only fellow humans but also the entirety of nonhuman creation. The process has resulted in the reification of a false assumption about the lack of agential potency in nonhuman animals. Consequently, the human species has justified thinking and actions that have contributed to devastating ecological and climate injustices. In response to this persistent phenomenon, I have proposed renewed attention to the complexity of nonhuman animals and their respective degrees of agency as one possible factor in the effort to correct our anthropocentric errors. Such an approach, drawing on the philosophical insights of Uexküll and others, opens up a space for our deploying strategies of decolonial resistance and renewing our discursive, social, and ecclesial practices.

In closing I would like to extend an invitation to readers of this volume. This is an invitation to engage in an exercise of imagination, something that I have elsewhere described as "strategic anthropomorphism," because it calls upon us to consider what it might be like to experience the world as a nonhuman creaturely agent in the world.[39] It is an invitation to let go of human-centered presumptions of meaning making and knowledge production, of human-centered perspectives about moral agency and cognitive range, and to do so in an effort to expand epistemological possibilities that exceed the bounds of our limited human horizon. Over the borderlands of our circumscribed worldview stands a panoply of world-making agents, whose being-in-the-world is neither "world-less" nor "poor-in-world," but robust, dignified, and meaningful. What would our advocacy on behalf of environmental justice look like if we took as axiomatic the agency of nonhuman animals? How might our discourse and discussions change? In what ways might this impact the formation of our Christian theologies of creation or environmental ethics? And how would such an exercise of decolonial resistance inform our understanding of ourselves as fellow creatures in God's community of creation?

39 See Horan, *All God's Creatures*, 226–227.

References

Agamben, Giorgio: *The Open: Man and Animal*, trans. Kevin Attell. Stanford: Stanford University Press 2004.

Boff, Leonardo: *Cry of the Earth, Cry of the Poor*. Maryknoll: Orbis Books 1993.

Brentari, Carlo: Jakob von Uexküll: The Discovery of Umwelt between Biosemiotics and Theoretical Biology, trans. Catriona Graciet. London: Springer 2015.

Buchanan, Brett: Onto-Ethologies: The Animal Environments of Uexküll, Heidegger, Merleau-Ponty, and Deleuze. Albany: SUNY Press, 2008.

Chryssavgis, John (ed.): On Earth as in Heaven: Ecological Vision and Initiatives of Ecumenical Patriarch Bartholomew. New York: Fordham University Press 2011.

Clough, David L.: *On Animals: Volume 1, Systematic Theology*. London: T & T Clark 2012.

De Waal, Frans: Are We Smart Enough to Know How Smart Animals Are? New York: W. W. Norton 2016.

Deely, John: "Umwelt," in: *Semiotica* 134 (1–4.2001): pp. 125–35.

Descartes, René: *Discourse on Method*, in: *Philosophical Essays and Correspondence*, ed. Roger Ariew. Indianapolis: Hackett Publishing 2000.

Edwards, Denis: Ecology at the Heart of Faith: The Change of Heart that Leads to a New Way of Living on Earth. Maryknoll: Orbis Books 2006.

Escobar, Arturo: *Territories of Difference: Place, Movement, Life*, Redes. Durham: Duke University Press 2008.

Freire, Paulo: *The Politics of Education: Culture, Power, and Liberation*, trans. Donaldo Macedo. Westport, CT: Bergin and Garvey Publishing 1985.

Friedman, Lisa: "What is the Green New Deal? A Climate Proposal, Explained," in: *The New York Times* (February 21, 2019), available online: https://www.nytimes.com/2019/02/21/climate/green-new-deal-questions-answers.html [accessed 24.05.2021].

Horan, Daniel P.: "Deconstructing Anthropocentric Privilege: *Imago Dei* and Nonhuman Agency," in: *Heythrop Journal* 60 (2019): pp. 560–570.

Horan, Daniel P.: *All God's Creatures: A Theology of Creation*. Lanham: Lexington Books/ Fortress Academic 2018.

Horan, Daniel P.: Catholicity and Emerging Personhood: A Contemporary Theological Anthropology. Maryknoll, NY: Orbis Books 2019.

Johnson, Elizabeth A.: *Ask the Beasts: Darwin and the God of Love*. London: Bloomsbury 2014.

Martínez, José: "Critical Anthropo-Geographies: Contested Place, Nature, and Development in the 'Zona Maya' of Quintana Roo, Mexico," unpublished PhD dissertation, Department of Anthropology. Amherst, MA: University of Massachusetts, 2004.

Mazzeo, Marco: "Il biologo degli ambienti: Uexküll, il cane guida e la crisi dello Stato," in: Jakob von Uexküll: *Ambienti animali e abienti umani: Una passeggiata in mondi sconosciuti e invisibili*. Macerata: Quodlibet Press 2010), pp. 7–33.

Meyer, Eric Daryl: *Inner Animalities: Theology and the End of the Human*. New York: Fordham University Press 2018.

Michelini, Francesca/Kristian Köchy (eds.): *Jakob von Uexküll and Philosophy: Life, Environments, Anthropology*. London: Routledge 2020.

Mignolo, Walter D.: The Darker Side of Western Modernity: Global Futures, Decolonial Options. Durham: Duke University Press 2011.

Plumwood, Val: "Decolonizing Relationships with Nature," in: William M. Adams/ Martin Mulligan (eds.): *Decolonizing Nature: Strategies for Conservation in a Post-Colonial Era*. London: Earthscan Publications 2003.

Pope Francis, *Laudato Sí'*, "On Care for Our Common Home," encyclical letter (June 2015).

Quijano, Aníbal: "Coloniality of Power, Eurocentrism, and Social Classification," in: Mabel Moraña/Carlos A. Jáuregui (eds.): *Coloniality at Large: Latin America and the Postcolonial Debate*. Durham: Duke University Press 2008), pp. 181–224.

Uexküll, Jakob von: *A Foray into the World of Animals and Humans and A Theory of Meaning*, trans. Joseph O'Neil. Minnesota: Univ. of Minnesota Press 2010.

Uexküll, Jakob von: *Theoretical Biology*, trans. D. L. McKinnon. New York: Harcourt Brace 1927.

Uexküll, Jakob von: *A Theory of Meaning*, trans. Joseph D. O'Neil. Minneapolis: University of Minneapolis Press, 2010.

Walsh, Catherine E./Walter D. Mignolo: *On Decoloniality: Concepts, Analytics, Praxis*. Durham: Duke University Press 2018.

White, Jr., Lynn: "Continuing the Conversation," in: Ian G. Barbour (ed.): *Western Man and Environmental Ethics: Attitudes Toward Nature and Technology*. Reading: Addison-Wesley Publishing 1973, pp. 55–64.

White, Jr., Lynn: "The Historical Roots of Our Ecologic Crisis," in: *Science* 155 (1968): pp. 1203–1207.

Winthrop-Young, Geoffrey: "Afterword—Bubbles and Webs: A Backdoor Stroll through the Readings of Uexküll," in: Uexküll, *A Foray into the Worlds of Animals and Humans*.

Eco-Justice as Mutual Participation?

Towards a Theological Vision of the Mutual In-Dwelling of All Creation

Michael Nausner

Abstract

For a theological vision of the mutual participation of all created, the stewardship paradigm as a description of a constructive relation between humankind and nature is acknowledged but deemed as insufficient. After a meditation on the framing of David Attenborough's film *A Life on the Planet* in which the wild is envisioned as mending humanity's destructiveness, the discourse of the Rights of Nature is discussed as an appreciation of nature's subjectivity, a subjectivity that is affirmed in various indigenous theologies as well, not least in Scandinavian Sámi theology. In conversation with this theology, the Swedish bishops' letter on the climate, the papal encyclical Laudato Si', and various eco-theologians, this article goes beyond the stewardship paradigm and argues for the necessity to accord nature its own voice.

Keywords

Climate justice; creation; Laudato Si'; participation; rights of nature; Sámi theology; stewardship

1 Responsibility for Creation/Creation's Responsibility

The emphasis in the ecumenical movement on justice, peace, and integrity of creation turns forty in 2023. At least since the ecumenical gathering in Vancouver 1983 the talk of responsibility for creation took center stage in the context of the World Council of Churches, and in times of accelerating climate change this challenge to worldwide Christianity and the world community at large has become even more urgent. It seems to me, however, that very much of the discussion on climate change circles around ethics and politics, i.e. the necessity for humanity to take its responsibility. And of course, this discussion is of key importance given the overwhelming evidence that humanity, at least humanity in the Western world, has not taken its responsibility when it comes to a sustainable lifestyle in the ecosphere. The paradigm

 | DOI:10.30965/9783657795314_009

of responsible stewardship is an important step toward sustainability, but from an eco-theological perspective it needs to be supplemented with a less anthropocentric view of just and equitable relations between humanity and non-human creation. Not only humans, but creation in its entirety is response-able to divine creative activity, and therefore the development toward just relations in creation cannot only happen via human techniques of stewardship, but needs to take into account the myriad and mysterious ways in which (divine) creativity occurs in the non-human world.

In this chapter[1], therefore, I want to join the chorus of theologians who search for ways beyond the stewardship paradigm by emphasizing the intimate mutuality of all life on planet earth. I start with a meditation on the visual framing of David Attenborough's film *A Life on the Planet* as a manifesto for letting nature do its work. In a second step, I reflect on the discourse around the *rights of nature* as a possible partner for a theology that strives to widen its understanding of agents and agency in the created world. I end up by arguing for an understanding of creation as an ongoing process of complex communication among all created beings in which divine-human exchange does not take center stage but is imbedded in a mutuality of becoming between humanity and non-human nature. Envisioning such mutuality is essential for the sake of a balanced community of creation in which human and non-human activity can co-exist in an equilibrium.

2 Embraced by the Ecosystem

In October of 2020 the film *A Life on the Planet* went online and became for me a unique and at the same time dramatic visualization of such mutuality. The 93 years old filmmaker David Attenborough understands the film as a witness statement and a vision for the future. In the trailer for the film he talks about humanity having run over the world and suggests we need to learn anew to live *with* nature rather than *against* it.[2] One of the strongest impressions the film left in me was its framing: It starts and ends with shots in the Ukrainian city of Chernobyl which since the explosion of the nearby nuclear plant in April of 1986 is uninhabitable. In the beginning we see Attenborough standing in one of the buildings that was hastily abandoned after the explosion and today

1 A first and much shorter version of the arguments in this article was published in Nausner, *Ökogerechtigkeit als gegenseitige Teilhabe?*

2 Cf. the trailer to David Attenborough's film *A Life on the Planet*: https://www.youtube.com/watch?v=64R2MYUt394 (accessed 08.05.2021).

stands in ruins. The building itself becomes a symbol for ecological devastation caused by humans. And at the end of the film we are back in Chernobyl, and still the city gives us the eerie sense of humanity's ability to make the planet uninhabitable. But the more the camera zooms out, it becomes apparent to which extent nature has started to embrace the human made infrastructure. Animals of a large variety scrimmage around between the house skeletons, and lush trees have grown so tall that they start to overshadow the high-rises in the abandoned city. As the camera drone slowly rises above the city, the viewers realize that the treetops have already covered many of the houses and streets. The stone skeletons and the asphalt strips are imbedded in a green web. It seems as if the remainder of human civilization is embraced by an ecosystem that has started to flourish again.

3 Subjectivity in Non-Human Nature?

A possible interpretation of this visionary framing of the film is that humanity's failed taming of nature here is juxtaposed with the carefree wild of nature. This is how Attenborough diagnoses one of our time's biggest problems: We substitute the wild with the tame. Today we know that because of the anthropocentrism of modern lifestyle much has been lost for good, not least biodiversity which is diminishing rapidly, and we also know that humanity's collective impact is causing the ecological equilibrium in the ecosphere to reach tipping points of various kinds. Due to the scale of humanity's impact on the ecosphere the talk about our current geological era as *Anthropocene* has become more and more common since its inception at the turn of the millennium. It is above all the exploitation and burning of fossil fuels that has wreaked havoc on the ecological balance in the ecosphere.[3] Why do I experience the visual impression of a greening Chernobyl as hopeful, nevertheless? Is it, because the wild—even after massive interference on the part of humans—still stuns us with its mysterious capacity to regenerate? Might it be the wonder at such creative and regenerative power amidst devastating destruction that will allow humans to "hear" nature anew, to interpret creatively and constructively how she "speaks" to us? And what kind of analogy exists between the respect for the freedom of human others and the respect for non-human others? What does the threefold relation God-human-nature imply for the subjectivity of non-human nature?

3 Sörlin, *Antropocen*.

With these questions I approach one key concern of this chapter: What kind of subjectivity do we humans, not least we Christians, grant non-human nature? And consequently: What kind of right are we prepared to grant nature and natural phenomena? Is the ascription of rights to natural phenomena maybe even a precondition for treating life on the planet justly?

4 Rights of Nature?

The discussion about the possibility to respect natural phenomena as bearers of rights in the face of ruthless exploitation of natural resources is half a century old and became notorious thanks to Christopher D. Stone's article *Can Trees Have Standing?* from 1972.[4] As a lawyer he argues that the circle of right holders has widened constantly throughout the history of law and that the inclusion of new right holders always has met with resistance. Given that "the world of the lawyer is peopled with in-animate right holders"[5] (corporations and other organizations such as nations etc.) he therefore does not hesitate to suggest to "give legal rights to forests, oceans, rivers and other so-called 'natural objects' in the environment—indeed, to the natural environment as a whole."[6] Unfortunately, however, natural objects have commonly been seen as "objects for man to conquer and master and use,"[7] a relation between humans and the non-human world that in eco-theological circles has been criticized for a long time as a misunderstanding of God's commandment to humans to subdue the earth, the so called *dominium terrae*, in Genesis 1:28. An objectifying attitude toward creation is the fruit of an unholy alliance between a modern separation of the human from the natural realm and a certain Christian interpretation of *dominium terrae*.

In his influential article *The Historical Roots of Our Ecological Crisis*, Lynn White already in the 1960s identified a ruthless interpretation of this *dominium terrae* on part of Western Christianity as partly responsible for the ongoing ecological devastation.[8] Many eco-theologians have chimed with this critique.[9] To counteract such objectification, Stone suggests the implementation of a guardianship for nature which would secure an effective voice for the environment in its own right.[10] In addition, it would counteract what he

4 Stone, *Should Trees Have Standing?*
5 Stone, *Should Trees Have Standing?*, p. 452.
6 Stone, *Should Trees Have Standing?*, p. 456.
7 Stone, *Should Trees Have Standing?*, p. 463.
8 White, *The Historical Roots.*
9 See for example: Moltmann, *Gott in der Schöpfung;* McFague, *The Body of God.*
10 Cf. Stone, *Should Trees Have Standing?*, p. 470.

calls exclusively "homocentric interests".[11] Humanity and its environment need to "compromise for the better of both".[12] At the end of his article, Stone goes beyond the notion of co-existence and dreams of the day when humanity comes "to regard the Earth, as some have suggested, as one organism, of which Mankind [sic!] is a functional part."[13] Here we can identify quite clear analogies to the Gaia hypothesis which James Lovelock developed roughly at the same time as Stone published his article. With his view of the planet as one living organism in which everything intimately interacts with each other, Lovelock has triggered a new approach in many disciplines regarding the symbiotic interrelation of all living.[14]

Since a bit more than a decade, the discourse of *rights of nature* has received new attention, and, as a group of legal scholars points out, in countries like Bolivia, Colombia, Ecuador, India, New Zealand, and the United States of America, legal rights for nature are tried with varying success in judicial systems. Major obstacles for the implementation of rights of nature are the difficulties to define a specific rights bearer and "how conflicts between rights of nature and corporate or human rights and interests will be adjudicated".[15] The law scholars explicitly cite religion as a motivating source for rights of nature legislation and claim that Enlightenment sources often see the biblical God as source of human rights, while the *rights of nature* discourse has stronger roots in non-Western and indigenous spiritualities.[16]

5 The Rights of Mother Earth and Sami Theology

While I am not in a position to make judicial judgments regarding the viability of Jewish-Christian sources for a *rights of nature* discourse, I would like to spend the rest of this chapter reflecting on some theological arguments that could give moral support for a *rights of nature* legislation.[17] Since 2010, when a large constituency of indigenous people signed the *Declaration of the Rights of Mother Earth* in Bolivia, the movement for the rights of nature has continuously enlarged its

11 Stone, *Should Trees Have Standing?*, p. 475.

12 Stone, *Should Trees Have Standing?*, p. 481.

13 Stone, *Should Trees Have Standing?*, p. 499.—Almost at the same time James Lovelock began to publish his findings on the intricate planetary symbiosis that became known as the *Gaia hypothesis*.

14 Lovelock, *Gaia*.

15 Chapron/Epstein /López-Bao, *A rights revolution for nature*, p. 1393.

16 Cf. Chapron/Epstein /López-Bao, *A rights revolution for nature*, p. 1392.

17 Always keeping in mind that there are hosts of challenges in terms of the practical implementation of rights of nature and how the necessary guardianship that needs to be involved can take shape in real life.—Cf. Bergmann, *Naturens rättigheter*, pp. 10–16.

circles. The declaration with its three articles *Mother Earth, Inherent Rights of Mother Earth* and *Obligations of Human Beings to Mother Earth* highlights the mutual interdependency between human beings and Mother Earth. Mother Earth functions as a metaphor for a living being, i.e. a community of interrelated beings who in turn are defined by their relationships.[18] It follows that rights are given to humans only as part of a larger community. Any ascription of rights, therefore, has consequences for the rights of interrelated beings, i.e. "rights specific to their species".[19] Thus, a key precondition for eco-justice is the recognition of the mutual participation between human beings and the created world they are a part of. Such recognition has remained alive in indigenous communities, as Stefan Silber points out in his reflection on liberating aspects in indigenous theologies which Western theology is in need of recognizing: According to the indigenous theologies of the Andes, Silber writes, "(h)uman beings are part of nature, not opposed to it. Nature itself is considered a being, an organism in which every part is connected to every other part."[20] Rights of humans and rights of nature cannot be separated.

That the concern of the rights of Mother Earth by now has reached the Western Christian world can be witnessed in the so called *Wuppertal Kairos Call for Creation* from 2019 which urges the World Council of Churches to support a juridically binding "Universal Earth Rights Charter" which explicitly builds on the *Declaration of the Rights of Mother Earth*.[21] But already the year before the declaration was signed by the Sámi Parliament of Sweden as the first democratically elected political entity in Europe. Marie Persson Njajta, a member of the Sámi Parliament, at this occasion called for a paradigm shift regarding humanity's relation to nature and emphasized the native view of humans as part of nature: "We as Sámi people understand ourselves as belonging to our land, our water and our landscape. […] Our deep connection to land and water connects us with native people across the world."[22] Such an understanding of humans belonging to the land and not the other way around is echoed by the voices of Sámi theologians in Scandinavia. One of them is Lovisa Mienna Sjöberg who in her study *To Live in Continuous Blessing. A Study of Sivdnidit as Religious Practice* probes into the religious dimensions of a northern Sámi understanding of humanity's relation to creation. *Sivdnidit,*

18 *Universal Declaration of Rights of Mother Earth*, article 1.1–3.
19 *Universal Declaration of Rights of Mother Earth*, article 1.6.
20 Cf. Silber, *Latin American Liberation Theology*, p. 183.
21 *Kairos for Creation.*
22 *Sametinget ger stöd till deklarationen om Moder Jords rättigheter.*

Mienna Sjöberg writes, is a religious practice that is "exercised by a person in communication with creation".[23] It is an age-old everyday practice that is integrated into lived Christian faith and thereby actualizes the colonial and ecological context of lived theology. Sámi Christians worshipping at an old sacrificial stone—*sieidi*—is an example for such contextualization in which the minister in the service seeks to reconcile Christian faith with the Sámi tradition to relate to non-human creation as animate. The controversy sparked by such celebrations show how theological condemnation and colonial subjection work together to this day in their rejection of land/nature as enlivened.[24] Colonial actors together with the Church of Sweden through the ages have consistently diminished and condemned the specific Sami way of communicating with nature as heathen, primitive religion or nature religion.[25] Against this, the Sámi theologian Tore Johnsen wants to reconstruct Sámi religious identity as a form of natural theology, i.e. a Christian response to God's call. Sámi religion is not an expression of paganism or—even worse—a response to the devil.[26] To Johnsen a necessary way for recognizing Sami contextual theology is to keep the width of the core of Christian theology, Christology, in mind. Reconciliation in Christ has cosmic dimensions (cf. Eph 1:10) and encompasses all of creation. Recognizing the ecological dimensions of reconciliation is of the essence to Johnsen:

> This is relevant when referring to reconciliation in Sápmi, as it creates a space for dialogue regarding the value and contribution of Sámi spirituality, which has been subjected to serious demonisation. The Sámi tradition has been characterised by a cosmological outlook where nature and places hold a sacred dimension, and where the human relationship with co-creation and Creator form an essential context for a reconciled life.[27]

Such mutual relation and communication, not least between humans and animals, is a recurring theme in Mienna Sjöberg's analysis of Sámi spirituality: Communication and even covenants between humans and animals can be initiated and terminated at the initiative of both animals and humans.[28] In an analogous way humans and land—with its subterranean inhabitants, the *hálddit*—are engaged in a mutual communication. Ancestors shape the

23 Mienna Sjöberg, *Att leva i ständig välsignelse*, p. 7.
24 Cf. Mienna Sjöberg, *Att leva i ständig välsignelse*, pp. 9–10.
25 Cf. Sundström, *Reconstructing Religious Identity*, p. 224.
26 Cf. Sundström, *Reconstructing Religious Identity*, p. 225.
27 Johnsen, *Acknowledged History and Renewed Relationships*, p. 121.
28 Cf. Mienna Sjöberg, *Att leva i ständig välsignelse*, pp. 154–55.

character of a certain landscape which therefore cannot be treated as object, but rather is approached as a collective subjectivity.[29] The kind of relation between humanity and nature that emerges here is witness to an understanding of mutual participation between humans and non-human creation, and the imagination of a mutual recognition of rights from such a perspective is not far-fetched. A one-way understanding of the relation between humans and nature as stewardship will not do justice to such lived interrelationality.

6 Is Stewardship *for* Creation Enough?

It seems to me, however, that in Western Christianity the paradigm of *stewardship* as the proper relation between humanity and non-human creation still is prevailing. On the one hand there is much to say in favor of it, especially when interpreted in terms of a caring relationship to creation as an expression of humanity created in the image of God. According to such an understanding of stewardship, the commandment to "subdue" the earth (Gen 1:28) may not be misinterpreted as an allowance for random exploitation. Instead, it needs to be seen in its relation to humans being created in the image of God (Gen 1:27) which in its depth dimension is not a matter of human *capacities* but rather "consists in a relationship in which the creature *receives* continuously from the Creator and mediates further what it has received".[30] The *imago Dei*, thus, means participation in the divine and it "is called to reflect the creator's governance of the world and is to be the channel through which God's blessings are to flow."[31] Responsibility for creation as mirroring God's creative activity is an important aspect in *A Bishops' Letter About the Climate* as well. This letter, authored by the bishops of the Church of Sweden, talks about human beings as *created co-creators*.[32] The term *created co-creator* indicates that such responsibility should not be misunderstood as human superiority over creation. Instead, such responsibility is rooted in a collective participation in "what has happened, what is currently happening and what the future will be like",[33] whether it is constructive or destructive. In the Eucharistic liturgy of the Church of Sweden the participation in destructive dynamics is expressed in the confession of sins in the following way: "I am complicit in the

29 Cf. Mienna Sjöberg, *Att leva i ständig välsignelse*, pp. 177–78.
30 Runyon, *The New Creation*, p. 18.
31 Runyon, *The New Creation*, p. 202.
32 Cf. Bishops of the Church of Sweden, *A Bishops' Letter About the Climate*, pp. 68–71.
33 Bishops of the Church of Sweden, *A Bishops' Letter About the Climate*, p. 55.

world turning its back on God."[34] In the Eucharist participation in the fallen creation and in the renewal of creation overlap.[35] But complicity or participation in the world's turning its back on God is not evenly distributed, and the ecological implications of Eucharistic communion often remain unnoticed. Ecological responsibility weighs heavier on the shoulders of the industrialized nations and is intimately connected to an unjust distribution of resources.[36] True mutuality in the community of creation needs to take account of such inequality, and the realization of the mutuality of all relations in creation can lead to a hopeful striving to give up an anthropocentric outlook on life in favor of a *creation-oriented outlook*.[37] Without any doubt, nature here is seen as more than something humans simply need to be stewards for. Fellowship and community with nature cannot simply be subsumed under the stewardship paradigm, which is recognized in the bishops' letter when they write about the risks and ambivalences of stewardship:

> The notion of stewardship has legitimised social structures characterised by subordination and oppression instead of community and cooperation. It has been used to defend colonial and hierarchical structures that have denied those at the lower end of the scale their full value: women, children, fauna, flora and minerals. In other words, the notion of stewardship [...] cannot serve as the sole model with which to interpret that responsibility.[38]

In its critique of the stewardship paradigm, the bishops' letter, therefore, stops short of affirming humanity's superiority over creation. This is in contrast to the papal encyclical *Laudato Si'* which for all its rebuke of "tyrannical and irresponsible domination of human beings over other creatures" still unequivocally assigns leadership position to humans and describes them as "called to lead all creatures back to their Creator".[39] Anthropocentrism is never criticized *as such*, but only when it is exaggerated, i.e. when it is tyrannical, distorted, modern, excessive or misguided.[40] At the end, human beings are described "as possessing a particular dignity *above* other creatures". Even though "our relationship with the environment [sic!] can never be isolated from our relationship

34 Bishops of the Church of Sweden, *A Bishops' Letter About the Climate*, p. 56.
35 Cf. Nausner, *Das geteilte Brot als Ausdruck gerechter Teilhabe*.
36 Cf. Bishops of the Church of Sweden, *A Bishops' Letter About the Climate*, pp. 56–58.
37 Cf. Bishops of the Church of Sweden, *A Bishops' Letter About the Climate*, pp. 69–70.
38 Bishops of the Church of Sweden, *A Bishops' Letter About the Climate*, pp. 67–68.
39 Pope Francis, *Encyclical Letter Laudato Si'*, 83.
40 Cf. Pope Francis, *Encyclical Letter Laudato Si'*, 68, 69, 115, 116, 118.

with others and with God",[41] at the end "responsible stewardship"[42] is the appropriate human relation to the "environment".[43] For all its affirmation of "mutual responsibility between human beings and nature",[44] the encyclical—a bit paradoxically—remains firmly rooted in the stewardship paradigm.

7 Allowing Creation's Voice to be Heard

Eco-theological voices, however, have for a long time now critiqued the stewardship paradigm as vulnerable for anthropocentrism, i.e. for an underlying assumption of human superiority over against non-human creation.[45] Jürgen Moltmann, for example, early on has suggested to abandon the talk about humans as the *crown of creation* and instead argued for humanity as a part of a *creation community*.[46] Sallie McFague in her own move against anthropocentrism elevates non-human creation by talking about the earth as the body of God, thereby taking seriously the planetary scope of Christology. The Christic paradigm is extended to oppressed nature, the "new poor".[47] Much later Elizabeth Johnson even more specifically chooses Christology as a starting point to protest the anthropocentrism in Western theology's focus on sin. That focus, she claims, had the consequence "that the wideness of God's saving mercy throughout the whole created order was by and large overlooked".[48] Johnson instead "envisions the living God actively accompanying the world in its evolutionary and historical breakthroughs" and develops "a theology of accompaniment ... that will support planetary solidarity and work for ecojustice."[49] The life of faith, she claims, needs to include "the very concrete good of the whole community of life on earth". Only then will we be able "at our crucial ecological juncture ... to discover that the beauty and power of our faith tradition is deepened by being rooted more firmly in the ecological reality of the earth."[50]

41 Pope Francis, *Encyclical Letter Laudato Si'*, 119 (my emphasis).
42 Cf. Pope Francis, *Encyclical Letter Laudato Si'*, 116.
43 Cf. Pope Francis, *Encyclical Letter Laudato Si'*, 236.
44 Pope Francis, *Encyclical Letter Laudato Si'*, 67.
45 Cf. Bergmann, *Naturens rättigheter*, p. 13.
46 Cf. Moltmann, *Gott in der Schöpfung*, p. 110.
47 McFague, *The Body of God*, p. xii.
48 Johnson, *Creation and the Cross*, p. xii.
49 Johnson, *Creation and the Cross*, p. xiii.
50 Johnson, *Creation and the Cross*, p. xvii.

Leonardo Boff in a similar vein as Sallie McFague makes the connection between the liberationist and the environmentalist discourse with his book *Cry of the Earth, Cry of the Poor* (1997), published after the Earth Summit in Rio de Janeiro (1992). With this book he "closed breaches between and within liberation theology and environmentalism",[51] as Dawn Nothwehr has it. Embracing the concept of panentheism that also can be found in process thought, he is able to show the intimate connections between the wounds of poverty and the wounds of the earth's devastation. In a more recent book he makes the explicit connection to the *Rights of Mother Earth*, endorsing the concept of *dignitas terrae* and thus the subjectivity of the earth as a living organism, arguing for a *bio-civilization* that builds on a mutuality between humanity and the earth.[52] Earth, Boff insists, can in accordance with a spirit of mindfulness no longer be left out of the societal contract, since "everything is mutually connected and mutually permeating".[53] Boff thus criticizes anthropocentrism by way of connecting the legitimate concern of social justice with environmental justice. Aware of its utopian character, he insists that the rain forest needs to be integrated into human community[54] and that some form of a "democracy of the earth" is needed, i.e. "the participation of *all*" in an overarching democracy in which "all participate and together search for solutions that as far as possible include all".[55] This vision is based on an understanding of "mutual belonging" between humans and more-than-human creation inspired by Sioux spirituality[56] and strives to connect the covenant with nature with the societal contract,[57] which means nothing else than effectively ascribing a voice to more-than-human creation.

Arguably one of the most influential proponents of an understanding of mutual interdependence between humanity and more-than-human creation was the "geologian" Thomas Berry. His ten theses on *The Origin, Differentiation, and Role of Rights* served as inspiration for the growing movement supporting the rights of nature. "The Universe", Berry maintains, "is composed of subjects to be communed with, not of objects to be exploited. As subject each component of the Universe is capable of having rights." (Thesis 3) In addition, the various components of the Earth have "intrinsic relations ... to each other". It follows that planet Earth "is a single community bound together with interdependent

51 Nothwehr, *Take and Read.*
52 Cf. Boff, *Achtsamkeit*, p. 69.
53 Cf. Boff, *Achtsamkeit*, p. 78.
54 Cf. Boff, *Achtsamkeit*, p. 79.
55 Boff, *Achtsamkeit*, p. 82.
56 Cf. Boff, *Achtsamkeit*, p. 84.
57 Cf. Boff, *Achtsamkeit*, p. 85.

relationships. No living being nourishes itself." (Thesis 9)[58] Reminiscent of Moltmann's talk about *creation community*, Berry talks about *Earth community* that challenges humans to foster "a mutually enhancing relationship with the other members of the Earth community".[59] Berry finds inspiration in various indigenous communities as well as in Eastern cosmologies where "the primary cultural referent as regards reality, value, and power for religious expression is the universe in its full plurality and integrity."[60] At the same time such cosmic orientation is not alien to the Jewish-Christian tradition. The problem to Berry is that the decidedly cosmological emphasis on seasonal celebration in the religion of Israel in the West shifted "toward an increasing emphasis on historical events".[61] This is the case both with the formative Exodus event in Jewish tradition and with the Christ event in the Christian tradition. Thomas Aquinas in the Middle Ages in his *Summa Theologiae* was still committed to a cosmic view. He understood divine creation as having the goal that "the whole universe together would participate in and manifest the divine more than any single being whatsoever."[62] The later move away from a seasonal and cosmological understanding of both the Exodus and the Christ event "set in motion those forces of alienation that would eventually lead in the West to our strong sense of anthropocentrism."[63] Berry is convinced that a new, cosmic understanding of Exodus is needed and therefore asks the rhetorical question whether it is possible "that we are being called to make an Exodus out of one sacred community locked in its historical self-salvific identity into the larger sacred community of life."[64] To Berry, this is in no way a matter of human agency only. Instead he formulates Christianity's necessary journey toward a more Earth related self-understanding in terms of mutual participation: "Absorption of the universe into the sacred realm of the human and absorption of the human into the sacred realm of the universe is required for any satisfactory way into the future."[65] Berry envisions such mutual absorption as *cosmic liturgy* in which it becomes clear that "the universe is not focused on any one single being, but depends on the entire multiplicity of beings."[66]

58 Berry, *The Origin, Differentiation, and Role of Rights*.
59 Berry, *The Christian Future and the Fate of Earth*, p. 97.
60 Berry, *The Christian Future and the Fate of Earth*, p. 102.
61 Berry, *The Christian Future and the Fate of Earth*, p. 103.
62 Quoted in: Berry, *The Christian Future and the Fate of Earth*, p. 107.
63 Berry, *The Christian Future and the Fate of Earth*.
64 Berry, *The Christian Future and the Fate of Earth*, p. 110.
65 Berry, *The Christian Future and the Fate of Earth*, p. 111.
66 Berry, *The Christian Future and the Fate of Earth*, p. 115.

This, of course, is a much more far-reaching critique of anthropocentrism than can be found in *Laudato Si'* as we have seen. For all its emphasis on humanity as integral part of creation by borrowing Francis of Assisi's terminology of "Mother Earth"[67], it remains firmly rooted in the anthropocentric paradigm, or even in *androcentrism*, to use Julia Enxing's classification. Enxing distinguishes between a necessary epistemological anthropocentrism (humans cannot avoid approaching the world *as humans*), a deplorable ideological anthropocentrism (humanity is seen as the center around which all other life is oriented and related), and finally androcentrism which shares with anthropocentrism the devaluation of non-human life but adds to it the devaluation of non-male human life.[68] Enxing commends *Laudato Si'* for its relational pathos but critiques it for its elevation of the human, and she extends the critique of anthropocentrism to a critique of its androcentrism. The encyclical remains male oriented. The "thought that God only can be incarnated in a human (and a male at that) is for a theology that wants to critique anthropocentrism absurd."[69] And indeed, the feminine notion of Mother Earth is neither connected in the encyclical to concrete women nor to any feminine aspects of the divine. Instead it continuously appears in a juxtaposition with God the Father whose "fatherly tenderness"[70] is an expression of "the paternal relationship that God has with all his creatures."[71] The feminine earth is here in need of masculine protection, as Sharon A. Bong observes, a metaphysical understanding undergirding the patriarchal pattern of male dominance over women and culture's superiority over against nature.[72] In addition "the voices of women are conspicuously absent from *Laudato Si'*", as Grace Ji-Sun Kim and Hilda P. Koster rightly critique in their edited volume *Planetary Solidarity*.[73] In this book the interrelation between colonialism, patriarchy, racism, and climate change is highlighted.[74] Planetary solidarity is envisioned as a solidarity that "requires that we give voice to these interconnected systems of life." Such solidarity "asks for nothing less than a *bio-cracy*, in which all life forms have a vote".[75] This clearly pushes the encyclical beyond its anthropocentrism and its cautioning

67 LS 1.
68 Cf. Enxing, *Anthropos—Anthropozentrismus—Anthropozän*, p. 4.
69 Enxing, *Anthropos—Anthropozentrismus—Anthropozän*, p. 16.
70 LS 73.
71 LS 96.
72 Ji-Sun/Koster (eds.), *Planetary Solidarity*, p. 89.
73 Ji-Sun/Koster (eds.), *Planetary Solidarity*, p. 2–3.
74 Cf. Ji-Sun/Koster (eds.), *Planetary Solidarity*, p. 5.
75 Ji-Sun/Koster (eds.), *Planetary Solidarity*, p. 7 (my emphasis).

against "biocentrism" as a reaction to "misguided anthropocentrism".[76] While acknowledging much of the relational thinking in the encyclical, the authors of the anthology identify in the subordination of non-human creation under human stewardship signs of a gender hierarchy. Like men talk on behalf of women, humans talk on behalf of creation. Consequently, feminist analysis of the ecological crisis is rendered invisible, as Rosemary P. Carbine laments.[77] Ivone Gebara sees as one of the consequences of the exclusion of feminist analysis an insensitivity for male hegemony and for an idealized depiction of women in the encyclical's Mariology.[78] But is bio-cracy a possible alternative to the paradigm of (male) stewardship?

To talk about a *bio-cracy* from a theological perspective may seem both far-fetched and quite utopian. Can an evolution, say from monarchy/aristocracy via democracy to bio-cracy, even be imagined, let alone theologically be justified? On the one hand, the abstract notion of a "rule of biological life/nature" will not lead us very far. On the other hand, there is a lot in the biblical tradition that witnesses of communication not only between God and humans, but also between God and animals and God and the wider creation. There are unmistakable signs of a wider and mutual participation between living beings in the Earth community. Already the book of Genesis witnesses of the human as intimately related to the rest of creation. God establishes a covenant which humans together with all of creation are a part of, not least together with the animal world (Gen 9:12). It is the same God's breath that gives life not only to human beings, but also to animals, and according to the psalms, animals praise God together with humans for nurturing them (Ps 148:10). In Job, God demonstrates power by showing God's intimate relationship with the wild animals (Job 40). Not least does the vision of the peaceable kingdom in Isaiah 11:4–11 encompass animals to the same extent as humans. And overall, the Bible is filled with animal metaphors from the beginning to the end.[79] Accordingly, we can talk about a biblical view of the human that does not contradict a theological *animalology*.[80]

I therefore agree with Terra Schwerin Rowe when she writes that Christianity in times of our current climate crisis is in dire need of rediscovering what she calls a *participatory ontology*,[81] an understanding of humanity as intimately intertwined with the rest of creation. The extent to which not only humanity as

76 LS 118.
77 Ji-Sun/Koster (eds.), *Planetary Solidarity*, pp. 64–66.
78 Cf. Ji-Sun/Koster (eds.), *Planetary Solidarity*, pp. 76–77.
79 Cf. Horstmann/Ruster/Taxacher, *Alles, was atmet*, p. 13.
80 Cf. Horstmann/Ruster/Taxacher, *Alles, was atmet*, p. 18.
81 Cf. Schwerin Rowe, *Genus Precarious*, pp. 331–6.

a whole (cf. all the science about humanity induced climate change and interdisciplinary and geological discussion about the *Anthropocene*!) but already individual humans (cf. the so called "scandal of the human microbiome") cannot even be thought as separate from the rest of the world is intriguingly demonstrated by new science. Evolutionary biologist Thomas Bosch describes the symbiosis of the human organism in the following way: Individual organisms (also the human organism!) "are multi-organismic. They form a complex community of life which are called meta-organism."[82] Humanity as a whole and human beings as "individuals" (if we still can imagine individuals amidst our intimate mutual entanglement with various other forms of life!) live in intimate mutual participation with a web of life to which they themselves belong. And such mutual participation is valid for humanity's relation to the Creator as well.[83]

Is not our mutual participation as a human species with the earth exemplified on a macro as well as on a micro level by the two major crises our world community is going through these days—the COVID-19 pandemic and global warming? There is, therefore, no way around letting the earth speak in order to achieve something that could be called climate-justice. Or better yet: We need to hear that it speaks already as Bruno Latour argues in his essay *Down to Earth*: The Terrestrial is "a new *political actor*".[84] It is not only that humans participate in the web of life, but "'geo' designates an agent that participates fully in public life", and the question is "how are we to act if the territory itself begins to participate in history, to fight back, in short, to concern itself with us"?[85] Given such mutual participation, the way forward must be to overcome the separation of social and ecological concerns. As Latour has it in his characteristically humoristic way: "(W)e don't have to choose between workers' wages and the fate of some little birds."[86] Instead, the decisive question of the current age is the *geo-social* question holding together social and ecological concerns,[87] which from a theological perspective also demands a reorientation in terms of understanding nature and matter as part of who we are as human beings. Amidst such entanglement we cannot be content with a definition of nature and matter as detached or with the process of defining as detached. To know needs to be more than the modern detached project of knowing *from the*

82 Quoted in: Lohmann/Graf, *Mikrobiome als Ressource*.

83 For a multi-facetted treatment of our "participatory predicament" on various levels, see Nausner, *Eine Theologie der Teilhabe*.

84 Latour, *Down to Earth*, p. 40.

85 Latour, *Down to Earth*, p. 41.

86 Latour, *Down to Earth*, p. 57.

87 Cf. Latour, *Down to Earth*, p. 63.

outside.[88] Humans as belonging to the Terrestrial, Latour maintains, cannot understand *from the outside* or *from above*. "The Terrestrial, for its part, does not allow this kind of detachment."[89] The challenge for humanity is to understand itself as part of nature-as-process and to acknowledge "living beings as agents participating fully in the processes of generating the chemical, and even in part the geological, conditions on the planet."[90] Such processes need to be seen as an integral part of our political and ethical co-existence instead of treating them as dynamics outside the social realm.

A "bio-cracy of all created" with full participation of non-human actors is, of course, far off as a realized political system, and my vision of an eco-justice of mutual participation is vulnerable to the accusation that human responsibility is underrated. But does it have to be a matter of either-or? Do we need to pitch humanity and nature against each other? I think, the challenge is to overcome the exclusive dominance of humanity and to acknowledge the devastating effect on nature performed by humanity *as a whole*. The role of humanity in Christian theology needs to remain *unique* (cf. Ps 8), but it does not need to be a *dominant* one. Neither should an advocacy of an eco-justice of mutual participation happen at the cost of certain social groups of human beings. One can detect a tendency toward such exclusivity in certain forms of deep ecology, but not least in various kinds of eco-fascism which partly harken back to the blood and soil ideology of national socialism.[91] Human rights and rights of nature should not be pitched against each other, even if this can and must lead to complicated juridical negotiations in concrete situations. The role of humans remains unique. [...] In the future, however, the uniqueness of humanity certainly should not only show itself in technical superiority, but more in the form of practiced restraint and attentiveness to non-human creation. I share Sverker Sörlin's vision who does not think that there is a way back from the *Anthropocene*. But there is still the possibility in this *age of humanity* to change course. Up to now, Sörlin maintains, the term Anthropocene has signaled humanity's capability to destroy. But Anthropocene "could also mean the opposite: that we refrain from doing what we are capable of".[92] Humanity

88 Cf. Latour, *Down to Earth*, p. 68.

89 Latour, *Down to Earth*, p. 72.

90 Latour, *Down to Earth*, p. 75.

91 Elizabeth Pyne discusses various forms of anti-human ecological thought. The eco-fascist manifest of the man who killed Muslims in two mosques in Christchurch, New Zealand on March 15, 2019 is an extreme example of such anti-humanism.—Cf. paper given at the *Doing Climate Justice* workshop at Leuven University, October 22–24, 2020; text in this volume.

92 Sörlin, *Antropocen*, p. 210.

in its capacity of being the image of God could practice *letting be* and *mindfulness*, not least mindfulness toward all the creative processes which continuously manifest themselves without human influence.

8 Creation as Communication

Catherine Keller for a long time now has given theological voice to such creaturely, political co-operation with panentheistic pathos claiming that creation continuously takes place as cooperation not only between God and creation but also between creatures. Creation is not just dead matter that God infuses with life. Instead, creation "takes place as invitation and cooperation" and "the creator lures self-organizing systems out of the fluctuating possibilities"[93], as Keller puts it in her characteristically theo-poetical way. Such lure, of course, is not only occurring "in the beginning", but as a continuous process of creation and creativity (lat. *creatio continua*) it belongs to the very nature of God. It is a process which is mirrored in many biblical passages which show that not only humanity reacts with lament and praise to God's creative activity. Instead, also non-human creation interacts with God in lament (cf. Gen 4:9; Rom 8:22) and praise (cf. Pss 103, 104, 148, etc.). In tune with Latour's claim of the earth as a political agent, Keller argues that we engage with the earth not as an object but as participant in it and that the earth therefore can be said "to be engaged in our political theology".[94] God is here not imagined as the ruler of heaven and earth, and creation is not a one-way process top-down. Instead, based on a specific reading of Genesis 1, creation is imagined as an "everlasting conversation".[95] Prior to the creation of humans, the earth community is included in such communicative creation. For all the human likeness to the creator, Keller writes, "the earth and the waters participate as invited in the creative process ('Let the earth bring forth,' etc.), with outcomes praised. Earth and ocean seem to mirror more directly than the human the character of the creator—to create. (Humans are not here invited to 'bring forth'.)"[96] Humans as *imago Dei* are not taken out of the creaturely web, instead, as Keller has it, our "theomorphism only matters within the context of our creaturely interdependence beastial and vegetal."[97] Human co-creation therefore should not

93 Cf. Keller, *Face of the Deep*, p. 195.
94 Keller, *Toward a Political Theology of the Earth*, p. 177.
95 Cf. Keller, *Political Theology of the Earth*, p. 43.
96 Keller, *Political Theology of the Earth*, p. 76.
97 Keller, *Political Theology of the Earth*, p. 77.

be misunderstood as an engagement over against other living beings but as a dynamic of continuous and subtle communication with all life. Humans in their "earthling *intersubjectivity*"[98] cannot pull themselves out of their divine and creational interrelations but need to act from within this web of mutual participation. Drawing on both Thomas Berry's call to earth mindfulness and the call to an "integral ecology" in *Laudato Si'*, Keller envisions a "complex human self-organization in mindful interdependence with the biosphere."[99]

If creation in a panentheistic spirit is conceived as an ongoing communication, as a process of mutual in-dwelling, if—in other words—Godself allows for creaturely freedom and creativity (cf. Gen 1:11–25), is it even conceivable to *not* afford voice and rights to non-human creation? There are strands also in the Rabbinic tradition that based on the plural in Genesis 1:26 ("Let Us make the human in Our image after Our own likeness") ascribes voice and agency to non-human creation. Rabbi Samson Raphael Hirsch for one suggests that the "Us" in Genesis 1:26 refers to the rest of creation: "Before creating the human, a being destined to develop the capacity to alter and possibly endanger the natural world, God sought the approval of nature itself. This interpretation implies that we could use nature only in such a way that is faithful to the purposes of its Creator and *acknowledges nature's consenting to humanity's existence*."[100] And could such an understanding of creation as a communicative process not give support for an inclusion of non-human actors into the realm of politics?

David Attenborough in his film *A Life on the Planet* has visualized such communication, such mutual participation, in a suggestive way, and I hope that I have been able to indicate in this chapter that Christian theology in an analogous way can inspire within us the imagination of a just and reconciled mutual indwelling of all created beings.

References

Bergmann, Sigurd: "Naturens rättigheter—i en rättsgemenskap av allt skapat levande," Unpublished manuscript 2020.

Berry, Thomas: "The Origin, Differentiation, and Role of Rights." http://www.ties-edu.org/wp-content/uploads/2018/09/Thomas-Berry-rights.pdf [accessed 16.06.2022].

Berry, Thomas: *The Christian Future and the Fate of Earth*. Mary Evelyn Tucker/John Grim (eds.). Maryknoll, NY: Orbis Books 2009.

98 Keller, *Political Theology of the Earth*, p. 86.

99 Keller, *Political Theology of the Earth*, p. 91.

100 Neril/Dee, *Eco Bible*, p. 11. (Italics added)

Bishops of the Church of Sweden: *A Bishops' Letter About the Climate. The Bishops of the Church of Sweden*. Uppsala 2020, pp. 68–71.

Boff, Leonardo: *Achtsamkeit. Von der Notwendigkeit, unsere Haltung zu ändern*. München: Claudius Verlag 2013.

Chapron, Guillaume/Yaffa Epstein/José Vicente López-Bao. "A rights revolution for nature. Introduction of legal rights for nature could protect natural systems from destruction", in: *Science*, 29 March 2019, Vol 363, issue 6434, 1392–1393.

Enxing, Julia: "Anthropos—Anthropozentrismus—Anthropozän: Eine komplizierte Gemengelage." Paper presented at the meeting with ITA (Interkonfessioneller Theologischer Arbeitskreis) on the topic "Anthropozentrik? Tiere, Menschen und Maschinen in der theologischen Diskussion" online January 14–15th, 2021, 1–16.

Horstmann, Simone/Thomas Ruster/Gregor Taxacher. *Alles, was atmet: Eine Theologie der Tiere*. Regensburg: Verlag Friedrich Pustet 2018.

Ji-Sun, Grace/Hilda P. Koster (eds.): *Planetary Solidarity: Global Women's Voices on Christian Doctrine and Climate Justice*. Minneapolis, MN: Fortress Press 2017.

Johnsen, Tore: "Acknowledged History and Renewed Relationships." In Daniel Lindmark/ Olle Sundström (eds.), *The Sami and the Church of Sweden: Results from a White Paper Project*. Möklinta: Gidlunds 2018, pp. 97–124.

Johnson, Elizabeth: *Creation and the Cross: The Mercy of God for a Planet in Peril*. Maryknoll, NY: Orbis Books 2018.

Kairos for Creation—Confessing Hope for the Earth. The Wuppertal Call. https://www.oikoumene.org/de/resources/documents/kairos-for-creation-confessing-hope-for-the-earth-the-wuppertal-call [accessed 16.06.2022].

Keller, Catherine: "Toward a Political Theology of the Earth." In Catherine Keller: *Intercarnations: Exercises in Theological Possibility*. New York, NY: Fordham University Press 2017, pp. 174–192.

Keller, Catherine: *Face of the Deep: A Theology of Becoming*. London&New York, NY: Routledge 2003.

Keller, Catherine: *Political Theology of the Earth: Our Planetary Emergency and the Struggle for a New Public*. New York, NY: Columbia University Press 2018.

Latour, Bruno: *Down to Earth: Politics in the New Climate Regime*. Cambridge&Medford, MA: Polity Press 2018.

Lohmann, Björn/Philipp Graf. "Mikrobiome als Ressource." https://biooekonomie.de/mikrobiome-als-ressource [accessed 16.06.2022].

Lovelock, James: *Gaia: A New Look at Life on Earth*. Oxford: Oxford University Press 1979.

McFague, Sallie: *The Body of God. An Ecological Theology*. Minneapolis, MN: Fortress Press 1993.

Mienna Sjöberg, Lovisa: *Att leva i ständig välsignelse. En studie av* sivdnidit *som religiös praxis*. Oslo: PhD dissertation 2018.

Moltmann, Jürgen: *Gott in der Schöpfung. Ökologische Schöpfungslehre.* München: Kaiser 1985.

Nausner, Michael: "Das geteilte Brot als Ausdruck gerechter Teilhabe. Über die sozialethische Dimension des Abendmahls", in: Michael Nausner, *Eine Theologie der Teilhabe*. Leipzig: Evangelische Verlagsanstalt 2020, pp. 169–183.

Nausner, Michael: "Ökogerechtigkeit als gegenseitige Teilhabe? Versuch einer theologischen Vision der gegenseitigen Durchdringung alles Erschaffenen," in: *Amt und Gemeinde* (70.1/2021), pp. 12–22.

Nausner, Michael: *Eine Theologie der Teilhabe.* Leipzig: Evangelische Verlagsanstalt 2020.

Nothwehr, Dawn: "Take and Read: Cry of the Earth, Cry of the Poor." https://www.ncronline.org/blogs/ncr-today/take-and-read-cry-earth-cry-poor [accessed 16.06.2022].

Pope Francis, *Encyclical Letter Laudato Si'* [LS]. http://www.vatican.va/content/francesco/en/encyclicals/documents/papa-francesco_20150524_enciclica-laudato-si.html [accessed 16.06.2022].

Rabbi Yonatan Neril/Rabbi Leo Dee: *Eco Bible. Volume 1: An Ecological Commentary on Genesis and Exodus*. The Interfaith Center for Sustainable Development 2020.

Runyon, Theodore: *The New Creation: John Wesley's Theology Today*. Nashville, TN: Abingdon 1998.

Sametinget ger stöd till deklarationen om Moder Jords rättigheter. http://www.naturensrattigheter.se/2018/05/29/sametinget-ger-stod-till-deklarationen-om-moder-jords-rattigheter [accessed 16.06.2022].

Schwerin Rowe, Terra: "Genus Precarious: Luther in the Anthropocene". In: Else Marie Wiberg Pedersen (ed.). *The Alternative Luther: Lutheran Theology from the Subaltern.* Lanham, MA: Lexington Books 2019, pp. 330–344.

Silber, Stefan: "Latin American Liberation Theology as a Transforming Political Theology: Diversity, Fragmentarity, Relevance," in: *Interreligious Studies and Intercultural Theology* (2.2/2018), pp. 177–192.

Sörlin, Sverker: *Antropocen: En essä om människans tidsålder.* Stockholm: Svante Weyler 2017.

Stone, Christopher D.: "Should Trees Have Standing?—Towards Legal Rights for Natural Objects." in: *Southern California Law Review* (45/1972): pp. 450–501.

Sundström, Olle: "Reconstructing Religious Identity Among the Sami of Scandinavia. Christian Sami Contextual Theology in the Twenty-First Century," in: *Senri Ethnological Studies* (93/2016), pp. 211–228.

Universal Declaration of Rights of Mother Earth, article 1.1–3. https://www.garn.org/universal-declaration/ [accessed 16.06.2022].

White, Lynn: "The Historical Roots of Our Ecological Crisis", in: *Science* Vol. 155 (1967): pp. 1203–1207.

PART II

Practices and Conflict Fields

Liberating Limits

How Acknowledging, Agreeing upon, and Adhering to Limits Can "Do Climate Justice" and Have Liberating Effects

Sebastian Salaske-Lentern

Abstract

The fantasies of limitless economic growth are putting the lives of today's most vulnerable members of humankind and future generations in peril. The mainstream of current economic, political, and public debates around sustainable development and climate policy focus on the idea of addressing climate change and other environmental challenges by means of ecologically friendly technologies and "green growth". Scholarly approaches by Niko Paech, Doris Fuchs and Antonietta Di Giulio make strong cases for the necessity of absolute reductions in material and energy use, as do the works of liberation theologians Ignacio Ellacuría and Jon Sobrino as well as Pope Francis. At the intersection of all four approaches, a common theme emerges: economic reductions and limitations do not necessarily reduce quality of life but rather have the potential to generate liberating effects.

Keywords

Post-growth economy; development; consumerism; sufficiency; sustainable consumption; shared austerity; eco-spirituality

1 Introduction

When I presented this paper at the *6th Workshop "Liberative Contextual Theologies": Doing Climate Justice* in October 2020, governments' responses to the Covid-19 pandemic around the globe had brought about heavy restrictions on personal freedom and civil liberties. Not just since the start of the pandemic, rigid border enforcement continues to limit people's freedom of movement and particularly their right to seek asylum and live in safety. With this in mind, it may seem odd or even cynical to suggest that limits could be liberating. The title "Liberating Limits" should make more sense, though, against a different, yet not at all unrelated backdrop: The fantasies of limitless economic

 | DOI:10.30965/9783657795314_010

growth and the unbounded intensity with which present societies—especially those so-called industrialized and increasingly those so-called emerging—keep exploiting and destroying Earth's systems, including the global climate, are putting the lives of today's most vulnerable members of humankind and future generations in peril. Against this background, protest movements like "Fridays for Future" or "Extinction Rebellion" call for radical change—and some scholars dare to spell out what such a change would need to entail: limitations, restrictions, and reductions instead of unlimited growth.

Human civilization is embedded in and deeply dependent on the network of planet Earth's systems, like atmosphere, geosphere, or biosphere. The ability of this network to carry and sustain humanity is, however, restricted by "planetary boundaries", beyond which the impact of human activities causes irreversible damage or loss and thus threatens to undermine the very foundations of human existence. Four of these boundaries have already been exceeded through human activities (the global climate being one of them), while the permanently damaging transgression of others is looming.[1] Consequently, acknowledging the planetary boundaries as well as agreeing upon and adhering to limitations to said human activities seems to be the obvious reaction to the threat. However, such limitations do not sound appealing to many citizens, business executives, and political decision makers especially in industrialized societies. They tend to trigger connotations of abstinence, asceticism, or loss of conveniences and freedom of choice.[2]

It is therefore not surprising that the mainstream of current economic, political, and public debates around sustainable development and climate policy focus on the idea of addressing climate change and other environmental challenges by means of ecologically friendly technologies and "green growth". The latter is supposed to be a form of economic growth that is successfully "decoupled" from any harmful impacts on the environment through efficiency gains, i.a. by employing said eco-friendly technologies. This idea promises to bring human activities back to and keep them within the "safe operating space" of the planetary boundaries without arduous changes to societies, economic systems, and lifestyles. It is becoming increasingly apparent, though, that such an approach is unrealistic, because efficiency gains tend to fall victim to an overcompensation through so-called rebound effects.[3] I therefore consider it important to bring back a discussion about limits to our affluent lifestyles. As

1 Cf. Rockström et al., *Planetary Boundaries;* Steffen et al., *Guiding Human Development.*

2 Cf. Paech, *Liberation from Excess*, p. 21.

3 Cf. Paech, *Liberation from Excess*, pp. 65–85.

a Catholic theologian, I also believe that Christians at large and theologians in particular should actively engage in this discussion.

Two scholarly approaches that dare to question, criticize, and dismantle the narrative of green growth are those of German political scientist Doris Fuchs and Italian Swiss philosopher Antonietta Di Giulio as well as of German economist Niko Paech. Both approaches bring a discussion about limits to human activities back to the agenda and make a strong case for the necessity of absolute reductions in material and energy use, respectively in industrial production and consumption. In this paper, I will outline these two approaches and pair them with themes from the works of liberation theologians Ignacio Ellacuría and Jon Sobrino as well as Pope Francis. Thereby, I am attempting to make two points:

- that social sciences as well as theological reasoning can explain how economic reductions and limitations do not necessarily reduce quality of life but rather have the potential to generate liberating effects;
- that the idea of reductions and adhering to limits resonates better with Catholic theology and social ethics than a pro-growth economic agenda, and that Christian churches and theologians should become allies to scholarly approaches and civil society movements that try to promote and practice a more frugal "life within limits".

2 Niko Paech: Transitioning Economic Development Towards a Post-growth Economy

Niko Paech's concept of a "post-growth economy" acknowledges the existence of limits to growth, which, according to him, "are not only seen in production systems but also in the hedonic overstimulation of people".[4] As Paech expounds meticulously in his writings and presentations, "greening" the present economic systems through innovative technologies and efficiency gains will not be enough to stabilize economic development within the "safe operating space" of the planetary boundaries. He explains: "As long as decoupling by technological means turns out to be impossible, sustainable development can only be understood as a program for economic reduction".[5] Therefore, technologically generated efficiency needs to be complemented by sufficiency.[6]

4 Paech, *Post Growth Economics*, p. 481.
5 Paech, *Post Growth Economics*, p. 477.
6 Cf. Gassner, *Gerecht Konsumieren*, pp. 12–13.

As a first rough indicator of the dimensions that such a reduction would need to have, Paech turns to the climate goal of keeping global warming within the temperature limit of 1.5 °C above pre-industrial levels. This results in an estimate according to which every person in a global population of 7 to 8 billion people would have to restrict their annual CO_2 emissions to approximately 2.5 tons by 2050.[7] While the societal equivalent of this individual budget would still allow economic growth in many of the less industrialized countries for several years, the highly industrialized parts of the world would have to shrink their economy immediately and significantly. The average central European person, for example, currently accounts for approximately 12 tons of CO_2 emissions per year through housing, consumption, mobility etc.[8] To achieve the necessary reductions, Paech suggests some of the following sufficiency measures:

- deglobalizing and regionalizing economic activities and production chains;
- halving industrial production;
- focusing the remaining production on maintenance, revaluation and enhancement of existing stocks of goods through "preservation, conservation, optimization, extension of lifetimes and intensification of benefits";
- reducing paid work to an average of 20 hours weekly, while releasing time resources for non-market activities;
- reducing the scope of individual mobility and practicing more settled lifestyles;
- replacing monetary wealth by a type of wealth that is based "on one's own ability to produce";
- substituting market-mediated consumption with …
  … self-production and exchange of services between neighbors, friends etc.,
  … extension of product lifetimes through care and repair,
  … and use intensification through communal use or "sharing" practices within the local community.[9]

The last-mentioned set of measures is particularly important. The combination of these different non-market activities, which Paech calls "creative subsistence", can replace industrially produced output and thus ensure that "a reduction in industrial capacity would" neither "entail a loss of consumption functions for the affected goods" nor a loss of material prosperity.[10] Moreover,

---

7 Paech, *Post Growth Economics*, p. 479; Paech, *Kleine Boote bauen*, p. 22.

8 Cf. Paech, *Einladung zur Produktivitätsverweigerung;* Paech, *Kleine Boote bauen*, p. 22.

9 Cf. Paech, *Post Growth Economics*, pp. 483–485 (direct quotes from this text); Paech, *Liberation from Excess*, pp. 51–56, 121.

10 Paech, *Liberation from Excess*, pp. 111–114.

he considers the necessary reductions and adherence to natural limits to be a "Liberation from Excess".[11] There is no doubt that they would be liberating for the earth as well as for the present victims and losers of the dominant economic systems and future generations. What Paech has in mind, however, is a liberation also for the present members of affluent industrial societies, who have to reduce their consumption and mobility levels.

This is by no means the rhetoric of lifestyle guides but rather an assessment based on valid economical and psychological reasoning. Relying on creative subsistence can, for example, liberate from the time demanding excess of consumption options as well as from the economic dependency on depletable resources like crude oil, rare earths, and other extractive commodities, on volatile market developments and a growing financial indebtedness. When freed from these dependencies, lifestyles become more autonomous, robust and resilient.[12] This may well be accompanied by a liberation from fear of loss and "an increasingly insecure future".[13] Moreover, creative subsistence facilitates experiences of self-efficacy and helps to reintegrate the social into the economic: "If simple manual work regains its status then this will open up the possibility of integrating those who are ostracized due to a lack of money, education or communicative abilities."[14]

Despite these and other liberating effects, a respective public and political will or democratic majorities in favor of a post-growth economy seem out of sight—let alone any sort of national or even global action plan. However, in the light of a continued and unrestrained exceedance of planetary boundaries and depletion of extractive resources, Niko Paech is convinced that reduction and sufficiency will eventually become a reality, "by design or by disaster".[15] He does not suggest, though, to resignedly or even cynically wait for the disaster to come. A post-growth economy can start in niches and be practiced as a form of self-empowerment by those who are ready to act out a lifestyle of creative subsistence and sufficiency: "The transition town, urban gardening and repair movements are examples of pioneering work that at least foresees some of what the rest of society will experience in future."[16] Politicians and citizens who are not "quite ready" yet, but want to support and promote a transition towards de- and post-growth, can at least support those movements and

11 Paech, *Liberation from Excess*.
12 Cf. Paech, *Liberation from Excess*, pp. 17–22, 57–64, 120–121.
13 Paech, *Post Growth Economics*, p. 485.
14 Paech, *Post Growth Economics*, p. 485.
15 Paech, *Liberation from Excess*, p. 131; Paech, *Kleine Boote bauen*, pp. 25, 39.
16 Paech, *Liberation from Excess*, p. 131 (direct quote from this text); Paech, *Kleine Boote bauen*, pp. 22–25.

activists through donations, advocacy, policy-making etc. Waiting inactively for a disaster to come would ignore "the already existing potential of an exemplary anticipation" of sustainable lifestyles. These "exemplary anticipations" could become the blueprints of a post-growth economy when its time has come.[17]

3 Doris Fuchs and Antonietta Di Giulio: Defining Sustainable Consumption Corridors

Doris Fuchs and Antonietta Di Giulio start from similar observations regarding the limits to growth as Niko Paech. While he conceptualizes his approach in a broader perspective of economics, theirs "moves the role that consumption plays in enabling individuals to live a good life and, at least, as importantly, in overstepping environmental and social limits to the center of attention". Furthermore, Fuchs and Di Giulio emphasize questions of societal and political discourse and deliberation, rather than economic strategies. Their concept of "sustainable consumption corridors" can thus complement Paech's approach. It is a fairly recent concept, which, however, draws on insights from works and debates around basic needs and capabilities.[18]

It integrates ideas of good life, justice, and planetary boundaries and proposes a joint societal discourse that should lead to an agreement on "sustainable consumption corridors". These corridors would be defined by both a minimum and a maximum threshold: a minimum level of natural and social resources that every individual is entitled to as the basis for a good life, and a maximum level to every individual's use of resources beyond which the integrity of the Earth systems is put at risk and "access to sufficient resources (in terms of quantity and quality) for others, both in the present and the future", is jeopardized. Different corridors could be defined for specific goods and services or bundles of the same. Every corridor would set a limit to consumption but guarantee that every individual is able to live a good life and free to realize their individual life plans and choices within a safe operating space.[19]

The last-mentioned condition is crucial to the concept. One of its fundamental assumptions is "that it is neither possible nor desirable to prescribe

17 Paech, *Kleine Boote bauen*, p. 25 (own translation).

18 Cf. Fuchs/Di Giulio, *Consumption Corridors* (direct quote: pp. 21–22); Fuchs, *Living Well within Limits*.

19 Cf. Fuchs, *Living Well within Limits*; Di Giulio/Fuchs, *Sustainable Consumption Corridors* (direct quote: p. 184).

specific 'sustainable' patterns of consumption and ways of living, but that we need criteria that leave room for individual life plans". The idea of sustainable consumption corridors does "not question individual freedom [...] but define[s] limits of individual freedom by taking justice into the equation".[20] It "neither implies a plea for asceticism nor a general rejection of consumption" but "pursues the aim of living well within limits".[21] Decisions "about adequate minimum and maximum consumption standards will need to result from processes of societal deliberation",[22] which have to "be inclusive in engaging with as representative a sample of society as possible, making sure that each voice is heard".[23] The concept of sustainable consumption corridors is context-sensitive and does not aim for a unified global implementation but encourages a contextual adaption in different parts of the world. It also needs to be reevaluated over time: Lower and upper consumption limits "have to be readjusted periodically according to social and ecological developments, new insights, and evolving value systems".[24]

Doris Fuchs and Antonietta Di Giulio do not stress the liberative effects of economical limits to the same extend as Niko Paech. However, to those who might consider minimum and maximum consumption thresholds an unjustified interference with individual freedom, they point out

> how much interference there already is, most importantly from market actors. Today, we can witness the powerful setting of consumption norms by enterprises with immense discursive power. [...] Rather than focus on our freedom from [...] intervention, we should retake our freedom in building the societies we want to live in [...] and our freedom to set limits to individual action for the sake of the joint pursuit of a collective goal.[25]

Similarly to Paech, they also suggest that on the one hand, "hoping for immediate all-encompassing change does not seem advisable", while on the other hand "we simply cannot wait for international negotiations and agreement on this". However, "local initiatives may well provide promising stepping stones".[26]

20 Fuchs/Di Giulio, *Consumption Corridors*, p. 18.
21 Fuchs, *Living Well within Limits*, pp. 298–299.
22 Fuchs/Di Giulio, *Consumption Corridors*, p. 20.
23 Fuchs, *Living Well within Limits*, p. 301.
24 Di Giulio/Fuchs, *Sustainable Consumption Corridors*, p. 188 (direct quote from this text); Fuchs/Di Giulio, *Consumption Corridors*, pp. 17–18.
25 Fuchs, *Living Well within Limits*, p. 300.
26 Fuchs, *Living Well within Limits*, pp. 301–302.

4 Ignacio Ellacuría and Jon Sobrino: A Civilization of Shared Austerity

Jon Sobrino, Jesuit and Salvadorean liberation theologian with Basque origins, has brought up the theme of a "civilization of shared austerity" in several of his writings. It is an adaption of Ignacio Ellacuría's vision of a "civilization of poverty".[27] With this notion, Sobrino's fellow-Jesuit did not envisage a "universal impoverishment".[28] He rather introduced it as a counter model to the prevailing "civilization of wealth", which promotes "the possessive accumulation [...] of the maximum possible wealth as the fundamental basis for one's own security and the possibility of an ever-increasing consumerism as the basis of one's own happiness".[29] Meanwhile, the civilization of poverty "makes the universal satisfaction of basic needs the principle of development, and the growth of shared solidarity the basis of humanization".[30]

In this context, Ellacuría did not refer to "poverty" as a state of deprivation of the bare necessities caused by unjust structures and exploitation, but as a voluntarily and actively accepted mode of life in which the goods of the earth are shared among all people in a way that enables everyone to live with dignity.[31] Sobrino speaks of a civilization of shared austerity to better capture this notion, even though this alternative term lacks the same sharpness and dialectical opposition to the civilization of wealth, as Sobrino himself has suggested several times.[32]

Clear parallels can be seen between Niko Paech's vision of a post-growth society and a theologically envisioned civilization of shared austerity, especially when the latter is described as

> a universal state of affairs which guarantees the satisfaction of basic needs, the freedom of personal choices, and an environment for personal and community creativity that permits the emergence of new forms of life and culture, new relationships with nature, with others, with oneself, and with God.[33]

---

27 Cf. Sobrino, *The Crucified People*, p. 9; Sobrino, *On the Way to Healing*; Maier, *Zivilisation geteilter Genügsamkeit*.

28 Sobrino, *On the Way to Healing*.

29 Ellacuría, *Utopía y profetismo*, p. 170 (English translation cited from Sobrino, *The Crucified People*, p. 9).

30 Ellacuría, *Utopía y profetismo*, p. 170 (English translation cited from Sobrino, *The Crucified People*, p. 14).

31 Cf. Ellacuría, *Misión actual*, pp. 119–120; Ellacuría, *El reino de Dios*.

32 Cf. e.g., Sobrino, *On the Way to Healing*.

33 Ellacuría, *El reino de Dios*, p. 595 (English translation cited from Sobrino, *The Crucified People*, p. 14).

Even though Ellacuría and Sobrino do not put ecological limits at the center of their concept like Paech, human embeddedness in and care "for nature and all creation" is certainly an important part of it.[34] Also, Paech's appreciation for the benefits of creative subsistence mirrors the founding of a civilization of shared austerity on "work that not only produces but also channels creativity and human fulfillment".[35]

The civilization of wealth, on the other hand, "does not build spirit or values that can humanize people and societies".[36] As a "civilization of the individual, of a selfish 'good life' and a type of success that excludes others and comes at their expense", it is rather "characterized spiritually by fear".[37] Its members, in their dependency on ever new options for consumption, are driven by a "desire […] for 'unlimited' wellbeing" which Sobrino characterizes as "truly compulsive".[38] The civilization of wealth is thus not only "dehumanizing […] for those who pay the costs" it generates, but also "for those who enjoy it".[39] However, a unique feature of Ellacuría's and Sobrino's liberation theological reasoning is the idea that healing and liberation do not primarily stem from self-empowerment in niches within the civilization of wealth. Far from it, they insist "that the new civilization be informed by spirit, a spirit generated mainly by the poor".[40] This counterintuitive postulate can be a critical reminder in debates around post-growth and sustainable consumption: Even though the industrialized countries and their citizens clearly are the main contributors to the present ecological crises—especially to climate change—and therefore bear the major responsibility for changing their economies and lifestyles, they may not be able to do it on their own. Rather they may need to seek support and inspiration from those who have experience in living within limits, because living as if environmental limits did not exist, has never even been an option for them.

5 Pope Francis: Sobriety as Part of Christian Eco-spirituality and Decreased Growth

It is of little surprise that a Catholic theologian would also consult Pope Francis' encyclical *Laudato Si'* of 2015 on the matter at hand. After having called for an

34 Sobrino, *The Crucified People*, p. 17.
35 Sobrino, *On the Way to Healing*.
36 Sobrino, *The Crucified People*, p. 9.
37 Sobrino, *On the Way to Healing*.
38 Sobrino, *The Crucified People*, p. 13.
39 Sobrino, *The Crucified People*, p. 13.
40 Sobrino, *On the Way to Healing*.

"ecological conversion" that draws motivation from a Christian eco-spirituality, the Pope comes to talk about "sobriety" as a part of said spirituality.[41] Earlier on, he had explained that

> if we no longer speak the language of fraternity and beauty in our relationship with the world, our attitude will be that of masters, consumers, ruthless exploiters, unable to set limits on their immediate needs. By contrast, if we feel intimately united with all that exists, then sobriety and care will well up spontaneously.[42]

He goes on to characterize sobriety as follows:

> Christian spirituality proposes an alternative understanding of the quality of life, and encourages a prophetic and contemplative lifestyle, one capable of deep enjoyment free of the obsession with consumption. We need to take up an ancient lesson, found in different religious traditions and also in the Bible. It is the conviction that "less is more". […] Christian spirituality proposes a growth marked by moderation and the capacity to be happy with little.[43]

Pope Francis states that "[s]uch sobriety, when lived freely and consciously, is liberating". It liberates from "unsatisfied needs, […] obsessiveness and weariness" and opens up spaces for finding "satisfaction in fraternal encounters, in service, in developing [one's] gifts, in music and art, in contact with nature, in prayer". Therefore, "living on little" does not constitute "a lesser life or one lived with less intensity. On the contrary, it is a way of living life to the full."[44]

Apart from the dimension of Christian spirituality, the Pope also comes to talk directly about respecting Earth's limits with regard to economic systems. He explicitly takes up growth critical debates, adopting his own critical stance towards the "idea of infinite or unlimited growth" and a "talk of sustainable growth", which "usually becomes a way of distracting attention and offering excuses":[45]

> In any event, if in some cases sustainable development were to involve new forms of growth, then in other cases, given the insatiable and irresponsible growth produced over many decades, we need also to think of containing growth by setting some reasonable limits and even retracing our steps before it is too late. […] That is why the time has come to accept decreased growth in some parts of the world, in order to provide resources for other places to experience healthy growth.[46]

---

41 Pope Francis, *Laudato Si'*, nos. 222–223. — Henceforth LS.

42 LS 11.

43 LS 222.

44 LS 223.

45 LS 106, 194.

46 LS 193.

6 Evaluation—Inspired by Feedback and Discussions during the Workshop

All four approaches to "liberating limits" were positively appraised by participants of the *6th Workshop "Liberative Contextual Theologies": Doing Climate Justice*. Some constructive criticism and queries were raised, however, which helped to detect some weak spots and clarify potential misunderstandings.

6.1 *Eurocentric Approaches, Unapplicable to the Realities of the Global South?*

A common concern by participants from parts of the Global South was the perception that Paech's vision of a post-growth economy as well as Fuchs' and Di Giulio's idea of sustainable consumption corridors are tailored to the situation in countries of the Global North, while not taking into account the realities in less industrialized societies. Therefore, these approaches came under suspicion of being either unfair or unapplicable to these realities. As one participant put it, "it is easy to say that we can live with less when you already have your needs covered, but for most of the developing world there is still a lot of room and need of economic growth". To some degree, this suspicion was also raised with respect to Ellacuría's and Sobrino's civilization of shared austerity and Pope Francis' talk of sobriety. Even though their theological thinking has been shaped by their experiences in contexts of the Global South, all three of them come from fairly privileged backgrounds and have enjoyed the relative comfort and security of being members of the Jesuit order.

As far as post-growth economy and sustainable consumption corridors are concerned, it has to be noted that, yes, Di Giulio, Fuchs, and Paech conceptualize their ideas from a European perspective. It can be added that both approaches stem mostly from academic debates. At the same time, it becomes apparent from their publications that Di Giulio, Fuchs, and Paech direct their suggestions primarily at industrialized societies of the Global North. They do not intend to prescribe a path of economic restraint to less affluent and industrialized parts of the world but rather try to challenge their own societies' current development path. Nonetheless, their concepts are not irrelevant for other contexts. They are, in fact, context-sensitive and encourage a contextual adaption in different parts of the world, as explained above with regard to the sustainable consumption corridors. The context sensitivity of Paech's considerations is noticeable when he takes the societal equivalent of a maximum of 2.5 tons of annual CO_2 emissions as a threshold that the highly industrialized parts of the world have to reach by shrinking their economy, while less industrialized countries can seek to meet it by following a path of economic growth.

Both approaches can be adapted and applied in the Global South as strategies to creating contextually appropriate and more sustainable forms of economic development that take the natural limits to growth into account, instead of simply reproducing the same mistakes that societies in the Global North have made for decades. One of the passages from Laudato Si' quoted above cautiously hints towards such a possibility when Pope Francis speaks of a "healthy growth" that "other places" should be able to experience. Meanwhile, the fact that the concepts of post-growth economy and sustainable consumption corridors originate from academic debates does not necessarily indicate that they do not resonate with real life experience. They are, indeed, both reflective of bottom-up movements like the voluntary simplifiers, and at least Paech's approach has been adopted by grassroots initiatives.

6.2 *Just Wishful Thinking?*

Another concern raised by various participants was the apprehension that all four approaches ultimately represent wishful thinking. The respective participants forecast a widespread resistance to these concepts, because of aversions either to the off-putting language of reductions, limitations, sobriety, austerity, and even poverty, or to the radical changes that would be required to put the approaches in practice. This is undeniably a weak spot of trying to "bring a discussion about limits back to the agenda". On the other hand, one could argue that precisely the aspect of radical change and the use of "radical language" might open up pathways for resistance to economic and cultural hegemonies and for necessary social struggle. This reasoning will be pursued further, below. Some participants, however, reacted to the concern of "mere wishful thinking" by pointing to certain provisions that could pave the way for an implementation of post-growth economics, sustainable consumption corridors, or even a civilization of shared austerity.

One example is providing people with opportunities to experience simpler lifestyles rather than letting them grapple theoretically with the idea of having to reduce their consumption and limit their wealth. It was pointed out that a lot of people who have been practicing simpler lifestyles for years can testify that they are indeed liberating. This is a valid point, which concurs with a widely held conviction in the field of Education for Sustainability (EfS) or Education for Sustainable Development (ESD), namely that it is important to not only help students develop an understanding and awareness of sustainability concerns, but also aim at building up their motivation and capacity by engaging them in actions towards sustainability.[47]

47 Cf. Delgado, *Education for Sustainability*.

For the context of Christian parishes or religious education, the season of Lent might be a suitable starting point for creating experience opportunities. These could be directed at rediscovering Lenten sacrifices not only as a religious deed but also as doing something positive for creation, in solidarity with others, and for one's own relationship with God and oneself. Other provisions within a Christian framework that were mentioned by workshop participants point in a similar direction: e.g., integrating simpler ways of living into a spirituality of Christian discipleship or learning from the example of monastic life, including the religious vow of poverty, which models that a different lifestyle from the mainstream consumerist society is possible. Participants drew direct connections to the concept of *Refigurative Religious Education in a Monastery* in Claudia Gärtner's contribution to the workshop.[48]

6.3 *Glorification and Spiritualization of Poverty?*

A third concern was raised from a particularly theological point of departure: Is a theological take on concepts like a post-growth economy not in danger of glorifying and spiritualizing poverty? The original labelling of Ellacuría's and Sobrino's civilization of poverty or the example of learning form monastic life and poverty could be taken as evidence to that effect. One participant considered this potential danger as "a kind of thin ice" with respect to the Global South, "where long-standing poverty is very much tied to colonial histories along with (Christian) mission history". It became clear in the following discussion that simplicity and especially poverty as voluntarily assumed lifestyles need to be linked to solidarity with the involuntarily poor. As expressions of solidary, they might also lead to civic engagement and action for a more just and sustainable society. Such an engagement can even turn into ways of taking a radical stance for and with those poor and marginalized communities who take up the social struggle for their own liberation from economic, cultural, and other forms of oppression. This leads to a fourth and last concern.

6.4 *Starting Points for Radical Critique and Social Struggle?*

In the follow up to the workshop, another probable weak spot was pointed out: The four approaches to "liberating limits", as they have been presented, do not appear to offer any starting points for a more radical critique of capitalism or neoliberalism as underlying ideologies behind the economic growth paradigm, nor for resistance to economic and cultural hegemonies or for social struggle. This seems to be true as far as Fuchs', Di Giulio's, and Paech's approaches are

48 See her article in this volume.

concerned.[49] However, it would certainly be possible to develop such a critique or social action building on Pope Francis, Sobrino, and especially Ellacuría. This would be a worthwhile project for future theological engagement with post-growth economics and sustainable consumption corridors. The assumption that starting points for radical critique and social struggle are needed, highlights the potential for conflict which arises from the idea of "liberating limits", and which even voluntary forms of post-growth self-empowerment in niches will have to face (e.g., when an urban gardening group is suddenly faced with the privatization of the public property that they use). This conflictive dimension has, admittedly, not been developed in this paper.

7 Conclusion and Outlook

Living well within limits and parting with economic growth imperatives corresponds to the Gospel message, which—as Ignacio Ellacuría puts it—is characterized by strong reservations towards wealth and affluence, even though it does not promote asceticism.[50] Post-growth economy and sustainable consumption corridors represent two promising approaches from different social science disciplines that bring a discussion about limits back to the agenda. Pairing them with Ignacio Ellacuría's, Jon Sobrino's, and Pope Francis' ideas has provided some first reinforcement that these approaches resonate well with Catholic thinking—actually better than a pro-growth economic agenda and affluent lifestyles.

More dialogue and collaboration on this would be helpful. Therefore, I want to encourage theologians to actively engage in the debates around post-growth and lifestyles of sufficiency, and become allies to those scholars who try to conceptualize and promote them. Societal change towards a life within limits and free from growth imperatives will continue to be difficult at a large scale. Paech, Fuchs, and Di Giulio agree on this and recommend taking quasi-subversive exemplary action in niches. Christian theologians, churches, and faithful in general would do well in becoming allies to social movements who try to flesh out such exemplary action.

---

49 Paech, in return, identifies certain shortcomings in traditional anti-capitalist agendas from a growth critical perspective, which cannot be elaborated in this paper (cf. Paech, *Liberation from Excess*, pp. 33–36, 60–61).

50 Cf. Ellacuría, *Utopía y profetismo*, p. 177.

Some examples of such collaborations exist already: The German church initiative "anders wachsen" ("growing differently") tries to promote ideas of alternatives to the economic growth paradigm within church and societal contexts. It is mainly supported by the protestant churches in Germany but also by some Catholic dioceses and organizations. The initiative has developed a concept for sustainable model parishes and congregations, so-called "anders wachsen-parishes", which has been trialing in congregations of the Evangelical-Lutheran Church of Saxony. More parishes and congregations are invited to adopt the concept.[51]

In 2018, an expert group to the German Catholic Bishops' Conference published an analysis of post-growth approaches and strategies from an angle of Christian social ethics. While the authors do not reject the idea of economic growth in principle, they praise the post-growth movement for bringing the serious flaws of current growth-based economic systems to attention and highlight that from the perspective of Catholic Social Teaching economic growth may never be an end in itself and thus is not to be absolutized.[52]

This paper has also shown how both social sciences and theologies are able to make a case that economic reductions and adhering to limitations do not necessarily reduce quality of life but rather have the potential to generate liberating effects. This is even more reason and incentive for Christians and particularly Christian theologians to engage in and become supporters of the idea of "living well within limits".

References

Delgado, L.: *Education for Sustainability in Local Government: Handbook.* Canberra: Australian Government Department of the Environment, Water, Heritage and the Arts/Australian Research Institute in Education for Sustainability, 2007, pp. 38–41, http://aries.mq.edu.au/handbook [accessed 24.05.2021].

Di Giulio, Antonietta/Doris Fuchs: "Sustainable Consumption Corridors: Concept, Objections, and Responses", in: *GAIA* 23, no. S1 (2014): pp. 184–192.

Ellacuría, Ignacio: "El reino de Dios y el paro en el Tercer Mundo", in: *Concilium* 180 (1982): pp. 588–596.

51 https://anders-wachsen.de.

52 Wissenschaftliche Arbeitsgruppe für weltkirchliche Aufgaben der Deutschen Bischofskonferenz, *Raus aus der Wachstumsgesellschaft?*, pp. 10, 52–53.

Ellacuría, Ignacio: "Misión actual de la Compañía de Jesús", written in 1983, published posthumously in: *Revista Latinoamericana de Teología* 29 (1993): pp. 115–126.

Ellacuría, Ignacio: "Utopía y profetismo desde América Latina: Un ensayo concreto de soteriología histórica", in: *Revista Latinoamericana de Teología* 17 (1989): pp. 141–184.

Fuchs, Doris: "Living Well within Limits: The Vision of Consumption Corridors", in: *Routledge Handbook of Global Sustainability Governance*, Agni Kalfagianni/Doris Fuchs/Anders Hayden (eds.). London: Routledge 2020, pp. 296–307.

Fuchs, Doris/Antonietta Di Giulio: "Consumption Corridors: Integrating the Good Life and Justice in Sustainable Development", in: *SCORAI Europe Workshop Proceedings: Sustainable Consumption and Social Justice in a Constrained World* (= Sustainable Consumption Transitions Series 6), Sylvia Lorek/Edina Vadovics (eds.). Budapest: SCORAI Europe 2016, pp. 14–24.

Gassner, Franz: *Gerecht Konsumieren. Sozialethische und theologische Perspektiven einer Ethik des Konsums*. Dissertation (Dr theol) at University of Vienna (2012), http://othes.univie.ac.at/25513/1/2012-05-02_8526403.pdf [accessed 24.05.2021].

https://anders-wachsen.de [accessed 24.05.2021].

Maier, Martin: "Zivilisation geteilter Genügsamkeit", in: *Stimmen der Zeit* 227, no. 1 (2009): pp. 1–2.

Paech, Niko: *Einladung zur Produktivitätsverweigerung: Grundzüge der Postwachstumsökonomik*. Presentation for Friedensbildungswerk Köln, October 15, 2016, https://friedensbildungswerk.de/Bilder/pdf/Vortrag-von%20Niko-Paech-am-15-10-2016.pdf [accessed 24.05.2021].

Paech, Niko: "Kleine Boote bauen zur Rettung der Welt: Postwachstumsökonomie als Programm zur Selbstermächtigung", in: *Ökonomie der Genügsamkeit: Impulse für eine Gesellschaft ohne Wachstum* (= Herrenalber Forum 85), Evangelische Akademie Baden/Freundeskreis der Evangelischen Akademie Baden (eds.). Karlsruhe: Evangelische Akademie Baden 2019, pp. 22–50.

Paech, Niko: *Liberation from Excess: The Road to a Post-Growth Economy*, 2nd ed. Munich: Oekom 2016.

Paech, Niko: "Post Growth Economics", in: *Handbook of Ecological Economics: Nature and Society*, Clive L. Spash (ed.). London: Routledge 2017, pp. 477–486.

Pope Francis, Encyclical Letter *Laudato Si' of the Holy Father Francis on Care for Our Common Home*, May 24, 2015, https://www.vatican.va/content/francesco/en/encyclicals/documents/papa-francesco_20150524_enciclica-laudato-si.html [accessed 24.05.2021].

Rockström, Johan, et al.: "Planetary Boundaries: Exploring the Safe Operating Space for Humanity", in: *Ecology and Society* 14, no. 2 (2009): Art. 32.

Sobrino, Jon: "On the Way to Healing", in: *America: The Jesuit Review* 211, no. 14 (2014), https://www.americamagazine.org/issue/way-healing.

Sobrino, Jon: "The Crucified People and the Civilization of Poverty: Ignacio Ellacuría's 'Taking Hold of Reality', in: *No Salvation Outside of the Poor: Prophetic Utopian Essays*, Jon Sobrino (ed.). Maryknoll: Orbis Books 2008, pp. 1–18.

Steffen, Will, et al.: "Guiding Human Development on a Changing Planet", in: *Science* 347, no. 6223 (2015): Art. 1259855.

Wissenschaftliche Arbeitsgruppe für weltkirchliche Aufgaben der Deutschen Bischofskonferenz (eds.): *Raus aus der Wachstumsgesellschaft? Eine sozialethische Analyse und Bewertung von Postwachstumsstrategien* (= Studien der Sachverständigengruppe "Weltwirtschaft und Sozialethik" 21). Bonn: DBK 2018.

Climate Crisis, Corona and Christianity

Religious Education for Sustainable Development in a Wounded World

Claudia Gärtner

Abstract

Education for Sustainable Development (ESD) has set itself the goal of empowering adolescents to achieve the Sustainable Development Goals (SDG) proclaimed by the UN. The following article discusses the extent to which Religious Education can be linked to ESD. It is shown that ESD sometimes does not make conflicts of interest or ideological blind spots transparent, which need to be critically analyzed by Religious Education. This reveals dilemmas that a politically oriented religious ESD has to deal with. How these dilemmas can be dealt with in Religious Education is finally illustrated by an example.

Keywords

Sustainable development; SDG; religious education; Capuchines

1 Introduction

This chapter discusses what Religious Education (RE) can contribute to mitigating the climate crisis and to promoting climate justice. In many debates about the importance of (religious) education in dealing with the climate crisis, the Sustainable Development Goals (SDG) of the UN "Agenda 2030 for Sustainable Development" are the horizon of the discussion. These 17 goals also represent my starting point: no poverty, no hunger, good health, quality education, gender equality, clean water and sanitation, clean energy, good jobs and economic growth, innovation and infrastructure, reduced inequalities, sustainable cities and communities, responsible consumption, protect the planet, life below water, life on land, peace and justice, and partnership for the goals.

These 17 SDGs are intended to lead to a sustainable global society by 2030. Quality Education is part of a sustainable world too. This fourth goal aims to "ensure inclusive and equitable quality education and promote lifelong

 | DOI:10.30965/9783657795314_011

learning opportunities for all."[1] At the same time, education is assigned a key function in achieving the 17 SDGs. Target 4.7 aims to "ensure that all learners acquire the knowledge and skills needed to promote sustainable development, including, among others, through education for sustainable development and sustainable lifestyles, human rights, gender equality, promotion of a culture of peace and nonviolence, global citizenship and appreciation of cultural diversity and of culture's contribution to sustainable development." (Target 4.7)

Because the 17 SDGs are so prominent and widespread in the sustainability discourse, RE should reflect on how it wants to or can contribute to achieve target 4.7. To do this, it is necessary in a first step to take an in-depth, critical look at the conception of Education for Sustainable Development (ESD) (paragraph 2). In a further step, I will outline guiding principles for a politically oriented RE (paragraph 3), and I will discuss problems that are related to them on the basis of four dilemmas (chapter 4). Finally, I concretize my considerations by means of a religious learning arrangement (chapter 5).

2 Education for Sustainable Development—Critical Remarks

In order to implement the ambitious goal 4 of the 2030 Agenda, UNESCO was mandated to initiate, coordinate, implement and evaluate a wide range of measures and actions.[2] In this regard, the UNESCO

> aims to improve access to quality education on sustainable development at all levels and in all social contexts, to transform society by reorienting education and by helping people to develop knowledge, skills, values and behaviours that are needed for sustainable development. It is about including sustainable development issues, such as climate change and biodiversity into teaching and learning. Individuals are encouraged to be responsible actors who resolve challenges, respect cultural diversity and contribute to creating a more sustainable world.[3]

I will now highlight and reflect on several aspects of this objective.

UNESCO wants people to "develop knowledge, skills, values and behaviours needed for sustainable development." Although—in contrast to AGENDA 2030—the development of values is an aim, the competences remain purely formal. No normative orientation is given, except for vague references to concepts of diversity and sustainability. In this way, ESD ties in with concepts of

1 UN, *Transforming Our World.*
2 UNESCO, *Education 2030.*
3 UNESCO: *Education for Sustainable Development.*

competence-orientated didactics, which are often criticized, especially from the perspective of religious and political education, as being content-free and uncritical. This would "dilute education to 'skills formulas'"[4]. Based on evaluated international ESD projects, Huckle and Wals conclude: "From the review it is quite clear that the ethical dimension is rather weak, if not absent, in most of the documents and cases reviewed."[5] In the following, we will show whether and how theology and RE in particular can offer more ethical guidance.

The second aspect to be emphasized in target 4.7 is the focus on the individuals who "are encouraged to be responsible actors." This individualizes the problem solving. "Instead of a critique of and sensitization to the contradictions of global socialization, the responsibility for balancing them is transferred to the subjects in the form of a 'competence to shape'."[6] Ideland and Malmberg coin the term "eco-certified child."[7] In this way, they express that such education primarily places the responsibility for sustainability on the growing subject. "The individual becomes responsible for 'everybody's' security and for the ecological system of the world. This individual focus tends to make conflicts of interests or ideological standpoints invisible."[8] In this way, ESD not only runs the risk of overwhelming children and young people and possibly overburdening them morally, but this can also be accompanied by a depoliticization of sustainability.

> The political muscles are atrophied when the problems are placed on the shoulders of individual children who, despite their lack of income, suffrage, and established channels for making their voices heard in society, are expected to be able to change the world through rational, individual actions. This means that the possibilities for real change may perhaps disappear.[9]

An ESD oriented in this way can then contribute to the stabilization of social conditions described by the concept of "sustainable non-sustainability".[10]

Even a brief glance at teaching materials underlines this tendency:[11] saving water, buying second-hand or ecologically certified clothes, collecting rubbish or eating a low-meat diet are suggestions for action that are mostly discussed

---

4 Euler, *Nachhaltigkeit und Bildung*, p. 171. All German quotations in this article are translated by the author.
5 Huckle/Wals, *The UN Decade of Education*, p. 500.
6 Kehren, *Bildung für nachhaltige Entwicklung*, p. 135.
7 Ideland/Malmberg, *Governing 'Eco-Certified Children'*.
8 Ideland/Malmberg, *Governing 'Eco-Certified Children'*, p. 181.
9 Ideland, *The Eco-Certified Child*, p. 136.
10 Blühdorn et al., *Nachhaltige Nicht-Nachhaltigkeit*.
11 Ideland, *The Eco-Certified Child*.

affirmatively in subject units on the preservation of creation. A (religious) ESD oriented in this way "helps to reassure and temporarily occupy children, but disguises the fact that the problems are bigger and thus overall reinforces a reassurance narrative."[12]

The third aspect to be highlighted is the solution-oriented perspective of target 4.7. EDS encourages individuals to "resolve challenges, respect cultural diversity and contribute to creating a more sustainable world." Accordingly, Haan and Kamp, who developed one of the most influential conceptions of ESD, state: Students

> identify and demonstrate procedures for reaching agreements on goals and processes of sustainable and equitable development in the face of normative and political differences (e.g. in the form of simulation games, mediations) [... and] can constructively manage differences of opinion and conflicts in relation to issues of (non-)sustainable development.[13]

Possible fundamental conflicts between the economic, ecological and social sustainability goals remain unnamed and tend to be concealed. Looking at the UN Decade of Education for Sustainable Development (2005–2014), Huckle and Wals therefore conclude: "UNESCO has trimmed and tamed the Decade of Education for Sustainable Development so that it does not challenge neoliberalism and fails to develop GESC [Global Education for Sustainability Citizenship]."[14]

It is insightful—and hopeful—that the latest UNESCO framework paper on ESD is unusually clear about the conflicting aspects of the SDGs, especially between individual sustainable actions and non-sustainable structures.

> As much as attention is required for what is happening at the individual level in relation to transformative decisions and experience, there is a need for ESD to focus more on deep structural causes. The relationship between economic growth and sustainable development is one of the pertinent issues in this regard.[15]

Here it becomes clear, at least to some extent, that the concept of sustainability as an *umbrella term* runs the risk of obscuring conflicting goals, which is probably why sustainability is currently met with such broad approval. Such a broad concept of sustainability is therefore compatible with the economy

12 Reuter, *Fridays for Future*, p. 322.
13 De Haan/Kamp, *Nachhaltigkeit und Gerechtigkeit*, p. 240.
14 Huckle/Wals, *The UN Decade of Education*, p. 497.
15 UNESCO, *Framework for the Implementation*, Annex II, Art. 4,8f.

without necessarily implying socio-ecological objectives. Therefore, UNESCO calls for ESD to "raise critical and structural questions".[16]

This brief analysis of target 4.7 already reveals sensitive aspects of ESD. Without going into these debates in detail here, general points of criticism of ESD can be summarized. ESD is the most widespread, influential concept that RE has to deal with. But the concept of sustainability that guides ESD has an economic origin.[17] ESD does not always make the possible dominance of economic goals transparent. Ultimately, ESD has a strong anthropocentric alignment and views nature as a resource for (only a few) people. At the same time, ESD can also be seen as an attempt to transfer the solving of ecological and social problems to future generations. Significantly, it is an Education *for* (!) Sustainable Development and thus already points to a possible functionalization of education in the title. Thus, RE should not seamlessly continue ESD. The following chapter therefore analyzes which accentuations RE can or should contribute to ESD.

3 Political Religious Education for Sustainable Development

RE has a normative orientation and is value-based. Religious ESD is to be oriented in this respect. Within the framework of this essay, I cannot explore the question of how RE can be normatively oriented not only in the denominational, catechetical context, but also in the state school system, in detail.[18] The following thoughts must therefore be reflected contextually in the respective education system.

Both biblical scriptures and Christian traditions offer great potential resources for overcoming the climate crisis. Since this potential has already been developed in other contributions to the multi-authored volume from a

16 UNESCO, *Framework for the Implementation*, Annex II, Art. 5.7.

17 The concept of sustainability originated in forestry and is subject to an economic logic in that nature is primarily regarded as a resource to be preserved for the economic system. Cf. Prescher, *Das Nachhaltigkeitsdogma*; Pufé, *Nachhaltigkeit*; Kluwick/Zemanek (eds.), *Nachhaltigkeit Interdisziplinär*.

18 In Germany, this is possible because RE is taught as a confession-oriented subject. RE teachers teach the subject from the perspective of the respective denomination, whereby they have to present and discuss the respective topics in a multi-perspective and also in a controversial way. Students must not be overwhelmed by the content and have the right to opt out of RE. Notwithstanding this, the confessional orientation of RE is not uncontroversial in Germany.

biblical, historical or systematic-theological perspective, I will content myself here with a few keywords on subjects that are particularly relevant for RE.[19]

- Christianity has many spiritual, liturgical and aesthetic resources. ESD often has a more cognitive orientation. However, attitudes that lead to changed, sustainable actions are hardly transformed by cognitive learning settings. What is needed here is experience-oriented, holistic learning. The spiritual, liturgical and aesthetic dimensions of Christianity offer rich learning opportunities.
- The Christian theology of poverty and fasting offers a link to current debates on sufficiency and *buen vivir*.[20] From the perspective of RE, it is particularly relevant that poverty in Christianity does not mean romanticizing the plight of the poor, stabilizing the gap between rich and poor or renouncing something, but rather freedom for something (new): to become free from abundance, from things that keep us from the essential, in order to become free for God and the world. Christian theology and spirituality can tie in with lifestyle movements such as *minimalism*, which seeks to reduce material possessions in order to achieve more freedom and quality of life.[21]
- Political theology, especially Johann Baptist Metz, has defined religion as "interruption"[22]. When adolescents are confronted with religious traditions or themes in RE, they can interrupt the daily life of the students. RE can invite students to try out looking at their lives from a different perspective. Religion can thus, at least temporarily, interrupt the usual view of the world and change familiar logics.
- At the Fridays for Future demonstrations there are posters that quote: "We are unstoppable! Another world is possible!" The conviction that the world can be different is a profoundly Christian hope, unfolded in theological concepts of otherness, eschatology and creation. The belief in God's otherness, in his eschatological redemption of creation, can release power to fight for precisely this other world. RE can encourage students that the present society, economy and politics are not without any alternative. The TINA-world view[23] is a deeply un-Christian perspective.

---

19 Cf. Gärtner, *Klima*, pp. 83–106.

20 Cf. Acosta, *Das 'Buen Vivir'*.

21 However, it cannot be overlooked that lifestyle minimalism has a materialistic and individualistic orientation that contrasts with a Christian theology of poverty. Smit, *Purpose-Driven Purging Minimalism*. Minimalism is marketed extremely successfully in the media and thus also closely rooted in the economic system, as the following bestsellers show: Becker, *The More of Less*; Carver, *Soulful Simplicity*; Kondō, *The Life-Changing Magic*.

22 Metz, *Glaube in Geschichte und Gesellschaft*, p. 166.

23 The acronym TINA alludes to the slogan "There is no alternative" often used by Margaret Thatcher, who gave economics a quasi-religious status: "Deregulation's good, if not God" (Flanders, At Thatcher's Funeral).

- From a Christian perspective, RE not only aims at changing individual actions, but is fundamentally based on ideas of a different, more just world. Jesus's message of the Kingdom of God calls Christians to engage in changing social, political, economic and cultural structures in order to preserve creation, even if in history and in the present, Christian practice does not always correspond to Jesus' message. RE has therefore always to be politically oriented and thus defies individualistic tendencies of ESD.

However, political Religious ESD gives rise to a variety of areas of tension. Four of the most important fields will be outlined below.[24]

4 Dilemmas of Political Religious Education for Sustainable Development

4.1 *Between Normativity and Plurality*

RE as well as Christianity and theology in general are challenged by a plurality of world views. RE must therefore ask itself if Christian concepts, traditions, values and beliefs are still relevant and plausible in a plural and (post-) secular society. RE must neither neglect this plurality nor overwhelm its students with these values and concepts. In this perspective RE can take up three ways of dealing with this tension between normativity and plurality: Firstly, the development of normative positions in RE contexts should be transparent, reflective and controversial in confrontation with other positions. Secondly, religious norms and themes can be translated into plural, connectable, secular discourses, as, for example, suggested by Jürgen Habermas.[25] And thirdly, as already outlined, religion can be offered as an interruption of non-religious discourses. However, it must always be examined to what extent the specifically religious logic is preserved by the three strategies. In RE, for example, it is possible to find learning arrangements in the field of creation theology that lead to saving water or collecting rubbish. This action-orientation can undoubtedly be justified in a secular logic and is broadly connectable. However, the social and political perspectives of the theology of creation are undermined here.

4.2 *Between Determinism and Hope of Change*

Ecological issues are closely interdependent with economic, social, political and cultural ones. The lives of students as well as the Christian message of hope are also deeply embedded in these diverse structures. In terms of social analysis, however, a dominance of economic logics can be recognized or one

24 Cf. Gärtner, *Klima*, pp. 131–35, where I elaborate six dilemmas.

25 Cf. Habermas, *Vorpolitische Grundlagen*.

can speak of a hegemonic neoliberalism or capitalism. The Christian message of hope, the ideas of a different, good life, as well as the many spiritual, liturgical and aesthetic dimensions of Christianity are interwoven in these hegemonic structures as well as the lives of the students who encounter RE. This field of tension cannot simply be resolved pedagogically. In fact, RE must deal with it. To do so, it is indispensable to know about the effectiveness of social and economic systems so as not to succumb to them blindly. Nevertheless, the awareness of problems does not yet lead to a permanently changed practice. This mind-behavior-gap is a serious problem for ESD as well as for a social-ecological transformation of society.[26] A theologically reflected way of dealing with this tension can best be described in eschatological terms. According to this, RE has to, on the one hand, deal with the tension that human thinking, behavior and attitude can be shaped by sustainability or a social-ecological practice. On the other hand, human beings will (presumably) not succeed in comprehensively realizing socio-ecological justice or climate justice, because their thinking, behavior and attitude are at the same time characterized by repeated failure due to freedom, sinfulness and structural human guilt. A redeemed creation will only be realized through God's saving action. RE thus moves between determinism and hope of change, it initiates a preliminary practice that is completed through God. At the same time, RE nudges a refigurative practice as a repetitive creation of a utopian present in a dynamic society.[27]

4.3 *Between Self-Purpose and Functionalization*

As already outlined, ESD tends to reduce education instrumentally to the accomplishment of future tasks. The term "Education *for* Sustainable Development" points to that. Theologically and in terms of RE, this functionalization of education can be rejected with reference to the openness and foreignness of future tasks as well as with reference to the eschatological proviso. And yet, a political religious ESD asks about the potential of religion to enable adolescents to deal with the challenges of the multiple crises. Especially with regard to spiritual resources, this tension between self-purpose and functionalization can be clarified. Spirituality might empower us to deal with environmental catastrophes although it does not solely have the function of

26 Cf. Kuckartz, *Nicht Hier, Nicht Jetzt;* Entzian, *Denn sie tun nicht, was sie wissen;* Kruse, *Vom Handeln zum Wissen.*

27 Cf. Deflorian, *Transformative Bewegungen?*, p. 219.

strengthening the resilience[28] of believers. With regard to the political dimension of religion and RE, the question also arises to what extent religion can be functionalized for political purposes. Thus, both remain: the possibility of being able to cope with present and future tasks in a more powerful and participatory way through religion and RE, and at the same time the danger of instrumentalizing religion through this. The harmonization of spirituality or mysticism and politics represents a basic tension of political theology and political religious ESD.[29]

4.4 *Between Truth Claim and Suspicion of Ideology*

Even if Christianity, in its self-understanding, no longer exclusively possesses the absolute truth, it still has a claim to truth that it can normatively bring into political religious ESD. In this way, it can, for example, relativize capitalist claims to absoluteness and break through structures that are supposedly without any alternative, which means that Christianity can certainly be seen as having ideology-critical potential. At the same time, this claim to truth raises suspicion at Christianity itself for being ideological. Thus, the dominion or "mastery over nature" interpretation of Genesis plays a significant role in the millennia-long exploitation of creation.[30] Only through constant self- and ideology-critical reflection can absolutist truth claims be avoided. This self- and ideology-critical reflection refers to theology, to Christian tradition, but also to the role of the RE-teacher and one's own religious practice. Political religious ESD must therefore deal with the tension between utopias of a good creation for all, which draw their visionary power from precisely this claim to truth, and its own ideological entanglements.

28 Cf. on the intertwining of the concept of resilience and neoliberalism Graefe, *Resilienz im Krisenkapitalismus*. "While the concept of resilience, as it is used today in neoliberal discourse, makes resilience an individual, learnable competence of individuals that enables them to survive in catastrophe, for Metz historical resilience means precisely the common struggle for all people to be able to be subjects. The decisive difference here is the link between becoming a subject and solidarity": Lis, *Subjektwerdung unter neoliberalen Bedingungen*, p. 288.

29 Cf. Sölle, *Mystik und Widerstand*; Kreutzer, *Mystik als Widerstand*.

30 Cf. Vogt, *Christliche Umweltethik*, pp. 190–204.

5 Refigurative Religious Education in a Monastery

In the previous chapters, I have highlighted that an ESD that is primarily strategically and formally oriented needs to be refined in terms of content. The outlined dilemmas of a political religious ESD also made it clear that these cannot be resolved theoretically, but must rather be dealt with in concrete practice. The following example of a monastery garden will therefore be used to illustrate how a political religious ESD can become concrete.[31]

At the beginning of 2020, the German Federal Minister for the Environment awarded the Capuchin monastery garden in Münster a special prize of the UN Decade on Biological Diversity,[32] recognizing the close link between social and ecological aspects of the monastery garden. In the middle of the city, the monastery is creating a biodiverse oasis that is a place of learning, encounter and recreation for the city's population. In addition, the monastery garden is managed inclusively by involving people with disabilities in the design and maintenance of the garden. But the experiences opened up by the monastery garden extend beyond biodiversity and social togetherness, for monastic life is also reflected there, as it also provides the nutritional basis for the monastery. This can lead to simple winter food, but also to surprisingly varied meals, as I was able to experience myself as a guest. In the middle of the week there was roast venison, donated by a forester from fallen game. The roast was prepared by a former hotel chef who prefers the monastery kitchen to the noble but hectic restaurant business. A life of poverty, living off what nature or fellow human beings give, can thus also be very opulent. Material poverty, as practiced by the Capuchins, goes hand in hand with a good life for employees and the urban population as well. The monastery garden can thus be a starting point to get to know the lived poverty, community and spirituality of the Capuchins. For a Christian understanding of poverty, as it exists especially in the mendicant orders does not primarily aim at a sufficiency-based lifestyle that is ethically justified, but has a spiritual focus that understands poverty as freedom for God and the message of God's Kingdom. But at the same time, such a radical life as an other-place is also a deeply critical foil for social logics, routines and normalities and thus has political implications.

What can be learned through political religious ESD in this place? On the one hand, the garden is open every day for the citizens as an ecological and spiritual oasis that they experience on an individual basis. Visitors will find spiritual (Franciscan) impulses in the garden, e.g. from the Canticle of the Sun of

31 Cf. Gärtner, *Klima*, pp. 138–42.

32 Spindler, *Vereinte Nationen*.

St. Francis. On the other hand, spiritual gardening courses for children, young people and adults are offered in cooperation with the Nature and Biodiversity Conservation Union (NABU) and the Institute for Theological Zoology. The offers are thus not exclusively aimed at Christian visitors, but at the heterogeneous public. The garden can thus become a meeting place: a meeting place of people, but also of Christian tradition and post-secular society, where sustainable ways of life can be sought and discussed together. The monastery garden and monastic life can be experienced as a heterotopia in a non-sustainable, capitalist society. The Capuchins lead a life that is good for them, sustainable, in community with each other and with nature, wanting to be free for God and the needs and concerns of fellow human beings. The monastery can be interpreted as a place of transformative, sustainable community that draws from a tradition that is thousands of years old. This life is provocative not only through its vow of poverty, but also by defying hegemonic aspirations for individualization und entrepreneurial acting. Instead of a bricolage identity, a lifelong vow of *stabilitas loci* is chosen.[33] Renouncing material wealth does not only represent renunciation, but also liberates for social, ecological and spiritual wealth. Transformation research emphasizes the relevance of such sustainable forms of life, even if they exist in the niches of society. For it is there that alternative forms of life would be discovered or preserved, which can be inspiring for a sustainable transformation society. But can this radical otherness, this monastic heterotopia be productively introduced into learning processes, since too much foreignness can also prevent learning processes?

The monastery garden is an encouraging example of how sustainable living can succeed. Encouraging learning settings are more likely to lead to learning successes than so-called "disaster didactics"[34], which can lead to reactance. In addition, visiting a monastery garden follows principles of holistic learning. The garden invites to discover and marvel at biodiversity and is a local place of sustainable living situated in the lifeworld. The ecological practice is impressive, possibly detached from its religious context. Accordingly, nature conservation associations are also offering learning arrangements here. But the monastery garden can open a bridge to spiritual perception and religious traditions as well. Thus, low-threshold offers for spiritual gardening are made for young people, and the religious roots of the monastery community

33 The innovative function of monasteries was already underlined by Johan Baptist Metz when he described them as productive role models of the church, which, however, are themselves always faced with the challenge of radically and consistently living the discipleship of Christ (Cf. Metz, *Zeit der Orden?*, p. 10).

34 Gagel, *Untiefen der Katastrophendidaktik*.

can also be experienced through participation in liturgy, prayer or pastoral opportunities—and this not in a purely cognitive mode, but through (voluntary) participation in a lived spiritual practice. In the monastery garden, it is thus possible to learn on a bodily-aesthetic or spiritual-liturgical level how sustainable life is lived in religious tradition.

But is a visit to a monastery garden interesting at all for children and young people today? Doesn't monastic life stand in such stark contrast to the lifeworld of adolescents that the sustainable life of the Capuchins cannot be a model for sustainable life outside the monastery walls? To what extent can a visit to the monastery garden therefore enable sustainable thinking and action?

Such a learning setting cannot be designed as model learning or learning by example, according to which the pupils learn about a sustainable way of life during their visit to the monastery, which they should imitate or adapt. This is because the Capuchin way of life contrasts with society in many ways. For example, it is based centrally on the *stabilitas loci*, which is diametrically opposed to the fragmented, fluid and individualistic lifestyles of most milieus.[35] In addition, pitfalls are known from diverse RE research on (biographical) learning on models. For example, "great" unattainable role models often offer little orientation for young people. These role models are too alien, too strenuous and often too moral for adolescents to want to emulate them. However, adolescents often deal productively with other people's biographies and life plans if conflicts or difficult dilemma situations are accessible.[36] They open up cognitive dissonances and areas of identification for their own searchings, so that experiences of difference can become relevant for their own lives.[37] A political religious ESD should therefore also question monastic life for possible points of conflict, failure and dilemmas. Precisely because sustainable other-places are part of an unsustainable society, they are in tension with this society both structurally-institutionally and biographically-individually. For students, it is important to perceive that religious orders also experience a "complex layering of asynchronies"[38] that produce diverse "experiences of irritation"[39]. Monastic forms of life face the challenge of "facing these conflicts and practicing living with dissonance"[40]. In doing so, dilemma situations can

35 This is also a central challenge for the religious orders, which are looking for new, more flexible social forms in the face of shrinking membership (Cf. Engel, *Jetztzeit der Orden*, p. 348).

36 Cf. Mendl, *Modelle—Vorbilder—Leitfiguren.*

37 Cf. Lindner, *In Kirchengeschichte verstrickt.*

38 Bucher, *Die Ordensgemeinschaften*, p. 18.

39 Bucher, *Die Ordensgemeinschaften*, p. 19.

40 Engel, *Das Andere*, p. 84.

become apparent that are also accessible to learners. Religious also study and work beyond the walls of the monastery. How can the demands of study and work, e.g. with regard to digitalization and internationalization, be combined with a resource-poor life? What can be done when the financial resources are not sufficient to renovate buildings to make them more energy-efficient? Or when the cherished monastery facilities are too large for the shrinking community and vacancy also entails ecological costs? At these and comparable dilemmas and questions, the boundaries between the monastery as a sustainable religious other-place and the non-sustainable living environments of young people dissolve. At these points it becomes clear that a sustainable life in a non-sustainable society is hardly possible. Monastic life is also entangled in different social, economic, ecological and religious logics. Therefore, even monastic life and monastic gardens cannot ultimately be interpreted as a prefiguration of a sustainable society, but rather as a refiguration, as the constant attempt to live sustainably in a non-sustainable society. "The existence of the order under postmodern conditions would then be understood as a vita consecrata situalis [...]. The first task of such a vita consecrata situalis would be to look for best-practice places where a different order of things can already be seen here and now."[41] The monastery garden described could be such a place where a sustainable order of things becomes perceptible. On the one hand, this view is entirely consistent with the described spirit of eschatological hope that permeates a theology of sustainability: "Another world is possible!" On the other hand, such a situational and at the same time refigurative practice offers RE connecting factors. For monastic life itself faces the second described field of tension between determinism and hope for change (chapter 4.2), in that the religious keep trying to live differently in the non-sustainable structures of this world. In the monastery, students can recognize that religious find orientation and hope in the messianic message of the Kingdom of God, of a good creation aiming at redemption. They strive for a different, good life, and at the same time they can fail again and again. The Capuchins have to figure out again and again, contextually, situationally and also biographically, how such a life is possible in a non-sustainable society. If it is thus possible to engage in conversation with Christians about these tensions and dilemmas in religious other-places such as the monastery, then these become places where political religious ESD is initiated in the form of a refigurative RE.

41 Engel, *Jetztzeit der Orden*, p. 348.

References

Acosta, Alberto: "Das 'Buen Vivir': Die Schaffung einer Utopie," in: *Juridikum*, (4.2009), pp. 219–223.

Becker, Joshua: *The More of Less: Finding the Life You Want Under Everything You Own*. Hove: Joosr Ltd 2016.

Blühdorn, Ingolfur/Felix Butzlaff/Michael Deflorian/Daniel Hausknost/Mirijam Mock (eds.): *Nachhaltige Nicht-Nachhaltigkeit: Warum die ökologische Transformation der Gesellschaft nicht stattfindet*. Bielefeld: Transcript 2019, http://www.transcript-verlag.de/978-3-8376-4516-3.

Bucher, Rainer: "Die Ordensgemeinschaften in der aktuellen Transformationskrise der katholischen Kirche: Vortrag am 20. November 2012 beim Österreichischen Ordenstag in Wien-Lainz," in: *Ordensnachrichten* 51 (6.2012), pp. 17–32.

Carver, Courtney: *Soulful Simplicity: How Living with Less Can Lead to So Much More*. New York: Tarcher Perigee, op. 2017.

De Haan, Gerhard/Georg Kamp: *Nachhaltigkeit und Gerechtigkeit*. Berlin, Heidelberg: Springer 2008). https://doi.org/10.1007/978-3-540-85492-0, 240 [accessed 13.09.2019].

Deflorian, Michael: "Transformative Bewegungen? Nischenaktivismus zwischen Management und Überwindung der sozial-ökologischen Krise," in: Ingolfur Blühdorn et al. (eds.), *Nachhaltige Nicht-Nachhaltigkeit: Warum die ökologische Transformation der Gesellschaft nicht stattfindet*. Bielefeld: Transcript 2019), pp. 205–226.

Engel, Ulrich: "Das Andere in der alltäglichen Ordnung ansichtig machen: Zur Pastoral der Orden in einer säkularen/religionsaffinen Welt," in: *Ordenskorrespondenz* 54 (1.2013), pp. 83–86.

Engel, Ulrich: "Jetztzeit der Orden: Plädoyer für eine 'Vita consecrata situalis' unter postmodernen Bedingungen," in: *Ordenskorrespondenz* 54 (3.2013), pp. 339–352.

Entzian, Annett: *Denn sie tun nicht, was sie wissen: Eine Studie zu ökologischem Bewusstsein und Handeln*, Transformationen Band 2, München: Oekom 2015).

Euler, Peter: "Nachhaltigkeit und Bildung: Plädoyer für ein sachhaltiges Verstehen herrschender Widersprüche," in: *Krisen- und Transformationsszenarios: Frühkindpädagogik, Resilienz & Weltaktionsprogramm*, Umweltdachverband GmbH, Forum edition Jahrbuch (ed.), Wien: Forum Umweltbildung 2014), pp. 167–174.

Flanders, Laura: "At Thatcher's Funeral, Bury TINA, Too," https://www.thenation.com/article/archive/thatchers-funeral-bury-tina-too/ [accessed 05.05.2020].

Gagel, Walter: "Untiefen der Katastrophendidaktik: Von der Ambivalenz des Begriffs 'Schlüsselprobleme', Politische Bildung", in: *Beiträge zur wissenschaftlichen Grundlegung und zur Unterrichtspraxis* 27 (2.1994), pp. 44–57.

Gärtner, Claudia: *Klima, Corona und das Christentum: Religiöse Bildung für nachhaltige Entwicklung in einer verwundeten Welt*. Bielefeld: Transcript 2020.

Graefe, Stefanie: *Resilienz im Krisenkapitalismus*. Bielefeld: transcript 2020.

Habermas, Jürgen: "Vorpolitische Grundlagen des demokratischen Rechtsstaates?", in: *Dialektik der Säkularisierung: Über Vernunft und Religion*, Jürgen Habermas/Florian Schuller (eds), Freiburg im Breisgau: Herder [7]2007.

Huckle, John/Arjen E. J. Wals: "The UN Decade of Education for Sustainable Development: Business as Usual in the End," in: *Environmental Education Research* 21 (3.2015): pp. 491–505, 500, https://doi.org/10.1080/13504622.2015.1011084 [accessed 14.11.2019].

Ideland, Malin: *The Eco-Certified Child: Citizenship and Education for Sustainability and Environment*. Cham: Springer International Publishing 2019), https://doi.org/10.1007/978-3-030-00199-5, 136 [accessed 07.12.2020].

Ideland, Malin/Claes Malmberg: "Governing 'Eco-Certified Children' Through Pastoral Power: Critical Perspectives on Education for Sustainable Development," in: *Environmental Education Research* 21, no. 2, 173–182, https://doi.org/10.1080/13504622.2013.879696 [accessed 07.12.2020].

Kehren, Yvonne: *Bildung für nachhaltige Entwicklung: Zur Kritik eines pädagogischen Programms*. Baltmannsweiler 2016.

Kluwick, Ursula/Evi Zemanek (eds.): *Nachhaltigkeit Interdisziplinär: Konzepte, Diskurse, Praktiken Ein Kompendium*, Wien/Köln/Weimar: utb Kulturwissenschaft/Böhlau/Vandenhoek&Ruprecht 2019.

Kondō, Marie: *The Life-Changing Magic of Tidying up: The Japanese Art of Decluttering and Organizing*, 1. American ed., Berkeley: Ten Speed Press 2014.

Kreutzer, Ansgar: "Mystik als Widerstand—Das Emanzipationspotenzial von Dorothee Sölles Politisch-Mystischer Theologie unter den Bedingungen 'Entgrenzter' Arbeit," in: Claudia Gärtner/Jan-Hendrik Herbst (eds.), *Kritisch-Emanzipatorische Religionspädagogik: Diskurse zwischen Theologie, Pädagogik und Politischer Bildung*. Wiesbaden: Springer 2020, pp. 273–290.

Kruse, Lenelis: "Vom Handeln zum Wissen—Ein Perspektivwechsel für eine Bildung für nachhaltige Entwicklung," in: *Bildung für nachhaltige Entwicklung: Aktuelle theoretische Konzepte und Beispiele praktischer Umsetzung*, Norbert Pütz/Martin K. W. Schweer/Niels Logemann (eds.), 1st, New ed., Psychologie und Gesellschaft 11, Frankfurt a. M: Peter Lang GmbH Internationaler Verlag der Wissenschaften 2013, pp. 31–57.

Kuckartz, Udo: "Nicht Hier, Nicht Jetzt, Nicht Ich—Über die symbolische Bearbeitung eines ernsten Problems," in: *KlimaKulturen: Soziale Wirklichkeiten Im Klimawandel*, Harald Welzer/Hans-Georg Soeffner/Dana Giesecke (eds.), *Sozialwissenschaften 2010*. Frankfurt a. M.: Campus Verl. 2010, pp. 144–160, https://content-select.com/media/moz_viewer/519cc3ff-8178-484a-831e-29115dbbeaba#chapter=177035&page=1 [accessed 29.04.2020].

Lindner, Konstantin: *In Kirchengeschichte verstrickt: Zur Bedeutung biographischer Zugänge für die Thematisierung kirchengeschichtlicher Inhalte im Religionsunterricht,* Arbeiten zur Religionspädagogik 31, Göttingen: V&R Unipress 2007 (also: Regensburg, Univ., Diss., 2006).

Lis, Julia: "Subjektwerdung unter neoliberalen Bedingungen. Politische Theologie im Kampf um das Humane", In: Hans-Gerd Janßen/Julia D. E. Prinz/Michael J. Rainer (eds.), *Theologie in gefährdeter Zeit. Stichworte von nahen und fernen Weggefährten für Johann Baptist Metz zum 90. Geburtstag,* Berlin/Münster: Lit-Verlag 2018, pp. 285–288.

Mendl, Hans: *Modelle—Vorbilder—Leitfiguren: Lernen an außergewöhnlichen Biografien,* Religionspädagogik innovativ 8, Stuttgart: Verlag W. Kohlhammer 2015.

Metz, Johann Baptist: *Glaube in Geschichte und Gesellschaft: Studien zu einer praktischen Fundamentaltheologie,* 5. Aufl., unveränd. Nachdr. der 4. Aufl. 1984, Welt der Theologie, Mainz: Matthias-Grünewald-Verl. 1992.

Metz, Johann Baptist: *Zeit der Orden? Zur Mystik und Politik der Nachfolge.* Freiburg: Herder [6]1986.

Prescher, Thomas: *Das Nachhaltigkeitsdogma: Wie wir lassen, was wir tun sollten, Versorgung gestalten.* Stuttgart: Kohlhammer 2019.

Pufé, Iris: *Nachhaltigkeit,* 3., überarbeitete und erweiterte Auflage, utb 8705. Konstanz/München: UVK Verlagsgesellschaft mbH; UVK/Lucius 2017, http://www.utb-studi-e-book.de/9783838587059 [accessed 26.05.2021].

Reuter, Ingo: "Fridays for Future"—Über Klimaschwankungen Im öffentlichen Diskurs angesichts des Widerstandes junger Menschen gegen den Totalitarismus der Sachzwänge," in: *Zeitschrift für Pädagogik und Theologie* 72 (3.2020): pp. 312–323, 322, https://doi.org/10.1515/zpt-2020-0035 [accessed 18.12.2020].

Smit, Harma-Mae: "Purpose-Driven Purging Minimalism Is Not the New Christian Approach to Managing Possessions," in: *Touchstone: A Journal of Mere Christianity* 32 (5.2019), pp. 42–45, http://www.touchstonemag.com/ [accessed 15.02.2021].

Sölle, Dorothee: *Mystik und Widerstand: "Du Stilles Geschrei",* Hamburg: Hoffmann und Campe [5]1999.

Spindler, Beate: "Vereinte Nationen zeichnen Klostergarten der Kapuziner aus," http://www.kapuziner.de/nachrichten/nachricht-einzelansicht/news/vereinte-nationen-zeichnen-klostergarten-der-kapuziner-aus.html?tx_news_pi1%5Bcontroller%5D=News&tx_news_pi1%5Baction%5D=detail&cHash=2056d90dfd936642a3ea1feff11f42a2 [accessed 20.03.2020].

UN, Transforming Our World: The Agenda 2030 for Sustainable Development A/RES/70/1 (2015), https://sustainabledevelopment.un.org/content/documents/21252030%20Agenda%20for%20Sustainable%20Development%20web.pdf [accessed 15.02.2021].

UNESCO, "Framework for the Implementation of Education for Sustainable Development (ESD) Beyond 2019," 2020, Annex II, Art. 4,8f [accessed 07.12.2020].

UNESCO, *Education 2030. Incheon Declaration and Framework for Action for the Implementation of Sustainable Development Goal 4* (Incheon, Republic of Korea, 2015).

UNESCO, Education for Sustainable Development, https://en.unesco.org/themes/education-sustainable-development [accessed 26.05.2021].

Vogt, Markus: *Christliche Umweltethik: Grundlagen und zentrale Herausforderungen.* Freiburg im Breisgau: Herder 2021.

With the Coronavirus Pandemic at the Crossroads: Reflections of Czech Students

Petr Jandejsek

Abstract

The article explores the coronavirus pandemic as a potential trigger of substantial changes in climate protection. In particular, it sees the promise of slowing down. It argues that the Covid-19 pandemic helps some of us realize in a unique way that our common home is endangered, and the experience of lockdown brings hope that achieving significant changes towards improving the environment could perhaps be realistic. Drawing on essays written by Czech students of social work and theology in spring 2020 and other sources (e.g., Jon Sobrino and Karel Čapek) the article finds possibilities for sharing Christian hope in a world of despair.

Keywords

Coronavirus; Czech students; faith; environment; transformation

Since its outbreak in 2020 the coronavirus pandemic has been generally regarded as a crisis which damages many aspects of human life, be they health, family, work, education, culture, or religion.[1] Unprecedented emergency measures, such as hard lockdowns, have also raised expectations that unquestioned patterns of behavior with implications for social and climate justice could eventually change. A temporary reduction of air pollution seems to point in this direction. Can the pandemic play an important role and become a reminder of an "urgent challenge to protect our common home", which Pope Francis expressed in his encyclical *Laudato sì*?[2] I want to argue that the Covid-19 pandemic has helped some of us realize in a unique way that our common home is endangered, and the experience of lockdown has brought hope that achieving significant changes towards improving the environment could perhaps be realistic.

1 This paper has been supported by Charles University Research Centre program No. 204052.
2 Pope Francis, *Laudato Si'*, art. 13.

 | DOI:10.30965/9783657795314_012

The key resources for the chapter are essays by Czech students written shortly after the pandemic had broken out. In March 2020 I became involved in an essay challenge proposed by St Chrysostom Orthodox Research Group under the title "How to respond to coronavirus faithfully?" Prospective authors were invited to "share some helpful thoughts and attitudes, to help ourselves rise up from the struggle for self-preservation which has paralyzed our spiritual forces."[3] I consulted a number of essays at the Jabok Institute of Social Pedagogy and Theology in Prague, Czech Republic.[4] They offered a striking collection of ideas. On the background of the then situation of lockdown the essays interwove reflections on the students' personal perspectives as well as the perspective of the whole society; they covered issues of practical mutual support as well as state politics, and they expressed fear of death as well as hope that the post-Covid world will be changed.

I will first introduce some facets of the students' essays, paying special attention to their intuition that the pandemic will stimulate transformation. However, that hope could be considered unwarranted or even naïve since the students insufficiently take into account the real socio-economic impacts of pandemic. Thus, secondly, some observations from a long-term research project "Life during pandemic" in the Czech Republic will be provided. On the background of deterioration exposed and deepened by the corona crisis and because of it, I will try to rehabilitate hope in the third section. Making an analogy with a story by Karel Čapek, I will propose a framework in which the pandemic as a trigger needs to be prophetically interpreted. Then there is an opportunity that the enforced temporary slowdown caused by the pandemic will transform into real and effective change for the benefit of the climate. Theological resources for this interpretation of the pandemic will be discussed in the final part. The students' "wrestle with God" shows both the way in which the pandemic has shaken their faith and also deepened their trust in the divine mystery.[5]

3 See the announcement of competition: Sevastyanova, *Theological essay challenge*.

4 Altogether seventeen students engaged in writing from March to May 2020. Fifteen of them were students of Jabok, and the remaining two studied at two different theological faculties of Charles University. All essays are available at Jabok Institute website: *Studenti píší na téma*. All but one are in Czech.

5 I would like to express my gratitude to the participants of the Liberation Theology Workshop: *Doing Climate Justice* organized by the Centre for Liberation Theologies, KU Leuven, in October 2020. Their insightful comments on the first version of this paper helped me elaborate it significantly. On several occasions, I quote from their comments.

1 Desire for a Slowdown that Will Last

In this part I will look at the corona crisis and the lockdown through the eyes of the students. Their contribution will be seen as a source of hope that the current corona crisis may trigger personal, social, and environmental changes that will last. First, I will quote a poem which one student included in her essay. It conclusively captures tension between fear and expectations in those first weeks of the lockdown.

> Jsme zklidnění a zpomalení
> tráva i stromy si mohou tiše vydechnout.
> Bez ptaní a dovolení vešel do našich životů
> zasel otázky a pootevřel bránu k smrti.
> Nervózně čekáme, až odejde
> a přitom se modlíme, aby přetrvalo
> to, co jsme v sobě najednou objevili
> tu jiskřičku věčnosti náhle probuzenou.
>
> We stay calm and slowed down.
> Grass and trees may sigh with relief in silence.
> It came into our lives without asking permission,
> Sowed the questions and half opened the gate of death.
> Nervously we wait until it leaves
> And still we pray that something remained with us:
> The spark of eternity, suddenly awake, we found inside us.

The poem reflects the experience of the pandemic and lockdown. It praises enforced slowdown and considers it positive for humans and nature alike. All may "sigh with relief". The pace of life has slowed down, fewer people are traveling, and less shopping has led to reduced consumption. The poem contains traces of desire to return to a previous life. However, also knowledge about our finitude is delivered by the experience of death. Strongly present is the feeling that, thanks to the crisis, we have glimpsed what transcends everyday concern and interest ("the spark of eternity"). Overall, there is a kind of spirituality of calming prevailing in the poem, which stands in contrast to the modern stress on progress.

The essays elaborate on what is only indicated in the poem. Reading the essays, I will focus on three aspects: feelings, complaints, and also that of looking for ways forward. In a sense, the poem and essays represent a path from the shock of presence to re-orientation in the future.

Each essay reveals the uniqueness of its author, his or her personality, forms of faith and motivation for writing. Students express their desires, what they mourn and long for. Typically, this level is not much elaborated and has to be searched for in short remarks and sighs.

"It came out of the blue."[6] Many essays reveal the experience of being surprised and caught off-guard. In the middle of everyday life something unexpected arrived and forced us to react. For the generation of millennials, it is the experience of finally coming up against one's limits for the first time. We may speculate that a similar experience of shock occurred after the bombing of Hiroshima or 9/11 in the U.S. In any case, for some students that was the reason for writing an essay. "I felt like locked in a cage", writes a student describing how she felt. The critical problem was not just the official recommendation to stay at home but most of all the uncertainty of how long it would last and how dangerous the situation was.

The next set of expressions regards the change of speed which is a topic strongly present also in the poem. "The world has stopped and heard the silence." Not that "the sound of silence" would have been absent before. But we hardly find time to listen to silence in the rumbling of day-to-day business. We may notice it only when we have time to listen. What is meant by the sound of silence? It ranges from God to "the important things in life". Unexpected time to stop and listen also enabled some to uncover their relation to nature: "Let us stop and search for the green".[7] Whereas coronavirus forced us to stop and soothe, the resulting silence is not necessarily void. It recalls the biblical prophet Elijah overhearing God's voice in a gentle whisper (1 Kgs 19:12).

Finally, the feeling of ambiguousness comes to the fore face to face with the reality of Covid-19. I could read: "Coronavirus showed us how vulnerable we are", but also "The coronavirus crisis teaches us to maintain our green planet". Something similar was present also in the poem: "We wait till it leaves and still we pray that something remained with us". Now the crisis as a pedagogue both uncovers our unpreparedness and instructs us in a unique way. With respect to the above-mentioned demand to stop, the crisis teaches us to maintain the environment by refraining from acting. Presumably, the students want to emphasize the need to refrain from that which is superfluous and harms the Earth. While this voice commendably calls for voluntary modesty, it is

---

6 While quoted expressions are taken from the essays verbatim (my translation) I decided to keep them anonymous and not refer to particular authors. Generally, my intention is to give an overview illustrated by several examples.

7 Bess Brooks, a participant at the Liberation Theology Workshop, 2020, commented on the experience of the beauty of nature as follows: "One of the harsh paradoxes of the current situation is that humankind is suffering terribly while creation, in some respects, continues to thrive. I was very conscious of the cherry tree in our garden blooming profusely during lockdown, almost in contradiction to my own 'plight'. Of course, this overlooks the bigger picture—the devastation caused by our collective behavior/climate chase".

insufficiently specific in terms of who should refrain from what. I will come back to the problem of unequal responsibility in the third section.

The second level of reading is what liberation theology calls "ethical indignation". Objects of accusations are more than one. There is a peculiar kind of impersonal accusation levelled against the coronavirus crisis itself: "The coronavirus crisis left some people in uncertainty and depression." I read this as a kind of outcry or lamentation. It is as if merely drawing attention to the misfortune helps us to remain human and compassionate. We may not be able to change things but we still witness that human beings are endangered. I find the same idea in Jon Sobrino. When he asks how the sick civilization can be re-humanized, he first suggests to give the poor and victims back their names.[8] By returning names to the victims instead of taking them as numbers or altogether disregarding them we claim their existence. By returning names we return them their dignity in the world of silence and disdain. One year after the beginning of the pandemic it is important to speak of the victims—be they the departed or any others affected by Covid-19—in a human, not just a statistical sort of way. A minute's silence to commemorate the victims of coronavirus held on 22nd March, 2021 was a chance to recover our humanity.[9]

When it comes to the issues of environment and social affairs it is first of all us humans that one essay charges with exploitation and neglect: "Nature is exploited. Drinking water is not available to all. We cannot see the blue sky because of smog." Elsewhere we read an explanation: "For long we have misinterpreted our role of stewards of creation." The general charges are sometimes more explicitly oriented at the power holders. They are accused of "the increase of social problems and unemployment". They caused the situation where we "lived in times when we had no time to stop and look back, we were always caught in stress and hurry". In addition, they are charged with "ridiculing of Greta Thunberg's plea". I will return to the role of power holders later in the chapter.

Finally, the third level of reading traces the ways in which the students interpreted the current crisis as an opportunity and chance. Some realize that without a massive impulse like Covid-19 we would hardly be willing to change: "Something big had to come that stopped the planet." With satisfaction and hope someone uttered: "Voices calling for change were heard at last." The environmental issues stand at the forefront, both in regard to the calming down of life and as a legacy of the experienced crisis: "Surprisingly it helped nature a lot", "Let the governments not subsidize companies that pollute the Earth".

8 Sobrino, *Eine kranke Zivilisation vermenschlichen.*

9 Cf. Dvořáková, *Minuta ticha za oběti pandemie.*

Students evaluate positively the role of shock which led to lockdown and had temporarily beneficial effects on the level of air pollution.

Development in the second half of 2020 shows a return to "normalcy". Carbon dioxide emissions have been increasing again, mainly due to the Chinese "dirty recovery".[10] There seems to be a significant finding here: it is futile to put hope merely in the shock generated by the pandemic. In order for the changes that occurred during the lockdown to be lasting, something more is needed.

However, there are other reasons to view the lockdown as an important period to learn from. Home office and home schooling allowed many people to spend more time at home with their families. Some students consider this a promising option for the future: "We lost time which we used to spend in jobs and we got time to be with our kids." This and also the experience of mutual support attracted many. They see it as a way of becoming more human: "People started to behave more like people, they became more human." The net of support comprised not only of kin but to some degree also the other: "Gradually people learned to pull together and cooperate; they helped one another including strangers".

Students generally agree that we cannot go back to the life we had before the crisis: "Maybe we will not return to where we were before."[11] Some students voice the need for a change of values: "Once the pandemic is over, we will have to reassess our present values." I want to deepen this insight and underline that to reassess the values only after the pandemic is too late. As demonstrated above in regard to climate protection there is a strong tendency to re-establish old patterns of behavior once things return to normal.

We have seen that students perceive the corona crisis as a kind of break, a healthy shock. They believe it may positively influence human and non-human beings alike and, generally, there is much to learn from it. Simply said, slowdown heals a too hectic lifestyle and healthily reduces the level of consumption. It also shows that abstention from acting is a path to face climate change. The other strong consequence of the corona crisis is re-humanization. In particular, the *homo economicus* changes back to a person, a human being in relations with his or her family and community. Restored humanity is also demonstrated by an interest in victims.

---

10 "After a steep drop in early 2020, global carbon dioxide emissions have rebounded strongly," IEA, https://www.iea.org.

11 The same idea was uttered by the Slovak president Čaputová: "We cannot go back to business as usual." Čaputová, *Potřebujeme globální soucit*. The speech with English subtitles is available on the same website.

However, there are important aspects of the pandemic that are missing on the horizon of the students' perception. When students call for a reduction in work and consumption, it is based on their situation. They do not take into account those who have limited revenues, limited access to financially rewarding work and public services, e.g., medical care and education. During and after the pandemic, these people are worse off. Roughly speaking it seems that the "sigh with relief" concerns only some people and some sectors of nature.[12] In the following section I will demonstrate this in detail. The point is not to downplay the hope which students shared. Rather, I want to offer a broader context in which the need for change becomes even clearer.

2 The Dark Side of the Corona Crisis

The poem contains these verses: "It came into our lives without asking for permission (...) and half opened the gate of death". The corona crisis brought fear, isolation, pain and loss. However, the poem and all the essays touched on the dark side of the pandemic only in passing.[13] In this chapter I want to argue that the pandemic has the potential to alert us that our common home is under threat and also that significant changes towards improving the environment could be realistic. So far, I have dealt mainly with the second goal using the students' essays. In this section I want to pay attention to the pains of our present that the crisis reveals and deepens. When the students predicted the future, they compared it to the pre-pandemic situation. Here I want to demonstrate that it is the pandemic itself that reveals the real social problems and, to some extent, the climate problems.

The plague of Covid-19 seems to be fair. But the reality is quite different. I will not deal with the medical but the social issues and limit myself to the

12 A little before the essays of the Czech students appeared, "A degrowth perspective on the coronavirus crisis" has been published, which formulated similar topics. Unlike the students, "A degrowth perspective" denies that the slowdown caused by the pandemic would be a desirable degrowth. "Instead, it's an example of why degrowth is needed; it shows the unsustainability and fragility of our current way of life". With the students—and President Čaputová, as will be shown later—it believes that "the response to Covid-19 has shown that degrowth is possible, because society (and the state) has demonstrated an ability to dramatically change the modus operandi in response to a major crisis": "A degrowth perspective on the coronavirus crisis."

13 This is not necessarily something to blame students for. They wrote their essays before the pandemic situation in the Czech Republic worsened rapidly in the second half of 2020.

context of the Czech Republic. According to the Czech research institute PAQ,[14] there are significant socio-economic impacts of the crisis that are distributed unequally. In what follows I utilize the results and comments of a PAQ long-term monitoring of life during pandemics. The research areas cover stability of work, impacts on households and household strategies.[15]

As for the stability of work, the least secure on the labor market is the position of those who are paid by their output or receive a part of their income as cash in hand. The pandemic has made them unemployed and economically inactive. Usually, they cannot make use of work compensation because these are designed for higher income workers (more than 400 Euros per month). Education is also proving to be an important factor. Higher unemployment has affected people with low levels of education whereas employees with university degrees have managed to return to full work activity more quickly.[16] Another factor is the amount of income. The crisis has considerably affected the lives of people from households with children who had an income below the median (less than half of Czech households). Forced labor restrictions without compensation most significantly affected people from households, which were already below the poverty line before the crisis. As regards the sectors of employment during autumn and winter 2020 the situation worsened especially for workers in the trade and services sector. In addition, as expected, working women encountered work restrictions (compensated and uncompensated) more often than men.

Regarding the impact on households, the PAQ research shows that one-seventh of Czechs live in households that, in the event of a loss of income, may be threatened by the absence of savings that will not last more than one month. This number corresponds approximately to the number of households under the relative income poverty line. These households face difficulties in living; they are more prone to debt or other problems. Researchers recognize that income poverty may actually be greater than official data show: in reporting, income is stated before any court ordered deduction for the repayment of

14 PAQ (Prokop Analysis and Quantitative Research) specializes in analyses and research in the areas of education, social problems and politics. In 2019 Daniel Prokop, the leading figure of PAQ, published an influential volume *Slepé skvrny*. Following Pierre Bourdieu (and also Mike Savage) with his distinction between the three types of capital—economic, social and cultural—Prokop described a new class structure of Czech society.

15 See the special website with research results: *Život během pandemie* (available in Czech).

16 The pandemic has also hampered equal educational opportunities which would enable children from disadvantaged families to achieve better education. It is estimated that 10,000 children dropped out of education in Spring 2020 as they were unable to take part in online schooling (cf. People in Need Czech Republic website).

debts; moreover, research does not include people living in hostels and shelters. As indicated above, the crisis has been more pronounced in households with children—partly because it includes single women who have lost a significant part of their income by switching to childcare allowance.

Following the decline in work activity and a drop in income, the same research indicates two negative tendencies for households. The first is an increase in debt and the threat of court ordered seizure of property. The second is a need to reduce consumption. While the first tendency directly threatens the household, the second may be reflected in a decline in domestic demand and thus a slowdown in the economy, which will lead to further shocks in the labor market.[17] These tendencies relate in particular to the groups already mentioned above. Roughly 13% of households are considering a loan from a bank or credit company or have problems repaying their liabilities. Further data show that the pandemic has exposed the vulnerability of the poor and exacerbated it. Whereas billionaires make money in a pandemic, low-income groups are losing their incomes and the scissors are widening.[18] This affects not only social justice, but also social cohesion and trust in democracy.

These research data materialize what students put very generally: "Coronavirus showed us how vulnerable we are." It is true that students called for solidarity with the victims of Covid-19 and for mutual support. The research data, however, expand the picture. Now it includes also those people stricken by social deterioration who remained "invisible" in the students' essays.

I still need to address the issue of climate change in regard to the pandemic. Above, I have already indicated that the beneficial effects of the lockdown on the level of air pollution were only temporary.[19] There is an even greater need for political voices that the fight against coronavirus needs to be linked to the pursuit of climate justice.[20] Although the European Recovery Pack for post-Covid-19 Europe requires fair climate transition, it is still under discussion regarding what kinds of changes will be considered green. Philippe Pochet believes that a related new socio-ecological contract should bring together questions of inequality, climate, and the digital economy. Drawing on Pierre

17 Concerns about the effects of reduced consumption go against the idea of students who saw a positive trend in reduced consumption during coronavirus. Of course, the problem is that the enforced reduction of consumption has been distributed unevenly, that is unjustly.

18 Gawlasová, *Bohatí jsou ještě bohatší.*

19 Cf. *COVID-19 measures have mixed impacts.*

20 Examples of initiatives pointing in this direction are For the Green Renewal of Slovakia of a Slovakian MEP Martin Hojsík (Kubala, Europoslanec Hojsík) and *Green Stimulus in the U.S., A Green Stimulus to Rebuild Our Economy.*

Charbonnier, he warns that these three aspects definitely do not have to go hand in hand. "There are other models—there is Biden's green capitalism or China's green surveillance society; some are more state-centric and some more market-led. It is by no means certain which of the competing visions of the transition will win."[21] The voices of students expressing hope for lasting change do not yet reflect reality. But they are on the side of those political initiatives, such as the Green New Deal and the new socio-ecological contract in the EU, that are striving for the same change, that is, so that previous patterns of behavior do not return.

The pandemic and lockdown have demonstrated that it all depends on political and economic decisions, be it social well-being of some segments of society and the level of air pollution. In the first case—as was demonstrated by PAQ research—what proved decisive was the degree of financial allowance. In the second case the suspension of manufacturing and the decrease in road traffic played a role. The question is whether more humane and fairer decisions will be made at the crossroads that the pandemic represents.

3 A Crisis with an Open End

In her apt speech on the occasion of the 75th anniversary of the founding of the United Nations the Slovak President Zuzana Čaputová expressed the same hope as the students. According to her, the pandemic opens up opportunity: "I would even dare to say that this pandemic crisis brought the best out of us".[22] In particular, she believes there is a lesson to be learned from Covid-19. Things unimaginable until then were suddenly possible. We were quickly able to change our behavior and work together in order to protect ourselves. "We can do it when it comes to other global threats (…) most notably the climate change, which is undoubtedly the greatest threat to our common future."[23] Non-standard time allows non-standard changes.

President Čaputová interprets the pandemic as a break. It opens space for significant positive resolutions as she—and the students—believe. The break by itself, however, does not guarantee the quality of the resolution, not even that any resolution will occur. There is also a possibility of the break being

21 Pochet, *A Socio-Ecological Contract.*

22 Čaputová, *Potřebujeme globální soucit.*

23 Čaputová, *Potřebujeme globální soucit.*

misused.[24] Conceptually this was developed by Naomi Klein.[25] Klein speaks about coronavirus capitalism and sees the current situation as another example of what happens when people are shocked, distracted, and disoriented. Certain political-economic groups are trying to take advantage of the situation and introduce drastic measures, which are normally unacceptable. They use moments of crisis—fear and chaos—and make such political and economic changes that benefit their accumulation of capital.[26]

In order to conceptualize the process of the response to the current crisis I suggest using a literary analogy. It is based on a story by Karel Čapek, an important Czech writer and playwright. His *Tales From Two Pockets* include one called "Murderous attack".[27] The story goes as follows (in my words): A venerable man, Mr. Tomsa, sits at home one evening listening to music. Suddenly someone fires at him from outside. The bullet misses him, but Mr. Tomsa experiences a shock. As an inexperienced person in these situations, he does not know what to do at first. Finally, he calls the police: "It's a scandal, shooting at a calm citizen out of the blue", he says, upset. After a while a policeman arrives. The policeman asks whom Mr. Tomsa suspects. Who might profit from his death? The question surprises him. "I have no enemy, I live for myself, I'm not involved in anything." The policeman leaves Mr. Tomsa alone. He regrets himself and laments the unjust world. Suddenly, however, the policeman's question makes him remember: recently he did a stupid thing to his friend. It initiates a process of self-reflection and repentance. Mr. Tomsa is sitting on bed having hard time. It is night and silence. Then in the morning he goes to the police station and asks the case to be dropped.

I understand the tale as an analogy to the discernment process that started in the pandemic. In many ways, it resembles the "journey" that students described in their essays. The "murderous attack" of the coronavirus brings shock and confusion. The attack by itself does not trigger reflection and change. In the story this comes about only after the policeman challenges Mr. Tomsa.

---

24 See, for example, the Czech Republic Supreme Audit Office news released in April 2021 stating that almost half of the increase in state budget expenditures was not related to the pandemic. This is contrary to how the state justified the increase in public spending. *Zpráva kontrolního úřadu.*

25 I am grateful to Dr Marion Grau participating at the Liberation Theology Workshop, 2020 for drawing my attention to Klein's work.

26 *Coronavirus Capitalism.* Klein introduced the concept of disaster capitalism in her book *The Shock Doctrine.* There she explored this deeply inhuman approach. Instead of mourning for victims of tragedies it welcomes opportunity for radical reforms. It drastically reduces social solidarity and massively invests in business for the benefit of few. It supports privatization of public goods and services, including health and education.

27 Čapek, *Vražedný útok.*

Strange as it may sound, the policeman plays the role of a prophet who asks critical questions and by this he opens a new reality. In the context of coronavirus the prophetic voices are represented by students ("we pray that something remained with us"), President Čaputová ("We can do it when it comes to other global threats, most notably the climate change"), or the degrowth initiative ("society has demonstrated an ability to dramatically change the modus operandi in response to a major crisis")—to name just a few.[28] As biblical tradition makes us aware, there come also false prophets, such as calamity capitalists to whom Naomi Klein drew attention. The interpretation of the pandemic is still at a crossroads. And who represents Mr. Tomsa in the pandemic story? It is those ("a venerable *man*") who say "I have no enemy, I live for myself, I'm not involved in anything". It is not the whole society indiscriminately but the power holders and decision makers who—like Mr. Tomsa—experience a changing encounter with an as yet unperceived reality.

The charming story by Čapek opens a more complex reading of the coronavirus crisis. As in the case of each analogy, this one is also incomplete. Certainly, it omits some important aspects of the present pandemic. Yet it includes that of the sacred silent night in which Mr. Tomsa underwent his transformation. In the last section I will focus on the spiritual sources for dealing with the pandemic as well as on how they are being transformed by the crisis.

4 Faith that Gives Birth to Hope

In the essays of the students, talk of God appears in roughly two forms. One form tries to "explain" the role of God whereas the other admits that the current conception of God is collapsing in crisis and proving insufficient. I will give examples of both.

There are attempts to see God as a behind-the-scenes actor: "It looked like a catastrophe but it was God who slowed down our world," and "God punished humankind with coronavirus because of our sins". It is a kind of rationalization justifying one's idea of God. But can we really think of God as one who sends disaster on people? The same idea, with only the opposite evaluation,

28 To them I add Pope Francis who says: "We are living during a historic moment, marked by difficult challenges, as we all know. The world is shaken by the crisis caused by the COVID-19 pandemic, which highlights yet an even bigger challenge: the socio-environmental crisis. And this requires us, all of us, to face a choice. The choice between what matters, and what doesn't. The choice between continuing to ignore the suffering of the poorest and to abuse our common home, our planet, or engaging at every level to transform the way we act." His Holiness Pope Francis, *Our moral imperative*.

appeared in another essay: "I accused God of what happened". Not only are these notions theologically problematic. But I find them quite unhelpful.

More students put emphasis on the ineffability of divine presence: "We squeeze God into our notions and thus we find simple solutions where there are not". The reality of the crisis overwhelms their religious imagination. Some continue to struggle and resemble the biblical Jacob wrestling with the Unknown (cf. Gen 32:24–32):[29] How can a good God allow this to happen? How can we see God's providence in this painful situation which even questions the very existence of God self? This is a struggle of faith motivated by the real experience of isolation and fear. I do not encounter a loss of faith in the essays. Rather, the reality of God gains a new practical sense: "God—not fear—has to be in the center". The experience of our limited ability to control coronavirus makes someone give up the hegemonic narratives of domination of nature: "We do not master the world and that leads to the trust in God". I believe these are important lessons the pandemic teaches us also for dealing with "an even bigger challenge: the socio-environmental crisis" (Pope Francis).

These two theological approaches—one of explaining God, the other struggling for faith on the background of suffering—can be further conceptualized using Jon Sobrino's distinction between European and Latin American theology.[30] When some students try to make sense of God in an adverse situation, they are close to the theology influenced by first Enlightenment. Shaped by Kant, this theology confronts the lack of meaning. The majority of students, however, do not seek in God primarily explanation but hope: hope against fear, hope that real and effective changes will occur. Their theology is that of the second Enlightenment. The world afflicted with misery calls for liberation that only makes a person free. Thus, the task of theology is not first to confront the absence of meaning, but to confront the reality of an inhuman world and transform it so that it may take on meaning.[31] "The first perspective leads to an effort to reconcile faith with the meaningless reality within the subject. The second believes reconciliation to be possible only if an attempt is made to solve the objective crisis", explains Sobrino.[32] Turning to God in search for meaning of the pandemic may serve our religious and intellectual appeasement. Does it,

29 Coincidently, this biblical passage, regarding the river called Jab(b)ok mentioned in the story, inspired the name of the Institute.

30 Sobrino, *Theological Understanding*.

31 Interestingly, Sobrino's criticism of European theology resembles Pope Francis' criticism of contemporary Gnosticism, for example, thinking faith separate from the flesh. Cf. Pope Francis, *Gaudete Et Exsultate*, art. 36–46.

32 Sobrino, *Theological Understanding*, p. 18.

however, suffice? When the world becomes an unsafe and chaotic place, faith is called to generate, first of all, hope and change.

Faith, as some students write about it ("We pray that something remained with us: the spark of eternity, suddenly awake, we found inside us."), has a typical feature. It is fragile, intimate. It is reminiscent of Elijah's encounter with God on Mount Horeb. There, the Lord appears to Elijah as a gentle whisper (cf. 1 Kgs 19:11–13). The shape of faith here described is what Czech theologian Tomáš Halík calls "timid piety". Halík believes it "denotes not only the style of piety of some Christians, but also the reserved attitude of a large part of the population in the Czech lands (and particularly influential and educated sections of society) towards ecclesial forms of Christianity".[33] Timid piety prefers apophatic God-talk. At first sight it may seem that such fragile faith insufficiently generates hope in times of crises, be it the pandemic or the climate crisis. And yet, there are examples of the opposite. In the difficult time of pre-war Czechoslovakia in 1938 Karel Čapek, often cited as an example of timid piety, wrote his Prayer for Truth in which he expresses hope that neighbor need not hate neighbor forever. Forty years later another representative of timid piety, Václav Havel, wrote: "Hope is simply not optimism. It's not the belief that something will turn out well, but the certainty that something will make sense—no matter how it turns out".[34]

The lockdown in 2020 overlapped with Lent and also the feast of Easter. One student commented on that in this way: "For me this Easter is different when compared to the previous years: most of all I think of hope and a challenge to change something". This chapter argued that the pandemic of coronavirus may bring hope for the wounded world, first because "it exposes our vulnerability and uncovers those false and superfluous certainties around which we have constructed our daily schedules, our projects, our habits and priorities" (Pope Francis' sermon on 27th March 2020), and second because we have experienced that previously unthinkable measures became possible very quickly. Ultimately this hope does not lie in the somewhat ambivalent phenomenon of the pandemic. It springs precisely from the mystery of Easter when life defeated death, the unthinkable has become a reality.

---

33 Halík, *Patience with God*, p. 63. The personalities of Czech history who are cited as examples of this piety, include Karel Havlíček, Karel Čapek, Tomáš Garrigue Masaryk, and Václav Havel.

34 Havel/Hvížďala, *Dálkový výslech*, p. 156–157. In Czech: "Naděje prostě není optimismus. Není to přesvědčení, že něco dobře dopadne, ale jistota, že má něco smysl—bez ohledu, jak to dopadne".

References

"A degrowth perspective on the coronavirus crisis," https://degrowth.info/en/blog/a-degrowth-perspective-on-the-coronavirus-crisis-2 [accessed 19.03.2020].

Čapek, Karel: "Vražedný útok," in: *Povídky z jedné a z druhé kapsy*. Praha: Československý spisovatel 1956), pp. 157–161. English translation: Karel Čapek, "Murderous Attack," in: *Tales From Two Pockets*, trans. by Norma Comrada, North Haven, CT: Catbird Press 1994.

Čaputová, Zuzana: "Potřebujeme globální soucit. Největší hrozbou je klimatická krize, řekla Čaputová v OSN," https://www.lidovky.cz/svet/potrebujeme-globalni-soucit-nejvetsi-hrozbou-je-klimaticka-krize-rekla-caputova-v-osn.A200923_210652_ln_zahranici_livs [accessed 23.09.2020].

"Coronavirus Capitalism—and How to Beat It," The Intercept, https://www.youtube.com/watch?v=niwNTI9Nqd8 [accessed 16.03.2020].

"COVID-19 measures have mixed impacts on the environment," European Environment Agency, https://www.eea.europa.eu/highlights/impact-of-covid-19-lockdown [accessed 18.01.2021].

Dvořáková, Petra: "Minuta ticha za oběti pandemie je šancí na návrat lidskosti," https://denikreferendum.cz/clanek/32486-minuta-ticha-zaobeti-pandemie-je-sanci-na-navrat-lidskosti [accessed 25.03.2021].

Gawlasová, Nicole: "Bohatí jsou ještě bohatší a chudých prudce přibývá. Pandemie přispívá k rozevírání příjmových nůžek v celém světě," Hospodářské noviny, https://archiv.ihned.cz/c1-66896750-bohati-jsou-jeste-bohatsi-a-chudych-prudce-pribyva-pandemie-prispiva-k-rozevirani-prijmovych-nuzek-v-celem-svete [accessed 22.03.2021].

Green Stimulus in the U.S. "A Green Stimulus to Rebuild Our Economy," Green Stimulus Proposal, https://medium.com/@green_stimulus_now/a-green-stimulus-to-rebuild-our-economy-1e7030a1d9ee [accessed 23.03.2020].

Halík, Tomáš: *Patience with God: The Story of Zacchaeus Continuing In Us*. New York: Doubleday 2009.

Havel, Václav/Karel Hvížďala: *Dálkový výslech: rozhovor s Karlem Hvížďalou*. Praha: Melantrich 1989.

IEA, https://www.iea.org/news/after-steep-drop-in-early-2020-global-carbon-dioxide-emissions-have-rebounded-strongly [accessed 19.03.2020].

Jabok Institute, "Studenti píší na téma 'Jak reagovat na koronavirus z hlediska víry?'", https://knihovna.jabok.cz/cs/koronavirus-a-vira [accessed 2.10.2020].

Klein, Naomi: *The Shock Doctrine: The Rise of Disaster Capitalism*. London: Penguin Books 2007. Czech translation: Naomi Klein, *Šoková doktrína: Vzestup kalamitního kapitalismu*, trans. Martina Knápková and Luděk Vacín. Praha: Argo/Dokořán 2010.

Kubala, Radek: "Europoslanec Hojsík: koronavirus déšť nepřinese, zelená transformace je nutná," Deník Referendum, https://denikreferendum.cz/clanek/31046-europoslanec-hojsik-koronavirus-dest-neprinese-zelena-transformace-je-nutna) [accessed 25.03.2021].

People in Need Czech Republic website: "Vyhlašujeme sbírku na pomoc českým dětem. Pomůžeme jim dohnat učivo, které zameškaly kvůli covidu," https://www.clovekvtisni.cz/vyhlasujeme-sbirku-na-pomoc-ceskym-detem-pomuzeme-jim-dohnat-ucivo-ktere-zameskaly-kvuli-covidu-7030gp [accessed 16.09.2020].

Pochet, Philippe: "A Socio-Ecological Contract for a Post-Pandemic Europe," Green European Journal, last modified February 4, 2021, https://www.greeneuropeanjournal.eu/a-socio-ecological-contract-for-a-post-pandemic-europe [accessed 04.02.2021].

Pope Francis, "Our moral imperative to act on climate change and three steps we can take," trans. by Elena Montrasio, TED Ideas Worth Spreading, https://www.ted.com/talks/his_holiness_pope_francis_our_moral_imperative_to_act_on_climate_change_and_3_steps_we_can_take/transcript [accessed 25.03.2021].

Pope Francis, Apostolic Exhortation *Gaudete Et Exsultate* of the Holy Father Francis on the Call to Holiness in Today's World. Rome 2018.

Pope Francis, Encyclical letter *Laudato Si'* of the Holy Father Francis on Care for Our Common Home. Rome 2015.

Prokop, Daniel: *Slepé skvrny: o chudobě, vzdělávání, populismu a dalších výzvách české společnosti / Blind spots: on poverty, education, populism and other challenges of Czech society*. Brno: Host 2019.

Sevastyanova, Olga: "Theological essay challenge," https://orthodoxresearchgroup.com/coronavirus-faithful-response-essay-challenge [accessed 02.10.2020].

Sobrino, Jon: "Eine kranke Zivilisation vermenschlichen," in: *Concilium 45 (1.2009), pp. 55–65. Czech translation: Jon Sobrino, "Duch dýchá otrávený vzduch," Getsemany 207 (léto 2009)*, https://www.getsemany.cz/node/2441 [accessed 02.10.2020].

Sobrino, Jon: "Theological Understanding in European and Latin American Theology," in: *The True Church and the Poor*. Maryknoll, N.Y.: Orbis Books 1984, pp. 7–38.

"Život během pandemie," https://zivotbehempandemie.cz/destabilizace-prace (available in Czech) [accessed 25.03.2021].

"Zpráva kontrolního úřadu: Téměř polovina navýšení výdajů státního rozpočtu nesouvisela s pandemií," Český rozhlas, https://www.irozhlas.cz/zpravy-domov/nejvyssi-kontrolni-urad-pandemie-koronavirus-cesko-hospodareni-vyrocni-zprava_2104060813_dok [accessed 06.04.2021].

PART III

(Future) Imaginaries

Implementing an Ecology of Hope for Greater Climate Justice

Susana Vilas Boas

Abstract

The theme of ecology has been strongly debated in various social, political and religious spheres. In Christianity, the theme gained a greater dimension with Pope Francis' Encyclical Letter Laudato Si' (2015), where the care for Nature is presented as a humanizing element and as a meeting point of God with the human being. In the light of Christian theology and in line with Laudato Si', this article defends the need for an ecology of Hope so that greater climate justice is possible. The argument follows three fundamental points: The ecological demands to be human, the ecology in view of the future and the urgency of the ecology of relationships. The development of these subthemes will support the thesis of the urgency and need to create an ecology of Hope, so that it becomes the essence of an integral ecology both with regard to the human being and with regard to his relationship with creation.

Keywords

Laudato Si'; Ecology of Hope; Apocalypse; human being; intellectus spei; intellectus amoris; human action

The subject of ecology has been widely debated. In Christianity, the theme has gained a greater dimension with Pope Francis' Encyclical Letter *Laudato Si'*,[1] where care for nature is presented as a humanizing element and as a meeting point of God with the human being, and of the human being with God. However, theological reflection and papal concerns on this issue have existed throughout history.

For example, with Saint Francis of Assisi, nature was presented as a sign and voice of God—the splendid book where God speaks to us[2], considering that "through the greatness and the beauty of creatures one comes to know by analogy their maker" (*Wis* 13:5). Alongside this reflection, the church has developed

1 Pope Francis, *Laudato Si'* (LS).
2 Cf. Celano, *Vita seconda di San Francesco*, p. 750.

 | DOI:10.30965/9783657795314_013

a theological and religious journey, making faith a place of communion with nature. However, with technological advance and scientific progress, the ecological question had to be worked out at different levels. For example, Paul VI, in 1971, insisted on warning of the destruction of nature and signaling this destruction as a sign of the very degradation of the human being[3]; John Paul II assumes a more proactive discourse, inviting humanity to a global ecological conversion.[4] From here on, it is no longer a question of looking at the destruction of the planet with regret, but of working actively on the ecological cause, accepting

> the world as a sacrament of communion, as a way of sharing with God and our neighbours on a global scale. [As Patriarch Bartholomew affirms] It is our humble conviction that the divine and the human meet in the slightest detail in the seamless garment of God's creation, in the last speck of dust of our planet.[5]

From this viewpoint, the Pope's voice on this topic is no longer exclusively directed towards Christians, but towards all human beings. Benedict XVI is an example of this, by proposing a large-scale action in which the whole of humanity commits itself to correcting and improving growth models that do not respect nature. Pope Francis is even more proactive in calling on the whole human family to unite around this cause for an ever more symbiotic, sustainable and integral development of human beings and nature. It cannot be forgotten that the human being is a natural being and not a being alien to nature. This is the emphasis of the *Laudato Si'*: the belief in humanity as a family capable of mutual care—a care that goes beyond human relations, since it takes into account the "common home" in which everyone lives.

The underlying theology of the *Laudato Si'* is an active theology of Hope.[6] The Encyclical exposes human reality, showing that the attacks on the environment and the social inequalities which we see happening daily before our eyes are not only the result of a lack of responsibility, nor of an unbridled thirst for greater economic power; but rather the reflection of the dehumanization of human beings and their loss of Hope in the present and the future.

3 Cf. Pope Paul VI, *Octogesima Adveniens* 21 (pp. 416–417).

4 Cf. Pope John Paul II, *Redemptor Hominis* 15 (p. 287).

5 Patriarch Bartolomeu, *Global Responsibility and Ecological Sustainability*.

6 Hope in the humanity of the human being which reveals itself as the starting point for an ecology of Hope, capable of facing up to the injustices committed against nature.

1 Ecological Demands: "Being Human" to "Human Being"

Pope Francis' pastoral action—and very specifically *Laudato Si'*—are indicative of a unique proposal for humanity. Against a parasitic model of human relations, the Pope proposes the family and unitary model, where everyone is interdependent and lives personal autonomy while respecting this interdependence. Rejecting an individualistic principle that would be either in the realm of dependence or in the realm of independence, the Pope speaks of the need for an integral ecology that promotes and gives human beings human authenticity. Thus, the awareness and acceptance of interdependence among the members of the human family (in communion with all that exists) is the way to go beyond a biologistic and scientistic idea of the human being. For this very reason, it is necessary to understand that, "an integral ecology calls for openness to categories which transcend the language of mathematics and biology, and take us to the heart of what it is to be human" (LS 11). From this perspective, the ecological question refers, above all, to what the human being is (much more than what the human being does).

This reflection linked to integral ecology seems to be in line with Böhme's thinking on the question of the paradigms that govern, and/or should govern, existence and the very concept of human being. In a manifest indivisible binomial between "human being" and "being human," Böhme speaks of the tension between what is natural in the human being and what is not.[7] A tension between facticity and project that develops and manifests itself through two paradigms that govern the way we see and understand what it is to be human: the paradigm of emancipation and the paradigm of reconciliation. The first paradigm (emancipation) concerns the nature of the human being according to the Aristotelian definition of "rational animal". Here the concept of the human being is understood through his specificity, that is, through everything that separates and distinguishes him from all other living beings (reason, sociability, mind). Through what is specific to him, the human being develops his self-formation, overcoming and emancipating himself from the rest of nature that surrounds him. On the contrary, the second paradigm (reconciliation) alerts to the need to overcome the tensions (and the very dichotomous idea) between mind and body, nature and culture. These tensions lead to the

7 Here, it will be important to realize that the references to human nature and to "becoming natural" do not have underlying the idea of a subjugation to the "primate" condition of the human being, nor the denial of the evolution of the human being as such. Rather, the concept of "natural" is equated to that of "essence", that is, to what the human being is integrally, as opposed to all the artificialism that can be incorporated into him through the use of technology and science.

alienation of the human being from what he is in his integral human nature. Through the paradigm of reconciliation, it is possible to open doors to the naturalization of the human being and the humanization of nature. This is a paradigm that, in some way, has already been pointed out by other thinkers (such as Schiller and Marx), but that also manifests itself in the biblical-Christian reading of Gen 1:26–28. Here, both the differences between human beings and other living beings are emphasized, as well as the necessary interconnection (interdependence) among all creatures and the human responsibility to—as human beings—take care of nature (a nature that is not alien to the human being, but in which the human being is inserted and is an integral part).[8]

Placing the human being in a human-divine sphere (cf. Ps 8:5–6), the biblical accounts present the human being as a being created for life, for the safeguarding of all that exists, without the pretension or illusion that a human authenticity can exist outside the relational sphere (between humans, between humans and God, and between humans and other creatures). It is important to keep in mind that this relational perspective is not something unique to religious thought. On the contrary, throughout history, thinkers from the most different areas (even thinkers opposed to the idea of religion) have defended this position, both to speak of the integrality of what it is to be "human", and to speak of the relational dimension that is the requirement and foundation for the safeguarding of all that exists. An example of this is Karl Marx when, in the middle of the 19th century, while ignoring the existence of God, he defends that every human being is a product and an integral phase of human society and that, consequently, "the real nature of man is the totality of social relations"[9].

The question of human nature has undeniably marked the philosophical-humanistic reflection of the last centuries as never before. In this sense, the call for an integral ecology becomes an urgency of the present time to which it is necessary to respond. Never before have human capacities to exploit and destroy the planet been so developed and, at the same time, has humanity been at risk of being turned into something inhuman and perverted by techno-scientific advances as now. In fact, Jean-Paul Sartre warned that "Man is condemned to be free"[10], today, freedom is allied to the desire for the beautiful, the strong, the unlimited ... to the unbridled desire for human immortality, even if this means giving up being integrally "human"! Trans-humanists and post-humanists have been developing an idea of the human being that moves away from the human dimension. Through science and technology (as in

8 Cf. Böhme, *On Human Nature*, pp. 4–5.
9 Marx, *Selected Writings*, p. 83.
10 Sartre, *Existentialism*, p. 29.

prosthetics, pharmacology, nanotechnology, surgery, computationalism, and genetic engineering), the human being is converted into a series of gadgets—of uploads—aimed at a (mechanistic) biological improvement that leaves aside the integrity of what it is to be human (vulnerability, compassion, authenticity ... the natural, as opposed to the artificial that now seems to want to impose itself as never before).[11]

As Hannah Arendt warns, it is not right to equate "the human condition" with "human nature", since they are different realities. The human condition refers to human capacities—such as rationality, work, action, thought, etc.—, but these are human characteristics, not constitutive elements of human nature. This is why changing the human condition (through techno-scientific implants, genetic manipulation, or even by altering the space where the human being is), would not lead to an "improved human being", but to a "human under condition" (something whose consequences we cannot fully anticipate). In turn, human nature is something unsolvable, that is, "if we have a nature or essence, then surely only a god could know and define it, and the first prerequisite would be that he be able to speak about a 'who' as though it were a 'what'."[12] From this perspective, the very idea of "human nature" is suspect, insofar as we cannot (do not have the criteria) speak of it with precision and clarity (at the risk of falling into its dehumanizing objectification). However, nothing prevents reflection on the human being from starting from the very concept of nature. In fact, the concept can be understood as a synonym for essence, or it can refer to something natural that is not the fruit of human production. From this perspective, human nature will always refer either to the essence of the human being—what the human being is as such, regardless of external factors such as culture or the environment in which he finds himself; or to his corporeal dimension, equating him to all other beings not made by human hand (mountains, plants, animals, etc.).

In line with the thinking of *Laudato Si'*, this question about the human condition and nature seeks to find and dialogue with the integrality of the human being. From this search, Pope Francis calls for integral ecology, that is, the retreat from the desire to "have more" (to have more vision, intelligence, strength, etc.) and the rejection of equating "more" (more years of life, more independence, etc.) with "better" (better human values, better relationships, better humanization, etc.). For this very reason, the Pope warns that the desire to be a better human being is not a technological facility; rather, it is a difficult and painful process (far removed from the idea of buying upgrades),

11 Cf. Böhme, *On Human Nature*, pp. 6–7.

12 Arendt, *The Human Condition*, p. 10.

since it presupposes a process of growth, effort and commitment to one's own humanity, and never an automatic and immediate principle of improvement (cf. LS 11).

This is not only the position of Christianity, but of so many humanistic thinkers (like Hannah Arendt, for example) who have looked into this problematic issue. In fact, despite so many forces in favor of an *in-human* vision of the human, there is no reason to despair. Rather, to believe and to follow a path towards an integral ecology is to go towards an ecology of Hope that is not alien to the biblical narratives and *Laudato Sí'*. However, it is necessary to rediscover in the human being all that is ancillary (and, therefore, false to the Hope that is the foundation of human integral ecology), all that is human authenticity (and which, consequently, raises ecological integrality to the altitude of a greater Hope—a humanizing Hope of the human being).

It is true that, at the present time, the meaning of life, truth and future seem to be intoxicated by a morbid discouragement. This is not yet the death of Hope, but a sign of the smog of despair that undermines contemporary life and insists on spreading, both in terms of socio-political relations and in terms of man's faith and relationship with God. A smog that blocks the vision of reality and genuine Life. This toxic environment makes everyday life asphyxiating, it forces the human being to wear masks, to avoid going out and relating to others. However, this is a smog of illusion. The brightness of Hope continues to shine, it is only clouded by the pollution that conceals it and blurs it. Along with the smog of despair, small hopes emerge, like *ignis fatuus*, from the swamps. They have a transient brightness and short duration. They are simulacra of hope, vain promises of an easy and happy future, but ultimately nothing more than a sign of the "desert of the real"[13].

Thus, contemporary society is characterized by the announcement of the immediately possible and immortality, the fulcrum of man's newest alliance with the virtual and the technical, constitutes the Holy Grail within reach of all those who wish to drink from it. However, *Gaudium et Spes* cautions us that:

> The modern world shows itself at once powerful and weak, capable of the noblest deeds or the foulest; before it lies the path to freedom or to slavery, to progress or retreat, to brotherhood or hatred. Moreover, man is becoming aware that it is his responsibility to guide aright the forces which he has unleashed and which can enslave him or minister to him (*Gaudium et Spes* 9).

Without noticing, mankind oscillates between the euphoria of the promise and the dysphoria resulting from the clash with reality. The promise of false

13 Baudrillard, *Simulacres et simulation*, p. 10.

immortality moves us away from the desire for eternity. The promise of popularity and the omnipresence of the "likes", deviate us from truth and a meaningful life. Hope, like friendship, becomes quantifiable, empty and hollow, enslaved by the clicks of others; it is experienced in a sensualist fashion measured in terms of wins and losses: How many clicks has my recent publication got?

The perishability of hope spreading in today's societies is tinged by a type of television and cybernetic schizophrenia. On the one hand, we have outrageous advertising schemes in which, for a given price, it is possible to buy an easy, carefree and alienated life without suffering and death; on the other hand, we have fatalistic news, which is the bearer of violence, destruction and the announcers of the end of the world. This schizophrenia creates a vicious cycle of fear and consumption. As our fears grow due to the news, the more we consume with the hope of achieving a carefree life; as our consumption increases, the more fearful we are that this hope will be shattered by the "enemies" presented in the news. The escape from reality seems to be inevitable.

In technologically advanced societies the confusion between virtuality and reality is increasing, because the smog of despair and fear limits our ability to distinguish them, to perceive the difference between Hope and hope. The consequence of this confusion is the gradual triumph of virtuality. The simulation, so characteristic of advertising schemes, precedes and determines the real (or what is considered as real), the simulation becomes, as argued by Baudrillard, "a strategy of the real, neo-real and hyper-real whose universal double is a strategy of deterrence"[14].

Marketing and advertising sustain an agonizing and dying hope which alienates humanity from the sense of God and other human beings, ultimately distorting its very existence. In this existential shipwreck, those who are drowning seek salvation by clinging to the first buoy that appears. In our days this buoy is a materialistic one, where human beings prefer to have rather than to be, to consume rather than serve, to escape rather than confront. Society has been plagued by the desire to forget, it is becoming an amnesiac society, marked by the desire not to see or feel suffering and death, the desire to be something other than itself. Like a castaway on the high sea, human beings no longer know what to believe, they are condemned to live the *carpe diem* of the present without a horizon of hope for the future. The *hic et nunc* of false promises pervert the meaning of Hope, condemning it to death, and corrupting the meaning of the divine promise. The era of simulation, the *smog* that chokes humanity, prevents the possibility of touching the real, the true and the

14 Baudrillard, *Simulacres et simulation*, p. 17.

pure. Virtuality becomes a "protected species" and overvalued in detriment of the real, "leaving space only for the orbital recurrence of models and simulated generation"[15]. There is no longer the desire for a breath of fresh air, an oasis of life. The habit of an agonizing life, behind the mask, contaminated and under epidemic threat, is an incubator of a desperation that is becoming more and more assumed as a way of life. This life is impossible to live (such is the horror of despair!) because of this the virtuality of a simulated happiness seems to be the only motivation for human beings to carry on, trying to achieve the promised easy happiness, if they are willing to pay for it, embarking on a roller coaster of emotional and existential ups and downs.

Faced with this desperate schizophrenia, how can we talk about Hope? To what extent can Hope be asserted as truth, as oxygen capable of dissipating the *smog* of virtualized and simulated hopes? Far from the temperamental oscillations of hope, Hope is bound to the divine promise. A promise for the present and the future, historical and eschatological, a promise of eternal life, of a fullness that takes into account the wholeness of the human being and which, therefore, elevates it to the sphere of the divine.

In this regard, perhaps it is also appropriate, in order to distinguish the apparent from the real, the pseudo-human from the human, and the utopian from Hope, to approach the notions of "action" and "behavior" from MacIntyre's perspective. In fact, this philosopher draws attention to what separates behavior from human actions, which is of capital importance for the present reflection, especially to abandon old conceptions that ecology is linked only to a series of learned and practiced behaviors (e.g., separating garbage, saving water, taking care not to pollute the environment in any way, etc.). Integral ecology—from which springs and in which a true ecology of Hope is concretized—is something human, in a comprehensive sense of the totality of the human being. It is not a unique dimension of the human, or an appendix of its humanity; rather, it is a vivid manifestation of the human being to be "human". The Hope that underlies the integrality of the human being is, therefore, a Hope that must be understood and lived beyond the adoption of behavior to safeguard nature. In fact, as the philosopher Alasdair MacIntyre warns, the notions of "human action" and "human behaviors" cannot be taken as synonymous. On the contrary, human behavior must be understood as something mechanical that the human being learns and does from social prejudices and determination; and it must be distinguished from action, since the latter derives from human values and a communitarian teleological view of the world and of life.[16]

15 Baudrillard, *Simulacres et simulation*, p. 12.

16 Cf. MacIntyre, *Freedom and Revolution*; cf. Lutz, *Reading*, pp. 12–17.

2 What Future? What Hope? What Ecology?

The actions we perform are revealing of the level of humanity that inhabits us. The ecology proposed by Pope Francis focuses precisely on this integral dimension of the human being. It is not about behavior, but about actions—ultimately, it is not about what a human being does, but what a human being is. Too often we are led to give up and give up in the face of so much destruction that reigns around us. We live in a Babylon and, it seems, we are facing a lost cause. However, if the reality in which we live is likened to Babylon—as it is described in the biblical texts—we must look at it from the same biblical perspective.

From a synchronic reading of the book of Revelation[17], we see that, for example, chapter 18 tells us that Babylon is a totally secularized city, where there is no room either for respect for life (vv. 12–13) or for a relationship with God (vv. 2–3; 5; 24). All that exists mirrors an idolatry of progress—a progress without limits (v. 7) and without respect for what it is to be human (vv. 21–23). All of this seems to be reflected in our day, both if we think about human relationships, and if we think about ways of life and *dis-respect* for the planet we inhabit. What hope could the Babylon of Revelation have? What salvation could there be for it? Perhaps understanding this Babylon should not be reduced to a simplistic view. Rather, since the book of Revelation holds an incomparable symbolic richness, perhaps what revealing is the human action that urgently needs to be rediscovered. It is not a matter of assuming behaviors that correct the mistakes that are committed against Creation, but of integrating actions capable of humanizing ourselves and, consequently, humanizing our relationships with God and with other creatures.

The symbolism of Revelation describes the Hope that underlies the intrinsic humanity of the human being. It is not a mere hope that things will not continue as they are. On the contrary, it is a Hope that starts from reality as it is at the present time. Although I do not intend to exegetize the book of Revelation, nor to develop the ecology of hope from these biblical narratives, it is important to understand some aspects that manifest the Hope that remains despite the dehumanizing reality in which we live.

Before even looking at the Babylonian reality in which we seem to be immersed, it is important to understand how Hope is understood in the book of Revelation. In chapter 6, the breaking of the first six seals reveals a statement of fact: there will be destruction and nothing will remain as before. However, the Hope that radiates here is far greater than the levels of destruction presented.

17 Cf. Oriol/Alegre, *Escritos Joanicos*, pp. 213–288; cf. Carvalho et al., *Apocalipse*.

Yes, much will be destroyed, but ... not ALL will be destroyed! The emphasis on partial destruction (vv. 6 and 8: "a loaf ... three pounds" ... "one-fourth") is contrasted with the totality of those saved (cf. Rev 7:4 (and Rev 4:12)—the symbolism of the 144,000 who are saved is based on the sacred numbers of totality: 3 × 4 × 12 × 1000). The same happens in chapter 12 (cf. vv. 3–6), where the imperfection of the dragon of destruction (7 heads, 10 horns, destruction of a third of the stars of heaven), contrasts with the total salvation (the child and the woman are saved in a magnificent and improbable way: the welcome in heaven and the abundance of food in the middle of the desert).

Notwithstanding this Hope unveiled in the midst of so much destruction, we cannot close our eyes to the reality described: suffering and death are abundant. Nature itself suffers in an incomparable and frightening way: "The sun became black like black cloth, and the moon was blood-red. Then the stars of the heaven appeared to be falling to earth—like green fruit from fig tree buffeted by mighty winds. And the starry heavens disappeared as though rolled up like a scroll and taken away; and every mountain shook and shifted" (Rev 6:12–14). But isn't there a language here that needs to be rediscovered? Is destruction so literal, or does it just point to the need to banish/destroy everything that dehumanizes reality and the nature of which we are a part?

If we want to equate, without drama, the plurality of what we experience today with the plurality of the nascent churches described in the book of Revelation, we can rediscover the operative (and not just disruptive) Hope by which we are guided and which enables a real transfiguration of what it is to be "human".

If we look, for example, at the church of Laodicea (Rev 3:15–22), we seem to glimpse the reigning apathy about the issues that Pope Francis calls "integral ecology". In the letter to this church, there is recognition of what that church is, and, given the actions it takes, a judgment is made: "I know you well—you are neither hot nor cold; I wish you were either one or the other! But since you are merely lukewarm, I will spit you out of my mouth!" (vv. 15–16). More than their behavior, what is at issue are their actions. Their actions reveal the dehumanization in which the people of Laodicea live: more concerned with economic issues and appearance than with authenticity of life (v. 17). However, the letter to this church is not only a look at reality and a judgment of disapproval. It is also a letter that counsels (v. 18), that is revealing of a true love—a love that goes out to the encounter and that seeks an authentic sharing of life (vv. 19–20)—and, even more, it is a letter in which the Hope that springs from love is mirrored: the promise of victory! The promise that, not only will there be no destruction, but that there will be such salvation that the people who are now apathetic and indifferent can *hope* to sit on God's lap (v. 21). The promise of victory is always present. One might think that, a different reality, might long for a greater promise or another mode of treatment. However, the principles of salvific Hope are always the same. For example, the church of Philadelphia (Rev 3:8–13) is commended for its action and receives no rebuke and/or warning, despite the recognition of its weakness (v. 8). However, the letter to this church is also marked by the call to faithfulness (v. 11), the assurance of love (v. 9b), and the promise of victory (vv. 10 and 12).

Given this coherence in the promise and this thread that is Hope, there seems to be, from these biblical narratives to our days (namely in the text of *Laudato Si'*), both the recognition that there is something wrong—something that has to be changed—since the planet is being destroyed by the dehumanizing action of human beings, and the certainty that life will be victorious as we become more human (and, consequently, true guardians of nature). Although there is much to be done—both at the level of behavior and at the level of human action—we must look at the ecological problem with this Hope and without giving room to fatalisms that are nothing but generators of apathy and resignation.

From this biblical-Christian perspective, it is important to remember that the challenge faced by Christians nowadays remains the same as always: the mandate to proclaim and bear witness to a Hope that is greater than what we can think or even imagine (cf. Eph 3:20), a mandate which presupposes that faith in Jesus Christ bears the mark of a greater Hope. To be conniving with the death of Hope is to affirm and work for the dissolution of Christianity. There is no Christianity without Hope, without the mark of Christ. Without this, Christianity would become an unruly message, without *arche* and *telos*. To speak of Christianity is to go beyond the ecclesial institution, to recognize Christ as the Lord of Hope and the Consummator of the Promise.

So, eschatological Hope is not (nor should it be) indifferent to history, to the daily life of all human beings. On the one hand, the eschatological dimension gives meaning and fullness to history (to the centuries); on the other hand, it is in history that the already / not yet of the Promise takes place. Without history the process of redemption and salvation would be absurd and incomplete. It is in seeking the encounter of eternity and history, particularly through the person of Christ, that humanity can build a full life. In the words of Benedict XVI,

> Redemption is offered to us in the sense that we have been given hope, trustworthy hope, by virtue of which we can face our present: the present, even if it is arduous, can be lived and accepted if it leads towards a goal, if we can be sure of this goal, and if this goal is great enough to justify the effort of the journey (*Spe Salvi* 1).

The promise that comes from God does not announce an easy path, or the foreshadowing of a bright future. One cannot confuse, in our process of achieving personal fulfilment, the aristotelic *eudaimonia* with the sensualist *hedonism* of the present day, where laughter and pleasure are confused with happiness (a happiness that is nothing more than a psychological pleasantness).

The redemption offered in the cross affirms the victory of Hope and the consummation of the promise. Nowadays, this redemption continues to be unsettling and presented as madness (cf. 1 Cor 1:21–24), because there are so many recent and different mechanisms of redemption, which try to establish themselves as the dominant paradigm of salvation in contemporary societies. However, through these mechanisms, redemption ceases to be conceived from an integral point of view, and is reduced to a *secularism of appearance* which confines human life to the slavery of fragmentation (aesthetics, power, fantasy, wealth, etc.), where the partial is considered or confused with the whole.

This desire for instant redemption, through the snap of a finger, has increased in recent times and we are now living the consequences. For instance, the false promises of the French Revolution led to the reign of terror, the Communist Revolution led to the Gulags, the transhumanist revolution seems to lead to the very negation of what it is to be human. Many were, and are, mechanisms of redemption that have proved fruitless. Rationalism gave way to Nihilism, the absence of being that prevents any hope and any desire for a full life. We are still living this dangerous nihilistic heritage. Since there is neither beginning nor end, as everything is secular, as everything depends on our will, we can, therefore, be whatever we want. There is no nature or essence that limits or hinders us. In the virtual world people can simulate themselves and their lives at will. Everyone can fabricate a second life, a life which for them is more "real" or "authentic" than their first life.

In this scenario, Hope maintains its traditional function as the counterweight against the flow of despair, reaffirming the words of Christ: "I have come so that they may have life and have it to the full" (John 10:10). Therefore, human life finds its source, foundation and meaning in Life, in God. So, its value can only be found beyond the transient sensations and experiences (see *Fides et Ratio* 46). The memory of the failed promises of modernity and the resulting mistrust of everything and everyone cannot paralyze us. The smog of despair can be dissolved and it is possible to attain clear and open horizons. It is necessary to realize that Hope congregates memory and eschatology, and we can only achieve this Hope in communities historically located.[18] It is, therefore, necessary to develop pragmatic articulations with everyday life and

18 Cf. Ricœur, *La mémoire*, pp. 642–643.

maintain an integral notion of the human being.[19] Only in the concreteness of people and communities can the smog of despair be dissipated and despair be transfigured into Hope.

It is not the intention of this reflection to establish norms and/or practical measures that could be implemented at the political or social level for greater climate justice. However, in light of this human—and planetary—urgency, we can consider some proposals to make this "ecology of Hope" effective. Something that, not being specific to the political, social, or ecclesial sphere—since it concerns, above all, the human being—when consummated, will have an unquestionable impact in the most different spheres.[20] Thus, in a more concrete way, I propose a line of thought similar to that which is revealed in *Laudato Si'*, since in it, Pope Francis not only presents environmental concerns, but more importantly alerts us to the problem that is "mental pollution", which prevents and corrupts interpersonal relations reducing them to virtual and cybernetic emptiness.

> True wisdom, as the fruit of self-examination, dialogue and generous encounter between persons, is not acquired by a mere accumulation of data which eventually leads to overload and confusion, a sort of mental pollution. Real relationships with others, with all the challenges they entail, now tend to be replaced by a type of internet communication which enables us to choose or eliminate relationships at whim, thus giving rise to a new type of contrived emotion which has more to do with devices and displays than with other people and with nature. Today's media do enable us to communicate and to share our knowledge and affections (LS 47).

3 Ecologizing Relations With God

The warnings of Pope Francis are not reduced to calling for "simple ecology" or maintenance (as if separation and recycling of waste solved everything).[21] On the contrary, the Pope speaks of an integral ecology which, given reality, "respects our unique place as human beings in this world and our relationship

19 Cf. Duque, *Ritualidade da arte*, p. 25.

20 It is true that the destructive action of the human being has been great in the last centuries. In terms of behavior, something is already beginning to be visible: never before have we separated and recycled waste; never before have international political agreements and national laws sought to safeguard the planet (see, for example, Palardy, *Science Study Shows*). The same happens with the documents of the magisterium of the church, in which, for example, the *Laudato Si'*.

21 Cf. Ribeiro, *Ambientalista Simplório*.

to our surroundings" (LS 15), and that is de way how I define ecology and the meaning of ecologizing.

To develop a humane and humanizing ecology is to be ready to walk a path of conversion and reconciliation with God. In fact, over time, especially with the processes of social secularization, the consequent substitution, or at least the attempt to replace the divine reference with the human reference, has led to the isolation of the human being and has increased the emptiness of his "I". Where does the human being base his nature and identity? In a perversion of the original process of creation, the human being has placed himself, with anthropocentrism, at the focal point of creation. Like God, the human being wants to create from nothing. But the latter, unlike the former, ends its creation with nothing. This is the triumph of the nihilistic will of the human being. He makes nothing out of nothing, for he thinks that if there is nothing to determine him, he can be anything he wants to be.

By "annihilating" God, the human being ends up annihilating nature. Take, for example, the paradox between the excesses of promises and the deficits of the achievements of modernity. If modernity promised the dominion of man over nature and over himself, which would be realized in social equality and perpetual peace between peoples (Eden on earth), in practice we see that the dominion of nature has led to its unbridled exploitation, to the growth of social inequalities, and we have never seen so many conflicts and wars in human history as after the Second World War (hades on earth?!).

From here on, dehumanization is practically inevitable, with destructive consequences for the inhabitants of the "common home" offered by God to His creatures, and which human beings have been entrusted to manage and care for. Hence the urgency of man's reconciliation with God, as well as with all creatures. It is a reconciliation which can only be achieved together, one being the expression and manifestation of the other.

The mandate "to grow and multiply" (Gen 1:28) is a clear call to develop the greatness of creation and is in no way dissociated from the mandate to "dominate the earth", a domain which is synonymous with care and not with possession or subjugation—it is a domain which can only be understood as a blessing. To accept and live this blessing is the first mission of the human being. That is why caring for Creation is based on the recognition of the dignity of every creature. This recognition, which in biblical accounts is translated by the nomination of each one of them (Gen 2:19–20), currently requires the human being to recognize his own humanity (Human Being = Being Human). Only in this way can the human being re-establish his relationship with God, as the founding relationship of humanity and of all creation, one and unique. The healthy recognition of this creature-Creator relationship places the human being back on his mission as guardian of an ordered nature; a nature that protects and nourishes him and, at the same time, a nature that demands his care and preservation. Moreover, as Hannah Arendt says, "the Earth is the very fifth essence of the human condition".[22] It constitutes one of the conditions of possibility for the human to be human. Ecologizing the relationship with God is precisely taking on this process of banning everything that filters, distorts, dilutes or impedes life's access to Life and consequently creates distancing artifices that hinder care for Creation.

4 Ecologizing Relations with Creation

In the *Laudato Si'* a relationship of continuity is established between the accounts of the book of Genesis and the present reality of creation. Here, Pope Francis links care for creation with the humanization of the human being, taking on the action of caring for nature as a manifestation and expression of human dignity. In this way, disrespect for creation becomes the first and foremost cause of inequality among human beings—an inequality in the way we live and in the way we look at each created being. The lack of recognition of the dignity of creation leads to blindness towards human dignity. It is not by chance that the Pope emphasizes the co-creative responsibility of the human being, not calling progress into question, but rejecting the idea that it can only happen if nature is devastated, corrupted and/or destroyed.

When we look at the world around us, we seem to feel the absence of something, the absence of a foundation for life. However, I would argue that the horrors of reality mainly demonstrate the lack of reigning humanity and the existential emptiness derived from insensitivity to God's presence. This is thought to be useless, absent or superfluous, but all the efforts devoted to replacing it only seem to widen the abyss into which we are plunged.

The reality that surrounds us is wounded. It needs not only to be cared for, but to be loved. Only by loving creation can one free oneself from the asphyxia of living without God and far from one's own humanity. Hope in human beings is the driving force behind the ecology of relations with creation and the only one capable of putting human beings back into their co-creative mission.

Yet we must be aware that the injustices done to creation will not be erased or corrected overnight. This is why Pope Francis' appeal is directed at the unity of the human family and not to a group. Humanity is called to grow and develop for the global good of the planet and not only to sectorize priorities which in

22 Arendt, *Condição Humana*, p. 12.

the medium and long term would mean not only disrespect for nature but the sectorization of the human person.

5 Ecologizing Relations with/as Human Beings

Indifference is not the badge of "being human". In indifference there is no place for authenticity. Therefore, the specification of anthropocentrism in egotism, in which the individual self does not see beyond its "world", the emptiness of its face reflected in the camera of its mobile phone or in the mirror of its room, declines into the blind and selfish reflection of one who, like Narcissus, lives only for himself. There is nothing beyond himself and his present time.

However, no matter how much human artifice (technology, hypocrisy, delusion, etc.) reigns, life is outside this artificial world. Therefore, looking for it in the artifice inevitably leads to disillusionment and nothingness. Human life, true life, remains linked to all living organisms and to the living source of life. The efforts to cut this bond objectify and coerce the human being, turning him into yet another artifice among other artifices. Authenticity is manifested in the ability to hear the cry of nature (of which the human being is an integral part), its cry for justice and for action in its defense. It is urgent to free creation from the slavery of the reigning egotism (cf. Exod 3:7–8).

Listening to the suffering of reality is the starting point for the re-humanization of the human being. In fact, "in the concrete situation confronting us, there are a number of symptoms which point to what is wrong, such as environmental degradation, anxiety, a loss of the purpose of life and of community living. Once more we see that 'realities are more important than ideas'" (LS 110). The apathy of indifference never generates life. Rather, it pulls the human being from the reality of what he is. Creation is no obstacle to the realization of humanity. On the contrary, it is there that the human being is realized and it is there that the human being develops and makes his humanity bear fruit, through humanizing progress and truly participating in the co-creative action of the human being.

From the Encyclical *Spe Salvi* of Benedict XVI and the Apostolic Exhortation *Evangelii Gaudium* of Pope Francis, it seems clear that Hope—understood from a Christian perspective—is both fundamental for the dignity of the human being (as a being in relationship with God and with the world), and for the assumption of a lifestyle far from the selfish ideals that fracture the integrity and authenticity of the human being. Only when the human being understands himself as part of creation and lives according to a greater Hope (a hope that persists even when surrounded by adverse circumstances) does it become possible to develop concrete actions in relation to the world that the human being is called to care for. An action that springs from the essence of the human being and not only from a desire that is external to him. It is an action that crosses the different areas of his life: at personal, social and/or political level.

6 Ecology of Hope—The Way to Human Authenticity

Hope in the authenticity of the human being leads Pope Francis to insist that this is not a condemned reality. Rather, this is the time to act and to live the present through the Hope in which we are created. A Hope that does not deceive us (Rom 5:5) and therefore does not allow fatalistic discouragement to condemn to death the planet and the humanity that lives on it. On the contrary, "Hope would have us recognize that there is always a way out, that we can always redirect our steps, that we can always do something to solve our problems" (LS 61).

It is therefore urgent to create an ecology of Hope, inasmuch as it is the only one capable of keeping humanity healthy and invigorating human authenticity in its action and mission on the planet. The ecology of Hope translates into a healthy balance which removes everything that corrupts the nature of the human being and, consequently, allows the human being to make his origin—his being created in the image and likeness of the Creator (Gen 1:26)—shine forth. The ecology of Hope is the dynamism that humanizes the human being, so that his actions do not result in a simple intellectualization about climate justice or in a selfish whim connected to individual and sectorized actions. An ecology of Hope will become the essence of an integral ecology, both in relation to the human being and in relation to his relationship with God and with creation.

As in all epochs of history, there is a small "remnant of Israel" that remains loyal to the experience of faith in the Lord of Hope. For these Christians, social despair leads to concrete actions. It is no coincidence that there is a growing missionary movement, a free gift of life far from the spotlight of the media. For example, last year in Portugal, at missionary laity level, more than a thousand people went on missions in developing countries. These figures contrast with those of five years ago, in which only four hundred and five people went.[23] The gestures of charity persist and refuse to become the "poster person" of

23 Cf. *1028 portugueses fazem voluntariado missionário*; cf. *405 portugueses participam em ações de voluntariado*.

an institutionalized and uncommitted solidarity. We continue to see, even at university level, a growing concern with the well-being of others, especially with those who come from other countries. I am thinking, in particular, of the Portuguese Catholic University in Braga, where the entire academic community comes together to help the many young Africans and Asians who come to the institution every year. Helping them to familiarize themselves with the institution and to cope with the difficulties of the language and culture.

Christian life must remain marked, however difficult the circumstances may be, by the question: "And who is my neighbor?" (Luke 10:29). Take the case of the refugee movement in recent years, to which there has been much opposition, because of religious and cultural differences or because of the fear of violence and loss of employment. Despite these fears, there are still countless voices that, guided by Hope, dare to see beyond fatalism, working to welcome the refugees and to demystify the idea that these people are enemies to be ostracized and expelled. They do this by showing society, in general, the benefits of receiving these people. For instance, in Portugal economic growth and population stability are at risk because of the low birth rate. The Portuguese government estimates that fifty thousand immigrants are needed to maintain the active working population.[24]

Guided by Hope, and in spite of the setbacks and challenges of reality, everyday life can be lived in happiness and the worship of God's love is increasingly linked with the love for others and the faith that unites the community. To the selfish desire for immortality, Hope answers with the gift of eternal life; to the desire for daily artificial joy, it responds, neither by rejecting nor inciting the existence of suffering, but through a dynamism of happiness that welcomes it, transfigures it and gives it meaning. In reality, Hope leads to a redemptive responsibility, a responsibility that goes against all fatalistic views. The Christian way of life defies contemporary society, which sometimes sees Christians as dreamers and believers in delusion and other times sees them as a threat to be contained or eliminated, so that the reign of fear continues and human beings remain "plugged to the machine" of advertising in a vegetative and dying way. It is imperative to keep in mind that Hope is under attack, but not extinct. Because, if it were, so would Christianity. In this manner, I argue, that it is necessary to recognize an *intellectus spei*[25] and an *intellectus fidei*, which work together to create a concrete understanding and *praxis* of hope, which removes itself from abstract perspectives and eschatological theorizations.

24 Cf. *Governo defende a entrada de 75 mil imigrantes.*

25 Cf. Ricœur, *L'Herméneutique Biblique*, pp. 111–128.

The dynamic nature of true hope ("the now" and the "not yet") shatters the crystallization of false hope and its inherent fatalism.

It should be noted that *intellectus spei* and *intellectus fidei* have a mutual implication and, therefore, give rise to an *intellectus amoris* that presents itself as the ultimate expression of a faith nourished by Hope. This is a correlation that cannot be ruled out in so far as it highlights the concreteness of Hope itself[26]. In the First Corinthians, St. Paul speaks of this intrinsic correlation between the theological virtues. This is a correlation that translates into concrete life. In fact, if we analyze this Pauline text closely, we find that the poetic sublimity of Love's hymn (1 Cor 13) does not appear as an explanation of the virtues, but as a synthesis of the previous chapters. These chapters speak of the dangers of idolatry and call for a persevering life in faith (1 Cor 10); of the rites that are practiced as means of manifestation of the Hope that inhabits the heart of the believer (1 Cor 11); and, finely, of the operability of love, since faith, nourished by Hope, always leads to concrete action in favor of humanity (1 Cor 12). It is only through this Pauline path that it is possible to understand chapter thirteen. The multiple "though I" expressions, present in the hymn of Love[27], are themselves revealing of a greater Hope. This Hope is not the greatest of the virtues, because when it achieves its plenitude it is no longer called Hope, but Love! It is not by chance that Hope is at the center of Christian virtues. It is the element which enables the realization of faith in gestures of love. In other words, Hope justifies living the faith in the here and now of the Promise. This is "the more" of Christianity in a world in despair.

Hope is the fountain and motivation for the belief in a real future and in a present that, despite the hardships, can fight and overcome the apathy that insists on regulating daily life. We cannot deny the harmful effects of high unemployment rates, the dangers and reasons for so much migration, the wars that persist in the world, the impact of global warming and the massive destruction of species. But, in a true Hope, we dare to row against the tide using faith as the anchor that prevents the world from remaining adrift. Therefore, an active Hope is fundamental. Without it faith will be vein, theology meaningless, the desires for change insipid, the gestures of love hollow. Hope brings back human dignity, it makes it possible to speak of God, eternal life, Christian

26 Cf. Mueller, *A teologia e seu estatuto teórico*, pp. 99–100.

27 "Though I speak with the tongues of men and of angels (...). And though I have the gift of prophecy, and understand all mysteries, and all knowledge; and though I have all faith, so that I could remove mountains (...). And though I bestow all my goods to feed the poor, and though I give my body to be burned (...)" (1 Cor 13:1a.2a–b.3a).

communities and even of Christianity. To live without Hope is to live without God, outside the spheres of the divine and of humanity.

The main reason for Hope in a world in despair, and devastated by climate injustices, is manifested from its origin and end: Jesus Christ. This concrete reason maintains the Gospel alive, prevents humanity from escaping from reality and keeps it from succumbing to the fear of suffocation. The world must be embraced and transfigured. It has an incomprehensible side, therefore, "the world perhaps exists not so much to be understood but more to be loved!"[28] So, Christians must be patient in tribulations, take every opportunity to be hospitable, bless even the persecutors, rejoice with others when they rejoice, and be sad with those in sorrow (cf. Rom 12:12–15), in the certainty that the God of Hope fills us all with joy and peace in faith, so that Christianity manifests and overflows with Hope through the power of the Holy Spirit (cf. Rom 15:13).

References

"1028 portugueses fazem voluntariado missionário," FEC-Fundação, Fé e Cooperação, https://www.fecongd.org/2018/07/23/1028-portugueses-fazem-voluntariado-missionario/ [accessed 31.05.2020].

"405 portugueses participam em ações de voluntariado missionário internacional," FEC-Fundação, Fé e Cooperação, http://www.plataformaongd.pt/noticias/noticia.aspx?id=719 [accessed 31.05.2020].

"Governo defende a entrada de 75 mil imigrantes," António Cotrim/LUSA, https://www.dn.pt/portugal/interior/governo-defende-a-entrada-de-75-mil-imigrantes--9502168.html [accessed 01.06.2020].

Arendt, Hannah: *Condição Humana*. Lisboa: Relógio d'Água 2001.

Arendt, Hannah: *The Human Condition*. Chicago: University of Chicago Press 1998.

Baudrillard, Jean: *Simulacres et simulation*. Paris: Galilée 1981.

Böhme, Gernot: "On Human Nature", in: A. Grunwald/M. Gutmann/E. M. Neumann-Held (eds), *On Human Nature. Anthropological, Biological, and Philosophical Foundations*, vol. 15. Berlin/Heidelberg: Springer 2002), pp. 3–14.

Carvalho, Carlos Pereira, et al, *Apocalipse. Novos Céus e Nova Terra*. Lisboa: Difusora Bíblica 1988.

Celano, Tomás de: *Vita seconda di San Francesco*, CXXIV, 165: *Fonti Francescane*.

Dinis, Alfredo: *O mundo é para ser amado. Textos de filosofia e ciência*. Braga: Aletheia 2014.

28 Dinis, *O mundo é para ser amado*, p. 11.

Duque, João Manuel: "Ritualidade da arte: performatividade da memória", in: *REVER*, No. 1 (Ano 18–Jan/abril 2018), pp. 11–30.

Lutz, Christopher Stephen: *Reading Alasdair MacIntyre's After Virtue*. USA: Continuum, A&C Black 2012.

MacIntyre, Alasdair: "Freedom and Revolution," in: *Labour Review* 5, N. 1 (February-March 1960), pp. 19–24.

Marx, Karl: *Selected Writings in Sociology and Social Philosophy*, translated by T. B. Bottomore, T. B. Bottomore/M. Rubel (eds.). London: Penguin Books 1963.

Mueller, Enio R.: "A teologia e seu estatuto teórico: contribuições para uma discussão atual na universidade brasileira." in: *Estudos Teológicos*, v. 47 n. 2 (2007), pp. 88–103.

Oriol Tuñí Josep/Xavier Alegre: *Escritos Joanicos y cartas católicas*. Estella: EVD 1995.

Palardy, Jim: "Science Study Shows That Nearly 80% of the Annual Plastic Flow Into the Environment Can Be Stopped Using Existing Technology", in: *PEW* [23-07-2020], https://www.pewtrusts.org/en/research-and-analysis/articles/2020/07/23/science-study-shows-that-nearly-80-percent-of-the-annual-plastic-flow-into-the-environment) [accessed 25.01.2021].

Patriarch Bartolomeu: "Global Responsibility and Ecological Sustainability", *Closing Remarks*, Halki Summit I, Istanbul (20 June 2021).

Pope Benedict: *Encyclical Letter Spe Salvi. On Christian Hope*, 2007. https://www.vatican.va/content/benedict-xvi/en/encyclicals/documents/hf_ben-xvi_enc_20071130_spe-salvi.html [accessed 25.01.2021].

Pope Francis: *Apostolic Exhortation Evangelii Gaudium*, 2013. https://www.vatican.va/content/francesco/en/apost_exhortations/documents/papa-francesco_esortazione-ap_20131124_evangelii-gaudium.html [accessed 25.01.2021].

Pope Francis: *Encyclical Letter Laudato Si' On Care for our Common Home*, 2015: https://www.vatican.va/content/francesco/en/encyclicals/documents/papa-francesco_20150524_enciclica-laudato-si.html [accessed 25.01.2021].

Pope John Paul II: *Encyclical Letter Fides et Ratio*, 1998. https://www.vatican.va/content/john-paul-ii/en/encyclicals/documents/hf_jp-ii_enc_14091998_fides-et-ratio.html [accessed 25.01.2021].

Pope John Paul II: Encyclical Letter *Redemptor Hominis* (4 March 1979), AAS 71 (1979), pp. 257–324.

Pope Paul VI: Apostolic Letter *Octogesima Adveniens* (14 May 1971), AAS 63 (1971), pp. 401–441.

Ribeiro, Luís: "Ambientalista Simplório", in: *Visão*, https://visao.sapo.pt/opiniao/ponto-de-vista/2019-06-05-0-ambientalista-simplorio-1/ [accessed 14.09.2020].

Ricœur, Paul: *L'Herméneutique Biblique*. Paris: Cerf 2005.

Ricœur, Paul: *La mémoire, l'histoire, l'oubli*. Paris: Le Seuil 2000.

Sartre, Jean-Paul: *Existentialism Is a Humanism*, translated by Carol Macomber. New Haven&London: Yale University Press 2007.

Apocalyptic Practice of Hope? Thesis on a Buried and Misused Biblical-Theological Resource

Gregor Taxacher

Abstract

The Anthropocene as an age of human ability for the destruction of the ecosystem "earth" represents a permanent secular end-time. It is the responsibility of theology to interpret such a global sign of the time in the light of the gospel, for which the categories of biblical apocalyptics are evident. But apocalypticism represents an often misused tradition and has a reputation for mythological dualism and pessimism. Authentic Judeo-Christian apocalyptic, however, represents a political prophetic theology of its present. It reflects the possibility of hope in situations of catastrophic gradient. It is astonishingly current and inspiring in the discourse around experiences of powerlessness and the impossibility of a "right life in the wrong one." In the face of climate catastrophe, it teaches a discernment of spirits between optimism for progress and a resistant practice of hope.

Keywords

Climate catastrophes; apocalyptics; eschatology; evolution; Anthropocene; hope; history

1 Introduction: Postapocalyptic Cows in Fukushima

Animals often appear in apocalyptic contexts, and mostly they are dangerous, aggressive and fantastic animals: winged lions and panthers, bears (Dan 7), rams and he-goats (Dan 8), locusts with scorpion spines, horses with dragon heads (Rev 9) or outright dragon creatures (Rev 12–13). However, only quite harmless, almost proverbial gentle animals survive the apocalyptic events: there even the lion of Judah becomes a lamb (Rev 5:5f.).[1]

Cows also seem to belong to these post-apocalyptic animals. At least, this is what German television recently reported from the area around Fukushima.[2] After the explosion and meltdown at the nuclear power plant, people hastily

1 On that point: Ruster, *Das Lamm Gottes*.
2 *Japan-fukushima*.

 | DOI:10.30965/9783657795314_014

evacuated the area. Farmers left their cattle behind, many of them died, wandered around, starved to death. Then came Satsuki Tani, a woman from the megacity of Tokyo who had never had anything to do with agriculture. But she saw the pictures of the cows from Fukushima. She began to gather the survivors and helped them to live after the disaster. Because products from the exclusion zone are not allowed to be marketed, these cows have lost their status as farm animals to be exploited. So, they not only have survived the nuclear disaster, but they have also escaped the fate of slaughter that would normally befall them. Now they live in peace with their rescuer Tani. She is now writing a children's book about the cows of Fukushima and says, "These cows are basically a miracle." Yes, they are a miracle, reminiscent and reminding us of those cows living peacefully with the lion and the she-bear, shepherded by children in the prophetically promised time of salvation (Isa 11:6f.).

Do animals first have to be potentially contaminated in order to escape the economic system of exploitation and simply be perceived as living beings? Do the apocalyptic catastrophes, that humans inflict the planet earth, have to actually happen first, so that salvation may occur? Will we only begin to tell our children other stories, stories of different and new possibilities of living together, after the interruption of the capitalist logic of growth by the worst-case scenario it has caused?

The disturbing story of the cows of Fukushima is for me an example of how the sceneries of our present and the apocalyptic texts of the Jewish and Christian tradition can illuminate and interpret each other in a surprising way. The apocalyptic texts resemble the interpreting angels that frequently appear in them, forcing us to look in a direction we are frightened by. But precisely when we see through their eyes, we can perhaps see more than just the frightful.

2 The Initial Situation 1: Unpopular Apocalypticism

The buzzword apocalyptic often has a bad reputation in the climate debate as well as in academic theology.

At first: In the political debate, it is used as a derogatory term for an alarmist evocation of ecological catastrophe that only spreads pessimism, feelings of powerlessness and resignation.[3] In fact, there is a danger that pessimistic forecasts function as self-fulfilling prophecy: If everything is too late anyway, there is no point in fighting against disaster anymore. Paralysis and indifference spread. Strategically and in terms of social psychology, when it comes to promoting changes in policy and our behavior in the climate debate, we

3 Taxacher, *Apokalyptischer Realismus*, pp. 46–47.

should avoid using a language of pure doom and gloom, a threat of the inevitable. Threatening messages do not have a motivating effect.

On the other hand, the apocalyptic character of the climate debate is one of numbers, of exact data. And year after year, these data turn out to be more sobering or alarming, whether they concern the melting of the Arctic and Antarctic and of mountain glaciers, the thawing permafrost or the instability of ocean currents such as the Atlantic Gulf Stream. Scientists, however, cannot tailor the publication of such results to what they do socially and psychologically. This creates a discrepancy between the rhetoric of the eleventh-hour decision, which always leaves just enough time for the message "Yes we can", and the scientific scenarios, in which the clock has already moved forward much further. This discrepancy does not go unnoticed by those who are interested, informed, concerned and passionate about change. So, the challenge of dealing with the "apocalyptic overtones" in the debate cannot simply be sidestepped. It cannot be contained, only suppressed—and that would not be good.

Secondly, apocalypticism is a topic that even in academic theology tends to be handled with pointed fingers—apart from purely exegetical-historical research. In the theological context, apocalyptics often appears as the domain of fundamentalist sects that justify an inhumane and anti-emancipative political theology. Of course, in contrast, it is obsolete for an enlightened, a hermeneutically and historically-critically informed theology to transfer apocalyptic texts directly to events of the present or the future, as if they had been prophesied in a literal sense. Such a fundamentalist approach to biblical texts, however, is not specific to the apocalyptics: prophecy as a whole and also the ethical statements of the Bible cannot be interpreted "literally" (which in itself is hermeneutical nonsense, because no text can be understood "literally" at all), and certainly not "applied" to the present time without turning them into reactionary ideology.

But the theological distrust especially towards the apocalyptic lies even deeper, namely in the newer German theology of both major denominations. Here, the alternative of "eschatological" versus "apocalyptic" has established itself as the rule for a non-fundamentalist interpretation of the biblical message. On the Protestant side, Rudolf Bultmann so influentially distinguished between an always mythological, falsely objectifying apocalypticism and an eschatology that is existentially and theo-logically qualifying the present (and not interpreting history).[4] This was received just as influentially on the Catholic side by Karl Rahner, for whom apocalyptic meant the misinterpretation of the

4 Bultmann, *Ist die Apokalyptik die Mutter der christlichen Theologie?*; also Bultmann, *Jesus*, pp. 22 and 38.

eschatological message of the Bible as a kind of report on future events.[5] This reading has had an impact on the rejection of apocalyptically inspired theology up to the present day.

However, this distinction between bad apocalyptic and good eschatology is based on inconsistent hermeneutics, which does not want to grant a certain text genre—the "apocalyptic"—the effort of demythologizing, post-enlightened translation and understanding work, which must be applied to other biblical text genres—prophecy, for example, or miracle narratives—in order to be able to receive them theologically today. In my opinion, this unequal treatment has deeper theological reasons: Biblical apocalypticism is opposed to an individualizing and spiritualizing Christian tradition of interpretation, which still characterizes modern and even more so post-modern Western theology. It is against doing theology in a supra-temporal and un-historical way. And it is against making theology seem harmless, "positive", comforting and edifying.

This is exactly the reason why Johann Baptist Metz raised an objection against the mentioned tendency of German theology with his *Theses on Apocalyptics.*[6] He understood apocalyptic as an interruption of a theology of "bourgeois religion", which recommends itself as a transcendence supplement to the existing conditions. Apocalyptic precisely forces the critical reference of the eschatological message of the Gospel to the real political, social, historical conditions. It represents, so to speak, their theological "negative dialectic".

Metz polemicizes against the "Evolutionslogik"[7] of an endless linear development prevailing in the *Zeitgeist:*

> Gleichwohl bleibt die theologische Uminterpretation der "Naherwartung" in eine "Stetserwartung" (oder "Stetsbereitschaft", kurzum: in ein zeitloses Existential) ein semantischer Betrug an der temporalen Grundverfassung des Christentums. [...] Alle vorherrschenden Spielarten gegenwärtiger Eschatologie [...] scheinen bereits erfolgreich einem ihnen fremden evolutionistischen Zeitverständnis eingepaßt, das sie nötigt, alle "Naherwartung" [...] extrem zu privatisieren—auf die Todessituation des einzelnen hin.[8]

Metz interprets apocalyptics now no longer as a pure myth, but as a political mysticism:

5 Rahner, *Theologische Prinzipien.*
6 Metz, *Der Kampf um die verlorene Zeit.*
7 Metz, *Der Kampf um die verlorene Zeit,* p. 214.
8 Metz, *Der Kampf um die verlorene Zeit,* pp. 215 and 216–217.

> Apokalyptik war mystische Entsprechung zu einer erfahrenen politischen Wirklichkeit; ihr Katastrophenbewusstsein unterbricht die Siegesgewissheit der Beherrschenden der Zeitläufte.[9]

In the last part of the aphoristic text, under the heading *Wider die falschen Alternativen in der christlichen Eschatologie*,[10] Rahner's establishment of the opposition between eschatology and apocalyptic is attacked without naming him, but nevertheless very explicitly. Metz means the worldlessness and individualization of this eschatology. In contrast to this, apocalyptics poses completely different, decisive questions: "Wem gehört die Welt? Wem ihre Leiden? Wem ihre Zeit?"[11]

However, Metz omitted to demonstrate this postulate concretely on the one hand relating the apocalyptic texts and on the other hand the present situation. Therefore, his theses did not have such an influence on theology as Bultmann and Rahner's "banishment" of the apocalyptic had. It seems to me that the present ecological catastrophe is the historical *kairos* to continue Metz' theses. We need them. The theses noted here serve this purpose.

3 The Initial Situation 2: Apocalypticism of the Anthropocene

The comprehensive discovery context of my theses consists in the correspondence between secular Anthropocene and theological apocalypse: Humanity is in a situation of permanent, self-produced end times, in a catastrophic gradient of its history, which it produces itself. This has the effect of a practical, factual demythologization of the apocalyptic discourse of the end times.[12]

There is substantial criticism of such a global diagnosis—first of all independent of its theological interpretation: Is the term Anthropocene not again installing a kind of "grand narrative", sometimes even with the purpose of accepting, even welcoming this situation as the highest increase of human disposal over nature—up to the consequence of fighting climate change in the same spirit that caused it: with geoengineering, through large-scale technology? The narrative of the Anthropocene would then be a kind of heroic legend

9 Compare Metz, *Der Kampf um die verlorene Zeit*, p. 218, where in thesis XXV also the displacement of apocalyptic is related to the Christian displacement of the Jews.

10 Metz, *Der Kampf um die verlorene Zeit*, p. 219.

11 Metz, *Der Kampf um die verlorene Zeit*, p. 220.

12 This based on: Taxacher, *Apokalyptische Vernunft*; also Taxacher, *Apokalypse ist jetzt*; also Taxacher, *God in Opposition*.

about the Anthropos, whose continuation would have to be an equally heroic rescue story.[13]

This is by no means intended by my use of this term. Thus, the term Anthropocene must not be affirmatively understood as "anthropocentrism"—after all, an anthropocentric worldview is precisely a central cause for the crisis that is indicated by "Anthropocene". Thus, for me, the term only states a situation into which humanity has factually brought itself and which it cannot get rid of, not even by denial, not even by a turn to a better ecological awareness of human embeddedness in nature (as desirable and saving as this would be). The possibility of the destruction of mankind by human abilities remains—and with it the responsibility that has fallen to us.

With the term "humanity", however, the second critical aspect of the term Anthropocene is already invoked: The ecological crisis is by no means the result of a practice of "humanity" as a whole and indiscriminately. It is the result of the capitalist-industrial mode of economy, which certain and determining actors promote and from which people benefit—or suffer—in very different ways. Thus, the diagnosis of the Anthropocene must inscribe the great inequality within humanity.[14] It is even aggravated by this situation, because cynically those who are affected first and most severely by the ecological catastrophe, in particular also by climate change, have caused this the least.[15] The climate movement has raised awareness of this situation by calling for climate justice. But it is precisely this inequality of those who cause and those who are affected that the situation remains a global one, affecting everyone and interconnecting everyone. That is why I consider the discourse of the Anthropocene appropriate and necessary.

As far as theological interpretation of the Anthropocene as an apocalyptic situation is concerned, it can be objected that the biblical apocalyptic texts speak of something completely different: of a judgment of God which ends and turns human history. My diagnosis, therefore, does not claim that the Anthropocene is "the apocalypse". This would only be a historico-theologically heightened way of the fundamentalist "application" of biblical texts. What I claim is the interpretability of the present situation in the light of these texts.

For a closer inspection, there is far less mythology in them than critical, political historical theology. And so even the biblical speech of God's judgment is quite open to a demythologization that takes the texts seriously. The texts

---

13 Haraway, *Unruhig bleiben*, pp. 66–73 and 81.

14 Neckel, *Scholastische Irrtümer?*; also Laux/Henkel (eds.), *Die Erde, der Mensch und das Soziale*.

15 Taxacher, *Apokalypse ist jetzt*, pp. 64–69.

of the Book of Daniel (Dan 7–12), for example, speak in code of the history of the successive empires of the Babylonians, Medes and Persians and finally of the Hellenistic rulers after Alexander of Macedonia—and they reflect this history from the point of view of the believers in YHWH in the tiny province of Judah, which seems to be a marginal part of these events.[16] Likewise, in John's Revelation, the Messianic Jesus community reflects their situation in the context of the Roman Empire as a new Babylon.[17] They ask about God's relationship to these disproportionalities.

Reading these texts in the situation of the Anthropocene, they interpretively destroy the impression of the naturalness of the relations. What constitutes the imperial structure of our contemporary relations? Who are the monster animals, the "powers and forces" of this time that trigger feelings of powerlessness? Who would currently be the addressees of apocalyptic thinking, who its genuine bearers? How do the circumstances relate to the will of God with his creation, as it is expressed in many voices in the biblical gospel? And to what extent do we recognize ourselves in the apocalyptic diagnosis that something is definitely and necessarily coming to an end in our societies? I suggest four theses for an actualized reading of the Apocalyptics.

4 Towards an actualized reading of Apocalyptics

4.1 *Biblical Apocalyptic Represents a Resource for the Theological-Prophetic Interpretation of the Signs of the Time*

Historically, biblical apocalyptic is a Jewish response to the imperialistic globalization of Hellenism, which was later continued in Christian terms in the context of Roman imperialism. This context forced biblical prophecy to think globally (in the ancient sense), to reflect its own prophetic message about the liberating God YHWH in the history of the universe.[18] Christian apocalyptics do so in the face of the discrepancy between the messianism of the dawning kingdom of God in Jesus' proclamation and the situation of the early churches in the midst of the permanent totalitarian power of the Roman Empire. It is precisely this contextualization that makes apocalyptic readable and accessible in the context of modern capitalist globalization and its ecological and social consequences.

---

16 Bauer, *Das Buch Daniel*, pp. 139–218.

17 Berger, *Die Apokalypse*, pp. 53 and 80–83.

18 Müller, *Studien zur frühjüdischen Apokalyptik*, pp. 35–173. My own point of view: Taxacher, *Apokalyptische Vernunft*, pp. 74–92.

"Apocalypse" literally means "revelation". In the biblical apocalypses, this revelation by no means refers only to the end-time events, but above all to the present and to history, which has allowed it to become as it is. Thomas Ruster interprets such texts from the perspective of contemporary systems theory.[19] According to this, the "powers and forces", the demonic magnitudes and monsters of the apocalypses, are personifications of the supra-individual dynamics that suggest our powerlessness. Today we call these "factual constraints," system laws. Apocalyptic deconstructs these as structures of sin, as delusional contexts. Of course, such deconstruction today must be done with social scientific, political analysis. This is what makes it different from a fundamentalist approach to apocalyptic texts. It is not about "literal" transmissions and identifications, but about the theological perspective on what is revealed in the secular world. Theology does not replace this analysis. But it does bring provocative categories of interpretation: those of creatureliness and fall (of "corruption"), of God's will, of God's kingdom, but also of judgment. Theology can "defamiliarize" contemporary secular discussions in a productive sense.

According to Vatican Council II, this is a central task of the church and thus of theology: "to investigate the signs of the times and to interpret them in the light of the Gospel" (*Gaudium et Spes* 4). In the two-step nature of this task—to investigate and to interpret—lies the rejection of a biblical fundamentalism. Researching the signs of the times is a step in its own right, requiring the appropriate tools from the empirical sciences, social theory, political economy, and others. This exploration is as convincing as its methods and arguments. What is to be said about the causes of the ecological catastrophe, about its entanglement with political, social and economic factors, cannot therefore be quickly skipped over in a theological moralism. What has been said above about the Anthropocene, then, must be neatly deduced, demonstrated—not simply ascertained. However, the two-step nature of this task also implies that the theological interpretation of the finding thus elaborated adds something new to it and does not merely repeat it in a heightened moral or religious tone. And here all biblical texts, through their model reference to time and history, but especially their apocalyptic passages, represent an important resource. Again, it is not enough to quote these texts in a correspondingly topical way. Rather, it must again be shown argumentatively to what extent they "reveal" (Greek: "apokalyptein") aspects of our contemporary situation that would otherwise remain concealed. This is exactly what "interpretation" means.

In view of the diagnosis that the Anthropocene is a threat to earthly life produced by the dynamics of human activity itself, which places our actions

19 Ruster, *Von Menschen, Mächten und Gewalten*, pp. 117–158.

under the pressure of permanent "eschatology," the biblical prophetic category of judgment, for example, brings a genuine theological interpretation into play. The fact that judgment does not mean an external punitive act of God, but rather the impact of the consequences of exploitative, (self-)destructive ways of life that have been practiced over long periods of time and maintained against better knowledge and prophetic pleas, can be shown in the biblical texts and then again translated concretely into today's situation.[20] It could be further shown what decisive significance the category of justice plays in this prophetic discourse—not as its abstract category of distribution, but as the ability to do justice to social needs and the conditionalities of creaturely finitude and vulnerability. The call for "climate justice" would certainly benefit from such Torah-knowledgeability.

4.2 *Apocalypticism Enables the Theological Distinction Between Optimism and Hope*

With the last remark I am already at the backdrop of my second thesis. According to my observation, the mainstream of climate policy protest movements—such as *Fridays for Future*—has so far sometimes shown a lack of reflection on their own position and participation in such contexts. The "imperial way of life" of industrial societies[21] is the cause of ecological and social crises and at the same time an achievement, which is supposed to be preserved and defended in these crises even by "environmental policies". Ecological movements especially of the north-western world are deeply involved in this way of life and its interests—and cannot simply discard it. This leads to a vacillation between fundamental criticism and rather technocratic proposals for solutions. It also leads to an internal dispute about how to address demands to politics on the one hand[22] and to one's own way of life[23] on the other. This entangles them in self-contradictions, makes them vulnerable—and characterizes an existential state of mind between euphoria about the new dawn and despair about their own ineffectiveness.

In the debate, an alternative is then often seen between the political and the "individual" side—which, however, notoriously does not disappear through the option for one of the two sides. The pursuit of sustainable lifestyles leads to the experience of powerlessness and entanglement; political activism does

20 I have reasoned that in Taxacher, *Apokalypse ist jetzt*, pp. 137–156.
21 On this: Brand/Wissen, *Imperiale Lebensweise*.
22 For example, the plea of Jan Steckel and Jörg Peters: Steckel/Peters.
23 On public awareness of this issue: Statista.

not absolve moral and existential questions. Adorno's verdict of the impossibility of the right life in the wrong[24] thus becomes a constant "feeling of life."

In this situation, a theology newly inspired by apocalyptic can give a voice to something otherwise unheard of. While we have just been talking about the category of judgment, it would be necessary here to bring in the New Testament—and likewise deeply apocalyptic—talk about the kingdom of God, its already present dawning and its location in or between the passing and the new "eon"[25]—and the question of what conversion (*metanoia*) means in this announcement of time. Jesus' basic message of the possibility of conversion, which breaks open through an approaching *basilaia* (Mark 1:15), cannot be interpreted without an apocalyptic time index.

Such a time index interrupts the experience of power continuity that shapes us, a kind of historical, social principle of inertia that keeps us collectively on a trajectory, even if its direction has long been recognized as fatal. This principle of inertia is a version of the historical image of modernity as an unstoppable trend "upward", now tilted into the negative, even catastrophic. The political-ecological struggles of the present still seem to move within a historical-philosophical paradigm of progress, of linear development towards new stages of human society—now, for instance, the "decarbonized" age—although this scheme no longer corresponds to the present perception of crisis.

Also theologically we have often equated progress with the work of God, especially in modern theology. Teilhard de Chardin wanted, very impressively, to think evolution and salvation history together.[26] Karl Rahner spoke of Christianity "within an evolutionary worldview."[27] Walter Benjamin, on the other hand, in his famous theses on history, saw in progress the violent action of the victors over the vanquished.[28] In this sense, an apocalyptic view warns, in my opinion, against equating the progress of human possibilities (technological, economic) with hope. But this also means, conversely, that if I am pessimistic about the future of our capitalist economic system, our society of constant growth, I don't need to be without hope. The undoubtedly frightening foreboding that many things are currently coming to an irretrievable end, that possibilities are literally "exhausted" and that we are facing "disruptions" that are completely different from those celebrated by the neoliberals, is then part of hope and not the opposite of it.

---

24 "Es gibt kein richtiges Leben im falschen": Adorno, *Minima Moralia*, p. 59.

25 Maurer, *Zwei Reiche*.

26 De Chardin, *Mein Weltbild*.

27 Rahner, *Die Christologie*; also Rahner, *Grundkurs des Glaubens*, pp. 180–202.

28 Benjamin, *Über den Begriff der Geschichte*.

The literary scholar Klaus Vondung called the modern use of apocalyptic in popular culture a "docked" apocalypse because it shows us only the catastrophic side.[29] In literature and cinema, apocalypse means only "Armageddon" and the end of the world. Yet the early Jewish and early Christian apocalypses are consistently meant as a message of consolation and a perspective of hope. They do not imagine an end, but a turning point—which, however, has to go through a downfall. To hope for this and to develop practice from this hope separates real hope, even in the face of catastrophic probabilities, from the optimism of "getting one more turn". Ultimately, such hope—even where it is not explicitly "religious"—has a transcending character. It does not result from the circumstances, but its light falls on them.

Thus, the gospel message of the kingdom of God does not speak about a world other (than ours), but it speaks from another world—illuminates this one world from God. "Kingdom of God," this central word of Jesus, is a term from early Jewish apocalyptic. (Ernst Käsemann has therefore called the apocalyptic "the mother of Christian theology"[30]). This kingdom means this world, but—as Jesus says in John's Gospel—it is not "of" this world (John 18:36). It does not bow to its criteria of success, of power. It frees us to hope, even in situations that seem outwardly hopeless. It establishes a practice of love for every threatened life that does not follow a calculation of "the greatest possible happiness of the greatest possible number." Especially in the environmental and climate debate, this also enables a discourse of renunciation, of quality instead of quantity, of sharing—a red rag in current politics.

4.3 *Apocalyptic Thinking Enables the Connection of Universal History and Resistant Marginal Stories*

The texts of the Bible, described by researchers as "apocalyptic," have a reconstructive context in which they establish hope, seek justice, and enable resistance. Their radical, pessimistic tone corresponds to the position of the groups behind these texts, which is actually perceived as powerless, marginalized, hopeless. Precisely for this reason, these texts were able to inspire modern liberation theologies, whose bearers—unlike Western, bourgeois theology—were able to recognize their own situation in the apocalyptic texts. Apocalypticism as a perspective of hope in a theology of liberation is not to be confused with simple optimism. Nor does it mean a defusing of the harsh apocalyptic images. But where the real situation itself is the horror, these images are not

29 Vondung, *Die Apokalypse*, p. 12.

30 Käsemann, *Zum Thema der urchristlichen Apokalyptik*, p. 130.

understood as a prophesied future to be feared, but as an interpretation of the present—and precisely in this way they can become a source of hope.

The early Jewish apocalyptics and already their predecessors in the literature of prophetic theology—for instant in the Babylonian exile, in the Diaspora as a minority in the Persian Empire, under the Hellenistic Diadochi or as Jesus' community under Roman emperors—experienced themselves powerless, in the military, political or social sense. Hence their imagery for the powers of their time: that of the great monster beasts, the great statue, the "whore of Babylon." But at the same time, this interpretation itself documents the "agency" of its authors. This arises from an attitude of looking through, of distancing. It is only apparently passive. A resistant practice can grow out of it. This is exactly why I see apocalyptic as a resource for the realization of the power of the powerless.

In the climate crisis in our part of the world, it is rather the other way around: people declare themselves powerless. "Individuals can do nothing about it." In this situation, there is a need for a liberation theology for "the affluent", for us collaborators of the imperial lifestyle. In its creative reception of apocalyptic language, the Rastafarian movement, for example in the lyrics of Reggae music, has called Western civilization "Babylon."[31] This intuitive hermeneutic of an apocalyptic metaphor gives a lot to think about. Is there a Babylonian captivity for Babylonians as well? An exodus for the "Egyptians"?

Walter Benjamin spoke of a "weak messianic power" that is given to "us as to every generation"—and that passes over to us from the past, from the hopes of the past.[32] He meant by this the unfulfilled hopes of histories that have not "made history." And it is in this perspective that I see today's Christian or ecclesial practice. We experience ourselves powerless in the face of global dynamics—for example, those that cause climate change. But we are also given this small messianic power to show in stories how history could also work.

Apocalypticism with its inherent theology of history, its urgent universalism, is endowed with a universal-historical claim long before this was theoretically formulated in historical-philosophical drafts (up to Hegel and Marx). Such universal-historical perspectives, the comprehensive narratives of a history in the singular, are today met very critically with good reasons—from the ideology critique of critical theory, from deconstruction or the critique of totalitarianism by Emmanuel Lévinas.[33] For such conceptions of history can

31 This symbolism should not be equated with its linkage with racist or anti-Semitic conspiracy myths that can be observed in pop culture today. To this end see: Buschbom, *Babylon*.

32 Benjamin, *Illuminationen*, p. 252.

33 I refer for this overall to Heinrich, *Grundriss einer Philosophie der Opfer*; also important to me are Adorno, *Negative Dialektik*, pp. 295–353 ("Weltgeist und Naturgeschichte. Exkurs zu Hegel") and Lévinas, *Totalität und Unendlichkeit*, pp. 318–365.

hardly do without teleological constructions, whose executors then declare themselves to be the victors of history. In contrast, the universal-historical perspective of apocalyptic represents a reversal, a negative dialectic: Universal history emerges from the doom into which all are banished, powerful and powerless, perpetrators and victims. This corresponds to the undeniability of the diagnosis of the Anthropocene: humanity is by no means united, but deeply torn and divided, and the Anthropocene is not a human project or the "world's spirit" peak. But the factually created conditions of the Anthropocene are subject to everyone, (still) profiteers and nameless victims, corporate leaders and climate refugees, industrial societies and extinct species.

Therefore, a "big" perspective—that of "history"—is indispensable, especially in critical-analytical intent. But the traces of salvation are not found in this perspective, but in that of the small counter-histories, the subcultures of the subalterns, the stories that cannot be leveled into the course of history just because they appear statistically irrelevant to the universal perspective. Apocalyptic thinking emerges where the marginalized appropriate a universal analysis while developing contingent practices.[34] The extent to which such resistant practices in climate justice movements actually bear apocalyptic traits would be worth empirical investigation. Such an investigation could be found, for example, in

- forms of refusal, of protest by omission, in policies of renunciation, in social projects of disengagement,
- the rediscovery of the meaning of a prophetic practice of signs, in the conscious real symbolic character of one's own practice (for instance in forms of artistic politics, "social sculpture" in the sense of Josef Beuys),
- new ecological relations of global and local contexts in practice, which also reflect the relationship between powerlessness and empowerment.

4.4 *The Theological Use of Apocalyptic Thinking Requires an Actor-related Differentiation of Spirits, a Hermeneutics of Apocalyptic in View of its Concrete Speakers and Addressees*

Skepticism about apocalypticism has its justified reason in its dangerous manifestations. There was and is a terrorist apocalyptic that ignites religious violence internally or externally. There was and is an apocalypticism of authority that religiously legitimizes imperial politics as mission. Ideology-critical hermeneutics of biblical apocalyptic deconstruct these uses.[35] It searches for

34 Siebenrock, *'Seht, ich mache alles neu'*.

35 Stobbe, *Bibelhermeneutik und politische Geschichte*.

that authentic "dangerous memory" (in the sense of J. B. Metz[36]) which preserves the apocalyptic of the oppressed and their resistance.

On the other hand, the extensive distance of at least German theology from apocalypticism is rooted deeper than in the justified rejection of an apocalypticism of terror or one of power. Johann Baptist Metz's theses on apocalypticism have remained lonely mainly because of the fear in our academic theology of speaking too mythologically, too pessimistically, too dualistically.[37] But this fear is also a reflection of an optimistic assessment of the given social conditions. In liberation theology, such fear plays a lesser role.[38] My assumption behind it: One's own location—political, social, economic—strongly determines the interpretation of the apocalyptic. For the oppressed, for groups with little to lose, texts about "disruption," a revolution announced by God, are more likely to be words of hope than for people in Western industrial societies, who tend to trust the mechanisms established in these societies for negotiating how the world is seen and shaped.

In the hermeneutics of apocalyptic, therefore, such questions are important: Who is speaking here and from which position? Whose violence is being spoken of (that of the oppressors, that of God)? In this respect, there are serious differences between the reception of apocalyptic by Thomas Müntzer, for example, during the peasant uprisings of the 16th century[39], and that during the Crusades and in the course of the Conquista of the Americas[40]—even if they both share the problematic trait of justifying violence theologically. But in one case it is about the resistance of desperate poor people, in the other about the violence of the conquerors and the legitimization of subjugation in the name of Christianity.

In this respect, the beatitudes of Jesus according to Luke are also an apocalyptic determination of the time. The "Blessed are the poor, the hungry" is there contrasted with a "Woe to the rich, to those who are now full …" (Luke 6:20–24). This, too, not only the mythological images of the apocalyptic, means an uncomfortable "dualism". How one receives the message depends on the status of the recipient. This can also be traced in the history of the impact of apocalyptic: As long as Christians were a persecuted minority, the Roman

---

36 Metz, *Memoria Passionis*, pp. 88–92.

37 Consider this skepticism in Johanna Rahner's response to Johann B. Metz's theses on apocalypticism: Rahner, *Apokalyptik*. More detailed in her textbook: Rahner, *Einführung in die christliche Eschatologie*, pp. 30–41 and 139–147.

38 For this purpose: Richard, *Eschatologie und Politik*; also García Roca, *Apocalyptic and Global Crisis*.

39 Strübind, *Eschatologische Konzepte*.

40 For this, compare my analysis: Taxacher, *Apokalyptische Vernunft*, pp. 190–201.

Empire a pagan, oppressive power, apocalyptic texts were read as promises of turning point and salvation. In the medieval imperial church—when Babylon had become "eternal Rome"—they were read more as threats, as accusations. The apocalyptic horsemen became figures of terror, apocalyptic was equated with the end of the world. What once meant promise was now feared.

If John's revelation ends with the request for the proximate coming of the Lord (Rev 22:20f.), now one strove for the preservation of the Christian Roman empire, which in a historical-theological interpretation of the "katechon" of 2 Thess 2:6f. could stop[41], postpone the apocalyptic labor pains at the coming of the Lord. This turn of the Christian reception of apocalyptic from the change of the real-historical role of Christianity already means the first step to the modern "docked" apocalyptic as a pure doomsday fear fantasy.

Also climate justice—namely the fundamental change of our power and living conditions, without which it cannot be realized—one may want to stop like the unlawfulness mentioned in 2 Thess 2, or long for it and fight for it, because one experiences exactly the existing conditions as the injustice mentioned there. To receive apocalyptic does not only require a discernment of spirits, but also causes such a discernment.

References

Adorno, Theodor W.: *Minima Moralia. Reflexionen aus dem beschädigten Leben*. Frankfurt a. M. 1951.

Adorno, Theodor W.: *Negative Dialektik*. Frankfurt a. M. 1966.

Anglet, Kurt: "Katechon—das/der 'Hemmende', 'Aufhaltende'", in: Kurt Anglet, *Macht und Offenbarung. Zum Geheimnis der Gesetzwidrigkeit*. Würzburg 2009, pp. 96–192.

Bauer, Dieter: *Das Buch Daniel*. Stuttgart 1996.

Benjamin, Walter: "Über den Begriff der Geschichte," in: Walter Benjamin, *Illuminationen*. Frankfurt a. M. 1977, pp. 251–261.

Benjamin, Walter: *Illuminationen*. Frankfurt a. M. 1977.

Berger, Klaus: *Die Apokalypse des Johannes. Kommentar Teilband 1*. Freiburg i.Br. 2017.

Brand, Ulrich/Markus Wissen: *Imperiale Lebensweise. Zur Ausbeutung von Mensch und Natur im globalen Kapitalismus*. München 2017.

41 Ebach, *Biblical Apocalyptic*, in particular pp. 25–26 ("Apocalyptic or katechontic?").—A contemporary historical-theological continuation of this speculation about Katechon is Anglet, *Katechon*.

Bultmann, Rudolf: "Ist die Apokalyptik die Mutter der christlichen Theologie? Eine Auseinandersetzung mit Ernst Käsemann," in: Rudolf Bultmann, *Exegetica, Aufsätze zur Erforschung des Neuen Testaments*. Tübingen 1967, pp. 476–482.

Bultmann, Rudolf: *Jesus*. Tübingen 1951.

Buschbom, Jan: "Babylon" als Bild für die westliche Zivilisation in HipHop und Reggae, https://www.politische-bildung-brandenburg.de/themen/zwischen-den-graeben/babylon-als-bild-fuer-die-westliche-zivilisation-hiphop-und-reggae [accessed 25.03.2021].

De Chardin, Pierre Teilhard: *Mein Weltbild*. Freiburg i. Br. 1976.

Ebach, Jürgen: "Biblical Apocalyptic, or 'It Won't Always Be Like That!'", in *Concilium* 50 (3.2014), pp. 19–29.

García Roca, Joaquin: "Apocalyptic and Global Crisis", *Concilium* 50 (3.2014), pp. 83–95.

Haraway, Donna: *Unruhig bleiben. Die Verwandtschaft der Arten im Chthuluzän*. Frankfurt/New York 2018.

Heinrich, Caroline: *Grundriss einer Philosophie der Opfer der Geschichte*. Wien 2004.

Japan-Fukushima: https://www.daserste.de/information/politik-weltgeschehen/weltspiegel/sendung/japan-fukushima-104.html [accessed 2503.2021].

Käsemann, Ernst: "Zum Thema der urchristlichen Apokalyptik," in Ernst Käasemann, *Exegetische Versuche und Besinnungen II*. Göttingen ^{3}1968.

Laux, Henning/Anna Henkel (eds.), *Die Erde, der Mensch und das Soziale. Zur Transformation gesellschaftlicher Naturverhältnisse im Anthropozän*. Bielefeld 2018.

Lévinas, Emmanuel: *Totalität und Unendlichkeit. Versuch über die Exteriorität*. Freiburg 1987.

Maurer, Ernstpeter: "Zwei Reiche. Apokalyptik in biblisch-theologischer Perspektive," in: Bernd U. Schipper/Georg Plasger: *Apokalyptik und kein Ende?*, Göttingen 2007, pp. 131–150.

Metz, Johann Baptist: "Der Kampf um die verlorene Zeit. Unzeitgemäße Thesen zur Apokalyptik", (first published 1977), in: Jürgen Manemann (ed.), *Befristete Zeit*. Jahrbuch Politische Theologie. Münster 1999, pp. 212–221.

Metz, Johann Baptist: *Memoria Passionis. Ein provozierendes Gedächtnis in pluralistischer Gesellschaft*. Freiburg i.Br. 2006.

Müller, Karlheinz: *Studien zur frühjüdischen Apokalyptik*. Stuttgart 1991.

Neckel, Sighard: Scholastische Irrtümer? Rückfragen an das Anthropozän. https://www.soziopolis.de/scholastische-irrtuemer.html [accessed 25.03.2021].

Rahner, Johanna: "Apokalyptik—Mutter der christlichen Theologie?", in: Jürgen Manemann (ed.), *Befristete Zeit*. Jahrbuch Politische Theologie. Münster 1999, pp. 225–231.

Rahner, Johanna: *Einführung in die christliche Eschatologie*. Freiburg i.Br. 2010.

Rahner, Karl: "Die Christologie innerhalb einer evolutiven Weltanschauung", in: Karl Rahner, *Schriften zur Theologie* Vol. V, Zürich 1962, pp. 183–221.

Rahner, Karl: "Theologische Prinzipien der Hermeneutik eschatologischer Aussagen", in: Karl Rahner, *Schriften zur Theologie*, Vol. 4, Einsiedeln 1960, pp. 401–428.

Rahner, Karl: *Grundkurs des Glaubens. Einführung in den Begriff des Christentums.* Freiburg i.Br. 1984.

Richard, Pablo: "Eschatologie und Politik. Befreiungstheologische Reflexionen über die Apokalyptik", in Jürgen Manemann (ed.), *Befristete Zeit.* Jahrbuch Politische Theologie. Münster 1999, pp. 51–59.

Ruster, Thomas: "Das Lamm Gottes. Ein Tier erklärt den Sinn der Welt," in: Simone Horstmann/Thomas Ruster/Gregor Taxacher, *Alles, was atmet. Eine Theologie der Tiere.* Regensburg 2018, pp. 323–339.

Ruster, Thomas: *Von Menschen, Mächten und Gewalten. Eine Himmelslehre.* Ostfildern 2005.

Siebenrock, Roman A.: "'Seht, ich mache alles neu'. Thesen zur Hermeneutik eschatologischer Bilder und Aussagen im Zeitalter der säkularen Apokalyptik. Ein Orientierungsversuch", in: Thomas Herkert/Matthias Remenyi (eds.): *Zu den letzten Dingen. Neue Perspektiven der Eschatologie.* Darmstadt 2009, pp. 24–37.

Statista: https://de.statista.com/infografik/17947/beim-klimawandel-ist-der-einzelne-gefragt/ [accessed 25.03.2021].

Steckel, Jan/Jörg Peters: https://www.zeit.de/wirtschaft/2019-09/klimaschutz-oekologischer-fussabdruck-industrie-co2-emissionen-verzicht-gewissen-verantwortung [accessed 25.03.2021].

Stobbe, Heinz-Günther: "Bibelhermeneutik und politische Geschichte. Eine kurze Auseinandersetzung mit der apokalyptischen Schriftauslegung christlicher Fundamentalisten", in: Bernd U. Schipper/Georg Plasger: *Apokalyptik und kein Ende?*, Göttingen 2007, pp. 191–206.

Strübind, Andrea: "Eschatologische Konzepte der täuferischen Tradition als Anfrage an aktuelle Perspektiven christlicher Hoffnung", in: Christoph Böttingheimer (ed.), *Was dürfen wir hoffen? Eschatologie in ökumenischer Verantwortung.* Leipzig 2014, pp. 17–42.

Taxacher, Gregor: "Apokalyptischer Realismus. Warum die Klimakatastrophe doch ein theologisches Thema ist," in: *zeitzeichen. Evangelische Kommentare zu Religion und Gesellschaft* (2/2020).

Taxacher, Gregor: "God in Opposition: The Value of a Critique of Apocalyptic Reason", in: *Concilium* 50 (3.2014), pp. 60–70.

Taxacher, Gregor: *Apokalypse ist jetzt. Vom Schweigen der Theologie im Angesicht der Endzeit.* Gütersloh 2012.

Taxacher, Gregor: *Apokalyptische Vernunft. Das biblische Geschichtsdenken und seine Konsequenzen.* Darmstadt 2010.

Vondung, Klaus: *Die Apokalypse in Deutschland.* München 1988.

Land as God's Common Good: Reframing the Logic of Nation State Territoriality with a Theology of Land as Shared "Creation"

Julia Blanc / Christian Kern / Ivan P. Khovacs / G. P. Marcar / Sofia Oreland / Christian Tauchner

Abstract

In this article we seek to question assumptions about territorial ownership and nation-state sovereignty over the use and exploitation of land as a first step towards doing environmental justice, turn to Christian sources prompting fresh thinking about land and human relationship to the natural environment, bring biblical and patristic thought into conversation with two contemporary Christian environmental justice responses calling us back to our creaturely connection to land, and, finally, rationalize an eco-theology and its implications for an ethic in which right relationship with God and neighbor demands a right and just relationship with the creation.

Keywords

Land ownership; nation state; territoriality; migration; book of Ruth; poor; Amazon synod; Christian environmentalism

1 Introduction

We watch small waves lapping water shallow enough that we catch a glimpse of what used to be farmlands just beneath. Over time the local villagers have seen rising sea levels slowly claim their land. The cutting back of nearby mangroves has only exacerbated the loss. The residents of this village on the eastern coast of India have been forced to move to new fields in order to secure a livelihood. Those fields are now themselves under threat as sea levels continue to rise unabated. Seasonal flooding has already wreaked havoc in these fields. In the meantime, salinization from advancing sea water has left water wells dry. Other land has unburdened itself into the sea through natural processes of erosion. So has the local mosque, it too has disappeared into the water. A cyclone made landfall here some years back, leaving the area even more vulnerable than it already was. The elderly in the village tell us all about progressively scorching weather making farming increasingly fruitless. Residents are desperate to experiment with new types of crops that might withstand such changing conditions.

 | DOI:10.30965/9783657795314_015

> They are also determined to rebuild the mosque. Hunger strikes have provided some measure of response from authorities in town: hopefully the villagers will get help securing access to fresh water. Others, however, have given up on the village and are taking their chances on migration to other parts of the country.

This memory collage from one of our contributors, a visiting church worker, describes the effects of land loss observed during a conference in India discussing the effects of climate change. Though distinctive to a village on the East coast of India, it is only one of many similar examples of environmental impact on populations the world over: sea levels rise, coastlines erode, salt concentration in the groundwater increases, water wells run dry, and people are as a result displaced from land they have inhabited and farmed for generations. The climate crisis is not just a matter of excessive carbon emissions resulting in atmospheric changes leading to unbearable weather patterns, it relates also to the land we live on. "Climate change" itself is a misleading term if it narrows our focus on the atmosphere. Should we speak more directly, in fact, about a crisis of the ground under our feet when tackling the full consequences of the climate crisis? If so, could we link land loss on the coast of India to Western attitudes about land and its uses? Paying attention to land and its protection as one of the essential features in the fight against climate change is in fact not new. The UN's Convention to Combat Desertification (1994), building on earlier research,[1] had made it clear that land degradation neutrality is crucial in the fight against climate change. The convention underlines the need for land protection and rehabilitation, along with biodiversity management, partly because "[r]estoring the soils of degraded ecosystems has the potential to store up to three billion tons of carbon annually" and prevent their release into the atmosphere.[2] Any discussion about land, however, carries underlying assumptions about the ownership, cultivation, and exploitation, we want to question from the start.

Western societies, it would seem, have simply taken for granted the idea that land can be owned, exploited as resource, commodified commercially, and put to utilitarian use. Politically, this goes back to what Nancy Fraser identifies as a "Keynesian-Westphalian" seventeenth-century emergence of a modern nation state constituted as a population inhabiting a land and sharing in an identity bound to territory held in common.[3] National sovereignty in this case presupposes representative government over both people and territory, and is the necessary condition rooting a population to their common share in

1 See below, *The Brundtland Report* (1987).

2 United Nations, *Global Sustainable Development Report 2019*.

3 Fraser, *Reframing Justice*.

the land and its natural resources.[4] An economy of ownership, in other words, is the lynchpin holding together the nation state and extraction industries as an inseparable whole. Individuals, of course, are also landowners in their own right, exercising agency under what the Keynesian-Westphalian frame guarantees in principle and the state enforces in law. Conceptually, however, once land becomes property, or mere property, our relationship with the earth is pinned to a logic of exploitation serving our material ends; land, that is, in the exercise of economic prerogative over its natural resources, comes to represent nothing more than the material and political strength of the state.

Our first aim in this chapter, then, is to link territoriality as a principle of the modern state to an ethos of land ownership and to the logic of dominion and exploitation this legitimates. Our working hypothesis is that just and effective climate action requires a *critique of modern land ownership* and of the interest of the nation state as a possessor of land. In doing this, we seek to overwrite the values underpinning the objectification of land, in order to overcome its logic of brute ownership with a Christian ethic that recognizes our sharing in the integrity of all God's creation, which in our argument is critical to any discussion about climate justice.

We do this in the forgoing sections as follows: in section (2) we sketch a critique of the principle of territoriality undergirding the modern nation state, in (3.1) we consider a theological reframing of land as common good in the Book of Ruth, (3.2) questions notions of ownership and possession with patristic thinking about sharing God's common goods, (3.3) incorporates the church's response to indigenous ideas about land in the Amazon, (3.4) finds resources for contesting contemporary attitudes of land exploitation in examples of climate activists disrupting the ideology behind territorial structures; finally, (4) offers alternatives for how to relate to land, no longer as an object rife for exploitation but as the wellspring of a common, human, providential good.

2 The Objectification and Exploitation of Land in Western Concepts of the Nation State

The rise of the Western political state can be told as a story of territoriality, in which land ownership is constitutive of the European understanding of political communities and principled on the idea of dominion over land. Roman law in late antiquity already saw the *civis* as a property owner whose status as a citizen was anchored to legally held material rights: whether individuals

4 Weber, *Eigentum an nicht-erneuerbaren natürlichen Ressourcen*, esp. Chapter 3.1–3.2.

possessed objects, slaves, or territories, it was their property-owning priority which made them legal persons, enabling, for example, recourse to legal action in cases of conflict with others.[5] Later, in the Middle Ages, the principle of territoriality spread throughout Europe, and gave rise to a powerful nobility whose status was a direct reflection of their vestment in land ownership. The German word "noble" itself is instructive: etymologically, the noun *Adelige* goes back to the expression *allod*, which is a reference to "the ground you possess."[6] The privileged status of the *Adelige* in the medieval society is partly an attribution of dignity and privilege ostensibly due those born of "blue blood", but it is ultimately a testament to the priority given to land possession and to one's right to rule over it.

In the 12th century, territoriality played an increasingly central role in ecclesial thought. By making use of the biblical image of the "flock in the fold", the church expressed its own institutional structure in topographical terms. There is nothing abstract in the portrayal of the souls under the curate's care as the flock: the image comes bundled with a portrayal of a penfold, which is, once again, an image of boundaries and fenced-in territory. It is this piece of land that holds the flock together and makes concrete the idea of the *communio ecclesialis*. The topographical structure of the parish church, then, translates the social imaginary of the flock in the penfold into a concrete organizational structure, mapping for the church its spiritual domain. Michel Foucault sees in this form of ecclesial organization a particular kind of power that prepares the ground for the emergence of the modern nation state.[7] Just as the pastor watches over the flock in the penfold the modern state joins a population to a defined territory, ensures their safety, watches over their health, and shapes their sense of national identity.[8] Those who live in the territory are seen as members of the nation state who are, thereby, entitled to the rights of citizenship. It is this principle of citizenship linked with territoriality Fraser's "Keynesian-Westphalian frame".[9]

This brief sketch of territoriality as a principle of Western-European socio-political organization calls for a critique about what counts as common possession of land and the implications for the ownership and governing of space. As we have seen, the state's claim over a defined territory, a claim vested with a corresponding governing authority, is predicated on clearly defined and

5 Pocock, *The Ideal of Citizenship*, esp. pp. 34–35.

6 Frank, *Kirchengeschichte des Mittelalters*, p. 34.

7 Foucault, *Sicherheit, Territorium, Bevölkerung*, esp. lecture 2.

8 Foucault, *'Omnes et singulatim'*.

9 Fraser, *Reframing Justice*.

defensible geographical boundaries. A nation's borders, however, are themselves in the employ of ideological parameters binding bodies in a common, national identity. In effect, that which the state names the state performs: territoriality as a claim on land is also a claim on the human bodies whose common identity is the ground they occupy. Territoriality, then, is both a physical and an ideological claim. This notional and corporeal claim on human lives extends to the objectification of land as such. Land which can be owned, and the parceling-out of which dispossesses others of competing claims, is land which can be used and exploited at will.

Territorial claims as they emerged with the rise of the modern nation state are premised on the valuation of land as a material possession. Societies marked by Western principles of territoriality have generally failed to propose even a nominal sense in which occupied land should have a "voice" in how it is farmed, mined, harvested, or lived on. Indeed, the legal processes governing the possession and use of land are premised on the image of a passive, etherized body of "real estate". Only in recent years, has it been possible to overcome the passive imagery of land, namely, in South American nations: around the year 2009, Bolivia and Ecuador adopted new constitutions scripted around ecological priorities.[10] Not only do the new constitutions emphasize environmental protection and sustainable development as a core value, they address for the first time "nature" or "Pachamama" as a juridical entity with a right to protection, regeneration, and respect.[11]

It is striking, however, that we should accept unquestioningly a view of land as having no more than inert, proprietary significance. There is no need to invoke naïve, anthropomorphic imagery in defending something other than a material valuation of land. It does need pointing out, however, that our inherited understanding of the land's passivity is a functional, political value, but it is not something we need to take as given. Theologically, in fact, we need to push back against the materialist, reductionist view if we are to critique unrivalled economic growth in the West funded by an excessive use of resources, which is to say funded ideologically by "territoriality" in the most damning sense of the term.

---

10 We note also that New Zealand in 2017 granted legal rights to the Whanganui river, one of the largest in the country, which the local Māori tribe in the North Island consider their "ancestor", a recognition for which they have fought for some150 years. Cf. O'Bryan, *Giving A Voice to the River*.

11 "Art. 72. La naturaleza tiene derecho a la restauración. Esta restauración será independiente de la obligación que tienen el Estado y las personas naturales o jurídicas de indemnizar a los individuos y colectivos que dependan de los sistemas naturales afectados." Asamblea Constituyente, "Constitución del Ecuador"; Gudynas, *Politische Ökologie*.

As examples of the Braunkohlerevier[12] in Nordrhein-Westfalen show, climate change is indeed about air pollution, but it is also a question of excessive land use and the result of the "objectification" of land in the "territoriality" framework we have described. If this is the case, then, climate justice is more than a corrective to carbon emissions but touches on fundamental questions of how we in the West have come to see ourselves in relation to the ground we walk on, and whether we can conceive of approaches to land use which go beyond the paradigm of material possession and objectification. Here is where the disruptive voices from often uncomfortable but nonetheless creative actions of advocates of the earth can help us to formulate alternatives to the principles of territoriality. The question for us is, then, how might these acts of resistance help to overcome the modern, instrumentalizing logic of objectification and exploitation of the earth?

3 Critical Resources for an Alternative Way of Living with the Land

In the sections that follow, we want to offer three vantage points from which we can consider the full implications of the question: (1) a biblical perspective drawing on the Book of Ruth in which the land is an agent of Gods' common good, (2) Basil's economic doctrine of gifting and grace, and (3) the church's response to indigenous notions of land custodianship we find the Apostolic Exhortation, *Querida Amazonia* as well as in the proceedings of the Amazon Synod. This should (4) enable us to imagine alternative ways of understanding land and our common interest in mitigating the human causes of climate change.

3.1 *Resource 1: Ethics of Environmental Justice and the Book of Ruth*

The term "environmental refugees"[13] first came into use in the mid-1980s in the UN's Brundtland Report, making the ethical case for a "sustainable" future in the face of climate change.[14] Those discussions made it clear that balancing

---

12 See the description and theological reflection on coal-mining in the Braukohlerevier by Benedikt Kern in this volume.

13 Brundtland, *Report of the World Commission*, I.2.16.

14 Cf. El-Hinnawi, *Environmental Refugees*. The term is not without controversy. Black critiques the paucity of "theoretical reflection about what constitutes a refugee," or a lack of "a conceptually coherent field of study" capable of interpreting "the personal histories and psychological or spiritual situations" of persons in forced-migration populations, given the driving needs of "researchers based within policy organizations" responding to "particular types of displacement" with "the documentation of empirical examples

economic needs with long-term environmental obligations would entail nothing less than a collective, moral vision of the oneness of the human race in all its diversity.[15] This section turns to the story of the biblical Ruth, seen from the perspective of the environmental refugee, to help outline a moral vision for Christian responses to climate change that can look past the limits of national borders.

Ruth's story brings into sharp relief a biblical moral landscape in which love of God and love of others is ethically of a piece with love of the land. At stake in this equation is the God of grace whose character demands a just relationship with the land. In the story, Ruth is the foreigner for whom the prospect of setting foot on Israel's soil is a matter of life and death. Ruth and her mother-in-law, Naomi, find themselves widowed, landless, and childless, in the middle of a disastrous drought, with no possibility of help in sight; Ruth famously opts to follow Naomi to Israel, setting off a chain of events in which her life is put at the mercy of people, country, and God not her own. In time, the question of whether Ruth, the landless Moabite incomer, will find sanctuary on Bethlehem's soil reveals also a question about Israel's future and their identity as people of God. The story tellingly plays on the fertile seeding of the royal family line in the womb of Ruth, the stranger who, pushed to by famine, embraces Israel's people and places her hope on Israel's God: "Your people will be my people, your God, will be my God" (Ruth 1:16). Crucially, in Ruth, the themes of fertility and harvest speak of land as the medium in which overturning widowhood and childlessness is the measure of God's grace. Israel's soil, far from being the backdrop against which Ruth's redemption drama happens to unfold, is in fact God's theatre of justice for the poor.

The juridical dimensions in Ruth's story become apparent in disputes about inheritance, right of abode, "levirate law" restrictions around a widow's remarriage, and so forth. At heart, however, Ruth tests the limits of statutes stipulating that tenancy on soil ultimately belonging to God must make Israel

---

of displacement" leading to evidence often made to fit a predetermined value of the term "environmental refugee". Black, *Fifty Years of Refugee Studies,* pp. 65–66. Cf. also Brundtland, *Report of the World Commission.*

15 Brundtland, *Report of the World Commission,* Ch.I.3.24. This is not without its problems: Brundtland's appeal on behalf of "humanity" is based on a notion of *rights,* a premise which needs to be questioned and cannot simply be taken as read: "All human beings have the fundamental right to an environment adequate for their health and well-being." "Our Common Future, Annexe 1: Summary of Proposed Legal Principles for Environmental Protection and Sustainable Development Adopted by the WCED Experts Group on Environmental Law"; I.1.

unflinching in welcoming the migrant worker, the landless sojourner, the refugee claiming sanctuary within its borders:

> When an alien resides with you in your land, you shall not oppress the alien: the alien who resides with you shall be to you as the citizen among you—*you shall love the alien as yourself*, for you yourselves were once aliens in the land of Egypt; I am the Lord your God. (Lev 19:33–34)

God's covenant is so concretely bound to justice and the ethics of land that even the most dispossessed among people wandering into Israel's soil must know that God's grace is real, providential, and absolute. This underlying premise levels with us in two ways.

First, *you shall love the alien as yourself* is as powerful an exhortation as we could have to look beyond national boundaries in constructing an ethical response to climate change and its consequences in our day.[16] Ruth's story, read in contemporary terms, delivers a concrete account that justice for the "environmental refugee" is justice that looks beyond national borders. Second, Ruth's story question assumptions about human relationship with land based on ownership rather than on the knowledge that our share in the land makes us morally accountable for being agents of a concrete, visible grace. Central to Ruth's argument is the obligation which sharing in the bounty of the land places on its occupants to practice something of Gods' open-handed grace. Walter Brueggemann refers to the "imperatives of divine grace" in which "grace is performed as an economic act of neighborly welfare toward those who are not yet neighbor."[17] We see this most vividly in God's command to leave untouched the fallen heads of grain or the grapes lying beneath the vine as a provision for the poor, for dispossessed persons gleaning their sustenance from what is left on the ground:

---

16 Rodd rightly cautioned against overstating our case by superimposing ethical implications in our notions of "ecology", for example, or of "equality" and concepts of "rights", on Old Testament religious morality: we cannot expect to derive a contemporary ethics from the Old Testament given the vast distances in contemporary and ancient "world views": "Poverty as such was not an issue, although it was accepted that weaker members of society ought not to be oppressed. War was a normal fact of life: why Yahweh permitted Israel to be defeated was the problem. Domestic animals were treated as superior and delicate tools, while wild animals were a continuous threat: rare indeed is any awareness that kindness should be shown to them, and isolated is the vision of peace with the animals and between them. Ecology and the equality of men and women hardly featured in the Old Testament at all… .": Rodd, *Glimpses of a Strange Land*, p. 272.

17 Brueggemann, *God, Neighbor, Empire*, p. 106.

> When you reap the harvest of your land, you shall not reap to the very edges of your field, or gather the gleanings of your harvest. You shall not strip your vineyard bare, or gather the fallen grapes of your vineyard; you shall leave them for the poor and the alien: I am the Lord your God. (Lev 10:9–10)

The imprint of God's grace in this command comes home to Ruth in what we could easily miss as an ordinary provision of food. Her handful of grain, however, is anything but a free hand-out: it is nothing less than God's radical grace reaching the neighbor with love, the stranger with mercy the alienated other with justice.[18] How radical this really is only comes into view when we see Ruth prostrate herself on the ground.

> Then she fell prostrate, with her face to the ground, and said to him, "Why have I found favor in your sight, that you should take notice of me, when I am a *foreigner*?" (Ruth 2:10)

We are of course right to read this as Ruth's recognition that a newly arrived asylum seeker is at the bottom of the social hierarchy. A stronger choice is possible, however, if we can see that, in lowering herself to the ground, Ruth is staking a claim on God's justice for the poor. The word "foreigner", *nokri* (נָכְרִי) denoting someone who has suffered calamity or misfortune, is key in this verse. *Nokri* describes Ruth, the asylum seeker and "environmental migrant", in every sense of the word. And we are right, once again, to see in Boaz a picture of charity, of love and upright principle doing right by the destitute Ruth. We must not miss, however, that when Ruth plants her hands in Israel's soil, she is taking hold of a God-given grace to be morally included in the blessings of the land. Marriage, then, is for Ruth not simply mercy but the very fulfilment of God's justice for the orphan, for the widow, for the landless poor.

It should be obvious by now that the principles of territoriality we are bringing into question cannot easily cope with an economics of grace in which land is no longer reckoned coldly in terms of market value, the profitability of its natural resources, and the politics of the nation state. Ruth's story, for its part, raises the stakes, amplifying Isaiah's vision of a common good in which what is freely given has been first freely received:

> Come, you who thirst, come to the waters; and you who have no money, come, buy and eat, come buy wine and milk without money and without cost. (Isa 55:1)

18 Brueggemann, *God, Neighbor, Empire*, p. 105 (adapted for present purpose).

This clearly speaks of an ethic in which God's grace is neither pinned to an economy of ownership nor to the confines of national identity or race. This is where the moral dimensions of the land, and the role this plays in Ruth's redemption story, becomes a counternarrative of God's love for those undergoing forced migration. Indeed, if Ruth is symbolic of environmental migrants in our day,[19] then her story invokes the God without borders who "redeems the world in suffering and will consummate the world in joyous well-being."[20] The moral scope in this horizon ought to make possible an ethic of land accountable, as a matter of environmental justice, to the people most vulnerable to forced migration and the consequences of climate change.

3.2 *Resource 2: The Bread that you Store is for the Hungry—Basil of Caesarea*

We are confronting the Western notion of the nation state as a paradigm predicated on land ownership and on its resources being seen in essentially commodified terms. The far-reaching consequences of this tenet in light of the environmental crisis includes the frequent rejection of those fleeing displacement because of climate change and seeking refuge within another state. This section seeks to highlight resources for a theological alternative in the fourth-century church father Basil of Caesarea (330–379).

Basil's perspective is premised on all things *qua* creation being gifted into existence by God, *qua* Creator *ex nihilo*.[21] As creatures made in the "image of God" with responsibilities of stewardship over the earth, moreover, human beings must remain cognizant that everything we have is to be related to, not as possessions, but as gifts to be used in service to others. For Basil, we are aware of who we are because we recognize *whose* we are: the divine Benefactor from whom all things come.[22] The extent to which we recognize and faithfully live by this reality is revealed by our attitude towards our possessions and, respectively, towards others who are in need.

In Basil's provocative sermon "To the Rich" (Matt 19), we find a commentary on the sad and dejected rich young man who purports to have kept the

19 It is important to understand forced migration is in the negative sense of loss of land and livelihood, but also per International Organization for Migration (IOM) as necessary "adaptation" and show of "resilience" of populations in the face of drastic displacement and change: "Prevention and preparedness can foster resilience to sudden-onset disasters and mitigate the impacts of displacement on vulnerable populations." Melde/Flavell, *State of the art*, p. 12.

20 Brueggemann, *Biblical authority*, p. 15.

21 See Schaff, *Basil*, pp. 180–259.

22 Basil the Great, *On Social Justice*, p. 61.

commandments and yet cannot bring himself to part with his possessions. The rich man's reaction, Basil remarks, revealed that he had not, in fact, faithfully adhered to God's commandment to love the neighbor as oneself—if he had, the man would not have had such an "abundance" of wealth and possessions to dispose of, and would therefore not have been sad at the prospect of unburdening himself in order to follow Christ.[23] Rather than being orientated in his attention towards the divine Giver of all good things, and recognizing in his reciprocity with others that everything which exists is a divine benefaction, the rich man shows himself to not simply be in possession *of* goods, but one who is, as it were, possessed *by* avarice *for* goods. Avarice, for Basil, is innately totalizing and oblivious to creaturely or natural limitations: "The sea knows its boundaries, but the avaricious person does not defer to the proper order of things, but rather imitates the violent nature of fire: spreading to all and devouring all."[24] Avarice utterly saturates one's attention and reduces everything to an order-defying desire for further possessions.[25] As such, it represents an apotheosing attitude towards temporal goods, making one cling to what one has and fueling a perpetual desire to take more, rather than acknowledging in gratitude that all one has is given by, and received from, God.

On this view, then, the self-orientated and self-consuming attitude of avarice represents the inversion of a creaturely acknowledgement that one only has anything at all through divine gratuity; nor do possessions lose their constitutive contingency and giftedness once possessed. Seen positively, the conditional nature of human ownership is precisely the basis for living in gratitude to God for all that one has. Extending this to its ethical implications, moreover, tells us that the attitude proper to human beings as creatures is one in which all material desires are subjugated in gratitude to the will of God and thereby reoriented towards the divine prescription of love for one's neighbor. In a homily on the "Rich Fool" (Luke 12:18), Basil insists that his hearers reconsider "what resources have been entrusted to you, from whom you received them, and why you received," so as to ethically recognize "the things in your possession as belonging to others."[26] Specifically, Basil exhorts the wealthy in his congregation to recognize their debt to their divine Giver, who, in fact, has blessed them so that they might give to others. As everything is given to humanity in common by God, moreover, everything which one has is, in this sense, *already* the property of those who need it:

23 Basil the Great, *On Social Justice*, p. 43.
24 Basil the Great, *On Social Justice*, p. 50. Cf. Job 38:8–11.
25 Basil the Great, *On Social Justice*, p. 51.
26 Basil the Great, *On Social Justice*, p. 61.

> The bread you are holding back is for the hungry, the clothes you keep put away are for the naked,[…] the silver you keep buried in the earth is for the needy. You are thus guilty of injustice toward as many as you might have aided, and did not.[27]

We learn from Basil, then, that the earth and its resources are constituent of God's economy of grace: all things are gifted for the common good of all humanity. Catholic social teaching on the "common destination of created goods"[28] is an example of a concrete alternative to the Western paradigm of land as the possession of the nation state. For not only does the refusal to share from our resources exhibit ingratitude towards the divine Giver, doing so sinfully forecloses God's gifting economy in which we are made but custodians of belongings which, rightfully, already belong to those in need.

3.3 *Resource 3: The Amazon Synod and the Custodians of the Forest*

A recent example of Christian response to environmental justice is found in the Apostolic Exhortation, *Querida Amazonia*,[29] with its underlying ethic of living in relation to land. Proceedings from the Amazon Synod are at pains to show that the very concepts of "land" and "soil" must be expanded to include rivers and bodies of water sustaining life in all its biodiversity, in line with thinking and traditions endemic to indigenous populations who have thrived on a symbiotic relationship with the land, its waterways and natural resources. Consequently, the papal document recognizes the hereditary inhabitants of the Amazon as the rightful "custodians of the rainforest and its resources."[30] This ethos of coexistence with the land, one might say "coinherence" in the land, is echoed also among indigenous cultures of the Andes for whom the concept of *Pachamama* speaks of Mother Earth's overabundance mediating human relationships with the mountain, the river, the forest, the land.

---

27 Basil the Great, *On Social Justice*, p. 69–70. This passage is utilized by Thomas Aquinas (1225–1274) in his *Summa Theologica* to assert that a person who takes a good essential for life (such as food or clothing) out of necessity is not guilty of theft under natural law. See *Summa Theologica* II-II, q. 66, a.7 (the passage from Basil appears to be mistakenly attributed to Ambrose (340–397), who in his discourse "On Naboth" (1 Kgs 21:1–16), makes a strikingly similar point; see Ramsey, *Ambrose*, p. 135.

28 See for instance Pope Francis, *Fratelli Tutti*, 119.

29 Pope Francis, *Querida Amazonia* [=QA].

30 In the *Preparatory Document* for the Synod Section I—Seeing, §2 Socio-cultural Diversity (Amazon Synod, *Final Document*; Amazon Synod, *Preparatory Document;* Pope Francis, *Querida Amazonia* [=QA]). This view is kept also in the *Final Document* of the Synod 6–14; 66–73 and in QA 34–40; 41–52.

In the Andes, tilling land for planting entails ritually asking permission to plough into the soil, because this is seen as an act of ripping into earth's "flesh" for its primal energies; communal acts of healing and thanksgiving are similarly observed in times of harvest.[31] Given this quasi-personifying ethic of the land (a quasi-vitalist sense in which land is perceived as being in some sense alive), we can perhaps understand why land ownership was a foreign concept to pre-Columbian cultures of the Americas. The idea that land should become a capital asset, and that the parceling of land would become the basis for development, was diametrically opposed to the sense of a communal relationship to land found among many indigenous peoples.[32] We can hardly begin to appreciate the extent to which colonial objectification of land as property, that idea that land could be possessed and owned by any one person, was from the standpoint of indigenous traditions simply unfathomable.[33] It may help, however, to understand that for indigenous communities, land simply could not mean "territory" in our common use the term, but something closer to "space", or perhaps even "space-time"[34] understood as a holistic dimension encompassing human relationships and human flourishing over time. Earth itself is seen existentially as "cultural ground, full of traditions, myths and history."[35] The concept of "Pacha" therefore militates against treating the earth in terms of production processes meeting human need, moreover, against placing individualistic gain above the community Mother Earth hosts in her "great, fertile, maternal womb."[36]

31 When "rational" production processes were forced upon indigenous groups in the early stages of the colony and the dilapidation of the products was forbidden, these indigenous peoples stopped working. For them, it did not make sense cultivating, planting and harvesting when it should not culminate in a feast. Only then, with the "rational" production of cultivation, harvesting and storing for later consumption, real hunger became possible. Partly in response to such insights, the traditional methodological approach of Liberation Theology—to see, to judge, to act—has been expanded to include also as a fourth moment "to celebrate" in a wide sense.

32 Barros/Caravias, *Teología de la tierra*, p. 21.

33 Barros and Caravias likewise "set out by recognizing humbly how far we have always been from starting to understand the meaning that everything related to earth has for an indigenous person." Barros/Caravias, *Teología de la tierra*, p. 73.

34 See Barros/Caravias, *Teología de la tierra*, p. 76–81. See also Estermann, *Apu Taytayku*, pp. 54–57; May, *Los pobres de la tierra*, pp. 11–13.

35 Some languages like Xavante do not even have a word for "territory". See Barros/Caravias, *Teología de la tierra*, p. 75.

36 Barros/Caravias, *Teología de la tierra*, p. 77. Consequently, problems, conflicts and divisions between members of a community impinge on their relationship to the land, and so acts of communal reconciliation within the community are a prerequisite for a fruitful relationship to Mother earth.

The complexities of the present situation in the Amazon, in principle subject to legislated recognition of ancestral indigenous land holdings, are clearly beyond the parameters of this chapter. It should suffice to say, however, that Regina Reinart's study of the Amazon Synod documents the way in which recognition of indigenous territory provided for in law is fraught by procedural issues[37] preventing at least forty-percent of such claims from being processed through the relevant authorities.[38] In the meantime, commercial interests forcing migrations within the forest and eventually into cities tell a story of further land loss and of further alienation of indigenous populations from ancestral lands.[39] We need to pull the lens back from these technical, political, and juridical particulars, however, in order to take in the overall picture.

This is in fact what the Amazon Synod did, building on the insights of *Laudato si'*, namely, by filtering overarching questions of justice through the concept of an "integral ecology."[40] This amounts to taking an ethical standpoint which refuses to compartmentalize people and land opting instead to recognize that all aspects of society, the health of its institutions and processes, "have consequences for the environment and [for] the quality of human life."[41] This all-encompassing ecology inevitably demands our reimagining of what the just society is. To this end, the Amazon Synod begins by asking what the poor make of the common good, how they might see "the good life" and how this might reorient society itself towards "good living" as the basis for a sustainable future. The document furthermore insists that the role of the church is to be "an ally of the Amazonian peoples,"[42] who, for their part, "want the church to accompany them, to walk with them" in serving their custodianship without the imposition of "a particular way of being."[43] The church has consequently committed to joining the peoples of the Amazon both in resisting unchecked "development" and safeguarding the "cultures, traditions and spiritualities" underpinning their "love," "protection," and "care" of the Amazon.[44]

At this point, we would do well to pause and appreciate the extent to which the dialogic character of these documents reflect an ethic of communal

---

37 Reinart, *Die Amazonien-Synode*, pp. 42–53.

38 Reinart, *Die Amazonien-Synode*, pp. 45. This is all the more astonishing and scandalous, as the Brazilian Constitution of 1988 stipulated a five-year period for the demarcation of (all) indigenous territories.

39 See the Amazon Synod, *Preparation Document* I.2 on "socio-cultural diversity."

40 See the Amazon Synod, *Final Document* of the Synod Ch. 4, §65–85. It refers to the Encyclical *Laudato si'* Chapter 4, §137–162: Pope Francis, *Laudato Si'* [=LS].

41 QA 23.

42 Amazon Synod, *Final Document*, 46.

43 Amazon Synod, *Preparatory Document*, 12.

44 Amazon Synod, *Final Document*, 74.

thinking placing indigenous peoples, their spiritual values and cultural interests on the same celebratory[45] and theologically incarnate footing as what the church has to offer.[46] Is it possible that, by appropriating and reinterpreting the notion of territoriality in the light of indigenous ways of relating to "territory", the church has provided us a scaffold on which to negotiate a common future?[47] If so, then, we may well be in a position to appreciate in our concluding section the way in which faith and spirituality might be the most radical, countercultural set of values enabling us to see that land has always been God-given and was only ever intended to be our common good.

3.4 *Resource 4: Eco-theology and Christian Activism on Behalf of God's Common Good*

One example of earth advocacy is the organization known as Christians for the Mountains (CFTM), a network of evangelical Christians in the Appalachia region of the United States fighting against the practice of Mountaintop Removal. To access coal, entire mountain tops are dislodged, trees are ripped from the ground, and dirt and rocks are removed to nearby valleys or tipped into the streams. CFTM contest that the aptly described method of surface removal in coal mining is not only changing topography, vegetation, and biodiversity, but is also eroding the cultural value of a life "centered around tending this commons, which brought communities and families together."[48] The coal industry may justify the consequences in these methods as necessary in America's goal to achieve energy independence, but CTFM criticize the harm to the environment, going so far as to describe Mountaintop Removal as a "crime against nature."[49] The cultural and communal element at play, moreover, goes hand-in-hand with the environmental concern: CTFM work to mitigate the loss of the mountain "commons," which they see as threatening "kinship and communal practices" such as hunting, and fishing, as well as harvesting of wild berries, mushrooms and indigenous plants. CFTM's protest against coal companies and what they see as wanton exploitation of the land is also a protest against government agencies for failing to enforce regulations, and against

45 Amazon Synod, *Preparation Document* III.15. "This is spirituality after the fashion of Jesus: simple, human, in dialogue, and Samaritan, allowing us to celebrate life, Liturgy, the Eucharist, and festivals, always in respect for the rhythms proper to each people."

46 QA 5–6.

47 The concept of 'territory' is significant to the Amazon Synod, particularly in its Working Document (Amazon Synod, *Instrumentum Laboris*, cap. II) and in the Amazon Synod, *Final Document*.

48 The CFTM activist Judy Bond died 2011, quoted by Jennifer Hattam, *Dethroning King Coal·*

49 *"Christians For The Mountains"*.

politicians who benefit from the backing of the coal industry.[50] CFTM's grassroots "tactics" include prayer and preaching at protest rallies, and producing worship materials and resources for theological reflection with the conviction that "God gave us everything that we needed in those mountains."[51] CFTM activists occasionally engage in nonviolent civil disobedience, leading in some cases to arrests or to harassment from coal industry supporters.[52] Despite these risks, however, CFTM continue engaging faith with activism, motivated by their Christian faith: "God compels me to keep fighting… . This is a spiritual issue as well as an environmental issue."[53]

The Christian impetus for CFTM's work for the protection of the environment speaks to their distinctive framing of the world through biblical imagery and, indeed, by drawing on sources of Christian spirituality. Elizabeth Bomberg and Alice Hague, accounting for "how and why church communities mobilize locally on environmental issues," describe spiritual resources as "a particular set of cultural resources linked to faith, inner belief and transcendence … the collection of spiritual beliefs, symbols and identities that facilitate collective action on specific issues."[54] Their study of Christian and secular environmental groups in Scotland finds that the view of the earth as part of God's creation calls the Christian actors to "respect and protect" nature in a way that "engenders love" of God, love of neighbor, and love of creation[55] They affirm, furthermore, that seeing the earth as God's creation forms the basis of spirituality understood in terms of "the *interconnectedness* of all things."[56] CFTM's activism, in sum, uses theological resources to challenge the ways in which the exploitation and objectification of land threatens a Christian investment in the indissoluble interconnectedness between land, community, faith, and culture. Their very mission is described in terms of the interconnectedness we read in the Bible citation used as the group's motto, "The earth is the Lord's, and everything in it, the world, and all who live in it" (Psalm 24:1).[57]

---

50 Billings/Samson, *Evangelical Christians*, p. 7.

51 Hattam, *Dethroning King Coal.*

52 Billings/Samson, *Evangelical Christians.*

53 Billings/Samson, *Evangelical Christians*, p. 2.

54 Bomberg/Hague, *Faith-Based Climate Action*, p. 583.

55 Bomberg/Hague, *Faith-Based Climate Action*, pp. 587–88.

56 Bomberg/Hague, *Faith-Based Climate Action*, pp. 587–88.

57 Billings/Samson, *Evangelical Christians.*

While *creation care* has been the heart of Christian advocacy in Appalachia,[58] the global Christian climate movement has put *justice* center stage.[59] What is particular here is that justice is no longer entangled in the kind territorial ethics we are bringing into question, but takes its stand outside the polity of the nation state. We have seen this in Nancy Fraser's own break from geographically bounded understandings of climate justice:

> activists contesting transnational inequities reject the view that justice can only be imagined territorially, as a domestic relation among fellow citizens [and posit] post-Westphalian views of "who counts", [thereby] subjecting the Westphalian frame to explicit critique.[60]

Some indigenous, rural communities in Honduras have drawn similar conclusions in confronting their own vulnerability to climate change. The scholar María José Méndez chronicles the way in which indigenous communities are testing the limits of land claims in order to resist the threat of climate-driven displacement and to plan their community's adaptation to new climate conditions. Driven by principles of "collective land" interests and understandings of land as common, they seek to safeguard land practices capable of ensuring reduced levels of climate emissions.[61] Justice, from this standpoint, must in the end be intra-societal, international, and inter-generational justice for those made most vulnerable to the impacts of climate change.[62] Climate justice must serve indigenous people, the poor, and all those confronted by social inequalities of gender and class, and this means that it must be transnational in reach

58 Yet, justice and other perspectives are included in their discourses; creation care appears to be in the center. For a thorough discussion on how this network relate to the Creation Care movement and the Evangelical Climate Initiative in the United States, please see Billings/Samson, *Evangelical Christians*, p. 6. For a brief overlook of the on-going discussion of the role of religions in climate activism in the United States, and different types of Christian environmentalism, please see Kearns, *The Role of Religions*.

59 Not at least since the mobilization around the OCPS-19 (Conference of Parties) in Copenhagen 2009. See for example: Glaab, *A Climate for Justice*, p. 1111; della Porta/Parks, *Framing Processes in the Climate Movement*.

60 Fraser, *Who Counts?*, p. 282.

61 To protect land is a central strategy to tackle both the adaptation to a new climate and to reduce the emissions, according to the UN "Land and Climate Change | UNCCD". Méndez highlights the specific strategy to protect land "as common good" in her report from Honduras. Honduras is a country especially vulnerable to climate change consequences. The country has been hit by several severe droughts, hurricanes, increased flooding, and coastline erosion. The people's livelihoods are endangered and entire villages are suffering from the sea-level rise, which causes forced migration. Méndez, *The Silent Violence*.

62 On the link between climate justice, social discrimination, and human rights, cf. Schapper, *Climate Justice and Human Rights*.

and trans-territorial in moral scope. Our argument is that seeing land as a common, human and spiritual good is the measure of that scope. This is where pressing the issues through a Christian, activist frame makes a difference. As was evident in Bomberg and Hague's case study, whilst secular environmental groups expressed their hunger for justice in largely consequentialist, instrumentalist terms, Christian actors located the issues at the level of the human and the spiritual. Drawing strength from their reflection on Scripture and a pragmatic faith, these campaigners aim to reorder our hierarchy of values so that land is no longer reduced to the status of a mere matter, an object for human exploit, but is properly seen a human, common good, as the way in which God cares for us.

We are seeing, then, how alternatives to an objectifying ethic of land proprietorship enable us to look past a Westphalian frame. Activists pave the way for biblical imagery informing notions of land, and for relationship with God speaking to the way in which the community bears responsibility for the care of creation. Fraser speaks of environmentalists and indigenous people "asserting their right to make claims against the structures that harm them" on the basis of principles otherwise invisible to the existing structures.[63] We may not be able to figure belief in God's love of the creation into our existing structures and ways of valuing land and its resources. However, we can at least agree that renegotiating a Westphalian understanding of land requires some recognition of faith as a resource in the concrete work of environmental justice in general and protection of land specifically.

In sum, Christians engaged in environmental causes, as in the example of churches in Scotland and Appalachia, that is, those prioritizing a human sense of connection to the land to such extent that some can say that "When these mountains go, our culture, our heritage, and our identity are gone,"[64] are telling us something about the value of faith in the call to environmental justice. Could we go so far as to say that the care of creation is, on one hand, about living out our ecological commitments and ethical convictions, but, at the same time, because it is about sustaining "community" with an encompassing vision of "neighbor care,"[65] it is ultimately a question of living an incarnate Christian faith? If so, can we conclude provisionally at least that faith practices of prayer, Bible reading, worship, and so forth, are not simply aspects of niche spiritualities inhabiting, unseen, personal, inner, private spheres, but are in fact catalysts generating concrete and very public practices in response to

63 Fraser, *Who counts?*, p. 15.

64 Hattam, *Dethroning King Coal*.

65 With reference to Matt 22:35–39; Bomberg/Hague, *Faith-Based Climate Action*, p. 588.

environmental justice; and that, indeed, to say "The earth is the Lord's" is the makings of a "lived theology" reflected with, and never apart from, human relationship with the earth?

4 Land, Relationality, Ethics, Climate: Beyond Ownership and Acquisition

In the discussion above we have freely referred to the just distribution of land, the ethics of a just occupation and use of land. In doing so, we have simply taken for granted the idea that land is some "thing" which is unilaterally acted upon by the human agent. We want to conclude our discussion, however, by taking a counterintuitive option and breaking from what Ferrando identifies as the "geological agency"[66] implied in the androcentric perspective. What in fact do issues of climate justice look like when, for once, we stop seeing land as something which is simply determined upon and done to by human actors? This is where we test the strength of the arguments we have explored so far, and see our way out of conventional ways of speaking of land in objectifying terms as a thing, in order to insert into the discussion the "role", as it were, which land itself has in God's provision of a human common good.

In a sense we are simply following a furrow ploughed by intellectual challenges to the anthropocentric primacy implied in the idea of "owning" land in the Keynesian-Westphalian frame: cultural studies as well as in environmental humanities have sought to establish a discourse in which nature itself has a certain kind of narrative agency in this story.[67] So for example, post-humanism, going beyond a notion of the Anthropocene in which the earth is measured strictly in terms of human impact on the planet, strives to tear down the line of demarcation separating the human from the non-human.[68] Old Testament notions of land explored here alongside a Patristic perspective on the givenness of goods, as well as the church's validation of Amazonian perceptions of nature set alongside contemporary eco-spiritualties, make it possible to raise the idea that land could be seen as our theological conversation partner. To be clear, we are avoiding the error, theologically, of creating earth in our own image; this is not an argument for a "humanification" of land as such. Jesus, the incarnate

66 Ferrando, *The Party of the Anthropocene*, p. 162.

67 Haidvogl/Winiwarter/Brumat, *Natural History of the Danube Region;* Knoll/Lübken/Schott (eds.), *Rivers Lost, Rivers Regained.*

68 Ferrando's idea of post-humanism mines the interrelated nature of human life and the natural environment which, in her in her argument, "evolves in relational, symbiotic, entangled intra-acting processes." Ferrando, *The Party of the Anthropocene*, p. 171.

Son of God, did not become land (any more than he became a non-human animal),[69] he became a human being living in and with nature as he found it, treating it respectfully as one sharing in its "createdness".

The term *createdness* should alert us to at least two things: first, the fact that we as well as land itself are created, and, second, that our shared origins in God's creativity means that recognizing our common creatureliness with nature is a necessary part of our human identity.

The existing religious reflection on ecology, and land in particular, may be succinctly summed up by their distinguishing features, with eco-theologies sharing one common content, whereas "eco-spirituality" seems to cover two quite different fields. Eco-theology might be understood as intra-theological reflections seeking to create new knowledge in the field of theology. Representatives of these approaches[70] would include Leonardo Boff[71], Teilhard de Chardin,[72] Markus Vogt.[73] Eco-spirituality, on the other hand, might refer in pastoral terms to drawing on connection with creation in prayers, through pilgrimage, or other "practical" approaches,[74] or it may speak to aspects in the field of alternative or new spiritualties placing an emphasis, not primarily on theological reflection, but on intuitive (re)connection with the natural environment.[75] In one sense, our contribution to this volume is a contribution to ongoing theological reflections building on, or responding to, critical insight from eco-spiritualities, some of which have engaged more recently in critical dialogue with Christian theology.

Our approach has shown, however, contrary to perceptions that eco-spiritualities are something novel or profoundly alien to Christian discourse, that there is good reason to root contemporary reflection on nature, ecology, and land in existing parts of the Christian tradition. *Laudato Si'* has therefore been an important vehicle in the transmission of Christian reflection on human relationship with land. This is why some have gone so far as to describe

69 On the theological implications for "animality" human share with other creatures, see Meyer, *Inner Animalities*, esp. Ch. 4.

70 To include in broad strokes Altner, *Zwischen Natur und Menschengeschichte*; Ganoczy, *Schöpfungslehre*; Moltmann, *Gott in der Schöpfung*; Pannenberg, *Beiträge zur Systematischen Theologie*.

71 De Chardin, *Le Phénomène Humain*.

72 Boff, *Ecología*.

73 Vogt, *Prinzip Nachhaltigkeit*.

74 Ostheimer/Blanc, *Challenging the Levels*.

75 Bloch, *Alternative Spirituality;* Hedlund-de Witt, *The Rising Culture*; Heelas/Woodhead, *The Spiritual Revolution*; Taylor, *Dark Green Religion*.

this turn to spirituality and eco-theology, and to the "greening" of religion on the whole, as the "Francis effect."[76]

We have seen, on the other hand, that a shift away from the "usefulness" of land arguments to a new vision of land as a theological dialogue partner is a recent development in Christian theology. Our challenge to objectifying views of nature and urging of a more humane, relational form of discourse about land, for example, have come from Christian responses to the challenges of the present age. Our reading of the biblical story of Ruth identified land as an agent of divine grace, and from Basil, we learned the virtue of living within our creaturely limits by accepting possession of things only to the degree that it grows in us generosity and communion with others; the Amazon Synod has taught us to read ancient cultures and spiritualities as extensions of God's book of nature. These theological reflections are as contemporary as they are rooted in a Christian tradition in which land is far from being defined as material possession or as a trophy for human conquest. Our initial steps in this direction required challenging the objectification of land; we offered in its place theological discourse in which the gravitational center is no longer the human and our material needs but the impact nature and humans have on one another, and in the end on the delicate interplay between nature as such and human responsibility for the care of God's creation, as such. We are at this point, then, miles away from seeing our place in the natural world as an intractable confrontation between the human and its earthly opposite. We recognize the value in asserting that humanity is interwoven with the fabric of nature itself. For as the American farmer and poet Wendell Berry tells us, we are beginning to understand the interconnectedness of all things, and so to know that

> nature includes us. It is not a place into which we reach from some safe standpoint outside it. We are in it and are a part of it while we use it. If it does not thrive, we cannot thrive. The appropriate measure of farming then is the world's health and our health, and this is inescapably *one* measure.[77]

If we are to learn from the environmental activists in Appalachia who, motivated by their Christian faith, see themselves as part of the land they occupy, and if our perspective has been subsequently enlarged by the properly speaking "catholic", which is to say, universal vision of *Laudato si'*, boundaries previously thought to rigidly separate the human from the "natural" become

76 Maibach et al., *The Francis Effect.*

77 Berry, *What Are People For*, pp. 207–208.

markedly porous and finally simply blur at the edges in the light of our shared creaturely origins in God's eternal purposes.[78]

This then gives us every reason to believe that there might be an environmental turn in the present Christian discourse, perhaps even one in which both nature and the non-organic members making up the wider natural "commons" (*vis.* rocks, mountains, rivers) could help bring about a renewed perspective on what we take to be normative in conversations about environmental justice and the Christian response to climate change. Others have taken up reflection on the non-animate part of the environment, for example, in the rights of nature movement leading to new legal frameworks around nature. We have seen how nations challenging the Keynesian-Westphalian frame have enacted constitutional frames that codify core enforceable rights of nature.[79] For our part, in this contribution, we hope to have shown that the aim of theological reflection *about* nature in the twenty-first century, beginning as reflection *with* nature, ought to follow the ethical implications of such questions in justice *for* nature, and so for land inasmuch as for its inhabitants. Biblical and patristic thinking have already challenged us to see ownership, of land or anything else, in terms of the responsibilities this implies to share from our sense of gratitude with our fellow others. Our argument, in sum, is that this attitude of sharing and of offering back from what is already God-given must be expanded to include our attitudes towards land itself. For in this co-creatural era, an ethic of sharing can no longer be limited to humans alone but must include our sharing as *one* with creation itself in God's economy of grace.

References

"Christian For The Mountains | The Earth Is the Lord's, We Are Caretakers", downloaded 31.03.2021, https://christiansforthemountains.org [accessed 31.03.2021].

"Constitución del Ecuador". Available on https://www.acnur.org/fileadmin/Documentos/BDL/2008/6716.pdf [accessed 21.05.2021].

Altner, Günter: *Zwischen Natur und Menschengeschichte. Perspektiven für eine neue Schöpfungstheologie.* München: Kaiser 1975.

78 Horstmann/Ruster/Taxacher, *Alles, was atmet*; Lintner, *Respect for the Proper Value*; Lintner, *Mensch—Tier—Gott*.

79 Movements in Bolivia deserve scrutiny. Cf. Constitution of the Republic of Ecuador; Villavicencio Calzadilla/Kotzé, *Living in Harmony with Nature?* The Church of Sweden, inspired by the Sami indigenous people (spread across Norway, Sweden, Finland and Russia) and the Sami Parliament's decision to support the Universal Declaration of the Rights of Mother Earth, have adopted the study of the rights of nature in their national Christian education curricula.

Amazon Synod: *Final Document.* Available at www.sinodoamazonico.va [accessed 21.05.2021].

Amazon Synod: *Instrumentum Laboris.* https://www.vaticannews.va/en/vatican-city/news/2020-02/final-document-synod-amazon.html [accessed 21.05.2021].

Amazon Synod: *Preparatory Document.* Available at www.sinodoamazonico.va [accessed 21.05.2021].

Barros Souza, Marcelo de/José Luis Caravias: *Teología de la tierra.* Madrid: Paulinas 1988.

Basil the Great: *On Social Justice*, trans. C. P. Schroeder. Crestwood, NY: St. Vladimir's Seminary Press 2009.

Berry, Wendell: *What Are People For.* San Francisco: North Point Press 1990.

Billings, Dwight B./Will Samson, "Evangelical Christians and the Environment: 'Christians for the Mountains' and the Appalachian Movement against Mountaintop Removal Coal Mining", in: *Worldviews* 16 (no. 1, 2012), https://doi.org/10.1163/156853511X617786.

Black, R.: "Fifty Years of Refugee Studies: From Theory to Policy", in: *The International Migration Review* Vol. 35, No. 1, Spring 2001. Special Issue: UNHCR at 50: Past, Present and Future of Refugee Assistance, pp. 57–78.

Bloch, J. P.: "Alternative Spirituality and Environmentalism", in Roger S. Gottlieb (ed.), *Religion and the Environment. Critical Concepts in Religious Studies,* Vol. IV. London and New York: Routledge, 2010, pp. 301–322.

Boff, Leonardo: *Ecología. Grito de la Tierra, Grito de los Pobres.*, Madrid: Trotta ⁵2011.

Bomberg, Elizabeth/Alice Hague, "Faith-Based Climate Action in Christian Congregations: Mobilisation and Spiritual Resources", in: *Local Environment* 23 (no. 5, 4 May 2018), https://doi.org/10.1080/13549839.2018.1449822.

Brueggemann, Walter: "Biblical authority: A Personal Reflection", in: *Christian Century* (3–10 Jan 2001).

Brueggemann, Walter: *God, Neighbor, Empire: The Excess of Divine Fidelity and the Command of Common Good.* Waco, TX: Baylor University Press 2019.

Brundtland, Gro H.: *Report of the World Commission on Environment and Development: Our Common Future.* United Nations General Assembly (doc. A/42/427) 1987 (The Brundtland Report).

Constitution of the Republic of Ecuador, Official Registry No. 449, 20 Oct. 2008.

De Chardin, Pierre Teilhard: *Le Phénomène Humain.* Paris: Oeuvres Édition du Seuil 1958.

della Porta, Donatella/Louisa Parks: "Framing Processes in the Climate Movement: From Climate Change to Climate Justice", in: Matthias Dietz/Heiko Garrelts (eds.): *Routledge Handbook of the Climate Change Movement.* Lonodon: Routledge 2014.

El-Hinnawi, Essam: *Environmental Refugees.* Nairobi, Kenya: United Nations Environmental Programme 1985.

Estermann, Josef: *Apu Taytayku. Religion und Theologie im andinen Kontext Lateinamerikas, Theologie interkulturell* 23. Ostfildern: Grünewald 2012.

Ferrando, Francesaca: "The Party of the Anthropocene: Post-Humanism, Environmentalism and the Post-Anthropocentric Paradigm Shift", in: *Relations. Beyond Anthropocentrism* (no. 4.2, 2016): pp. 159–173, https://doi.org/10.7358/rela-2016-002-ferr.

Foucault, Michel: "'Omnes et singulatim': zu einer Kritik der politischen Vernunft" (1981), in: *Schriften in vier Bänden: Dits et Ecrits*. Frankfurt a. M.: Suhrkamp 2005, Vol. 4, pp. 165–198.

Foucault, Michel: *Sicherheit, Territorium, Bevölkerung: Geschichte der Gouvernementalität I*. Frankfurt a. M.: Suhrkamp [3]2014.

Frank, Isnard W.: *Kirchengeschichte des Mittelalters. Leitfaden Theologie* 14. Düsseldorf: Patmos [4]1997.

Fraser, Nancy: "Reframing Justice in a Globalizing World", in: *New Left Review* 36 (2005). Available on https://newleftreview.org/issues/ii36/articles/nancy-fraser-reframing-justice-in-a-globalizing-world_[accessed 21.05.2021].

Fraser, Nancy: "Who Counts? Dilemmas of Justice in a Postwestphalian World", in: *Antipode* 41, no. s1 (2010): pp. 281–297, https://doi.org/10.1111/j.1467-8330.2009.00726.x.

Ganoczy, Alexandre: *Schöpfungslehre*. Düsseldorf: Patmos 1983.

Glaab, Katharina: "A Climate for Justice? Faith-Based Advocacy on Climate Change at the United Nations", in: *Globalizations* 14 (no. 7, 10 November 2017), https://doi.org/10.1080/14747731.2017.1308060.

Gudynas, Eduardo: "Politische Ökologie: Natur in den Verfassungen von Bolivien und Ecuador," in: *juridikum* 4, no. 4 (2009). Available on https://www.juridikum.at/fileadmin/user_upload/ausgaben/juridikum%204-2009.pdf [accessed 21.05.2021].

Haidvogl, G./V. Winiwarter/S. Brumat: "Natural History of the Danube Region", in: Christian Hanus et al.: *Danube: Future Interdisciplinary School Proceedings 2017. Cultural and Social Implications of Global Change on the Danube River Basin*. Donau-Universität Krems 2019: pp. 42–53.

Hattam, Jennifer: "Dethroning King Coal: A miner's daughter stands up for Appalachia's mountains", Sierra Magazine—Sierra Club, http://vault.sierraclub.org/sierra/200311/profile.asp [accessed 12.04.2021].

Hedlund-de Witt, Annick: "The Rising Culture and Worldview of Contemporary Spirituality: A Sociological Study of Potentials and Pitfalls for Sustainable Development", in: *Ecological Economics* 70 (2011): pp. 1057–1065.

Heelas, Paul/Linda Woodhead: *The Spiritual Revolution. Why Religion Is Giving Way to Spirituality*, Religion and Spirituality in the Modern World. Oxford et al.: Blackwell Publishing 2005.

Horstmann, Simone/Thomas Ruster/Gregor Taxacher: *Alles, was atmet. Eine Theologie der Tiere*. Regensburg: Pustet 2018.

Kearns, Laurel: *The Role of Religions in Activism*. Oxford University Press 2011.

Knoll, Martin/Uwe Lübken/Dieter Schott (eds.): *Rivers Lost, Rivers Regained: Rethinking City-River Relation*. Pittsburgh, PA: Pittsburgh University Press 2017.

Lintner, Martin: "Respect for the Proper Value of Each Creature. An Animal-Ethical Rethinking of the Encyclical Laudato si'", in: *Louvain Studies* 43 (2020): pp. 26–48.

Lintner, Martin: *Mensch—Tier—Gott. Interdisziplinäre Annäherungen an eine christliche Tierethik*. Baden: Nomos 2021.

Maibach, Edward/Anthony Leiserowitz/Connie Roser-Renouf/Teresa Myers/Seth Rosenthal/Geoff Feinberg: *The Francis Effect: How Pope Francis Changed the Conversation about Global Warming*. Fairfax, VA: George Mason University/Yale University/George Mason University Center for Climate Change Communication: 2015.

May, Roy: *Los pobres de la tierra*, Colección Ecología-Teología. San José: DEI 1986.

Melde, S./A. Flavell, "State of the art: Impacts of environmental and climate change on human mobility", in: *Migration Policy Practice* Vol. X (No. 1, Jan-Mar 2020).

Méndez, María José: "The Silent Violence of Climate Change in Honduras", in: *NACLA Report on the Americas* 52 (no. 4, 1 October 2020): pp. 436–41, https://doi.org/10.1080/10714839.2021.1840175.

Meyer, Eric D.: *Inner Animalities: Theology and the End of the Human*. New York: Fordham University Press 2018.

Moltmann, Jürgen: *Gott in der Schöpfung. Ökologische Schöpfungslehre*. München: Kaiser 1985.

O'Bryan, Katie: "Giving A Voice to the River and the Role of Indigenous People", in: *Australian Indigenous Law Review*, Vol. 20 (2017), pp. 48–77. Available on https://www.jstor.org/stable/10.2307/26913618 [accessed 21.05.2021].

Ostheimer, Jochen/Julia Blanc: "Challenging the Levels: The Catholic Church as a Multi-Level Actor in the Transition to a Climate-Compatible Society", in: *Sustainability* 13, no. 7, 2021.

Pannenberg, Wolfhart: *Beiträge zur Systematischen Theologie 2: Natur und Mensch—Und die Zukunft der Schöpfung*. Göttingen: Vandenhoeck & Ruprecht 2006.

Pocock, J. G. A.: "The Ideal of Citizenship Since Classic Times", in: Ronald Beiner (ed.): *Theorizing Citizenship*, SUNY Series in Political Theory: Contemporary Issues. Albany, NY: State Univ. of New York Press 1995.

Pope Francis, Encyclical letter *Laudato Si'* of the Holy Father Francis on Care for Our Common Home. Rome 2015: https://www.vatican.va/content/francesco/en/encyclicals/documents/papa-francesco_20150524_enciclica-laudato-si.html [accessed 21.05.2021].

Pope Francis: Encyclical Letter *Fratelli Tutti:* https://www.vatican.va/content/francesco/en/encyclicals/documents/papa-francesco_20201003_enciclica-fratelli-tutti.html [accessed 21.05.2021].

Pope Francis: Post-Synodal Apostolic Exhortation *Querida Amazonia:* https://www.vatican.va/content/francesco/en/apost_exhortations/documents/papa-francesco_esortazione-ap_20200202_querida-amazonia.html [accessed 21.05.2021].

Ramsey, B.: *Ambrose*. London: Routledge 1997.

Reinart, Regina: *Die Amazonien-Synode als Chance und Herausforderung der Mission. Der Imperativ des Umweltschutzes, der Stärkung der indigenen Völker und des Aufbaus indigener Ortskirchen*, Studia Instituti Missiologici SVD 118. Siegburg: Franz Schmitt Verlag 2021.

Rodd, Cyril S.: *Glimpses of a Strange Land: Studies in Old Testament Ethics*. Edinburgh: T&T Clark 2001.

Schaff, P.: *Basil: Letters and Selected Works*. Edinburgh: T&T Clark 1985.

Schapper, A.: "Climate Justice and Human Rights", in: *International Relations* Vol. 32 (3, 2018): pp. 275–295.

Taylor, Bron: *Dark Green Religion: Nature Spirituality and the Planetary Future*. Berkeley/Los Angeles/London: University of California Press 2009.

UN "Land and Climate Change | UNCCD"; https://www.unccd.int/issues/land-and-climate-change [accessed 12.04.2021].

United Nations: *Global Sustainable Development Report 2019: The Future is Now—Science for Achieving Sustainable Development*. Available on https://catalogue.unccd.int/1229_FutureIsNow_Science_SDGs_report_2019.pdf [accessed 21.05.2021].

Villavicencio Calzadilla, Paola/L. Kotzé: "Living in Harmony with Nature? A Critical Appraisal of the Rights of Mother Earth in Bolivia", in: *Transnational Environmental Law* 7 (no. 3, 2018): pp. 397–424.

Vogt, Markus: *Prinzip Nachhaltigkeit. Ein Entwurf aus theologisch-ethischer Perspektive*. München: Oekom 2013.

Weber, Christoph F.: *Eigentum an nicht-erneuerbaren natürlichen Ressourcen: Umwelt- und wirtschaftsethische Reflexionen über die gegenwärtige Eigentumsordnung*, Beiträge zur sozialwissenschaftlichen Nachhaltigkeitsforschung. Marburg: Metropolis-Verlag 2020.

Doing Climate Justice from the Manifold Perspectives of Liberation Theologies

Editorial Team

Jan Niklas Collet / Judith Gruber / Wietske de Jong-Kumru / Christian Kern / Sebastian Pittl / Stefan Silber / Christian Tauchner

Abstract

Liberating theologies focus primarily on the poor and the relationship between reality and faith perspectives. The editors of this volume present their shared views while sticking to their different theoretical approaches regarding universality and particularity, epistemology, culture and economy. Taking reality and particularly climate issues seriously as well as the consequences for the poor, different social actors, including academia are seen in their different roles in the engagement for a world the humans share with other kinds of being.

Keywords

Liberation theologies; option for the poor; interconnectedness; coloniality; Eurocentrism; vulnerability; buen vivir; anthropocene

The intrinsic relation between Christian faith and the intricate realities of injustice is the core concern of liberation theologies. Similar to other perspectives on justice, the notion of climate justice links scientific questions of anthropogenic climate change with deeply ethical and political ones. Considering the uneven impacts of climate change, climate justice calls for a "common but differentiated responsibility"[1] for the prevention and reparation of the negative effects of climate change. The central focus of the project of climate justice is to "reveal and directly confront the disproportionate impacts of climate disruptions on the world's most vulnerable peoples."[2] Thus prioritizing vulner-

1 United Nations (1992), *United Nations Framework Convention*.
2 Tokar, *Climate Justice and Community Renewal*, p. 2.

© BRILL SCHÖNINGH, 2022 | DOI:10.30965/9783657795314_016

able peoples as those who are most affected by climate change, the notion of climate justice gains urgency in theologies of liberation.

Unsurprisingly, given the variety and complexity of the issues at stake, theological reflection on climate (in)justice involves a certain degree of theoretical pluralism. Such theoretical differences also exist among the editors of this volume. We conclude this volume with an editorial chapter in which we embrace our commonalities while we avoid smoothing over our differences. Despite our different theoretical approaches, we find common ground in our shared exploration of liberation theological perspectives on climate justice. What we have in common is, above all, an emancipatory epistemic interest: we seek to anchor our theological reflections in the primacy of praxis, thus prioritizing the lived realities of those who are displaced and dispossessed. Our common focus is on the complex and precarious relation of knowledge and power, and on the critique of Eurocentric epistemologies and their materializations within historical structures (and vice versa). The reader will find that some of us make explicit references to each other's contributions, thus marking further commonalities. Notwithstanding our shared perspectives, however, the reader can hardly overlook the differences in the way we explore climate justice as theologians. Our differences involve e.g. notions of universality and particularity, and the complex interrelations of epistemology, culture, and economy. Different conceptions of liberation and emancipation follow from different understandings of universality, and of whether culture or economy (or both, or neither) are dominating factors in generating climate injustice.

At first sight, the differences between our approaches could appear to overshadow and to all but negate the aforementioned commonalities. But, while it is not our goal to minimize our differences, or to downplay the tensions between them, we recognize the importance of remaining in dialogue. Our methodological differences are not harmonized, but valued as incentives for dialogue and critical self-reflection. As we discover fault lines in our contributions, we become aware of possible blind spots that prompt further reflection. In this dialogical approach, different conceptualizations, theories and emphases, *qualify and bring nuance to* our commonalities. The pluralism of our approaches and theories does not obstruct debate. On the contrary, a controversial and creative pluralism allows for the carving out of differences, thereby opening up pathways for further reflection on the issue of climate justice in particular, and on adequate theoretical frameworks for liberation theologies more generally. This further reflection is part of the debate that we see as our continued task for the future. In this light, our contributions are not harmonized nor unified in their writing styles, but they are offered to our readers as moderately reflexive of the abundance of activist and academic projects, including liberation theological perspectives, that publicize the urgency of climate justice.

In the following contributions, *Christian Tauchner* identifies the contemplation of self and nature as creation to be the primary feature of a liberation theology that starts from the interrelatedness of climate change processes. His approach centers the plight of Amazon peoples and understands the wisdom that traditional indigenous worldviews offer in face of the challenge to acquire a lifestyle of joyful sobriety. *Stefan Silber* identifies academic theology, and liberation theology in particular, as a location where local processes of analysis of (and resistance to) climate injustice can be interwoven with other global contexts, especially those most vulnerable for and most wounded by the climate catastrophe. In liberation theology, the cry of the earth and the cry of the poor are united. At the same time, Silber criticizes Western academia's insufficient recognition of voices and wisdoms that are critical of Western epistemologies, and which contribute decisively to the analysis of the impact, causes, effects of climate change, and to the analysis of possible solutions. *Sebastian Pittl* pays heed to the 2019 Amazon Synod as he identifies the task of doing climate justice from the place of academia, as theologians, as one that requires a profound process of "unlearning" (*verlernen*). *Christian Kern* sensitizes us to the need to reconnect discourses of climate justice, theoretical frameworks of liberation theologies, and the language we use as academics, to concrete, singular, and unique situations and practices, localized forms of knowledge, practices, art, lifestyles and wisdoms. *Judith Gruber* takes the majority Western European participation in the 2020 workshop as an incentive to reflect on the challenge to address localized responses to the climate crisis in Western European societies. The fact that climate denial is still considered an option here, prompts her to consider the longue durée of colonial history as she lays out the tasks of a liberative European climate theology. *Jan Niklas Collet* acknowledges the structural critique of intertwining dimensions of racism, gender, and coloniality in the injustices of the climate crisis. At the same time, however, he elaborates a cautionary stance against uncritically identifying capitalism as being inherently Eurocentric. Finally, *Wietske de Jong-Kumru*'s contribution closes this chapter with reflections on what kind of theology can offer a logic that counters the human malleability myth in the face of the climate crisis, and can accommodate thinking anew about the world that we share with other kinds of beings.

1 Shifting Grounds

Developments in (Catholic) theology and the self-understanding of the church have undergone major shifts in the last half century. The Vatican Council II has turned out to be one of the entry points and gates into new avenues—not only the windows of a sticky and dusty institution were blown open at the Council: The big doors were opened for a positive approach to the "world" with its "joy and hope, the grief and anguish" of our times (GS 1). The Council acknowledged developments in society and the contributions of sciences in their own value. The church was supposed to wake up to these developments and accept them as valuable contributions to revelation and to its self-understanding. Social and human sciences became interesting also for the church, and the findings from these disciplines should contribute to the advance of humanity and its salvation, in the sense of achieving a good life for all. The 1960s were also an over-all decade of hope for social change and development—Paul VI proclaimed "development, the new name for peace" in *Populorum progressio* 76: "When we fight poverty and oppose the unfair conditions of the present, we are not just promoting human well-being; we are also furthering man's spiritual and moral development, and hence we are benefiting the whole human race" (*Populorum progressio* 76). The perspective of the poor is present from the outset of the Council, with John XXIII's quest for a "church of the poor"[3] and its confirmation and explanation at the Medellín conference in 1968—centered particularly on justice and the demand that the church take the side of the poor and marginalized—and at Puebla in 1979 with the "option for the poor."[4] This option oriented the church as the people of God on its historical process towards liberation and full humanity, even as it was severely opposed and criticized by the traditional powers outside of the church and within.[5] This view of the poor inspired actors also beyond the church, for example in the pedagogy of oppressed, in order to empower these classes to take care of their development and liberty.[6] So, this initial process actually placed the person in charge of their history and historical liberation, and the poor and marginalized

3 See Bettazzi, *Church of the poor*; Planellas Barnosell, *The framers of the Pact*.

4 I omit the "preferential" etc., as an option always is a choice and the "preferential" etc. in reality means bypassing it as an option and commitment: Vigil (ed.), *Sobre la opción por los pobres*.

5 This explicit opposition became evident rather soon in the Rockefeller Report of 1969 as well as in the Santa Fe documents of 1983 to the US government, and within church in the intentions to divert the proposals for Puebla. See Boff, *Teología desde el cautiverio*.

6 See Paulo Freire's *Pedagogy of the Oppressed* and the process around formation.

classes in Latin America—by far the vast majority in each nation—were encouraged to become the agents of their development.

In the course of expanding and consolidating the theological framework, liberation theology started to specify the category of "the poor" and to treat each actor's particular situation. It had soon become clear that among the poor, women lived particular and specific situations of oppression and had different roles to play, but it became clear also that it made huge differences whether the discourse on "woman" was set in rural or urban, white or black contexts or according to family status, as examples.[7] Thus, the acting subject of liberating processes became much richer and diversified, and it had shifted to the poor and marginalized of traditional society.

Over the decades, in many countries the subaltern classes achieved political and social victories in the changes of governments. Brazil in times of the PT (Workers' Party) governments is an example. Similarly, in Bolivia and Ecuador indigenous aspirations were taken up; in both countries, new constitutions were drafted and they introduced the notion of "good life" (in Bolivia in 2009, in Ecuador in 2008). However, the transformation of societies did not advance sufficiently to be able to guarantee "good life" for everyone. Many poor still are forced to try to make their living by migrating within their countries and open new frontiers. This has been particularly visible in Brazil where it has been specially the poor who have cut down large sections of jungle and rainforest for their subsistence economy, only to sell their newly acquired land off to bigger corporations and latifundia with large scale monocultural production cycles or meat production once they had cleared the space. And they themselves moved on, deeper into the forests for a new cycle. So, the poor are used for the ecologically damaging tasks of destroying the rain forests, because they can't find alternatives to secure their survival.[8]

The Amazon Synod with its long preparation process could build on Pope Francis' insistence on ecology (*Laudato si'*; LS) and the view of sharing a common house and belonging to wider networks of relations. These relations go beyond the social ties to humans and includes a creative blending into mutual dependencies, and for society, the task consists in assuming stewardship. The failure of such creational integration and care leads to a "cry of mother Earth"

---

7 The recognition of diversity in "the poor" can be seen from early on, por example in the different faces of Jesus in the Puebla conference in 1979 ("concrete faces in real life which we recognize as the faces of the suffering Christ:" #31–39).

8 For an indication of the awareness regarding land, the poor and development see May, *Los pobres de la tierra*.

(cf. LS 2; 117; QA [*Querida Amazonia*] 42) and renders the earth and nature a *subject* to take into account for articulating the relationships.

Such a new relationship is suggested in QA when development projects are supposed to be tied into the cultural particularities of the native populations and the requirements of the poor. Often, these insights are expressed from the negative side as an opposition to consumerism (e.g., QA 33 [LS 144], 41; more clearly expressed in the Amazon Synod final Declaration chapter 4 on an ecological conversion; see #82ff.).

This awareness of the interrelatedness of all things in creation has consequences for action. The first element is a more contemplative approach, the awareness of self and nature as creation. With relation to the Amazon peoples and their ancestral cultures, the synodal process highlighted the wisdom of the original populations. They pursue a life in fullness, their "buen vivir," "good living" (*Final Document* #9).

Against this background of balanced interrelations, LS calls for caution in human action: "Often a vicious circle results, as human intervention to resolve a problem further aggravates the situation" (LS 34). Therefore, the Amazon Synod speaks frequently of the requirement of conversion on all levels, personal, social and structural, with a "call to unlearn, learn and relearn, in order to overcome any tendency toward colonizing models that have caused harm in the past" (*Final Document* #81).

In the context of "doing climate justice", the first step consequently is not action but contemplation[9] and the building of an awareness of the interrelatedness. This goes against the grain of Western technological confidence in being able to organize a rational dealing with natural resources, and discover and fix problems on the way. Indigenous peoples and traditional settlers in the Amazon region used to manage their environment wisely within their world view and cosmos, but nowadays their cultures are severely interrupted. Due to modern technological management and exploitation of the different resources, their traditional worlds and possibilities of "good living" are being overturned and they themselves become a new strand of poor even without meaningful references to their shattered world views, for example when they are driven out of their destroyed environments and have to settle precariously at the margins of exploding towns and megacities and their production circles. Instead, the task of "all persons of good will,"[10] not only the Christians, will consist in learning from the aboriginal peoples and take on their "example of a joyful sobriety," as "they have much to teach us" (QA 71, with reference to EG 198).

9 Contemplation in the sense of discerning and understanding the signs of time, see e.g. Segundo, *Revelación, fe, signos de los tiempos*.

10 The addressees of *Querida Amazonia*.

The workshop on "doing climate justice" has underlined this requirement of a renewed awareness of the interrelatedness of processes. Even if it is hard to adopt such traditional and all-encompassing worldviews as are upheld by some indigenous peoples, the challenge of learning and acquiring a lifestyle of "joyful sobriety" stands before us, as an immense task.

Christian Tauchner

2 Theological Relevance in Global and Local Power Structures

Our house is on fire. There is no need to recur to Greta Thunberg and her insistence on this affirmation to ascertain its validity. It is sufficient to pay attention to the news about wildfires in different parts of the world, about hurricanes, droughts, floods, loss of biodiversity, and other signs of disastrous climate change in order to confirm the necessity to react to the growing reality of climate injustice, that will be the great challenge for the 21st century.

Climate change is not only a threat to humanity, but also a very serious aspect of global injustice. It affects some people more seriously than others. For many people in the world, it is already more accurate to talk about a climate catastrophe. Climate change kills people, by means of hunger, diseases, natural disasters, war, repression, migration, and many others. Most people in industrialized countries however, enjoy comparatively privileged positions. Despite globalized connectivity in media, people in Europe and North America, for instance, can still easily deny or ignore, at least practically, the reality of human induced climate change. Political and economic leaders still propose measures that will exacerbate the problems rather than help to solve them, while insisting at the same time, that they are paying attention to climate change and heeding international resolutions.[11]

The assessment of climate injustice must therefore take into account these differences based on localizations, the contexts of any discussion of the problem, and the relations that places and contexts entertain with certain forms and contents of the climate discourse. While some people and some cultural and economic regions are more responsible for the causes of climate change, others suffer more from its effects. Moreover, both responsibilities and sufferings entertain relationships with racialized, gender, and postcolonial issues. Hence, climate injustice must be approached by interdisciplinary and intersectional means.

11 The idea of privilege is developed further below by Judith Gruber.

Globalized issues—like climate change—cannot be solved by any local strategy alone, as is obvious. Global strategies, however, must necessarily be based on local praxes, although these are always liable to include global perspectives and an assessment of global differences in the impact of climate injustice. Particularly in industrialized countries, it is extremely important to listen to the voices of the people who are suffering most from climate injustice. These voices from "the reverse side of history"[12] contribute decisively to the analysis of the impact, the causes, and the effects of climate change, and to the possible solutions to it. Surely our 2020 workshop on "Doing Climate Justice", localized in Central Europe, could have been more dialogical in this respect.

In the global discourse on climate injustice, these voices most significantly demonstrate that Western epistemology does not efficiently address the causes, scopes, dimensions and effects of climate injustice.[13] The analytical rationality of the West caused this crisis, but is unable to deal with it. Because of this, it is necessary for Western thought to listen to alternative discourses, life praxes, resistance, and wisdom, and accept their criticisms. While Gayatri C. Spivak links this openness to "the unlearning of our privilege as our loss"[14], Ignacio Ellacuría speaks of the necessity of "self-emptying"[15].

So, for instance, Creation, the world and humans must be envisioned more comprehensively, in their infinitely diverse interrelationships[16], in their vulnerability and woundedness, in their potential for resistance, in their own irreducible but interrelated rights, and in their fertile beauty. At the same time, deep-rooted Western anthropocentrism (or even androcentrism) must be opened up to ecocentrism and a deep respect for everything created. Indigenous voices, ecofeminist and indigenous feminist voices worldwide are contributing notably, at present, to this important global discourse.[17]

These local processes of analysis of (and resistance to) climate injustice can and must be realized anywhere. In order to be effective, however, it is of utmost importance that these processes are linked to other global contexts, especially those most vulnerable for and most wounded by the climate catastrophe.[18]

---

12 Gutiérrez, *La fuerza histórica de los pobres*, p. 301 [my translation].

13 See Mies/Shiva, *Ecofeminism;* Mellor, *Feminism and Ecology*; Gebara, *Longing for running water*.

14 Spivak, *The Post-Colonial Critic*, p. 9.

15 Ellacuría, *Escritos Teológicos*, p. 257 [my translation]. On Spivak, Ellacuría, "unlearning" and "self-emptying" also see Sebastian Pittl below.

16 Juan Almendares uses the term "Holobiocenosis" to characterize this infinity of relationships. Cf. Almendares, *Holobiocenosis*.

17 See, e.g., Birgit Weiler, *Gut leben*.

18 See, below, Christian Kern, regarding the connections between local and global actions.

One of the potential locations of these interwoven processes, in my opinion—and this was the experience of our workshop—is academic theology.

From the perspective of liberation theology, a theological assessment of climate catastrophe is a relevant praxis. Liberation theology can ascertain that the cry of the earth and the cry of the poor[19] are the same cry: it is the cry of G*d who is wounded by climate injustice. This injustice injures G*d who is present in the body of G*d's Creation and in the body of the poor. In this way, theology is not only challenged and entitled to create its own response to climate injustice. In doing so, theology also urges the church (as a community of believers) to fight against climate injustice,[20] and points to the two main foci of liberating praxis: the earth (understood as the complex interrelation of everything created) and the poor (in an intersectional sense). Indigenous theologies worldwide are contributing their share of alternative knowledge, such as the sacredness of ecology, the *buen vivir* ("good living"), the universal destiny of creation and its goods (*casa común*), and the interbeing of everything to a global eco-theological discourse.

Theology, however, as well as the whole of academia,[21] cannot be considered a discourse or a space free of power. Doing Climate Justice in academic theology, hence, needs to take into account privileges in academia with respect to color, gender, level of formal education, employment, denomination, clerical status, among others. Western academia is embedded in postcolonial power structures that communicate with neoliberalism and resist critical assessments of Western responsibilities in climate issues. This auto-critical reflection on power and privileges is a fundamental requirement for an academic praxis of climate justice. Academic eco-theological reflection should, therefore, relate dialogically and listen attentively to the voices of everyone less privileged, especially the ones most affected by climate injustice, and of the earth.

Academic theology alone will not revert climate change nor mitigate its consequences. But it can assume its own responsibility and contribute its own share to a global praxis needed in these present multiple crises.

Stefan Silber

---

19 Cf. Pope Francis, *Laudato Si'* #49; Boff, *Cry of the Earth*. See, above, Christian Tauchner's reflections on Liberation Theology and the Synod for the Amazon.

20 Below, Wietske de Jong-Kumru advocates other necessary lines of praxis as well, like "to stay with the trouble".

21 See the following part of Sebastian Pittl on academia and climate justice.

3 The Challenges of *Doing* and (*Un-*)*Learning* Climate Justice in the Academia

My reflections focus on the challenge of *doing* climate justice from the place of the academia. This not a navel-gazing exercise (which is always somehow a temptation of academic work) but a way to address some of the contradictions inherent in the concrete place from which our 2020 workshop engaged the issues of climate justice. Indeed, each attempt to engage questions of climate justice is located in a specific place with specific possibilities, sensibilities and resources, specific contradictions and ambivalences. For the future, much will depend on if and how the multiple struggles for climate justice will succeed to critically engage with each other, and on whether or not they will be able to build solidarity networks that are resilient and flexible enough to allow for real steps towards greater climate justice despite the persistence of hegemonic structures and their sophisticated strategies of co-optation. As organizers, in preparing and doing our workshop we had to struggle with the potentials and resources, the contradictions and ambivalences coming from this place of academia and, more specifically, of theological departments within a (predominantly) Western European context.

Contradictions and ambivalences of (Western) academia with regard to questions of climate justice can be found on a number of levels. They have to do with the fact that academic life and research (despite being of course indispensable to engage issues of climate justice in a critical and effective way) are themselves entwined with the structures and dynamics of "imperial modes of living"[22] in numerous ways. First, not only the personal lifestyle of many academics (in the so-called "West" as well as in many other parts of the world), but also the daily routines of academic research presuppose a disproportionate access to global resources, which cannot be universalized. This includes the ecological costs of academic traveling, as well as access to an often invisible infrastructure that provides academics with goods, facilities, and time by externalizing ecological and social costs[23] to other contexts (cf. the ecological costs of the extraction of rare earth elements used in electronic devices, the externalization of care work[24] etc.). Second, on a more institutional level, the increased importance of third-party funding in today's academia has intensified the

22 Cf. Brand/Wissen, *The Imperial Mode of Living*.

23 Lessenich, *Living Well at Others' Expense*.

24 The ecological costs of the externalization of care work became especially palpable during the first pandemic lockdowns, when special charter flights were rented to fly in much needed carers from e.g. Romania to Austria.

entanglement of academic research with economic interests, thereby deepening the dependence of academic research on economic structures, which, as Stefan Silber points out, are predominantly governed by a neoliberal logic. Third, academic research during the last decades has increasingly embraced the dynamics of a "cultural capitalism" and highly competitive global "visibility markets", which reward those who successfully achieve to distinguish their "singularity" from the "average" by rendering the latter invisible.[25] The dynamics of cultural capitalism foster specific forms of (creative) "collaboration,"[26] but simultaneously obstruct a necessary opening up of academia to other places of reflecting upon and struggling for climate justice—especially if these places possess less (financial, symbolic, social and cultural) capital and if their engagement is not likely to develop into "gains of distinction". Against this background the task of *doing climate justice* from the place of academia requires in my opinion a profound process of "unlearning" (as the integral part of both "learning" and "learning to learn differently"). This process of unlearning may take on different forms depending on concrete circumstances and contexts. On an individual level, it appears in practices of refusal with regard to opportunities and institutional expectations, which are connected with disproportionate socio-ecological costs (which of course is far easier for tenured academics than for junior researchers). It appears in practices of "affirmative sabotage"[27] which use the privileged positions and possibilities of academia in order to make visible and transgress the exclusionary dynamics which are inherent in the structures of academic work itself. It appears in the search for more inclusive, horizontal, and solidary forms of collaboration, in the critical opening up of academic discourse to non-academic forms of knowledge and to agents of civil society. And it appears in a constant attempt to remain sensible to the blind spots inherent in the own social positionality.

On an institutional level, processes of "unlearning" are closely related to the struggles for diversification and restructuring of academic institutions as part of their decolonization. To expose and dismantle the exclusionary structures which regulate (although in more subtle forms now than in the past) access to academia along the categories of "race", "gender", "class", "ability" etc. is today a necessary task in order to better reflect the plurality of perspectives, situations,

25 Cf. Reckwitz, *The Society of Singularities*, pp. 81–162.
26 Cf. Reckwitz, *Practices of Labor*.
27 For the notion of "affirmative sabotage" cf. Spivak, *An Aesthetic Education*.

different vulnerabilities and challenges of people from diverse backgrounds with regard to issues of climate justice within academic work.[28]

From a theological perspective, the processes of "unlearning" are closely related to—and indeed may be enriched by—the notion of conversion or "metanoia". In order for theology and the churches to contribute to the necessary processes of unlearning within academia and society in general they have to draw from their own traditions and resources, and they have to address the task of metanoic unlearning also within themselves. The Amazon Synod of 2019 was very clear on this, when it connected its call for a profound conversion on all levels of society with the emphasis that "[t]he Church is included in this call to unlearn, learn and relearn, in order to overcome any tendency toward colonizing models that have caused harm in the past. In this vein, it is important for us to be aware of the power of neo-colonialism which is present in our daily decisions [...]."[29]

Unlearning, like conversion, is not something that can be achieved individualistically. It is a process which is reliant on others, whose interpellations and different experiences are essential to become sensitive to the blind spots of one's own perspectives and practices. A process of opening up to others is therefore an integral part of any process of conversion. To make sure that this opening up to others does not remain confined to the narrow boundaries of self-affirming social bubbles (including academic bubbles), however, a renewed articulation of liberation theology's insistence on the "option for the poor" is in my opinion of crucial importance—this not in the sense of "a new exploitation of the poor [...] as a methodological resource of theology [...] but [...] as a [form of] self-emptying of [...] theology and theologians (who ought to [...] go out of themselves and their assimilation to intellectual groups from which they seek their worldly recognition)"[30]. Each reference to the "option for the poor" must, of course, be sensitive to tendencies of homogenization and romanticizing of the "poor" and engage critically with the complicated issue of (mis-)representation. However, a critical contextualization of questions of climate justice which does not want to elude global entanglements and dependencies, is necessarily required to open up its academic discourse to experiences and perspectives of the local and global "peripheries" (which

---

28 Cf. in this regard Stefan Silber's emphasis on the need to critically reflect on the embeddedness of academia within postcolonial power structures and Judith Gruber's reflections on the theological importance of critical whiteness studies below.

29 *Final Document of the Amazon Synod*, Nr. 81. Cf. also Christian Tauchner's reflections on the Amazon Synod above.

30 Ellacuría, *Los pobres, 'lugar teológico'*, p. 155 [transl. SP].

are largely produced by the efficient externalization of eco-social costs by the hegemonic "centers").[31]

In 2017 the "Wiener Festwochen" (a prominent cultural festival in Austria) established an "Academy of Unlearning" [German: "Akademie des Verlernens"]. At its inauguration the postcolonial scholar Gayatri Spivak, who has reflected extensively on the challenges of unlearning during the last decades, took up the German term "verlernen" to point to the complexity and difficulty of processes of unlearning in contexts that are marked by great power asymmetries. Drawing on her teaching experiences in rural areas in West Bengal she somewhat corrected her earlier account of "unlearning one's privilege as one's loss":

> [...] 'verlernen' and 'unlearning' are not the same. 'Ver' has a different kind of nuance altogether in German from 'un' [...] in English. [...] mere unlearning is very narcissistic and is possible only for the elite. [...] it is not possible to unlearn one's privilege. Privilege is historically given. Therefore rather than focus on myself and unlearn and unlearn I should use my privilege against the grain [...] This is the biggest challenge in the sense of 'verlernen' [...] learn to learn how to work with mind machines that have been destroyed by your own ancestors.[32]

If this notion of *ver*learning is taken seriously and not just as a fashionable paradox it might give us a hint about what could be the task of theological departments within the contemporary academia in the horizon of the current climate catastrophe: to be places which, by drawing on their own traditions and resources as well as their local and global networks, try to create spaces where people from different backgrounds can meet and learn together how to learn to unlearn in order to learn to learn *differently*. This is not to say that theological departments should claim to be a sort of avantgarde in these processes of metanoic *ver*learning and the related struggles for greater climate justice. However, they certainly could occupy a very valuable place in these struggles—together with and amidst others.

Sebastian Pittl

31 Cf. the above-mentioned studies of Lessenich and Brand/Wissen.

32 Spivak, *What Time Is It*.

4 Reconnecting the Global and the Local, the Theoretical and the Practical

The discourse about climate justice has a tendency to disconnect the global from the local, the theoretical from the practical, and to superimpose the first on the latter. On a basic level, this tendency emerges in the concept of justice itself. Justice as a normative concept implies equality and universality, thus drawing attention away from the singular, individual, the incalculable, to the more general. It is about "justice for all", realized in generally applicable rules or distribution systems. In the wake of this generalization, justice disconnects from individual, local, singular/unique situations and practices and sums up the latter in a more general practice of "just" calculation.[33] With regard to climate justice, one can observe a familiar tendency, at least on the level of climate negotiations, policies or regimes. In 1992, the UNFCCC established the classic definition of climate justice as a "common but differentiated responsibility" (art. 3, §1) as a general principle of action on the international level. Nation states were/are called to engage in the fight against climate change and to contribute means and resources in proportion to their historical contribution to CO_2 emissions and to their current economic, infrastructural, political capacities. As the UNFCCC addresses primarily nation states as principal actors of climate mitigation, offering a platform especially for national interests, it moves away from particular local situations and establishes on the sub-national level and brings about a certain homogenization of interests and representation. Again, a *logic of disconnection* between theory and practice applies, the global and the local: in order to be able to represent interest on the international macro-level, issues and perspectives from the meso-level and micro-level tend to be blinded out.

The original and critical approach of our 2020 workshop was, in my opinion, that we applied (more or less consciously) a counter-logic in regard to this logics of disconnection in justice affaires and its tendency to superordinate the global/theoretical to the local/practical. In contrast to this, the workshop wanted to draw *the attention to concrete situations*, local forms of knowledge and concrete resistant practices of particular agents. Against a generalizing logics of climate justice on the international level, it created a platform on which local perspectives and experiences should/could become more visible, together with their entanglement with macro structures and challenges. The articles in this volume give testimony to the degree to which this broadening and change of perspective was successful.

33 Rancière, *Das Unvernehmen*, pp. 17–19.

With its particular perspective, the workshop raised further questions that were present already during our preparation process—at least latently.

1) If the outlined danger in "doing (climate) justice" to favor the global and theoretical over the local and practice does exist, a really "just" understanding and practice of justice has to integrate a self-critical attitude with regard to its own tendency of blinding-out certain facets of local life, and calls for a permanent practice of *re-connecting the local and the global, the theoretical and the practical* as concrete form of this (self-) critique. This implies a modified understanding and practice of justice: Justice is not done only or primarily in generalizing ways of reflection or organization, but with a permanent, and ever new movement into the concrete, particular, singular situations of knowledge, beliefs and lives. This *incarnative logic of justice* implies distancing oneself from normative images of a perfect, innocent world and taking the risk to stay with the trouble.[34] It is only with such a utopia-critical stance that liberation theologies will be able to contribute to climate/social justice. There is no perfect world. But there should be a constant move into the details of a given condition and thus to reconnect the global and the local, the theoretical with the truly practical.
2) With regard to academic theology, one might ask more specifically: Are academic discourses as such, with their own tendencies of theorizing, able to do this kind of justice? Do they not contribute to the avoidance of a true exposure to the incalculable, singular local? Scientific practices aim at producing reliable knowledge that is valid beyond the context of its "original" production. With its claim of generalization, scientific knowledge carries in itself the impulse of dominion over space and time, which tends to blind out the irritation by the local and the concrete. Which form of knowledge would be able to avoid this hegemonic force in its own production process? Which kind of knowledge—of academic theology—would be sensitive and weak enough to give space to the local and concrete without losing its validity or relevance?

The provisional character of my reflections does not allow me to analyze and criticize in detail the complex connection between reliability, knowledge and power in space and time. However, it points to two challenges that academic (liberation) theology could—or has to—confront when it reflects on "justice" in context of climate change.

The first is a methodological one: certain traditions of liberation theologies apply frameworks taken from political theory, like dependence theories,

34 Haraway, *Situated Knowledges*.

in order to reconstruct interconnections between different agents and to highlight power asymmetries in transnational structures. In this way, a generalized logic of interaction in terms of a "structural dependence" on a meta- and meso-level is applied. This logic might capture important dynamics on a national, international and global scale and help to criticize them, but it might also contribute to the above-mentioned disconnection between the local and the global, the universalized and the particular. In terms of methodology, it seems to be important to connect such more abstract, transnational theoretical frameworks with lenses, methods and questions that move into concrete situations and pay attention to localized forms of knowledge, practice, art, lifestyles and wisdoms.

The second challenge goes deeper and touches the quality or form of knowledge itself. If we want to do justice to the things, situations, and lives we are talking about, we have to take account of their unique individuality, their singularities—and ungraspability. Yet, how should this be possible, as we are tied to the languages (of science and everyday life alike) by which we have shared access to the word, represent and communicate "things" among us in transferrable ways? Knowledge, language that pays attention to—and does "justice" to the individual, local, unique—seems possibly impossible/impossibly possible.[35] However, this *aporia* is something we shouldn't ignore, instead we should be aware of it. It could serve as an entry point of a permanent (self-) critical unrest that brings up—again and again—the question of how to do and talk *otherwise* and confront the un-justice in our words anew. Theology as such is particularly suited to cultivate such a form of weak, self-critical knowledge—as the ungraspable other is at the center of their own performance, always leading ahead to new beginnings. This weak, un-stable form of knowledge would then serve a basis for a reframed and modified understanding of how we access the world—and make use of the resources, not as something that we possess, as passive objects that can be exploited, but as something with which we enter in a carefully and possibly always respectful interaction, vulnerable and open for surprise.

Christian Kern

35 Derrida, *Der "mystische Grund der Autorität"*, p. 79.

5 Losing our Innocence. Climate Justice and the Problem of Epistemic Privilege/Violence in the Wake of Colonial Trauma

The climate crisis is a "planetary emergency"[36]—changing the conditions of survival on Earth, it impacts all its human and non-human life forms. Yet, responsibility for and vulnerability to the climate crisis are not shared equally across the globe. The causes and effects of these changes of planetary scale are distributed unevenly according to specific geographical, topographical and infrastructural conditions. As Stefan Silber put it quite memorably in a preparatory meeting for the Workshop: the climate crisis "kills thousands each year through starvation, natural catastrophes, war, repression and migration; it destroys ecosystems and annihilates species and biotopes. Yet, we in the Global North even have the privilege to deny climate change". One of our major points of attention in the conceptualization of the workshop was to address these differences as a matter of justice; our goal was to lift the experiences of those who bear the brunt of the crisis, in order to discern, from their practices of resistance, resources to tackle the catastrophe in transformative ways. It was a crucial point of discussion among the members of the preparatory team *where* these practices can be found and *who* the major stakeholders are in this search for transformation of a lopsided crisis. While we envisioned a global debate that also, and particularly, should include participants from regions where the effects of climate change are already strongly felt, a majority of the workshop participants then came from a Western European context. In the reflection afterwards, we considered this limitation as problematic for its exclusionary effects (how, for example, does the relatively homogeneous circle of participants indicate academia's exclusionary drive towards its own self-reproduction along established boundaries of race, gender and class?[37]). Yet, most of us also embraced this limitation as a necessary contextualization—in view of a global crisis that affects the whole planet, albeit in different ways, we need *localized* histories and futures that enable us to account in nuanced ways for the complex asymmetries of responsibility and vulnerability[38] at the heart of the climate catastrophe.

What is at stake in addressing the climate crisis specifically in Western European societies? As a starting point, I choose Silber's astute insight that the Global North has the privilege to deny climate change, and complement it with the observation that in European public climate discourses, not only

36 Cf. Keller, *Political Theology of the Earth*.

37 Https://www.chronicle.com/article/how-the-academic-elite-reproduces-itself/.

38 Fineman, *The Vulnerable Subject*.

outspoken denial but also more subtle forms of knowledge are at work: more often than not, the prevalent response to the climate crisis is a practice of ignorance, shaped by an attitude of "not wanting to know". Describing these responses as a privilege afforded by the unjust distribution of vulnerability to the climate catastrophe, Silber challenges us to understand climate change denial/ignorance as powerful knowledge practices that intimately tie into the distinctions which distribute causes and effects of the climate crisis unevenly across the planet. The climate catastrophe, we can thus argue, is not only a matter of social in/justice, but also gives rise to questions of epistemic in/justice that need further scrutiny.

In order to unpack these power/knowledge constellations in European climate discourses, we can turn to Afro-Surinamese Dutch anthropologist Gloria Wekker. Responding to a different (but not unrelated) problem, she has coined the term "White innocence" to conceptualize the more or less subtle forms of knowledge with which the dominant majority population immunizes itself against questions of justice that emerge in view of the deeply rooted racism in European societies with colonial legacies. For Wekker, this "innocence" is anything but—she defines it as an epistemic privilege that is tied to epistemic violence: speaking of white innocence as an aggressive rejection of "the possibility to know"[39], she describes it as a constitutive component "of a white supremacist state in which the human race is racially divided into full persons and subpersons. Even though—or more accurately, precisely because—they tend not to understand the racist world in which they live, white people are able to fully benefit from its racial hierarchies, ontologies and economies."[40] White innocence, for Wekker, is thus a particular form of knowledge that distributes resources in asymmetrical ways and so shapes the modes and materialities of our being in the world. It is a powerful epistemic practice that reproduces social and economic privilege in violent ways.

Wekker's concept of White innocence offers important perspectives for understanding the unjust distribution of responsibility for and vulnerability to the climate crisis. Elucidating the powerful connections between social, economic and epistemic privilege, it challenges us to analyze more carefully what sustains the dominant practice of climate denial/ignorance: how is this form of (not-)knowing sponsored by an unjust distribution of resources, and how is it, thus, intimately tied to violence?[41] Importing Wekker's race-critical concept

39 Wekker, *White Innocence*, p. 18.

40 Wekker, *White Innocence*, p. 17.

41 This is in line with Jan Niklas Collet's contribution to this chapter, which argues more substantially for the need to connect epistemic critique to a political-social analysis of the climate crisis.

into the climate justice debate further invites us to investigate how epistemic privilege in the climate crisis is bound up with other schemata for the unjust global distribution of power, resources and vulnerability to violence, such as distinctions along lines of species, race or gender. Analyzing the uneven access to the privilege of denial/ignorance through such multiple lenses of discursive categorizations allows for a more nuanced and flexible mapping of the global distribution of climate change responsibility and vulnerability that goes beyond a mere geographical differentiation between "North/South". Rather than relying on vague and essentialized notions of "North" and "South" that are prone to reinscribing the powerful distinctions with which modernity/coloniality has divided the world into civilized and wild, master and slave, it unearths a complex and thick history of intersecting lines of exclusion that determine Western Europe's specific position in the current global climate crisis.

In fact, such a complexified historiography (and geography) of climate change denial may expose that a myopic concentration on a North/South division may actually sustain, rather than disrupt, its colonial legacies and their uneven distribution of epistemic, social and economic privilege. When the argument that the Global North enjoys the privilege of denial is made in an all too sweeping way, and accompanied with the expectation that marginalized communities offer resources for tackling the climate crisis, it can perpetuate, rather than transform, the dominant epistemic practice of violent innocence. Nolens volens, it participates in a discourse that refuses to acknowledge—and consequently fails to tackle—profound social, economic and cultural shifts in Western European societies as effects of the climate crisis. The "migration crisis", for instance, is a clear indication that the global impact of climate change is also already felt in the "global North"; it shows that "we" in Western Europe cannot escape the consequences of our climate policies (which are in direct continuation of the expansion, extraction and exploitation economy of modern colonialism[42]). Ultimately, it demonstrates that the climate catastrophe materializes in different ways across the globe—and therefore calls for *localized* responses: providing resources to tackle the climate crisis in transformative ways is not only the responsibility of communities in the Global South, but such responses have also to be developed from and for the specific Western European situation.

From this, we can glean trajectories for developing a liberative theology that responds to the climate catastrophe from a Western European context. Crucial is a critical account of the complex entanglements of social, economic and epistemic privilege/violence that perpetuate the unjust distribution of

42 Cf. Brand/Wissen, *Imperiale Lebensweise*. Cf. also Sebastian Pittl's contribution to this chapter.

vulnerability to climate change. In searching for resources for a sustained transformation of the crisis, it cannot solely rely on additional, alternative knowledge practices that it seeks to import from the "peripheries". Rather, it has to engage in a critical reckoning with epistemic practices of denial/ignorance that sustain a long history of colonial trauma. Hence, it is the task of a specifically European climate theology to trace the colonial origins and on-going circulation of White innocence in order to show how it decisively shapes current climate policies in Europe. Part and parcel of this epistemic-social-economic critique is a critical-constructive reflection of how theological knowledge production has contributed to the asymmetrical distribution of privilege and vulnerability along religious, geographical, cultural, and economic distinctions that have divided the world into colonizer and colonized, redeemed and unredeemed, civilized and wild, free and enslaveable.[43] Such critical re-reading of the past is by no means a mere end in itself, but rather the condition of the possibility for the emancipative transformation of the powerful, but contingent, upkeep of epistemic, economic and social privilege through the uneven distribution of vulnerability.

Judith Gruber

6 Reclaiming the Commons
Brief thoughts on Epistemological and Politico-Economic Groundworks of a Liberation Theology of Climate Justice

A number of the diverse contributions at the 2020 conference focused on the particular importance of *epistemologies* regarding the notion of climate (in)justice. Questions raised included those about anthropocentrism, the problematic dichotomy between subject and object and the exclusion of those knowledges which are not in line with the corresponding figure of rationality. This figure of rationality was, not without justification, often related to a deeply rooted Eurocentrism in large sections of contemporary theology (and scholarly thought in general). The critique, then, referred to the intertwining of racism, the modern/colonial gender system and climate injustice. In the following, I want to draw some thoughts on the advantages and disadvantages that come or may possibly come with such critiques when they are elaborated incautiously.

---

43 Cf. Jennings, *The Christian Imagination*; Grosfoguel, *The Structure of Knowledge*.

If one takes an honest look at the facts of climate injustice, the intermeshings of gender, race, and class divisions cannot be neglected. Only by ignorance and indifference towards tremendous global inequalities and violence could these divisions and their interconnectedness be denied. The fact that such denial is actually happening highlights the importance of reflections on the epistemological features informing it, and on the conditions and possibilities of an epistemological turn to break with one's own entanglement;[44] it also draws attention to the "contradictions and ambivalences of (Western) academia with regard to questions of climate justice,"[45] and it stresses the importance of a deepening of the mentioned epistemological questions and the urgency to effectively "turn history around" because another world is not just possible but necessary (Ignacio Ellacuría). It marks the imperative to widen our figures of rationality so that various forms of knowledge can be appreciated and anthropocentrism can be effectively transcended.

At the same time, the notion of Eurocentrism needs to be worked out carefully to prevent it to unwittingly reinforce, rather than interrupt, regressive dynamics of Modernity. I see at least two interconnected risks to be aware of: a "culturalization of capitalism" and an "essentialization of the situatedness of knowledge". To be more specific, the usage of the notion of Eurocentrism has itself a dangerous side, when it does not distinguish clearly between the epistemological and political economy. This is because when the difference between the two is not worked out carefully, theory runs into danger to create yet two other dichotomies: first, an *ill-conceived* version of the difference between "the West and the Rest" (Hall), where both sides are imagined as if they would substantially exist and were not specters brought about in the first place by certain discursive formations (essentialization of the situatedness of knowledge); second, the illusionary idea that what is needed to gain climate justice would be some kind of *return to the origins*, to some kind of idealized past where there allegedly were no division between subject and object and where the human and the non-human coexisted peacefully in perfect harmony. In this view, then, the catastrophic status quo can only be regarded as the result of the epistemological hegemony of the "*substantialized West*." The problem is that this cuts the difference between epistemology on the one hand and political economy on the other. What difference would it actually make to talk about capitalism or about the substantialized West?

---

44 Cf. Judith Gruber's and Stefan Silber's thoughts on various forms of denial of climate change and some of their epistemological and cultural roots.

45 Cf. Sebastian Pittl's reflections on the relationship between different "places" of knowledge.

According to Marx, "a capitalist economy consists of many separate enterprises, each controlled by a capitalist owner, linked together by market exchange, which is not controlled by anyone; capitalist production is anarchic and is governed by the blind working of economic laws independent of the will of any individual."[46] If, on the other hand, the notion of capitalism is transferred from political economy to some kind of a pure form of a "capitalist worldview", it lacks substance. The notion does not serve the understanding of processes of concentration and centralization of capital, rivalry between different fractions of capital, the transformation of non-capitalist societies or individual sectors of societies by capitalism with or without extra-economic force and so on.

Against this background, it is of particular importance to be clear that capitalism is not a conspiracy. Capitalism has no "purpose", no *telos* in itself; it is an "anarchic" economic structure of production and realization of (surplus) value by complex processes of exchange (circulation), mediated through quite abstract market mechanisms; these mechanisms are themselves *not* culturally or politically controlled and operated in a strict sense of the term. Naturally, this does not impede that economy, as an important substructure of historical reality as a whole, co-constitutes other relatively autonomous sub-structures in a profound way (and is itself co-constituted by them).[47]

So, to be clear, my point is not to defame the necessary critiques of epistemological blind spots or to underestimate the impact of, above all, Eurocentrism in theory and practice. My only concern is, though, that the indeed urgent rethinking of epistemologies needs to be accompanied and informed by a suitable understanding of political economy and a clear notion of capitalism. This is because I worry that, if epistemological reflections bare of any such understanding of political economy, they *might* abet a culturalization of capitalism which at worst *might* lead to another mythologization of domination, exploitation and oppression as well as resistance and solidarity. Theorizing capitalism and Eurocentrism in theory are two different things. While it may be so that some theories of capitalism are eurocentric, it is not a sufficient analytical basis for liberation theology neither to identify capitalism and Eurocentrism and assume this a valid theory of capitalism nor to lay the critical approach to such politico-economic understandings of capitalism aside. Both a culturalization

---

46 Brewer, *Marxist Theories of Imperialism*, p. 29.

47 See Ellacuría, *Filosofía de la realidad histórica*, pp. 564–577. A good example of how, for instance, gendered and sexist ideologies and the accumulation of capital can go hand in hand, is still the study of Mies, *The Lace Makers of Narsapur*. Later works of Mies concentrate, probably not by accident, on ecofeminism. See Mies/Shiva, *Ecofeminism*.

of capitalism and an economization of culture can, I think, only be avoided if epistemological and politico-economic reflections go hand in hand.

Against this background, I advocate a reinforcement of politico-economic reflections in the conceptual groundworks of liberation theology without discounting epistemological reflections or cultural studies. One of the most important issues at stake seems to be the complex reciprocal relationships between different dimensions of what Wallerstein and others called the modern, capitalist world system (economy, culture, state politics, etc.). The climate crisis and the deeply rooted injustices it brings about, strengthen the need for deepened politico-economic reflections since its main driving forces do not primarily seem to be cultures but, for instance, emissions, extractivist modes of production and extra-economic but growth-oriented force.

From a liberation theological perspective, capital's universalizing tendency thus can be regarded as a negation of God's universal salvific will. This is why liberation theology needs to counter capital's universalizing tendency by seeking to historicize God's universal salvific will, which includes the struggle for universalizable economic structures on a world scale. In this perspective, liberation theology agrees with the imperatives of the global movements for climate justice which are "bound to touch upon and confront all issues regarding fair distribution, energy use, technology, infrastructure, urban reorganization, and agrarian reform, as well as the reclaiming of the commons and the potential for a participatory politics."[48] This does not necessarily include homogenization. On the contrary, it contains in itself a strong focus on local practices[49] since if economic structures tend to violently homogenize cultural difference and/or if they destroy natural living conditions they certainly are not universalizable.[50] This is where indeed the risen epistemological questions about, for instance, the Anthropocene are deeply interconnected with politico-economic analyses and counterhegemonic practices and strategies.[51] What is at stake, then, is the notion and realization of what I would call "universalizable universality."[52] This notion of universality should not be given up but deepened and clarified in favor of a liberation theology of climate justice, since it provides criteria for intervening in the various divisions that capitalism not only meets but also

48 Eigland, *Introduction*, p. 8.

49 Cf. Christian Kern's reflections on the local and the global.

50 Cf. Christian Tauchner's plea for "active passivity".

51 Cf. Wietske de Jong-Kumru's contribution; see also Angus, *Facing the Anthropocene*.

52 Cf. Wallerstein, *Die Barbarei der Anderen*, p. 8. While Wallerstein pleads for a "universal universalism", I prefer "universalizable universalism" because of the more active and dynamic dimension of the term as something still to be realized.

brings forth and to critically reflect on the contents and discontents of one's own critical approaches to climate justice.

Jan Niklas Collet

7 Theology and the Anthropocene

And the wounded skies above say it's much, too much, too late
Well maybe we should all be praying for time
George Michael[53]

In our deep future, we may be sponges.[54] At the heart of the 2020 online workshop on *Climate Justice* stood the paradox that the modern world has become increasingly shaped by human activity and has also grown increasingly outside human control.[55] In our present age, which is often referred to as the Anthropocene, humans are asserting their influence on earth like never before with catastrophic consequences: climate change, mounting carbon emissions, rising sea levels, the extinction of other species, cross-species viral epidemics. In the face of overwhelming environmental change and its unpredictable generativity, we seem to be wandering without knowing what we are doing with planet earth; we experience a fundamental disorientation.[56] What are we humans going to do now, as we face (the possibility of) ruination and extinction? Perhaps, as a theological intuition, the challenge is first to learn to endure our disorientation, to accept the unpredictability of our actions and to realize that we cannot rely on ourselves for a quick fix. Human and other critters' worlds are interdependent.[57] Human beings, including the very poor, depend on healthy ecosystems for their livelihood. Liberation theology can therefore accommodate the turn to climate justice, as my co-editors rightly hold in this editorial chapter.

As we are impelled to rethink our more than human relations, anthropologies and theologies built around the capacities that make us distinctly human no longer suffice.[58] In fact, many of our traits are not distinctly human at all:

53 Lyrics from the song *Praying for Time* by George Michael, from his 1990 album *Listen Without Prejudice*.
54 Pratt, *Coda*, G171.
55 Cf. Bubandt, *Haunted Geologies*, G124.
56 Ten Bos, *Dwalen in het Antropoceen*.
57 Haraway, *Staying with the Trouble*.
58 Kohn, *How Forests Think*.

e.g. the "orchestration of desire", the "impulse to attract", is "the way of life" in all its forms.[59] Birds as much as people resort to music, color, and dance. Fragrant flowers erupt to attract the animals that pollinate them. Even our understanding of care can shift to include human non-intervention and non-human agency.[60] Christians in the West may not be able to relate to their sisters and brothers in the South who continue to believe deep down "that rivers are alive, lakes are sacred, animals are like humans and the skies can talk back when upset."[61] When will African, Asian, Latin American, and other theologies finally receive recognition as theologies in their own right? For as we try to grasp what doing climate justice entails, we must not just be wary of being anthropocentric, but we must be particularly careful not to leave modern, Occidental humans at the center of our narratives, as Judith Gruber rightly insists in this chapter. History tells us that whenever European civilization has tried to conquer the darkness with its light, the supposed forces of light ended up as forces of violence and destruction.[62] However, the myth of white innocence (which Gloria Wekker has coined and which Gruber embraces in this chapter) seems to be so strong, that in Western Christianity too, no historical evidence to the contrary can overpower the belief that, essentially, Christian faith is, and always has been, about love. Postcolonial and decolonial theologies help to unlearn conventional Western narratives that are built on the myth of white Christian innocence. Yet for privileged white European theologians such new perspectives remain non-innocent efforts to affirm marginalized voices; as committed methodologies may well run the worst risk of appropriation.[63]

So, what new ways can we develop to think about the world that we share with other kinds of beings?[64] As we look for new creative concepts to imagine worlds that are possible, we try to think human and non-human agency together. Thus, landscapes are not seen as detached from humans but rather as populated by the ghosts of human activity. While we try to rediscover beauty in a place like Chernobyl, we also narrate the humanmade terrors.[65] We can lament the damage done, the death of species that are not able to survive. As we contemplate multispecies' shared histories, such as we find them in Chernobyl, and our unpredictable futures, we try to grasp the scale of death

59 Pratt, *Coda*, G173; Rose, *Shimmer*.
60 Puig de la Bellacasa, *Matters of Care*.
61 Maluleke/de Jong-Kumru, *Mirror of the Past*, p. 162.
62 Borgman, *What Does it Mean*.
63 Cf. Ouig de la Bellacasa, *Matters of Care*, p. 86.
64 Kohn, *How Forests Think*.
65 Cf. Attenborough's 2020 Netflix documentary *A Life on Our Planet*.

and ruin. At the same time, Donna Haraway encourages us to seek new practices of living as pose the question: how do we live and die well in our age?[66]

Our common experience is that time is running out. We need to act quickly to limit the consequences of climate change. On the other hand, contemporary economies' demand for increased production and innovation has made the clock run wild. Social polarization is deepening. We are desperately trying to keep up, panting as we race against the clock. Fearful to lag behind or be sidelined completely. Time is scarce. Emptiness, rest and inactivity are no longer sources of inspiration, but sure signs of failure and social marginalization.[67] The capitalist regime of the clock has displaced our other, intuitive experience of time, our inner sense of time. Hermsen advocates finding a new balance between the two. The dominant capitalist and economic clock leads to alienation, cynicism, indifference, acceleration, a loss of self and a way of living beyond hope or beyond faith in change. Our inner time enables contemplation, creativity and humanity. It is only when we do nothing that we can reflect and think and become creative. A functioning democracy promotes rest.

In line with this plea to re-appreciate our inner sense of time over capitalist clock time, I interpret Haraway's impatience with "a comic faith in technofixes, whether secular or religious" on the one hand, and with "a position that the game is over, it's too late," on the other hand.[68] Both the attitudes of faith in a quick fix and that of succumbing to despair are trying to avoid a true confrontation with the challenge we are facing. Both attitudes can be seen to result from the human malleability myth. The current climate and Covid crises are only the latest reasons for us to finally unlearn the modern conviction that with our human effort we can fix almost anything, including ourselves. We can't.

Haraway proposes a process of learning *to stay with the trouble* of living and dying together on a damaged earth as one that will lead to more livable future. She insists that neither hope nor despair is sensible, is tuned to the senses.[69] The practice of staying with the trouble requires learning to be truly present. That is not a self-evident theological praxis. As Kierkegaard has lamented, Christian preaching is quick to jump from problem to solution, from suffering to healing. As we preach about God's command to Abraham to offer his son as a sacrifice, we are inclined to accelerate the part of the biblical story that speaks of his three-day journey of silence, because we already see in our minds the image

66 Haraway, *Staying with the Trouble.*
67 Hermsen, *Stil de tijd.*
68 Hermsen, *Stil de tijd*, p. 3.
69 Hermsen, *Stil de tijd*, p. 4.

of the ram in the thicket that will replace Isaac.[70] As we follow the three-day liturgy of Easter, especially in Protestantism, we neglect Holy Saturday. We'd rather not dwell on the edge of the abyss, as we leap from cross to resurrection. If we wish to attune our theologies to the concept of learning to live and die well with other species on a damaged earth, we can start by learning to be truly present, to ponder on the secrets hidden in the dark experience of Holy Saturday without anticipating the light of Easter.[71] Perhaps we can learn not to think we can conquer the dark by claiming the light, but to dwell in the dark so that the light may find us. Looking at the tombstones, we are reminded of death, but in the lichens that grow on them, eternal life presents itself.[72]

Wietske de Jong-Kumru

References

Almendares, Juan: "Holobiocenosis: una reflexión englobadora pertinente", in: *En el Volcán insurgente* 58 (2019), pp. 68–70.

Angus, Ian: *Facing the Anthropocene. Fossil Capitalism and the Crisis of the Earth System.* New York: Monthly Review Press 2016.

Bettazzi, Luigi: "Church of the poor. One of the signatories of the Pact," in: Xabier Pikaza/José Antunes da Silva (eds.): *The Pact of the Catacombs. The mission of the poor in the Church.* Estella: Verbo Divino 2015, pp. 27–41.

Boff, Leonardo: *Cry of the Earth, Cry of the Poor. Ecology and Justice.* Maryknoll: Orbis 1997.

Boff, Leonardo: *Teología desde el cautiverio*, Colección Iglesia nueva 23. Bogotá: Indo-American Press Service 1975.

Borgman, Erik: "What Does it Mean to Be a European Theologian?" In: Religion and Identity in Post-conflict Societies. *Concilium* 2015/1: pp. 132–140.

Brand, Ulrich/Markus Wissen, *Imperiale Lebensweise: Zur Ausbeutung von Mensch und Natur im globalen Kapitalismus.* München: Oekom Verlag 2017.

Brand, Ulrich/Markus Wissen: *The Imperial Mode of Living. Everyday Life and the Ecological Crisis of Capitalism.* London: Verso 2021.

Brewer, Anthony: *Marxist Theories of Imperialism. A Critical Survey.* London/New York: Routledge 1990.

70 Cf. Kierkegaard, Die Opferung Isaaks.

71 Cf. Rambo, *Spirit and Trauma.*

72 Cf. Pringle, *Establishing New Worlds*, G157–G167.

Bubandt, Nils: "Haunted Geologies. Spirits, Stones, and the Necropolitics of the Anthropocene", in: Anna Tsing et al. (eds.), *Arts of Living on a Damaged Planet. Ghosts of the Anthropocene.* Minneapolis/London: University of Minnesota Press 2017, G121–G141.

Derrida, Jacques: *Der "mystische Grund der Autorität".* Frankfurt am Main: Suhrkamp, ^{8}2017.

Eigland, Eirik: "Introduction", in: Brian Tokar, *Toward Climate Justice. Perspectives on the Climate Crisis and Social Change.* Porsgrunn: Communalism Press 2010), pp. 7–12.

Ellacuría, Ignacio: "Los pobres, 'lugar teológico' en América Latina, in Ignacio Ellacuría: *Escritos Teológicos I.* San Salvador, UCA 2000, pp. 139–162.

Ellacuría, Ignacio: *Escritos Teológicos. Tomo II.* San Salvador: UCA 2000.

Ellacuría, Ignacio: *Filosofía de la realidad histórica.* San Salvador ^{2}2007.

Final Document of the Amazon Synod, Online accessible at: http://www.synod.va/content/sinodoamazonico/en/documents/final-document-of-the-amazon-synod.pdf [accessed 20.02.2020].

Fineman, Martha A.: "The Vulnerable Subject: Anchoring Equality in the Human Condition," *Yale Journal of Law and Feminism* 20 (no. 1, 2008): pp. 1–25.

Freire, Paulo: *Pedagogy of the Oppressed.* Bloomsbury Academic 2000 [1970].

Gebara, Ivone: *Longing for running water. Ecofeminism and liberation.* Minneapolis: Fortress 1999.

Grosfoguel, Ramón: "The Structure of Knowledge in Westernized Universities: Epistemic Racism/ Sexism and the Four Genocides/Epistemicides of the Long 16th Century," in: *Human Architecture: Journal of the Sociology of Self-Knowledge* 11 (no. 1, 2013): pp. 73–90.

Gutiérrez, Gustavo: *La fuerza histórica de los pobres. Selección de trabajos.* Lima: CEP 1979.

Haraway, Donna J.: *Staying with the Trouble. Making Kin in the Chthulucene.* Durham/ London, Duke University Press 2016.

Haraway, Donna: "Situated Knowledges: The Science Question in Feminism and the Privilege of Partial Perspective", in: *Feminist Studies* 14 (3, 1988), pp. 575–599.

Hermsen, Joke J.: *Stil de tijd. Pleidooi voor een langzame toekomst.* Uitgeverij De Arbeiderspers 2009.

https://www.chronicle.com/article/how-the-academic-elite-reproduces-itself/ [accessed 20.02.2021].

Jennings, Willie James: *The Christian Imagination: Theology and the Origins of Race.* New Haven [Conn.]: Yale University Press 2010.

Keller, Catherine: *Political Theology of the Earth: Our Planetary Emergency and the Struggle for a New Public. Insurrections: Critical Studies in Religion, Politics, and Culture.* New York, Chichester, West Sussex: Columbia University Press 2018.

Kierkegaard, Sören (1843/1844): "Die Opferung Isaaks", in Rose and Emanuel Hirsch (eds.), *Sören Kierkegaard. Auswahl aus dem Gesamtwerk*. Wiesbaden: VMA-Verlag 1964, pp. 243–247.

Kohn, Eduardo: *How Forests Think. Toward an Anthropology beyond the Human*. Berkeley/Los Angeles/London, University of California Press 2013.

Lessenich, Stephan: *Living Well at Others' Expense. The Hidden Costs of Western Prosperity*. Cambridge: Polity 2019.

Maluleke, Tinyiko/Wietske de Jong-Kumru: "Mirror of the Past and Window to the Future. A Century of Postcolonial Theology in Africa", in: Madelon Grant (ed.), *In the Image of God. The Worldwide Church and its Political Mission*. Sallux Publishing 2020, pp. 152–162.

May, Roy H.: *Los pobres de la tierra*, Col. Ecología-Teología. San José: DEI 1986.

Mellor, Mary: *Feminism and Ecology: An Introduction*. New York: Univ. Press 1998.

Mies, Maria: *The Lace Makers of Narsapur. Indian Housewives Produce for the World Market*. London: Zed Press 1982.

Mies, Maria/Vandana Shiva: *Ecofeminism*, Critique. Influence. Change 5. London: Zed 1993.

Planellas Barnosell, Joan: "The framers of the Pact. Origin, evolution and decline of the group called "the Church of the poor", in: Xabier Pikaza/José Antunes da Silva (eds.): *The Pact of the Catacombs. The mission of the poor in the Church*. Estella: Verbo Divino 2015, pp. 73–100.

Pope Francis: Encyclical Letter *Laudato Si'* of the Holy Father Francis on Care for Our Common Home, Vatican City, May 24, 2015.

Pratt, Mary Louise: "Coda. Concept and Chronotope", in: Anna Tsing et al. (eds.), *Arts of Living on a Damaged Planet. Ghosts of the Anthropocene*. Minneapolis/London: University of Minnesota Press 2017, G169–G174.

Pringle, Anne: "Establishing New Worlds. The Lichens of Petersham", in Anna Tsing et al. (eds.), *Arts of Living on a Damaged Planet. Ghosts of the Anthropocene*. Minneapolis/London: University of Minnesota Press 2017, G157–G167.

Puig de la Bellacasa, María: *Matters of Care. Speculative Ethics in More than Human Worlds*. University of Minnesota Press 2017.

Rambo, Shelly: *Spirit and Trauma. A Theology of Remaining*. Louisville: Westminster John Knox Press 2010.

Rancière, Jacques: *Das Unvernehmen. Politik und Philosophie*. Frankfurt am Main: Suhrkamp ^{7}2018.

Reckwitz, Andreas: "Practices of Labor and Organization in the Creative Economy", in: Andreas Reckwitz: *The Society of Singularities*. Cambridge: Polity 2020, pp. 135–144.

Reckwitz, Andreas: *The Society of Singularities*. Cambridge: Polity 2020.

Rose, Deborah Bird: "Shimmer: When All You Love is Being Trashed", in Anna Tsing et al. (eds.), *Arts of Living on a Damaged Planet. Ghosts of the Anthropocene*. Minneapolis/London: University of Minnesota Press 2017, G51–G63.

Segundo, Juan Luis: "Revelación, fe, signos de los tiempos," in: Ignacio Ellacuría/Jon Sobrino (eds.), *Mysterium liberationis* I. Madrid: Trotta 1990, pp. 443–466.

Spivak, Gayatri C.: *The Post-Colonial Critic. Interviews, Strategies, Dialogues*. London: Routledge 1990.

Spivak, Gayatri Chakravorty: "What Time is it on the Clock of the World?", Inauguration of the "Academy of Unlearning", Wiener Festwochen 2017, online accessible at: https://www.youtube.com/watch?v=fi99qcIDZxw [accessed 20.02.2021].

Spivak, Gayatri Chakravorty: *An Aesthetic Education in the Era of Globalization*. Cambridge, Mass., 2012.

Ten Bos, René: *Dwalen in het Antropoceen*. Antwerp, Boom 2019.

Tokar, Brian: "Climate Justice and Community Renewal", in: Brian Tokar/Tamra Gilbertson (eds.): *Climate Justice and Community Renewal. Resistance and Grassroot Solutions*. Abingdon, Oxon/New York, NY: Routledge 2020, pp. 1–16.

United Nations (1992), United Nations Framework Convention of Climate Justice, Art. 3, online: https://unfccc.int/resource/docs/convkp/conveng.pdf [accessed 14.05.2021].

Vigil, José María (ed.): *Sobre la opción por los pobres*, Iglesia, Pueblos y Culturas 50–51. Quito: Abya Yala 1999.

Wallerstein, Immanuel: *Die Barbarei der Anderen. Europäischer Universalismus*. Berlin: Wagenbach 2002.

Weiler, Birgit: *Gut leben—Tajimat Pujút: Prophetische Kritik aus Amazonien im Zeitalter der Globalisierung*. Ostfildern: Grünewald 2017.

Wekker, Gloria: *White Innocence: Paradoxes of Colonialism and Race*. Durham/London: Duke University Press 2016.

Authors of this Volume

Julia Blanc
PhD, Postdoctoral Assistant at the Center for Religion, Economy and Politics at the Faculty of Theology, University of Basel (Switzerland). Research interests include the environment, animals, and the SDGs, as well as norms and their empirical verification and the role of the Catholic Church in Europe.

Jan Niklas Collet
is research assistant for systematic theology at the Institute for Catholic Theology (TU Dortmund, Germany). His research focuses on political theology and liberation theology in dialogue with critical development research (especially de- and postcolonial theory), theological understandings of and contestation to the global rising of far-right policies, and theological approaches to climate justice.

Claudia Gärtner
Prof. Dr., Professor of Practical Theology/Religious Education, Faculty of Humanities and Theology, Department of Catholic Theology, Technical University Dortmund (Germany). Her main research interests are Religions Education for Sustainable Development, Didactical Design Research, Religious Education with Art.

Judith Gruber
PhD in Systematic Theology, University of Salzburg (Austria). From 2012 to 2017, she was Assistant Professor of Systematic Theology at Loyola University, New Orleans (USA). She joined the KU Leuven (Belgium) in 2017 as a Research Professor. She is a member of the Research Unit Systematic Theology and the Study of Religions, Faculty of Theology and Religious Studies. In her research, she brings Catholic theology into conversation with critical cultural theories.

María Fernanda Herrera Palomo
finished her Studies of Regional Science of Latin America at the University of Cologne (Germany, 2009). She participated in the Environmental Movement in Germany supporting the struggle of indigenous peoples like the Embera, Wayuú and Lakotas. She presented the situation in Colombia at the annual general meeting from RWE, Uniper and Eon in 2017. She joined climate camps in Germany and Poland as well as climate justice movement meetings in Holland. She has visited villages and communities in Colombia and transmitted their

concerns to German audiences. She also participated in the film "Still Burning" (2020).

Daniel P. Horan, OFM
PhD, is Professor of Philosophy, Religious Studies and Theology, and Director of the Center for Spirituality at Saint Mary's College, Notre Dame, Indiana (USA), and the author of several books, including *All God's Creatures: A Theology of Creation* (Lexington/Fortress, 2018) and *Catholicity and Emerging Personhood: A Contemporary Theological Anthropology* (Orbis Books, 2019).

Petr Jandejsek
PhD., is a lecturer in systematic theology at the Protestant Theological Faculty of Charles University in Prague and at Jabok Institute of Social Pedagogy and Theology (Czech Republic). His research interests comprise liberation theology, contemporary Christology, reconciliation and human rights. He is currently engaged in a project on theological anthropology.

Wietske de Jong-Kumru
holds a PhD in Theology from the Protestant Theological University in Amsterdam (Netherlands). Her dissertation was published as a book entitled *Postcolonial Feminist Theology* (2013). Until 2020, she was a Professor for Protestant Theology at Europa-University Flensburg, Germany. Her main research interests are religion, postcolonialism, and gender.

Benedikt Kern
is a Catholic theologian and member of the liberation theology inspired *Institut für Theologie und Politik* (Institute for Theology and Politics) in Münster (Germany). He works at the intersection of theology and social movements mainly on the topics of migration and deportations, church asylum, climate justice and civil disobedience. Most recently published: *Radikal Welt verändern. Papst Franziskus und die Sozialen Bewegungen* (Edition-ITP-Kompass, Münster 2018).

Christian Kern
(PhD, Salzburg University, Austria 2018) is research assistant at the Institute for Catholic Theology, TU Dresden (Germany). His research combines systematic theology and performative political theories. His current PostDoc-project reconstructs performative dynamics of artistic protest performances and develops a performative approach for political theology.

Ivan P. Khovacs
(PhD, St Andrews, Great Britain) researches primarily in practical and pastoral theology and theology and the arts as Senior Lecturer at Canterbury Christ Church University. He has directed formation for Anglican ministers, and is presently an advisor for national theological education in the Church of England. His teaching includes Christian Ethics with a special focus on ethics of the environment and the care of creation. He is an ordained priest serving in St James Piccadilly, a church in central London with a history of ministry with refugees and asylum seekers.

Irmgard Christine Klein
Dr. Mag., is a teacher for Religious Education and German literature at a high school in Innsbruck (Austria). In 2014 she obtained her doctorate at the Institute of Practical Theology at Leopold-Franzens-University in Innsbruck (Austria). She worked as Post doc at the same University (2017–2020).

G. P. Marcar
is the Harold Turner Research Fellow at the Centre for Theology and Public Issues (CTPI) in the University of Otago (New Zealand), where he is also a Teaching Fellow within the Theology Program. His research interests include theological and philosophical anthropology, animal ethics, legal philosophy, religious freedom, and human rights.

Michael Nausner
PhD, is a systematic theologian who between 2005 to 2017 was professor of Systematic Theology at Reutlingen School of Theology. From 2017 to the present, he works as senior researcher at the Church of Sweden's unit for research and analysis in Uppsala. His research interests lie in the intersections of theology, culture and ecology. In his latest book *Eine Theologie der Teilhabe* [*A Theology of Participation*] (Leipzig 2020), he explores theological, social, and spiritual implications of participation.

Sofia Oreland
is a PhD student at Uppsala University (Sweden), writing and researching about Christian climate activists' theological discourses expressed in their climate advocacy work. Her PhD project is an intercultural theological study of theological discourses expressed in Sweden and South Africa. Her research interests are to be found in public theology and in the intersection between the theology of culture and environmental thought. She is an ordained Lutheran

priest and previously worked within the global ecumenical movement explicitly in the area of climate justice.

Sebastian Pittl
(PhD, University of Vienna, Austria, 2016) is head of the Department of Dogmatics at the Faculty of Catholic Theology (University of Tübingen, Germany). His research focuses on liberation theologies, postcolonial theologies, political theologies and the relationship of theology and university

Elizabeth Pyne
(PhD) is Assistant Professor of Religious Studies at Mercyhurst University (Pennsylvania, USA). Her research focuses on Christian ecotheology and political theology, which she engages together with critical theory, feminist and queer studies, and the environmental humanities. She is the author of several publications on the theology of Edward Schillebeeckx and a forthcoming monograph, *Suspended Nature: Theology, Ecology, and Creaturely Politics* (T & T Clark).

Sebastian Salaske-Lentern
Dr. theol., works as "Peace, Justice and Ecology Coordinator" for the Catholic Diocese of Parramatta in Greater Western Sydney (Australia). His research interests include Christian social and environmental ethics (especially questions of sustainability, consumer ethics, and global social justice), theologies of creation, and liberation theologies (with a focus on the Latin-American context). Most recent publication: *Nachhaltiger Konsum und Beteiligungsgerechtigkeit. Impulse aus der christlichen Sozialethik zur Stäkrung kritischer Konsument*innen* (München: Oekom, 2021).

Stefan Silber
Prof. Dr. theol. habil., was Professor of Systematic Theology at the Catholic University of Applied Sciences in Paderborn (Germany) and visiting professor at various universities in Latin America. He specializes in Liberation and Postcolonial Theologies. Most recent publication: *Postkoloniale Theologien. Eine Einführung* (Tübingen 2021).

Christian Tauchner SVD
is a Divine Word Missionary from Austria. From 1982 to 2005 he lived in Ecuador and engaged in communication work, human rights and missiology (as the editor *Spiritus,* 1996 to 2004). Since 2013, he lives in Sankt Augustin (Germany) and works at the SVD Missiological Institute.

Gregor Taxacher
Dr. theol. habil.; research associate at the Institute of Catholic Theology at the TU Dortmund University (Germany). Main research areas: Theology after Auschwitz, Apocalyptics and theology of history, post-anthropocentric theology, political theology, doctrine of redemption.

Sibylle Trawöger
(Jun.-Prof. Dr.) studied Bio- and Environmental Engineering and Catholic Theology. She is Assistant Professor for "Systematic Theology and its Didactics" at the University of Würzburg (Germany).

Susana de Sousa Vilas Boas
with a five-year mission experience in the Central African Republic, has a PhD in Theology from the Portuguese Catholic University, Faculty of Theology (attended one semester at the Katholieke Universiteit Leuven). She has several scientific publications in the area. She is a member of the European Association of Catholic Theologians, collaborates with the Faculty of Theology (Braga), is Director of the Library of this Faculty and trainer at the Portuguese Association of Ethics and Practical Philosophy.